06/24
STAND PRICE
$ 5.00

Comedy
from Shakespeare
to Sheridan

Comedy from Shakespeare to Sheridan

*Change and Continuity
in the English and European
Dramatic Tradition*

ESSAYS IN HONOR OF EUGENE M. WAITH

*Edited and with an Introduction by
A. R. Braunmuller and J. C. Bulman*

Newark: University of Delaware Press
London and Toronto: Associated University Presses

Associated University Presses
440 Forsgate Drive
Cranbury, NJ 08512

Associated University Presses
25 Sicilian Avenue
London WC1A 2QH, England

Associated University Presses
2133 Royal Windsor Drive
Unit 1
Mississauga, Ontario
Canada L5J 1K5

The paper used in this publication meets the minimum requirements of the American National Standard for Permanence of Paper for Printed Library Materials Z39.48-1984.

Library of Congress Cataloging-in-Publication Data
Main entry under title:

Comedy from Shakespeare to Sheridan.

   Bibliography: p.
   Includes index.
   1. English drama (Comedy)—History and criticism—
Addresses, essays, lectures.   2. European drama
(Comedy)—History and criticism—Addresses, essays,
lectures.   3. Waith, Eugene M.   I. Waith, Eugene M.
II. Braunmuller, A. R., 1945– .   III. Bulman,
James C., 1947– .
PR631.C64   1986   822′.0523′09   84-40464
ISBN 0-87413-276-2 (alk. paper)

Printed in the United States of America

Contents

CONTENTS

Acknowledgments

The contributors and editors rejoice in this opportunity to honor a colleague, teacher, and friend who has shared so much of his learning, critical acumen, theatrical experience, and wit with us all. Our tribute's title is also the name of a course that Eugene Waith taught for many years at Yale University, and we dare hope that this collection will have at least some of the success and influence that class so notably did. To include contributions from everyone who acknowledges Eugene Waith's influence and shares in his friendship would produce not one ample volume but a shelf to rival, even surpass, the five feet once issued by The Other Place. The volume we offer here can only be an emblem, a token of affection and respect.

The editors thank the authors of this volume for their patience and good humor. We are especially grateful for the advice and encouragement of David Bevington, Ellen Graham, Jay Halio, and Maynard Mack.

Los Angeles and Meadville
Spring 1984

Foreword

From a profession so given as ours to preening, it is a special joy to single out for tribute a self-effacing scholar of the finest grain. Having had the honor to be a colleague of Eugene Waith's for forty years, I can testify that no one has ever been more loved and admired than he. Loved for his honesty and his independence of professional gimcrackery. Admired for his skill in breaking new ground through scrupulous research and criticism. In our world, as we all know, there are books with immediate flash, self-destructing artifacts, meteors to which the light of day is never kind. (What exactly *was* phenomenology?) And then there are the books with staying power, like Gene's own studies of the Beaumont and Fletcher plays, of the overweening hero, of dramatic definitions of greatness, and, most especially for this reader, of what were, until he wrote, the impenetrable murky fastnesses of *Titus*.

Perhaps a similar cleavage obtains among personalities. Let it be said, at any rate, that were I ever to serve in the armed forces of this country—which heaven forbid if it intends to win its wars—I should choose Gene for my commanding officer. He is one of those rare persons who would never ask a subordinate to do anything he had not already done himself—one of those still rarer persons who would have planned every detail of the campaign down to the crossing of the last "t" and land-mine—and one of those all but unique persons who, when the mission was accomplished, would recommend you for the Congressional Medal without saying anything of himself. Gene entered the army in 1943 as a buck private, though as a Yale instructor he could easily have pulled strings for officers' school, and emerged in 1946 as a First Lieutenant with the Croix de Guerre and other honors. This is a distinguished but not in itself amazing record. What is amazing is that Gene worked throughout the war in Intelligence, yet is one of only two men of my acquaintance who have never by a wink or a nod, or, as Hamlet says, a "Well, well, we know" or a "We could, an if we would," or some such other ambiguous giving out, conveyed the news that without their personal derring-do Goering would now be lunching in the White House.

Teacher, scholar, captain, friend—under whatever title you prefer, we salute you.

Maynard Mack
November 1984

Introduction

A. R. Braunmuller and J. C. Bulman

One of the most tantalizing promises in all classical writing, followed by one of the most notable lacunae, occurs at the beginning of *Poetics*, 6: "Well then, about the mimetic art that works in hexameters, and about comedy, we shall speak later; let us now discuss tragedy."[1] Aristotle's surviving text never does return to discuss comedy, and this gap has plagued Western comic theory far more than Aristotle's treatise ever stifled or narrowed later thought about tragedy. The *Poetics* does, it is true, refer to comedy. Comedy "tends naturally to imitate men worse . . . than the average" (2.4; 1448a16–18), although comic defects are ugly or ludicrous rather than "painful or destructive to life" (5.1; 1449a35). The comic poet achieves universality and probability differently from the tragic poet: the comic poets "construct the plot with the use of probabilities, then (and not until then) assign whatever names occur to them" (9.5; 1451b12–14). In the *Ars Poetica,* Horace expanded on some of these fragmentary observations when he emphasized the rhetorical and persuasive importance of decorous characterization and endorsed the use of type characters. These and other Horatian views were better known to, and more influential on, English Renaissance dramatists than any other ideas (most of them even more fragmentary than Aristotle's) that survived from the classical period.[2] Later antiquity offered Renaissance writers one further influential statement about comedy: the "De tragoedia et comoedia" (ca. A.D. 350) attributed to Aelius Donatus and containing the celebrated and supposedly Ciceronian dictum that comedy is "imitatio vitae, speculum consuetudinis, imago veritatis" (the imitation of life, the mirror of custom, the image of truth).[3]

If, as F. L. Lucas assures us, "Aristotle was little thumbed on the Bankside," we may suppose that his Renaissance commentators and imitators were even less perused.[4] Frequent imitations and adaptations from Machiavelli to Gascoigne to Shakespeare demonstrate, however, that Renaissance playwrights studied classical comic practice—the legacy of Menandrian New Comedy—even if they ignored classical theory.[5] Terence and Plautus were easygoing masters, and Elizabethan playwrights had a further stock of literary models provided by contemporary, especially Italian, versions of classical comedies. English comedy also found sources far indeed from either classical theory or classical practice. Magpie dramatists turned to native farce, the Corpus Christi cycle plays, prose romances, fabliaux, the jests of street and tavern for their material, much to the despair of a classicizing defender of poetry like Sir Philip Sidney. Seeking "exact" models for comedy and tragedy, Sidney found even the best observed "rules neyther of honest ciuilitie nor of skilfull Poetrie" and that all contemporary plays "be neither right Tragedies, nor right Comedies" but "mungrell Tragycomedie."[6] If Sidney's classicism proved inadequate to embrace the variety and eclecticism of English comedy extant when he wrote, later criticism fared little better. Today, critics still tend to discriminate and compartmentalize comedy into types— farcical, satiric, festive, romantic—with a Polonian rigor that might amuse even Sidney.

In the first essay of this volume, G. K. Hunter challenges some of our favorite assumptions about the genre. Arguing that neither an Aristotelian focus on plot nor a more recent (particularly nineteenth-century) focus on character suffi- ciently explains the workings of comedy, he posits a plot-and-character complex in which the two work integrally. He defines two basic structures: the farcical, in which character is presented as a series of ad hoc assertions of self against the continuous processes of action through time (or plot); and the romantic, in which character has the apparent power to hold up the plot and to impose on us a consciousness that abolishes time. All comedy, Hunter suggests, springs from these two ways of synthesizing plot and character. A writer may choose to emphasize one over the other, but both are always—at least implicitly—present. Jean E. Howard, employing a more theoretical vocabulary than Hunter, argues similarly that it is too easy to regard Shakespearian comedies as "festive," as mechanisms for containing the eruption of disorder within a social and aesthetic harmony. Instead, she sees an "inherent tension" in his plays "between comic expectations concerning conformity to socially prescribed roles" and a contrary "impulse to play with roles and to assert individuality through their subversion or self-interested manipulation." In Hunter's terms, one might say that Shake- speare strikes a balance between the structures of farce and of romance. By insisting that these structures ultimately determine comic form, Hunter makes secondary the distinctions that arise among the aesthetics of particular writers or the positions of plays in the pattern of historical development. We may dis- tinguish among types of comedy, writers of comedy, even entire periods, without having to bring to each an entirely different set of critical terms and expectations.

Two motifs—in practice and in theory—can help reveal the change and con- tinuity of English comedy: comic drama depicts a form of generalized everyday life (as opposed to tragic "reality," which, at least for the Renaissance, required some historical verisimilitude), and comic drama investigates the audience's relation with the play far more frequently than do other genres. As Jonas Barish observes in his essay on Caroline "defenses" of the stage, comedy lends itself better than tragedy to a study of its function within society. Amid the in- creasingly effective Puritan hostility toward drama, several Caroline dramatists discussed and represented antitheatricalism in their plays more explicitly and more discursively than their predecessors had done. Barish shows that this development, however understandable in the playwrights' cultural context, nonetheless "comes up against resistances and ineptitudes" in the plays them- selves.

Although comic worlds are insistently "like" their audiences' real environment, comedy again and again points to its own artificial nature, its "made-ness." This second motif (metadramatic or metacommentary) eventually turns to the question of laughter, its origin and its purpose. That issue confounded Sidney himself: "our Comedians thinke there is no delight without laughter; which is very wrong, for though laughter may come with delight, yet commeth it not of delight, as though delight should be the cause of laughter; but well may one thing breed both together" (*An Apologie*, 1:199). Of course, "one thing" may produce both delight and laughter, but "our Comedians"—the dramatists and actors—are equally right and plainly more generous, despite Sidney's preemptive caricature. Many theories define comic reactions as perceived differences between audience and comic substance: "Laughter is nothing else but sudden glory arising from some sudden conception of some eminency in ourselves, by comparison with the infirmity of others, or with our own formerly" (Thomas Hobbes, *Human Nature*, chap. 9). Perceived difference also underlies Bergson's explanation of laughter: "The comic is that side of a person which reveals his likeness to a thing, that aspect of human events which, through its peculiar inelasticity, conveys the impression of pure mechanism, of automatism, of movement without life."[7] Finally, Freud chose *Differenz* (a quantitative term rather than the qualitative *Unterschied*) to describe the "comparison . . . indispensable for the generation of this [comic] pleasure"; that pleasure derives from "the *difference* between the two cathectic expenditures—one's own and the other person's as estimated by 'empathy.'"[8] In a later essay, "Humor," Freud develops his ideas beyond these early economic explanations, but he retains the metaphor of comparison. The "humorous attitude . . . emphasizes the invincibility of . . . [one's] ego by the real world [and] victoriously maintains the pleasure principle" by "withdraw[ing] the psychical accent from . . . [the] ego and . . . transpos[ing] it on to . . . [the] super-ego." In effect, the humorist and, by sympathy, his audience belittle the ego's concerns, adopt a "parental" attitude toward them, and thereby protect, comfort, and give pleasure to the ego.[9]

As Freud's use of *empathy* makes clear, we all see the similarities even as we estimate the comparative differences between ourselves and that which we find comic. The comic writer introduces various degrees of difference, from the mechanical extreme (Chaplin's tick-tock walk, or Epicure Mammon's obscenely material dreams in *The Alchemist*) to the less obtrusive expedient of lightly characterizing type-names (Phebe and Sylvius in *As You Like It*, or Malvolio in *Twelfth Night*). Once more, we have crossed from the motif of the audience's relation with comic drama (difference-similarity) to the motif of the comic world's fundamental everyday-ness (how else may the majority discern similarity in order to erect difference?).

Even arguments that purport to reject comparison as a source of humor are usually disingenuous. Like other writers of satiric comedy, Ben Jonson disavows personal reference, and, as Jonas Barish notes, asserts that his plays "do not 'glance at' specific individuals, but deal in types, against whom the onlookers may (if they wish) measure their own lives." "What broad reproofs have I us'd?" Jonson demands to know; "Where have I been particular? Where personal?" Then he immediately admits that his audience has, in fact, so understood him:

"Yet, to which of these [comic "creatures"] so pointingly, as he might not, either ingenuously have confes'd or wisely dissembled his disease?"[10] Universalizing or abstracting the folly never will prevent comparison, the finding of difference (Jonson's defensive bulwark) or similarity (Jonson's true aim). If it did, comedy would fail.

These two interrelated motifs will, again, both temporarily support and ultimately dissolve most common distinctions among types of comedy. A traditional distinction has been drawn between Jonsonian "humours" comedy and Shakespearian romantic comedy—the one satirizing the mores of contemporary society, the other depicting a world archaic, allegorical, and full of wonder. Essays in this volume challenge that distinction. Alvin B. Kernan finds that even in Shakespeare's most romantic comedies there lurks social commentary once thought to be the exclusive province of Jonson. The opposition of court and country allowed Shakespeare to comment "on the central political issues of his day"—issues such as tyranny, abuse, and courtly extravagance—"issues that were of vital importance to the monarchs and to the many aristocrats," figures such as those who populate Shakespeare's "green worlds," "who had left their country estates and gathered in the court." In a complementary essay, John Lemly shows that Jonson, ostensibly and loudly hostile toward the conventions and attitudes of romance, in fact incorporated many of them into his plays, including those plays regarded as his most "humourous." Even as Jonson condemns the excesses and artifices of romance and masque, "he borrows their least naturalistic elements: allegory, nostalgic movement toward a pastoral landscape, deliberate archaism, sudden revelations, music and dance, and incredible, convoluted plots." The traditional barriers separating Jonson from Shakespeare begin to crumble under the pressure of such evidence, and we find ourselves having to reassess traditional generic distinctions.

The tendency to split English Renaissance comedy into rival camps has had unfortunate consequences. It has, as we have seen, simplified and suppressed the complex network of influences and analogues that makes Renaissance comedy a more cohesive body of work than critics usually admit. Perhaps worse, it has so elevated Shakespeare and Jonson that all other dramatists necessarily appear paltry. If lesser contemporaries imitate, their work is derided as derivative; if they strike out on their own, it is said that their work does not measure up. This fate has especially afflicted Middleton and Massinger, whose citizen comedies have long suffered by comparison with Jonson's comedies. Gail Kern Paster takes issue with such traditional disparagement by arguing that citizen comedy, far from being a pale imitation of Jonsonian satire, developed as a genre both allusive and independent. The stereotypical plot and "humourous" characters of the comedies Middleton wrote at the beginning of James's reign, she claims, admirably reflect conventional and conservative notions of class, social climbing, and appetitive behavior. By the end of the reign, however, after a long period of aristocratic compromise with an aggressive middle class, citizen comedy in the hands of Massinger had become more than a social document. No longer predictable, Massinger's characters, though borrowed from Middleton, are complex psychological portraits; Massinger's plot, however derivative, now "has less to do with class dynamics at a specific historical moment than with the permanent human fantasies about self-transformation which manifest themselves . . . in terms of class division." In Hunter's terms, Middleton and Massinger might be said to test different weights on the scales of plot and character; yet each writes within a genre too long regarded as simple and derivative. Examining Massinger's "strong determination . . . to make the materials of comedy subserve moral and social argument," Philip Edwards too defends the inventiveness and integrity of the dramatist's achievement. While Massinger often followed Jonson's and Shakespeare's lead, Edwards establishes Massinger's serious, sometimes overly serious, but independent contribution in comedies "concerned with abuses of common life" and in "comical histories"—*The Great Duke of Florence* and *The Guardian*. In these latter plays, we can observe the drift of Massinger's comedy toward tragicomedy and notice once more how much we miss when we allow Jonson and Shakespeare to overshadow later Jacobean and Caroline comedy.

*   *   *

The cursory history of English comedy sees Restoration and most later comedy as arising from various mixtures of the original fonts, Shakespeare and Jonson, with an admixture of French wit and decorum. Even if Jonson and Shakespeare had not already sketched their own Restoration comedies in *Epicoene* and *Much Ado about Nothing,* the sharp distinction dulls the more it is examined. Not only does seventeenth-century comedy resist this easy categorization, but it fails to make any very illuminating distinction between Jonson and Shakespeare themselves. For example, C. L. Barber's justly famous formula for Shakespearian "festive" (and largely romantic) comedy—"through release to clarification"—almost sounds like a psychological or moral gloss on parts of the comic plot Jonson himself named, following Donatus and Scaliger, as the *epitasis* ("or business of the Play"), the *catastasis* ("some fresh cheat," or new complication), and the *catastrophe* ("or knitting up of all").[11] Certainly the Forest of Arden cannot be too far from Bankside or we could not recognize (and simultaneously *not* recognize) ourselves in Rosalind, Orlando, Jaques, and the rest. Similarly, Malvolio *(Twelfth Night)* and Don John *(Much Ado)* might migrate without too much difficulty to Jonson's Blackfriars, and the entire cast of the romantic *Love's Labour's Lost* would easily slip into a comedy of humours,[12] as would most characters in Shakespeare's comic subplots.

A proliferation of terms—for example, the *comedy of manners*—really marks the impossibility of more than ad hoc, perhaps propaedeutic, distinctions. A late bloom like *The Importance of Being Earnest* effortlessly blends ageless elements of romantic comedy (Jack Worthing: "My name is Ernest in town and Jack in the country," for example, or the long-lost-child ploy) with overt social satire (Lady Bracknell: "Was he born in what the Radical papers call the purple of commerce, or did he rise from the ranks of the aristocracy?") with delightful reminiscences of Restoration comic contract scenes and obsessive concern for social status and manner.[13] Wilde's play does show, however glancingly, that another attractive, provisional distinction between Renaissance and Restoration comedy—the former often concerns individual identity, the latter the individual's proper place or status in the hierarchy of wit and of society—will prove useful but not definitive. The distinction broadly identifies the two periods' use of literal and figurative disguise, for example. Elizabethan disguises are most often correlated with a character's psychological state, and the dropping of disguise often marks a transformed psychology: Rosalind benefits from being Ganymede and Orlando from being "Orlando" to Ganymede. In Restoration comedy, disguise often assists the individual's socially defined hunt for station or for socially proscribed satisfaction: Horner gets what he wants disguised as a man who cannot, and Lady Fidget asks, "Why should you not think that women make use of our reputation as you men of yours, only to deceive the world with less suspicion?"[14] Similarly, in *The Rivals*, Captain Absolute evades Lydia Languish's inverted social disdain by assuming the disguise not of a different identity, but of a different social status. Yet the exceptions also crowd to mind: Malvolio disguises himself for social (and mercenary) purposes, as does the triumvirate of *The Alchemist;* and Fidelia's disguise in *The Plain Dealer* has no more and no less psychological resonance than Euphrasia's in Beaumont and Fletcher's *Philaster.*

The distinction between Renaissance comedy's concern with individual identity and Restoration comedy's concern with social identity is borne out in Robert Hogan's study of comic language in Sheridan, a playwright who often recapitulates Restoration practices. There are two essential comic languages, Hogan suggests: the language of humor, which ignorantly diverges from a norm of commonly accepted good speech and yields, at its funniest, Mrs. Malaprop; and the language of wit, which uses devices of grammar and rhetoric with such uncommon fluency that it diverges from ordinary speech in the opposite direction, namely, superiority. Sheridan "places" his characters both socially and morally through such language: wit implicitly springs from excellence of character; humor, from faults of character. Such judgments are conventionally held to typify Restoration and eighteenth-century comic writers—more social than psychological in nature, and (to use Henry Fielding's words) truer to the species than to the individual.

Rose Zimbardo disagrees with such thinking. By tracing how critics from Ben Jonson to Samuel Johnson responded to Shakespearian characterization, she discovers that the notion of "character evolved not towards a more social, but towards a more psychological definition." In the Restoration alone, she argues, the concept of what character was—an "imitation of nature"—first meant (as it did to Dryden) a representation of abstract idea or design; then, a representation of "the actual"; and finally, the "penetration of an assumed 'internal arena' in characters." This evolution in part determined which of Shakespeare's comedies were popular in which decades of the late seventeenth and eighteenth centuries. Anthony Kaufman concurs that comic writers in the Restoration had not altogether forsaken the Renaissance fascination with the "internal arena" of the individual. He focuses on one character type, the Don Juan figure, and follows his progress from Tirso's *El burlador de Sevilla* (published in 1630), through

Molière's *Dom Juan* (1665), and into the English Restoration drama, where elements of Don Juan's character inform rakes such as Horner, Dorimant, and Nemours. Shadwell's *The Libertine*, however, best belies the idea that the Restoration univocally conceived of comedy as social. Shadwell, according to Kaufman, was fascinated with his character's psychology: his Don Juan lives at the center of a bizarre fantasy of sexual hostility and aggression that "speaks to our deepest emotional selves." And although the playwright carefully controls our response to that fantasy by manipulating comic elements, his treatment of the myth is as much romantic as satiric. Once again, revisionist criticism points out that conventional distinctions between types of comedy often do not hold up under careful scrutiny.

Just as a single figure may span numerous types of comedy usually regarded as distinct, so too there are comic patterns that cross traditional boundaries of culture and period and genre. Kenneth Muir's wide-ranging survey finds that much of the greatest comedy centers on one such pattern, the test of love. "The mutual happiness of lovers, expected by the audience at the end of the last act, may be postponed by quarrels, misunderstandings, separations, disguises, and accidents. But the most interesting comedies are those in which the plot is not merely a device to postpone happiness, but those in which one or both lovers are rigorously tested, emerging more worthy of their partners in the process." Marjorie Garber discusses one such test in *As You Like It*. Rosalind persists in her disguise as Ganymede after Orlando has discovered her in the forest, Garber suggests, because she wishes to educate him in the ways of love and make him worthy of her. In Congreve's comedies, as Albert Wertheim shows, the test of love comes to include the crisis of finance. Dedication to an individual may require the apparent abandonment of the social sine qua non, money; and generosity as much as superior wit distinguishes his most admired characters. Garber's and Wertheim's analyses of love tests in individual comedies demonstrate how fruitful Muir's line of inquiry can be. By drawing on works of dramatists of various nations and periods—Calderón, Chapman, Marivaux, Middleton, and Molière among them—Muir shows that love tests manifest major cultural differences, but those differences finally indicate how similar in theme and design the best comedies often are. Muir does not argue for cases of direct influence, although we have seen that ample evidence exists. Rather, he suggests analogies, and by doing so, he promotes a view of comedy more inclusive and continuous than has been customary. He encourages us to see how much comedies by diverse hands—distinct in form, period, and subject—have in common.

* * *

In the great stretch of superb examples from the Elizabethan period through the eighteenth century, then, English comedy and comedies shimmer, dissolve, and recombine in ways that make even the most diversified critical approaches not helpless, but humble. No type of English comedy has proved more humbling to critical study, or more consistently fascinating, than the most mixed type of all, tragicomedy. Sidney lambasted almost all the Elizabethan drama he knew as "mungrell Tragycomedie," and the decades after *An Apologie* would have offered him little solace. About eighty years later, Dryden's Lisideius complained,

> There is no theatre in the world has any thing so absurd as the English tragicomedy; 'tis a drama of our own invention, and the fashion of it is enough to proclaim it so; here a course of mirth, there another of sadness and passion, a third of honour, and fourth a duel: thus, in two hours and a half we run through all the fits of Bedlam.[15]

In the same dialogue, however, Neander "cannot but conclude, to the honour of our nation, that we have invented, increased, and perfected a more pleasant way of writing for the stage than was ever known to the ancients or moderns of any nation, which is tragi-comedy" ("Of Dramatic Poesy," 1:58). Dryden himself could flatly declare, "the genius of the English cannot bear too regular a play; we are given to variety, even to a debauchery of pleasure" (Preface to *Don Sebastian* [1690], 2:49).

At the turn of the seventeenth century, various European literary controversies and especially Guarini's *Il Compendio della poesia tragicomica* (published in 1601) had begun to give the term new currency and new content.[16] Guarini's defense of *Il Pastor fido* (1585) contains a famous passage that probably influenced Fletcher's defense of *The Faithful Shepherdess* (c. 1609). Guarini claims that the tragicomic poet mixes comedy and tragedy thus:

> from the one he takes great persons but not great action; a plot which is verisimilar but not true; passions, moved but tempered; the delight, not the sadness; the danger, not the death; from the other, laughter which is not dissolute, modest amusement, a feigned complication, a happy reversal, and above all, the comic order.[17]

The recipe was influential, not only for its list of ingredients but also for its absence of quantities. Whether aware of Guarini or not, and many authors must have known his ideas only second-hand or through various plays he had influenced first- or second- or even third-hand, English playwrights spent the first three decades and more of the seventeenth century exploring tragicomedy's possibilities. By increasing the danger, even unto death, one might produce *Measure for Measure* or *The Winter's Tale;* by taking great persons and a bourgeois action, one might produce tragedy of the peculiar Jacobean sort represented by *The White Devil;* by violating "the strict rigor of the *comic* law" (Guarini's "comic order") one might produce—as Jonson worried he had in *Volpone*—a comedy of very mixed effect.[18]

Starting from Guarini's observation that tragicomedy displays "above all, the comic order," R. A. Foakes attempts to trace how developments in Jacobean comedy and satire lent to tragicomedy its distinctly comic shape. The most significant of these developments were: the devices by which dramatists expressed their increasing self-consciousness as manipulators of fiction; the popularity of scurrilous satire, which emphasized sex rather than love; the impact of the private theaters and the court masque; and a preoccupation with artifice (long a concern of comedy, as we noted earlier) both on the stage and in life. These developments, Foakes suggests, are interrelated in complex ways; together they made the emergence of tragicomedy not an aberration, but a likely consequence of cultural change.

If Foakes locates the dominant aesthetic of tragicomedy in Jacobean comedy and satire, Lee Bliss finds a predominantly tragic morality, at least in the plays of its chief Jacobean practitioners, Beaumont and Fletcher. Like Foakes, Bliss acknowledges the importance of satirical conventions in creating an aesthetic distance between audience and event; but the world of Beaumont and Fletcher, she argues, is far from comic. "The standard of virtue by which characters condemn each other is not a 'natural' one. Beyond the court lies neither moral nor physical comfort, only bestial sexuality or the primitive, virtuous, but ugly peasant life. . . . Despite their happy resolutions, the tragicomedies do not imply a world order fundamentally different from that of *The Maid's Tragedy*." In arguing her case for the tragic spirit of Beaumont and Fletcher's work, however, Bliss is careful to draw distinctions between it and Shakespeare's mature tragicomedy. Whereas Shakespeare "gradually submerges us in romance," Beaumont and Fletcher manipulate the *surfaces* of romance. Whereas Shakespeare uses "a self-conscious primitivism" to achieve dramatic sophistication, they use a more conventional form, closed to any sense of unforeseen human potential. Whereas he dramatizes a humane faith in the power of art to heal the wound in nature, Beaumont and Fletcher insist that art and nature remain separate and irreconcilable. Foakes and Bliss thus view tragicomedy through the lenses of discrepant dramatic traditions. But in doing so, they advance on previous assessments of tragicomedy as merely tragedy with a happy ending tacked on; by their differences, they attest to how rich and varied a form tragicomedy in fact was.

Exploring "a plot which is verisimilar but not true; passions, moved but tempered," writers of English tragicomedy encroached on the surrounding and supposedly well-defined generic territory. These invasions illustrate once again how truly ill-defined the borders were—and remain. Those invasions also return us to our two motifs—the everyday-ness of the comic world and comedy's profound interest in the audience's relation with the play. A Polonian term—*romantic tragicomedy,* for instance—might serve for a play that mingles romantic plot with verisimilar detail. *Cymbeline* could represent the combination: verisimilar Roman Britain provides a locale for the separated royal children, the near-escapes, the expansive time scheme of romance. Tragicomedies also, as Foakes makes clear, specialize in one form of comedy's relation with its audience, the conscious posing of its own artistry. Here the issue becomes not laughter but the still more puzzling mixture of laughter and tears. A modern master of the form allows his character a typically tragicomic acknowledgment: "Nothing is funnier than unhappiness. I grant you that . . . Yes, yes, it's the most comical thing in the world. And we laugh, we laugh, with a will, in the beginning . . . Yes, it's like the funny story we have heard too often, we still find it funny, but we don't laugh any more."[19] The bias may be slightly wrong for earlier tragicomedy, but the emphasis on our repeated swings from one emotional extreme to the other suits Renaissance tragicomedy very well. Indeed, the movingly and hilariously prolonged *denouement* of *Cymbeline* approaches and withdraws from and approaches (and again withdraws from) the mingled extremes of the funny unhappy story and the pathetic funny story. So, too, Viola and Sebastian, joyfully reunited at the end of *Twelfth Night*, cannot forbear—or their author cannot forbear—winking at romantic convention: "My father had a mole upon his brow. . . . And so had mine."[20]

This last example comes from a play few would call a tragicomedy, but it reminds us again of comedy's capaciousness. This capaciousness, this resistance to definition, can be defined as variously as there are major comic playwrights and comic masterpieces. Comedy eventually embraces its generic opposite: "tragedy is really implicit or uncompleted comedy . . . comedy contains a potential tragedy within itself."[21] Two examples: the Pyramus and Thisby story becomes now a joke playlet, now *Romeo and Juliet;* the old *True Chronicle History of King Leir* (c. 1588–94) with its happy conclusion becomes the new *King Lear* with an unhappy conclusion, which in turn becomes the newer *History of King Lear* (1681) with a comic ending. Indefensible as *King Lear* makes Nahum Tate's adaptation, the course of Shakespeare's later career helps us see (past Tate's blinkers) that in one sense at least the tragedy is an uncompleted comedy.[22] Perhaps the most spacious meaning of comedy—as in Dante's *Divine Comedy*—is the best after all, so long as we remember the other possibilities, including Balzac's *Comédie humaine*.

NOTES

1. Gerald F. Else, *Aristotle's Poetics: The Argument* (Cambridge, Mass.: Harvard University Press, 1967), p. 221 (*Poetics* 1449b21–22). All subsequent quotations of Aristotle are from this translation, with chapter and section numbers added.

2. See, for instance, M. T. Herrick, *The Fusion of Horatian and Aristotelian Literary Criticism, 1531–1555* (Urbana: University of Illinois Press, 1946). In *An Aristotelian Theory of Comedy* (New York: Harcourt, Brace, 1922), Lane Cooper attempts to reconstruct Aristotle's comic theory from the fragmentary references in the *Poetics* and elsewhere.

3. The essay—probably a conflation of two authors' work—was often reprinted with Renaissance editions of Terence and consequently itself gained classic status. In "Ancient Theories of Comedy: The Treatises of Evanthius and Donatus," S. Georgia Nugent discusses the document's textual history and gives both the Latin texts and a translation (see Maurice Charney, ed., *Shakespearean Comedy*, New York Literary Forum, 5–6 [1980], 259–80); the same volume contains essays by Ruth Nevo and Susan Snyder, respectively, applying Donatan precepts to Shakespearian comedy. For an excellent, wider discussion of ancient comic theory and its possible influence on English and Continental dramatists, see Madeleine Doran, *The Endeavors of Art* (Madison: University of Wisconsin Press, 1954), passim, but esp. pp. 70–84 and 105–11.

4. F. L. Lucas, ed., *The Complete Works of John Webster*, 4 vols. (London: Chatto and Windus, 1927), 1:19; Lucas continues: "and those who lament this, might with poetic justice be condemned to read *Catiline* once a week for life." Sidney, Chapman, and Jonson are among the exceptions to Lucas's claim (and our own).

5. Machiavelli's dramatic technique in *Mandragola* derives from Terence's *Andria;* Gascoigne's *Supposes* is indebted to Ariosto's *I Suppositi* and hence to Plautus (e.g., *Captivi*); Plautus's *Menaechmi* and *Amphitruo* served as sources for *The Comedy of Errors*.

6. Philip Sidney, *An Apologie for Poetrie* in G. Gregory Smith, ed., *Elizabethan Critical Essays*, 2 vols. (London: Oxford University Press, 1904), 1:197 and 199. Further quotations from this edition are noted parenthetically.

7. Henri Bergson, *Laughter: An Essay on the Meaning of the Comic*, trans. Cloudesley Brereton and Fred Rothwell (London: Macmillan, 1911), p. 87.

8. Sigmund Freud, *Jokes and Their Relation to the Unconscious,* in *The Standard Edition of the Complete Psychological Works of Sigmund Freud,* trans. James Strachey, 24 vols. (London: Hogarth Press, 1960), 8:195–96; Strachey makes the point about *Differenz* on 8:195 n.1.

9. Ibid., 21:163–64, and see 21:166.

10. From "To . . . The Two Famous Universities . . ." prefixed to *Volpone* (1616 Folio), reprinted in James D. Redwine, ed., *Ben Jonson's Literary Criticism* (Lincoln: University of Nebraska Press, 1970), pp. 114–15.

11. See C. L. Barber, *Shakespeare's Festive Comedy: A Study of Dramatic Form and Its Relation to Social Custom* (1959; Princeton: Princeton University Press, 1972), p. 4 and passim. The phrases quoted from Jonson occur in "The Argument" and the Chorus after act 4 of *The Magnetic Lady* (in Redwine, ed., *Ben Jonson's Literary Criticism,* pp. 122 and 130; see also Redwine's helpful discussion, pp. xx–xxiv). On the origins and development of the terms, see T. W. Baldwin, *Shakspere's Five-Act Structure* (Urbana: University of Illinois Press, 1947), pp. 295–332.

12. G. R. Proudfoot writes that in *Love's Labour's Lost* Shakespeare "takes a step towards the first comedy of humours, Chapman's *An Humourous Day's Mirth* (1597)—a play pervaded with minor verbal correspondences with *Love's Labour's Lost.*" See *"Love's Labour's Lost:* Sweet Understanding and the Five Worthies," *Essays and Studies,* new series 37 (1984): 17.

13. Oscar Wilde, *The Importance of Being Earnest,* in *Plays* (Harmondsworth: Penguin, 1954), pp. 267 and 258, respectively.

14. William Wycherley, *The Country Wife,* ed. David Cook and John Swannell, The Revels Plays (London: Methuen, 1975), 5.4.105–7.

15. John Dryden, "Of Dramatic Poesy," (1668), in George Watson, ed., *Of Dramatic Poesy and Other Critical Essays,* 2 vols. (London: Dent, 1962), 1:45. Further quotations from this edition are noted parenthetically.

16. See E. M. Waith, *The Pattern of Tragicomedy in Beaumont and Fletcher* (1952; reprint, Hamden, Conn.: Archon Books, 1969), pp. 42–85, for a comprehensive discussion of Guarini, his English influence, and the complication of tragicomedy with pastoral and satire in the period.

17. Translated in ibid., p. 48.

18. The quoted phrase comes from Jonson's "To . . . The Two Famous Universities" (in Redwine, ed., *Ben Jonson's Literary Criticism,* p. 116).

19. Samuel Beckett, *Endgame* (New York: Grove, 1958), pp. 18–19.

20. The example comes from G. R. Hibbard, "Between a Sob and a Giggle," in *Shakespeare, Man of the Theater,* ed. Kenneth Muir, Jay L. Halio, and D. J. Palmer (Newark: University of Delaware Press, 1983), p. 122; the same page contains Hibbard's astute commentary on the sob and giggle of Viola's response to word of Olivia's infatuation: "Poor lady, she were better love a dream."

21. Northrop Frye, "The Argument of Comedy" (1948), reprinted in Alvin B. Kernan, ed., *Modern Shakespearean Criticism* (New York: Harcourt, Brace, and World, 1970), p. 169.

22. See David Young, *The Heart's Forest: A Study of Shakespeare's Pastoral Plays* (New Haven: Yale University Press, 1972), pp. 76–87 and passim for an argument that *King Lear* defines itself in terms of pastoral, romance, and comic traditions.

Overviews

Comedy, Farce, Romance

G. K. Hunter

When we ask what kinds of plays were commonly written in the sixteenth and seventeenth centuries in England we are liable to be given an answer that is a curious mixture of formal or generic terms and of terms that reflect content or subject matter. The Harbage-Schoenbaum *Annals of English Drama* has an item called "type" attached to each play mentioned, and the words that appear under this heading give us a fascinating conspectus not only of the variety of plays but also of the limitation of vocabulary. Here "Classical Legend" meets "Biblical History" and "Heroic Romance" and "Realistic Tragedy." Are we being shown here the separate parts of an organized system of describing plays or only a set of ad hoc terms? The evidence seems to point more to the second possibility, for the categories—Romance, Legend, History, Tragedy—do not spring from a common basis and can hardly be related to one another as the elements of a systematic vocabulary. The mongrel quality of such a list might seem to be justified enough as the reflection of a "mongrel" drama.[1] Indeed the connection can certainly be made; but perhaps only in terms of expectation rather than reality. The modern scholar who reads through a body of Elizabethan drama soon becomes aware of more than random mixing in the relationship between one play and another. He comes to recognize family connections in form as well as content. What seems to be lacking is not so much organic interconnection but rather the existence of an organized vocabulary that would facilitate a more systematic description.

The absence of such a vocabulary was not cripplingly important in the period itself. The social condition of the playwrights was not such as to encourage aesthetic self-consciousness. The actor-shareholders or theatrical entrepreneurs were the persons in charge. They knew what their public would pay for (more or less). They could recognize fat parts and exciting situations without needing a vocabulary to describe them, and they could appreciate skillful play construction that would hold together such excellencies. And playwrights who preferred not to starve soon learned to please the purse-bearers and to accommodate their talents to the theatrical understanding the actors brought to them. Acting was, after all, conceived as a trade like carpentry, with a guild structure and a system of apprenticeship developing toward the clear standards of competence that marked the master craftsman. Those who were in the actors' supply business had to come to terms with the informal understanding of such experienced craftsmen, who knew as if by instinct what would work and what would not, what would hold together and what would fall apart, what would mature with time and what would warp and disjoint. Even the playwrights themselves, forming a small, tightly knit community, tied together by habits of collaboration, watching one another's successes and failures for inside references, for plagiarism, past or to come, and for technical innovations, seem to have been more aware of the immediate practicalities of their work than of the theoretical understanding a later age might find desirable.

For us today to say this may be to approach historical truth, but an appreciation of the playwright's "mystery" does not excuse us from an attempt to describe the actual objects made in a generalizing vocabulary. For only in generalizable terms can we hope to describe the formal structures that recur in example after example, describe the criteria that will allow us to classify. Such an aim, thus expressed, is, of course, liable to be misleading: it suggests that exactness is available. The more exact the system is made, the more, in fact, it becomes detached from the plays themselves, and in the end the preservation of the system may seem more important than the truth it refers to. Nonetheless, there is more space for system building than has been usually allowed. In what follows I will attempt to describe certain recurrent formal elements inside one traditional genre—comedy—but using only the standard vocabulary of formal play description such as even the playwrights of the sixteenth century could have recognized.

The basic vocabulary in talk about drama, from the time of the Greeks till now, has been that which was invented or at least adapted by Aristotle. It is true that our modern sense of plot, character, spectacle, and so on, differs in emphasis from *muthos, ethos, opsis,* and so on; but the idea of a group of such terms, used to handle the basic elements of all drama, has remained remarkably constant from that time to our own. To take more out of the *Poetics* than simple definitions is, however, far beyond my purpose, since this runs us into a difficulty I have already mentioned. Having described his basic group of what he calls "parts" *(mere),* Aristotle proceeds like a good anatomist to deliver a separate account of each part. Having defined plot, he then looks at the variety of plots and considers their advantages and disadvantages. Then he takes up character and explores the implications of that "part"; and so on. In pointing out this I am far, of course, from denying that Aristotle, here as elsewhere, has an overriding interest in organic form. But the method he employs has a certain inertia and conditions the reader (and more especially the writer who follows him) to advance through one set of connections and avoid another one. So it has proved among treatises on drama. Aristotle is very shrewd about actual plays; he cites their texts tellingly to exemplify one or another of his comments on his basic set of parts. But the chief interest of his treatise derives not from his treatment of actual plays taken as wholes but from the system he erects, the taxonomy he sets out and the vocabulary that allows us to talk about the separate elements found recurrently in plays.

The Aristotelian method thus shows us the reverse side of the phenomenon cited at the beginning of this essay. On one side of the coin we have a body of plays, powerful in range of effects but hard to describe in terms other than those of mere content: "Another play about Roman History is . . . in which . . . happens." On the other side we find a taxonomy of dramatic parts that is impressive in its comprehensive coverage and in its coherence, but that disappoints by its limited capacity to describe the actual experience of particular plays. This is, of course, by no means an unfamiliar dilemma. In a famous early Leavisite essay, C. H. Rickword's "A Note on Fiction,"[2] the author speaks of plot and character as only available to us as "precipitates from the memory"—the residue left when the experience of the work has boiled away. "Character," Rickword tells us, "is merely the term by which the reader alludes to the pseudo-objective image he composes of his response to an author's verbal arrangements," and "schematic plot," he adds, "is a construction of the reader's that corresponds to an aspect of that response and stands in merely diagrammatic relation to the source."[3] Rickword's suggestion is that words like *plot* and *character* make it possible for criticism to deal with the actual experience of art, but only by simplifying and distorting it. And certainly it is not difficult to find these words used by critics of Shakespeare so as to achieve such simplifying clarity. One critic, who wishes to describe the character of Hamlet, tells us that a certain episode shows us one personality trait while another repeats or develops the same trait, while a third piece of evidence may seem to contradict it but can eventually be argued into unity. The effect of a discussion in these terms, however scrupulously conducted, is to suggest that the episodes exist in order to show us the character. But that is not the effect made by these episodes in the theater. Another set of critics will tell us that "the revenge motive" governs the action or explains one episode as "the climax" or the turning point. Once again this approach seems to oversimplify the variousness and indeterminacy of our actual responses "in solution" as Rickword calls it. When we see Hamlet watching and Claudius praying we understand what is going on because we perceive (through the language used) a confirmation that Hamlet and Claudius are persons of a certain kind. But at the same time we see that the things they say (and do) at this point develop and change the play's capacity for forward momentum, canceling old possibilities and creating some new ones. Viewpoints conducted from the angle of plot or from the angle of character give us insights; but neither is adequate in isolation. For the actual experience of the play depends on their simultaneity, on the tension and cooperation between them in every moment of their existence, so that we can respond both to character in action and to action through character.

In an attempt to deal with this difficulty it may be appropriate to seek a vocabulary that allows us to describe plot and character in terms that show their interpenetration and do not set one in opposition against the other. Thus we may say that plot and character represent the synchronic and diachronic aspects of the same situation. In synchronic terms we lay out the play's movement as the revelation of a single unified mind or as the unfolding of the ethos inherent in a unified society. The ethos was, as it were, always there and always the same (in actuality or potential). Hamlet was always Hamlet; and the apparent movement through time that we follow is (in these terms) only the ingathering of information that allows us to see the static object (Hamlet, for example) with greatest fullness. In diachronic terms the characteristics involved are expressions of the local imbalances that lead to general movement through time. From this point of view the idea of Hamlet can never be isolated from the idea of Elsinore. By creating tension and pressure the opposition between these two creates movement, and by creating movement it allows us to see what is going on. Only in that social context of opposition and inside the shifting pattern of tensions is it possible to speak of Hamlet's resolution or achievement—ideas often associated with character but requiring a development through time in the sense we are given of the shifting balance between individual and society. I am presenting the playwright, in other words, as always required to combine incommensurates, obliged to convince us of the static unity of the world he has created, but needing to show us, at the same time, that each moment of the play is a moment of indeterminacy inside the lives of each of its individuals; their freedom to go any way at that point is essential to the experience, and their freedom is only demonstrated by the choice to move in one direction or another.

In terms of the interpenetration of plot and character that I have already spoken about we are liable, as modern readers, to suppose that the individual character must naturally provide the focus for the values that attach our hopes and fears to the dramatic action. We are equally predisposed to think of the society that tries to control the instability of individual wishes as mindlessly oppressive in its demand for conformity and accommodation. But this expectation by no means covers the actual ground of drama. The polarity of ethos and muthos is narrowed intolerably if we think of the concept of ethos only in terms of individual "character." If we translate ethos rather by "set of beliefs" or even "value system" (as seems quite justifiable), it becomes easier to see how the coexistence of ethos and muthos can provide a formal matrix not only for that kind of play in which the valued man sets himself against society but also for that in which the valued society succeeds in taming or expelling the irritant or objectionable individual; and we can see that in some cases the claims of ethos can even encourage us to dispense (more or less) with the sense of dramatic advance through conflict and allow us to find theatrical satisfaction in the contemplation of a static world where change (if it occurs) only confirms a basic stillness. *Hamlet* will serve (once again) as a play of the first kind where the ethos, the perceived and static system of values, is incorporated inside the valued character (Hamlet) and where such values can only be maintained by a continuous process of action for and against the devalued world of Elsinore. In the second kind of play the ethos or value system belongs to the normative social group whose capacity for a static preservation of values is knocked out of balance by an aberrant individual—Don John, or Duke Frederick, or Shylock—so that plot and counterplot must be used to threaten or confirm the stability of society. My last case is regularly exemplified in contemporary drama. In Beckett's plays for example we are given to understand how the world is but not how it can be changed; the scene revealed is an object of contemplation but not of possible development. The Elizabethan theater offers us less extreme examples, but we may notice how the pastoral ethos of *The Faithful Shepherdess* or *As You Like It* restricts our expectation of change; our contemplation of the woodland world assures us that only limited and appropriate developments will be allowed.

How do the distinctions I have been making match the traditional separation of plays into tragedy and comedy? The instances I have given might suggest that plays in which the value system attaches to the individual will be tragedies, while those that endorse society's values will be comedies. The idea has a certain force; certainly the endings of plays tend to support it. But a closer look suggests that the different emphases that can be given to ethos may appear in any genre. My concern here is with comedy; and it is easy, I believe, to see that in comedy the interconnection of ethos and muthos can be handled in any of the various ways I have described. There seems in fact to be a spectrum of comic forms running from the dynamic at one end to the static at the other, from the mode of farce in which the individual cannot exercise ethical[4] choice but must intrigue continuously just to survive, and stretching to the mode of romance at the other end where space and freedom from the pressure of intrigue allow us to contemplate a static world of values we are meant to endorse. For the professional *farceur* like Feydeau the story is almost entirely a story about running away from the assumed value system and is liable to end with nothing more than the status quo ante (as in *Occupe-toi d'Amelie* for example). The danger to the self that Feydeau's plots impose can only be averted by action so perpetual and so demanding that no process of ethical choice can be made visible. Under these circumstances the highest objective imaginable is mere recovery. At the other end of the spectrum lies what we easily recognize as the form of romance, where plot action is so slowed down or so evaded that we seem to be given an object of ethical contemplation rather than a process of change. In Peele's *The Old Wife's Tale*, for example, the use of a frame plot (the pages come to the Old Wife's cottage and listen to the story she tells to pass the night) denies us any real progression; it angles and distances the plot told so much that we pay more attention to its ethos (this is the kind of story an old wife would tell) than to its suspense. Moreover, the story told is one in which everything happens by unpredictable magic, so that our capacity to anticipate development is impeded even further; instead of expecting what *will* happen (as in Feydeau) we register the nature of what is happening.

The examples I have given might suggest that the distinction between the farce mode and the romance mode is simply a formal expression of a distinction of content—between realism and fantasy. There is undoubtedly a connection, but it is by no means necessary. The formal features of the romance mode I am describing can in fact accommodate a great deal of antiromantic sentiment. The comedy of George Bernard Shaw shows us a social world very like that of Feydeau. In both we see characters thrown back and forward between the shocking polarities of forced marriage or social disgrace, equally undesirable, equally unavoidable (so that farce's limitation of choice could hardly be better illustrated). But in Shaw the playwright's art concentrates our attention on the threats as objects of contemplation rather than causes of action. In *The Philanderer* (as so often in Feydeau) we see predatory women and unwilling men setting up traps of jealousy and misunderstanding, threatening marriages that can only be evaded at the very last minute, and all against the inevitable backdrop of tut-tutting respectability. But the interest or power of Shaw's play does not rest in any of this. It derives rather from its static demonstration of the "Ibsenite" ethos through which the advanced or independent woman demonstrates her sense of herself and of the world she lives in. Charteris, the passive recorder of this advanced world, has indeed to spend much of the play running away from the terrible Julia Craven, but even the fun of the chase is more a picture of what Ibsenism is like than an attempt to secure Charteris anything for himself.

In *Mrs. Warren's Profession* Shaw has moved his antiromantic vision even more obviously into the romance mode. The play shows us its young lovers, Vivie and Frank, confronted by the standard threats and shocks that should, in farce, galvanize them into panic. Their romance is threatened first by the comic discovery that the vicar/father is a former brothel haunter and then by the knowledge that Vivie's mother is an international madame, and finally the lovers are faced by the possibility that they are brother and sister. But, though the starting gun is fired again and again, nobody in this play runs very far, for Shaw is always providing space for thought and discussion about ethos. The center of the play and the issue it comes to rest on is, once again, the ethos of the new woman, exemplified by Vivie's decision to forgo love and pursue accountancy.

To say that Shaw is no "mere farceur" is to delight Shavians, for farce is a word that seems to invite condemnation. That farce is more shallow and primitive than romance is so widely assumed indeed that argument seems almost impertinent; and though I am speaking here not of farce and romance considered as classes of entertainment but of the farce mode and the romance mode as formal structures of comedy, I must seem to be laboring a paradox when I give the two of them an equal status. Our attachment to the truth of ethos and our modern sense of the individual consciousness as the center of all profundity drive us to assume that our response to a mode dominated by action, achieve-ment, intrigue, and change must be lacking in seriousness. The evidence, how-ever, is not all one way. I forbear to raise the issue of Greek comedy (Old or New); but early Tudor comedy (or farce) brings the matter to our attention in its own way, and in a way more germane to the period covered by this essay. In a play like John Heywood's *The Four PP* it is hard to think of plot or character in their usual modern senses. But the tension set up between the four individual characters and the governing values of the world we know they live in is much the same as we find in more modern plays. As in Feydeau the social expectations that attach to the individuals drive their attempts to achieve personal desires into impossible comic subterfuges. But in Feydeau, Parisian respectability is only a notional social value and is not mandatory; space is allowed for hoping that something will turn up to change the rules. In Heywood, however, Christian piety is presented as an absolute; the rules cannot change. Throughout the play the explicitly Christian content of the language draws our attention to the omnipresence of what the characters are so anxious to avoid; and this is, of course, highly comic, as well as strongly doctrinal. We can foresee that the only possible completion to a unified picture of life in this play will be the collapse of all the characters into the Christian piety that is waiting for them all the time.

There can be little doubt that Heywood saw the farce mode as providing an accurate and, indeed, profound picture of the world as it was. Fallen mankind has been shown and told the truth; the characters (and no doubt the audience) acknowledge this. But the action shows human nature (in its natural state) to be quite incapable of reaching or resting in the acknowledged ideal, indeed only capable of betraying it and so mocking it. The competition to tell the biggest lie, which supplies the major part of the action, is a close parody of the necessary irrationality of faith *(credo quia impossibile)* yet is handled in such a way as to mark not the closeness of the two impossibilities but only their divergence. We see how individual behavior ought to fit into the perfect pattern but see also how uncontrolled human nature makes the individual run in the opposite direction from every ideal that is set up. The form thus allows the comic free play of human nature, yet does not require such freedom to turn into a disconnected series of jokes,[5] for the jokes and escapisms are always seen in the context of the ideals they try to ignore but which we can never forget. The characters try to assert freedom and we see that they are never free. The hunted characters of the farce mode have, recurrently, this same double relation to what the audience can see: they run and hide from the ethical demands of an organized social system to which, nonetheless, they clearly belong. They are simultaneously aggressive and dependent, like rebellious children inside a family, who demand both that the others ignore them and make room for them. It is this perceived duplicity that makes their subversions merely comic, "unthreatening" *(ou phthartikon)* in Aristotle's phrase.[6]

The effect of such farcical structures on Shakespearian comedy is not hard to discover. In the Shakespeare comedies that are closest to the farce mode—*The Comedy of Errors, The Taming of the Shrew, The Merry Wives of Windsor*—we see marked structural similarities linking one play with another and recalling the farce forms we have looked at already, even though the social references of the three plays are widely various. All three plays show their central characters—the Antipholi, Kate, Falstaff—hounded by plots that, moving fast and furious, force them to run just as fast. The worlds they are found in demand that they accept an ethos that they barely understand and that they would rather exploit than accept. Their careers are marked by a series of attempts to impose themselves on an environment that can only regard them as aberrant. And being aberrant they are too weak to succeed in their impositions. One is a puzzled foreigner, one is a woman self-exiled from supposedly normal femininity, one is a self-deceiving and rootless intruder into bourgeois homogeneity. There is thus a comic disparity between the view of self that the protagonist holds and what we are given to understand about the nature of the society. Energy, willfulness, determination to keep on moving, may allow the protagonist to win the occasional battle, but he or she is bound to lose the war, for all the eventual advantages lie with the social body. Yet not one of these figures is merely a victim. To say that Kate wants to be tamed is to say more than the play allows; but her relation to the world she inhabits, to father, sister and to suitors, has much of the air of a deliberate challenge, "tame me if you dare." I call this a challenge because the hunted person in all these cases really belongs with the hunters and understands the rules of the game as well as they do, so that we are watching an occasion of complicity as well as hostility. The comic energy of self-assertion may be doomed to failure from the start; but the action is continuous because each "set" or "innings" in the game ends not only with failure but also with an assertion that the two sides really belong together—which generates a further bout of self-assertion and opposition. In *The Comedy of Errors* each discovery by an Antipholus that the world is alien is complemented by an assurance that it is familiar and welcoming. Each rebuff that Falstaff endures in *The Merry Wives* is followed by a renewed invitation to visit the wives. Each deprivation that Kate suffers is expressed by Petruchio as an aspect of his concern for her dignity. The unceasing and manic energy of farce in these plays comes from the central characters' unrelenting determination to reject complicity with the world around them. But we can see well enough that complicity is the only fate available. The unity of the play's world demands that the opponents finally admit that they belong to one another. Antipholus of Ephesus rejects with a torrent of vituperation the kindly-meant diagnosis of Doctor Pinch, wife, and neighbors; but the community is not put off by his rejection. They think of his "madness" as simply the deprivation of their "normality," their efforts being bent entirely toward what they see (properly enough) as his recovery of full status as a healthy and accepting member of society.

The plots of these plays are generated out of the opposition between individual self-assertion and the ethos of a coherent social group. The action is continuous and gives little or no space for ethical choice or audience contemplation of the worlds depicted, because the ethos is presented mainly as a means to stimulate recurrent rejection. It is necessarily late in the action when the protagonist discovers that complicity is possible and rewarding. But the audience has always known this. We have watched all the running and passing with a clear sense that there is only one way to go. The concluding movement in the farce mode thus fulfills the duplicity that I have seen as inherent in the relationship between the plot and the ethos, the movement and the place being moved from. The comic economy of these fictional worlds frustrates the attempts of individuals to disrupt social values but preserves their right to live freely inside such values. The end of the play is rewarding because it shows how the aggression of the individual and the self-protectiveness of the system (its need to isolate and to punish) can come together in a final satisfactory unity. The plays we have looked at show different methods of solving the problem of ending which they all share. In *The Comedy of Errors* the opposition between the mercantile world of Ephesus and the merchants from Syracusa turns out to be only an error. The need for understanding and for self-protection that both sides share is only formally disjunct; once the accidents are removed it is clear that there is an essential identity. In *The Merry Wives of Windsor*, on the other hand, there is no error; the attempt at subversion was real. But among the resourcefulnesses of the subverter we must note a powerful capacity to switch reality into play and vice versa. In this ability Falstaff is at one with the merry wives themselves as well as with the host and the parson. The elaborate last scene eventually allows (or forces) Falstaff to join the community he has tried to exploit and permits the townsfolk to turn their need for revenge into a self-strengthening ritual or play, which at once transforms and absorbs their enemy. The fact that the entire play is only a play makes it easy to turn what is threatening Windsor's "reality" into the threatless fantasy of self-conscious comedy. The possibility that Falstaff was only playing at seduction is a fictional half-truth that the protagonist and the community can embrace as a sufficient truth. And the fictionality of the whole enterprise allows the audience also to accept this without feeling betrayed. The cast of actors belongs together as a cooperative group; the tensions of their fictional existence dissolve into daylight as they confess their theatricality. This, we may note, is a recurrent device in Shakespeare's epilogues. Allowing for differences of situation we can see something of the same movement of aggression into accommodation brought to satisfactory ending in *The Taming of the Shrew* by a similar transformation of real life into play. Petruchio tames Kate by a "play" of aggression that drowns her "real" tendency to violence under the full flood of commanding and socially approved masculine terror (alias husbandly authority). Petruchio's tactic of terror remains, however, so clearly under conscious control, so limited in its actual physical expression, and so completely in the service of social conformity that it can be allowed to be playful, unthreatening, and so comic. And Kate is presented as quick to see the advantage of an aggression that carries social approval along with it and is therefore merely "playful." The end of Shakespeare's play is very different from that of Charles Marowitz's graffito parody in which Kate becomes an obedient zombie after being traumatized by anal rape. Shakespeare's Kate is no less zestful at the end than she was at the beginning. But she has moved her zest from the side of the hunted to that of the hunters. Whether she believes in her strongly worded final position on wifedom or merely plays at believing is a question that cannot be answered. The more interesting point is that Shakespeare has so arranged things that it need not be asked. Shakespeare's comic worlds move toward closure very regularly by turning purpose into play and emotion into performance (as is obvious enough at the end of *Much Ado*, for example); but they seldom ask us to consider how far playfulness is unreal. It is not by being herself that Kate (or any other of these characters) can secure the stability of a comic ending; for what we seek to know at this point is not what the characters really stand for but what they have learned about how they can all live together, on one level if not another.

After all this to turn back to *The Four PP* is to see how far the brilliance of these Shakespeare plays depends on the variety of levels on which the tension between plot and character, individual and society, is handled. Shakespeare depicts a relationship between a set of social values—Ephesian mercantilism, Padua's marriage market, Windsor's system of community support—and aggressive individuals anxious not to belong; but behind the aggression he allows the indeterminacy of human motives and the uncertainty that attaches to anything we can say about that. And behind the social values he asserts nothing more than the consensus of individuals who support them. The opposition is thus set up between two points that are multivalued and can be variously redefined in the course of the action, clear enough as opposites for the purpose of the play but neither rigid nor doctrinal. Heywood, on the other hand, depicts an essentially doctrinal world, seen clearly enough in the professional lives and professional language of those who live in the service of the church, the Palmer and the Pardoner most obviously. But the professionals are also ordinary sensual men more anxious to win in the short term as individuals than to belong eventually to the congregation of saints (but hoping to be able to achieve both ends). The desire to win is displayed, entirely characteristically, in the commercial relationships that dominate even so church-oriented a world as this one. It is the power to sell and so to cheat the others that unites Pothecary, Pedlar, and Pardoner. The individuals here show all the taste for compromise and flexibility that can be imagined, but the opposites they live between are too absolute to accommodate them. The opposition of sacred and secular cannot be compromised. Heywood cannot give us the richness and variousness of Shakespeare, and presumably does not wish to give it; for the absolutes of Christian doctrine are no doubt too important to him (and to his audience) to allow shuffling with sin and salvation. The only space he can create is the space to turn round at the end, deny the secular values that have hitherto dominated the activities, and allow his escapees to embrace the sacred opposites, which still allow them to use their "vertues" (capacities), though under a new heading:[7]

> These, with all other vertues well marked,
> All-though they be of sondry kyndes,
> Yet be they nat used with sondry myndes;
> But, as God only doth all those move,
> So every man, onely for his love,
> With love and dred obediently
> Worketh in these vertues unyformely.
> Thus every vertue, yf we lyste to scan,
> Is pleasaunt to God and thankfull to man.

The final lines make what looks like a Shakespearian point about pastime or play:

> And all that hath scapet us here by neglygence,
> We clerely revoke and forsake it.
> To passe the tyme in thys without offence,
> Was the cause why the maker dyd make it.
>
> (ll. 1230–33)

But the similarity to Shakespeare is only superficial. Shakespeare offers us playfulness as a kind of reality, asking us to note our human capacity to play with possibilities as one of our basic qualities. In this sense playfulness is not an opposite to seriousness but a version of it. But Heywood must mark a clear limit to the number of things that can be played with; his play is humble and apologetic (as his last lines show), whereas Shakespeare's play is bold and unashamed. Shakespeare achieves his freedom, of course, by a resolute secularism, so that the conflict between protagonist and the surrounding world of values is a conflict of wills rather than doctrines. In terms of doctrine, however, will is largely irrelevant: the individual either conforms to or rejects the Truth and so is right or wrong. But a conflict of wills leaves open what doctrine closes down. Characters in this system can promulgate doctrines (or rather, ideologies) as instruments of their wills, but in such a case the doctrines are inside the drama and judged by dramatic criteria ("did this character really mean that?") not outside the drama, making an external judgment on that. Shakespeare's plays in the farce mode give their characters so much power over play and ambiguity that they seem always on the verge of escaping from the rat race of the farce plot, reimagining the situation around them and so giving themselves freedom from its compulsions.

The brilliance of Ben Jonson's plots has often been cited as the main reason for his theatrical power. Coleridge on *The Alchemist* and Dryden on *Epicoene* agree about the unique quality of these as structures. What may be said in the terms of this essay is that the so-called perfection of Jonson's best plots derives from the extent to which the characters (and the ethos they share) fit precisely inside the space the plot allows them. A group of people, elaborately cross-related, hunt one another and are hunted, manipulate and try to avoid manipulation, all inside an unchanging and explicit set of valuations. The obvious difference between these plays and Shakespeare's plays in the farce mode that I have discussed earlier lies in the restriction Jonson's plots impose on Jonson's individuals. A power to retreat into the mystery of oneself and so to modify the external conditions seems always to be available in Shakespeare, even though it is not always followed through; but in Jonson change is presented as social rather than psychological, as when Face escapes into the persona of Jeremy the butler. There is, however, an extraordinary continuity between the authors in the ways in which their farce plots express both the basic conflict between protagonist and society and the congruence that holds them together. The ambiguous vitality of Face, Doll Common, and Subtle, both subversive and supportive of social values, makes modern attempts to explain them by doctrinal analogies rather misplaced. To see the three of them as the World, the Flesh, and the Devil adds a momentary frisson to our perception, but cannot be taken beyond that. Neither their diabolical nor their antibourgeois status has doctrinal force. If they are devils they are only comic devils and their Pandemonium crumbles around them as they try to occupy it. They live in daily terror of being undone, betrayed by one another or by the loss of their house. Using this as their foothold they can exercise superior talents and exploit the bourgeois greed of the respectable citizens around them. But the foothold is too insecure to allow more than brilliant individual cheats; by overreaching they fall down. They cannot achieve the staid condition of bourgeois continuity in exploitation; and in so far as Jonson makes Lovewit the householder a representative of this condition he does not seem to be requiring us to condemn it. The play sets Face, Doll, and Subtle against the petty respectability of their victims, as cheats and liars against "good men and true." But at the same time, and at a level below that of mere social distinctions, what we are shown is a unified society. As in *The Beggar's Opera*, here too the criminal is only a capitalist in a hurry. The speed and boldness, the extent of risk-taking in the syndicate's operations, cut them off from the respectability of the London bourgeoisie around them, and so (we are shown) cut them off from long-term profitability. Thus they are society's victims as much as they are society's victimizers. They can only live by panic, and, as Michael Frayn has recently remarked, "Farce is about panic."[8] This is how the play rivets our attention: the house is not their own, all the rooms are full, the doorbell is ringing, the master is outside, and the whole structure so carefully built up begins to sway and teeter. At this point doctrine may seem, once again, to threaten the balance and ambiguity I have detected. The master returning to find the neglected property and the frolicking servants may well remind readers of the parables of the vineyard or the talents, and Jonson's heavy moralism might suggest that we are about to see a final judgment scene of reward and punishment. But the comic logic of the farce mode does not allow this. When Lovewit returns he does not show us a genuine opposite but only a different aspect of the same ethos. The doctrinal distance between master and servant in the biblical stories is clearly inappropriate to this "real" world of economic accommodations. Master and servant are here as necessary to one another as host and parasite in nature. Lovewit and Face have a common cause—to transfer the spoils of criminal activity into the mode of respectable profit taking.

When criminal greed is translated into capitalist enterprise at the end of *The Alchemist* we are not left with a world whose values have doctrinal certainty but only with values that are provisional and yet defensible because self-aware. Face is able to rejoin "good" society while the less agile Doll and Subtle skulk in outer darkness and gnash their teeth. We allow this because we allow that speed and agility are genuine values and, moreover, are the only values by which the world of this play has been controlled. The case is the same with Surly, who has an identical aim to Lovewit's but proves too slow and morally pedantic to win the prize. So he "deserves" to lose. The end of the play is phrased, in other words, as another kind of game, in which the values are like the rules in a game. But where in Shakespeare the game is like a team game in which "you precious winners all" share the rewards of victory, in Jonson we are watching an individualistic game in which each player plays for himself. At the end of *The Alchemist* we are invited to share the significantly named Lovewit's pleasure in his winnings and to allow that the exclusion of Doll and Subtle is a laugh which appropriately completes the joke that they were trying to play against the world. In the deliberately demoralized world of this comedy perhaps a joke is the most we can expect. For the dramatist too is a jokester. Here, as even more obviously in *Epicoene*, the outwitting inside the plot reflects the trickery by which the dramatist outwits our expectations about the play. If we do not blame the witty Jonson for deceiving us why should we blame the witty Face? Playfulness is more akin to exploitation here than Shakespeare ever allows it to be, just as the game played is closer to a real Darwinian struggle for survival. But *The Alchemist*'s final reference to the play as only "play" has the same effect on our capacity to allow the conclusion as we find in Shakespeare. When we learn that the characters in *The Alchemist* have all been, in fact, game players playing the same game, it comes to seem only proper that the play should end with some winning and some losing according to the rules of the game. Reconciliation between situations wholly opposed becomes possible when we see them distinguished as the devices of art rather than the reflections of life.

What I have called the de-moralizing (or perhaps it should be the de-romanticizing) of the world in which Jonson's mature comedies operate is often seen as part of an inevitable historical process by which the seventeenth century replaces fantasy by realism. The movement from Lyly to Shakespeare, Shakespeare to Jonson, Jonson to Etherege, can certainly be viewed as one in which the claim that "this is life as it is actually lived" becomes increasingly important. But this characteristic is only one among many and needs to have set against it some other compensating changes. The choice to isolate the manners of the town as a picture of life requires (or perhaps is required by) a change in the nature of the expectable plot as well as a change in the mode of utterance and the range of verbal effects available. To believe in the probable characteristics inside the town ethos it seems we have also to believe in the improbable plots that estrange people and bring them together. The narrow capacity for change and so for action that is allowable inside the homogeneous world of town realism imposes plot types marked by extremes of ingenuity and coincidence, convulsions of intrigue to produce the most modest of social displacements. Wycherley, like Jonson, presents comedy as a revelation of apparent difference but basic congruity between the trickster (Horner, Face) and "respectable" society, which has, it turns out, no differentiating values. But in Jonson the substratum of greed that provides the rules still allows the game to be played with an infectious pleasure in wit and manipulation, exploiting the large variety of voices required to express the great variety of social types involved. When the great variety disperses at the end of a Jonson comedy we are given a sense of pleasure in their sheer diversity and in the incapacity of judgment to control them all. In *The Country Wife* on the other hand, the contract by which wit does not so much deny judgment as run past it in a crowd is impossible to sustain. Horner's game is less to win than to deface. His stratagem, to gain access to the women of the town by having it spread abroad that he has been made a eunuch, sets up his plot as a subversion of an expected social ethos, and clearly we might anticipate that we will be seeing him chased from bedroom to bedroom as the stratagem works or is endangered. This is not, however, the main effect made. Horner is much more intensely an antagonist of false morality (and so a proponent of the absent true morality) than a bare account of the plot would suggest. The Fidgets and Squeamishes may be the targets of sexual adventure, but they are also the objects of moral disgust. The aim revealed is less to enjoy the women than to triumph over their husbands and the whole bourgeois conspiracy of respectability and complacent self-regard. The mainspring of *The Country Wife* is the male rivalry between the roughly equal members of a homogeneous society claiming to represent social life as it actually exists. The game being played here is the only game in town and there is no escape from it. Horner's superiority must be shown (as his name suggests) by his demasculating the others—giving them the horns. But this sexual superiority can only be seen as a displaced version of a desired moral superiority that society does not permit. Horner's belief in honor, manliness, liberality, and good sense has to operate in a world where "honor" is Lady Fidget's word for well-concealed appetite and where liberality describes Sparkish's imbecile negligence. As a frustrated moralist Horner can only show himself as a savage exposer of moralism. Wycherley's stern limitation on the possibility of change is somewhat concealed by the variety of the situations he shows us. But the material is in fact more repetitive than seems to be the case at first glance. The three overlapping plots (Fidgets, Sparkish, Pinchwife) are simple transformations of one another. The Fidget plot and the Pinchwife plot both revolve round Horner as cuckolder, but in opposite directions, the first depending on his supposed impotence, the second on his reputed potency. Likewise, the Fidget plot repeats the Sparkish plot in the foolishness with which the husband and the husband-to-be treat the matter of the wife's liberty. Sir Jasper allows his lecherous womenfolk the freedom to cuckold and disgrace him because he believes rumor; Sparkish imposes on Alithea a freedom she does not seek because he is entirely self-deceived. Thus, for all the complexity of its plotting, the world of *The Country Wife* turns round a very small number of possibilities. The freedom of these "free spirits" to choose one thing rather than another is the usual nonfreedom in the plot of farce.

Given the power of *The Country Wife* in study as on stage, critics have difficulty in allowing the word *farce* to describe its mode. At the mere level of mechanism, however, it proclaims its genre: locked doors, back entrances, observers behind screens, intercepted letters, fake parsons, wives disguised as boys—all these traditional elements are found here. And they are here appropriately because they represent not simply the mechanisms but also the unifying vision of farce. The play's power is not a result of its escape from the mode. It is, rather, due to the extent to which the traditional vision of farce—life as a plot of hunting, running, panicking, exploiting, being found out, running again—is savagely and enthusiastically endorsed. Horner's dominance in this world, his command of its ethical tone, does not exempt him from its limitations and its contradictions. His rational manliness and his personal superiority derive only from the fact that he knows better than to expect any freedom of ethical choice, knows that he is a mechanism in a world of mechanisms. This imposes the usual problem for the ending of plays in the farce mode; and it is at this point that the figure of Alithea must be introduced as modifying in some degree the stern logic of the farce plot. Perhaps only a well-bred woman could achieve in this tightly defined world the sufficient combination of detachment and belonging. Certainly Harcourt, her male counterpart, is too much part of the town world in language and behavior to modify our sense of what is possible. Alithea is by no means an untraditional figure. Her goodness is largely continuous with that standard form which equates female virtue with the power of resolute denial. But the mode of her expression sets her apart from the tradition. She is a free woman; she does not blush at the thought of vice, nor does she seek to live inside the boundaries that parents or family have laid down for her. Her right actions derive from her own mind, the limitations she creates for herself. Her refusal to abandon Sparkish, however foolish he shows himself, derives from her assumption that she has entered independently into a binding contract (thus, in the eyes of the law, taking up a masculine prerogative). It is only when Sparkish himself breaks the bond that she allows herself to be free to choose another. Thus the idea of rational contracts freely entered into appears as a quasi-ethical escape from the cycle of appetite that farce displays. We are shown that ethical choice is possible even in the town world of *The Country Wife;* but the choice exercised is virtually without effect in the rest of the world we see. Sparkish is not going to suffer and convert; in particular, the life of Horner is untouched by it. At the end of the play he escapes detection, but only just; and the minimal nature of his "success" hardly provides the kind of agreement that will require the plotting to end. In several comedies we have seen several means by which the farcical plot can cease to hunt down the errant individual, absorbing his energies into a sense of community. The realistic world of *The Country Wife* imposes particular problems on the fulfillment of this pattern: it gives greater power to the aggressive drives of the individualist, and as if in compensation it weakens our sense of a possible communal agreement. Were all women as cool and clear-headed as Alithea, the play seems to say, then marriage could be a match as rational as male companionship. But this is not the reality that is shown in the play. The true discovery of self that affects the four PP, Kate, Falstaff, the Antipholi, even (in a different sense) Jonson's Face, so allowing their plays to end in reconcilement, is not possible for Horner or for the other town men in Wycherley, for the town self is the only true self we are shown. The most the play can present is an exception. The action turns on the necessarily exploitative relations between men and women. But then we are shown a woman of "masculine" temperament, who cannot be exploited. The possibility of an ideal relationship is flashed at us but not explained. The stasis that derives from Alithea is allowed, but only as an isolated and particular ideal. A brand is plucked from the burning and shown us, but only to make us forget that the rest of the world is still on fire.

*   *   *

The mode of farce, I have argued, is one in which the complex of plot and character is dominated by its plot aspect, so that characters are shown making a series of ad hoc assertions of self against the dominant process of social events moving inexorably through time. In my remaining pages I wish to turn to a parallel exposition of what I am calling the romance mode. I am applying the word *romance* (as I have indicated) to that comic form in which the complex of plot and character is read primarily in terms of character, and is properly so read because the ethos exhibited on the stage has the power to hold up the processes of movement through time or to impose on us a consciousness that makes us forget time. Thus in *The Winter's Tale* we may see Leontes as a man driven as hard by events as Face is in *The Alchemist;* but the pressures on Leontes are internal, not derived from his social context, and are changed by a transformation of mind that is hard to anticipate and impossible to fix as part of a process of time. The overall economy of Shakespeare's play is one that eventually discounts progression, making the present more significant as a repetition of the past than as a development out of it—the great gap in time in the middle of the play helps, of course, to encourage this. Or we may consider the role of Rosalind in *As You*

Like It, who (once again) exerts her power to stop the plot and make the action turn round and around the ethical fact of love. I stress the point that I am speaking here of plot movement being held up or frustrated, not controlled or redirected; I am describing an overall effect of stasis or balance rather than a particular (romance) form of movement.

The power given to romance characters to stop the plot does not mean that they appear to us as of necessity more effective or lifelike than the characters of farce. This is one of the points at which the use of Shakespeare as a measuring rod distorts the scale. Shakespeare has a marked taste for romance forms in comedy and is also the creator of unforgettable characters. But the ethos that dominates a romance plot may be that of a situation as easily as that of a person (see my earlier remarks on *The Old Wife's Tale*). The mechanism is the same in either case. The individual (or group) is given free space in which to choose what can be made out of the given events, and time not dominated by plot movement is made available to us so that we can contemplate the meaning of that choice. It follows that the plot of romance is characteristically leisurely and even diffuse, putting little pressure on the characters to move ahead smartly before the next social demand arises. A satisfactory end can only be reached in such a plot by allowing a considerable amount of freedom in the connections made between the intentions of individuals and the way the action works out.

In order to show a conspectus of romance structures in the seventeenth century that corresponds to the one I have already essayed for the mode of farce I wish to concentrate (once again) on texts from Shakespeare, Jonson, and Restoration Comedy, therefore parallel to those already considered. I choose these texts to make the point that the modes of articulation I am talking about can declare their separate presences inside a single oeuvre and quite independently of supposed historical development. An expressive interrelation of plot and ethos is possible at a number of alternative points of balance; and the choice is not determined simply by the taste of one period for one view of life or another (fantastic, hard-boiled, cosy). This is not to say that there is no connection between social outlook and aesthetic mode; but it is certainly not correct to allege that the mode that shows ethos at the mercy of plot is always required by what is usually understood as realism (as I have argued already), or that the mode that allows ethos to dominate plot must be used to express love. Thus, among the romance plays I shall discuss in this section I include Jonson's *Bartholomew Fair.* This play is usually considered (and properly enough) a masterpiece of realistic portraiture. But it is held together formally by the mode of romance—by its stasis in time; by its unpredictable swirl of events, making expectation impossible to sustain; by its emphasis on chance; by the natural sympathy established between characters and background. The material of the play, I am arguing, is absorbed and structured by the form, not selected or eliminated.

The Tempest, on the other hand, is often thought of as the archetypal romance (and Jonson so presents it in the Induction to *Bartholomew Fair*); yet its often-remarked tight control of time and space and the impersonal precision of the plot that Prospero has set up to deal with those around him seem to point away from ethos and toward a plot-controlled type of structure in which little or no space is given for ethical choice or the contemplation of values. As often in the best plays there is an element of technical teasing in this—the structure points in one direction and the play advances in the other one. For once the motive-force of plot movement is identified as a particular person—in this case a person with a remarkably complex attitude toward his own power of control—our attention to his plot is liable to be undercut by our interest in the character of the plotter. *The Tempest*'s presentation of time assists in this effect. The plot (we are told) was conceived before the play begins and what we see in the play's real time is only the fulfillment of what has been set up. There are occasional points at which the plot is shown as reaction to immediate events (Prospero remembers the Caliban-Trinculo-Stephano plot), but by and large the events proceed like clockwork once the spell's wound up. We are never on the edges of our seats to know who will survive or how. The neoclassical unities of place and time are not invoked here to show their traditional function of allowing muthos to dominate ethos, pressing the small space of present experience under the accumulated weight of the past, forcing moves and evasions that are thus explicable to us, even when the characters themselves cannot see the chain of cause and effect. In *The Tempest* the wrongs done in the past still rankle in the mind of Prospero, but those malev-olences have already, we can see, turned into benefits and lost their consequential force. In theory we ought to be watching the characters guilty of past crimes harried into repentance (at the very least); but in fact the opening up of the play is toward an understanding that such an end cannot be achieved by such means. We see Prospero's commitment to his plot of revenge fading away before the discovery that revenge (bewitching the sinners, afflicting Caliban with cramps) cannot achieve anything real in terms of the dominant ethos. The world of the play has to be allowed to be a free world of genuine individual choices, for the people in it turn out to be uncontrollable. ⸺

The plot movement of *The Tempest* is in fact so little committed to forward impetus that it seems to be recurrently on the verge of losing direction or running down. I have already mentioned the most striking example—the sudden interruption of Prospero's timeless show of the gods by a memory of necessary action—against Caliban's time-bound plot. But Caliban himself has had to push his plot past the becalming influence of ethos when Trinculo and Stephano show themselves more interested in the bottle than the murder; and at the climax of their plot they show themselves again more susceptible to the pleasures of the moment (the "trumperies" on the line) than to the opportunities of the future. Everywhere we look in the play we see the attempt to control the future by planning ahead from the present subjected to frustration: Antonio and Sebastian cannot achieve their murder, Ariel cannot achieve his freedom, Ferdinand cannot achieve Miranda. Above all, Prospero cannot achieve his intention of complete control and has to confess that his grand plan is pointless. There is plenty of frustration in farce where one person's intention is regularly crossed by another's. But this is not the mode of *The Tempest*, whose whole action points up the inconsequentiality of human plans and offers us stasis and con-templation as the unifying focus on what happens. The end of the play achieves in some degree what Prospero planned, but it is also an acceptance that what is planned can only be part of what is happening, only part of the larger and vaguer sense of life's meaning that we are required to contemplate. The epilogue turns around the usual relationship that is established in Shakespeare's epilogues between the play's fiction and the actor's reality. Earlier epilogues (to *As You Like It* for example) move the plane of the action from a lesser to a greater reality: in reality the actor is not imprisoned in his role; he and his fellows are human beings like the members of the audience, and the epilogue invites the audience to celebrate their shared humanity by joining the company (clapping their hands). At the end of *The Tempest,* the actor playing Prospero is presented instead as an isolated and problematic figure reduced to impotence by the loss of the magic of his fictional role. The audience's plaudits no longer give him a new and more assured life; the most they can do is to allow him to escape from fiction to absence. *The Tempest* ends with the power of the magician to plan ahead revealed as only the power of the human being to suffer, allowing us to contemplate (in terms of ethos) the static condition of wishing, hoping, fearing, loving, hating.

Throughout his dramatic career as a writer of comedy Shakespeare shows a marked reluctance to allow sharpness of expectation too dominating a hold on his actions. It seems to be his characteristic technique to avoid giving us too precise connection between the different elements or persons who appear. He tends to put together persons with little coherence ab initio, and he is wary of contexts that tell us too clearly what we should expect. He regularly leaves his transitions open and unexplained, and he changes frequently or renders vague the places where such action could be expected to occur. He wrote no London citizen comedies, and, given his preferences, we need not wonder why; for in such plays the narrow range of the social context sharpens our expectations of action, allowing only a small number of plausible alternatives. *Twelfth Night* is a good example of a comic organization that stands quite opposite to this kind of restriction. Not only are the place and time of the action left obscure, but the very form of the action is created by piling up matters only loosely connected. We advance into the play by way of an extraordinary range of apparent incompatibles—a bereaved and shipwrecked maiden, a lovesick duke, a drunken uncle, a self-deceiving votaress, a foolish knight, a professional entertainer, a puritan steward—all talking in the divergent languages of their separate obsessions. Though these characters soon settle into a system where centrifugal and centripetal forces balance out to produce stable orbits, the action continues to be characterized by distance rather than proximity. Each of these separate characters has a strong tendency to pursue his own course as if the world elsewhere were void; and collisions when they occur seem like bumps in the night between drunk men—temporary displacement followed by attempts to resume the former motion—rather than systems of cause and effect. So multicentered a world offers so many possibilities of conjunction that it becomes impossible to forecast what will happen. Such anticipation as the play allows derives from an understanding of its ethos more than from any perception of its plot movement. We cannot anticipate the role of Antonio in the history of Viola, but we can expect that the action will eventually fulfill the ethical goals that her free space has given her power to choose. This is what she demands of time:[9]

> O time, thou must untangle this, not I,
> It is too hard a knot for me t'untie.

—where *time* is seen as an unstructured element in which good (and bad) things will turn up rather than a developmental process leading from then to now.

In such a structure as *Twelfth Night* turns out to be we recognize the movement through time as having a certain mysterious independence from the intentions of the characters who are pressing on it. One way in which character-centered criticism has tried to deal with this quality in the play is by absorbing plot direction into our sense of character development, often speaking as if this were the most profound and most laudable form of development available. Real instances of development of character are in fact rather hard to find. At the end of *Twelfth Night* Orsino discovers that he does not really love Olivia and pledges himself to Viola instead. Does he do this because he has "developed"? There is no evidence that requires us to think so. All one can say is that a pattern of persons used to integrate relationships has been developed out of elements chosen originally, it appears, for disparateness. The separate elements are (by and large) in stable position at the end of the action, as they had not been at any earlier point, but this evidence can hardly lead us to suppose that the ending worked out that way because the qualities of characters caused it to happen. We have seen characteristics exposed and tested throughout the play—Viola's resilience, Malvolio's self-love, Feste's disengagement, Sebastian's willingness to take chances. The results of these testings may have told us who deserves what fate, but some other and more mysterious cause must be held responsible for such fates being fulfilled. We may say that we come to know such people, but we know them as people carried to their fates rather than people achieving them. We see them as static objects, faces at the window of a train hauled past us to a destination ("happiness") via a route that we cannot describe.

We may look at another example of what is called character development in Shakespearian comedy that allows an even clearer image of the objections I raise against it. In *Much Ado about Nothing* Benedick ends the play by accepting the matrimony that he had earlier sworn to avoid. Can we say that this time we have seen "character development"? The question points up the contrary demands made by ethos and muthos. The demand of ethos is that we accumulate the evidence dropped piecemeal along the play and fit it into some deep structure of notional ethical unity (Benedick was always, in some sort or other, the same, always in love with Beatrice). At the same time we are meant to respond to the contradiction between earlier and later statements and to the changes in role that are involved. The role, we may say, has developed, though the character has not. The comedy arises, it seems, from such impossible opposites—a character who is both responsible and irresponsible, the same man and a new man. In the mode of farce self-contradiction is a sign of incapacity to measure up to the demands of the fictional world; but Benedick's self-contradiction is endorsed by the play he is in as an appropriate ethos, and we are invited not to laugh at weakness but to share the pleasure of being free to live with contradictions, the pleasure of defying, or at least distancing, the necessity to conform to progressive adaptation.

The standard map of seventeeth-century drama sees Shakespeare as the poet of such moments of character and self-assertion and Jonson as his polar opposite, the poet of plot and logic. At an earlier point in this essay I have argued that Shakespeare must be allowed to have written plays in the mode of farce, plays that give characters little freedom from the necessities of the plot. I wish now to consider an obvious corollary to that argument—to look at Jonson's *Bartholomew Fair* as a play that gives sufficient scope to its characters to allow them to distance the pressures of plot progression. The Induction to *Bartholomew Fair* is much exercised to separate this play from those that "make nature afraid . . . [and] beget tales, tempests and such-like drolleries."[10] Certainly the presented material of this play is quite distinct from that of *The Winter's Tale* or *The Tempest.* But if we look beyond content or social presentation we may come to see that there is much in the structure of *Bartholomew Fair* that aligns it with the romance genre, indeed, even with such extreme examples as *Pericles* or *The Tempest.* The technique of setting a large gallery of disparate persons in a loosely structured but rigorously testing environment is one we have already noticed in *Twelfth Night;* and we may notice it again in *Bartholomew Fair.* In *The Alchemist* (and even more obviously in *Volpone*) Jonson controls the ethical diversity of his persons by subjecting them to the close proximity of their stage manipulators and masters. It is true, of course, that Lovewit is not on stage for much of *The Alchemist;* but his existence and his rights hang over the action from the beginning. A plot so pressed upon by intrigue behind intrigue holds our attention focused upon probable outcomes that will untie the knot, and we can judge the events as they pass before us in terms of their power to promote or distance or divert such likelihoods. But in *Bartholomew Fair* the diversity of ethos or intention is not controlled by any given perception of likely developing outcome. Time as chance may not seem to be as deliberately invoked as in *Twelfth Night;* but the plotting by which Winwife marries Mistress Grace and by which Quarlous secures Dame Purecraft is made out of a series of deliberately exposed opportunisms and inventions, appearing amid the swirl of random characters across the stage (Captain Whit, Val Cutting, Bristle and Haggis, Sharkwell, Puppy, and so on) whose local color diverts our attention from the likelihood of planned progression. It is characteristic that the play begins with Winwife as the preferred suitor to Purecraft but keeps us uncertain whether he or Quarlous is advancing or retreating in the pas de trois, or, indeed, what advance or retreat would be like. In this context we should remember Grace Wellborne's method of "choice" between these two suitors, submitting their romantic pseudonyms of Argalus and Palamon (ideal lovers) to the scrutiny of the random next arrival on the scene. The play thus reaches the realist assumption that marriage is a lottery by a specific devaluation of high-stretched romance, and yet by a process more akin to fairy tale than to rationality. And the fact that the random chooser is a madman who does not even pretend that he can understand the names further downgrades the importance of purpose or intention. Indeed Quarlous the master plotter, who obtains both Cokes's license and Overdo's blank charter, has to be content for all that with the lottery's superior power to give the more passive Winwife the top prize.

The tendency in *Bartholomew Fair* to present devaluations of romantic attitudes inside structural systems that characterize the romance mode is everywhere evident. Courtship and marriage are presented as only admirable when wholly rational. Quarlous and Winwife begin their suit with the standard vocabulary of passion: "'Sblood we love you," but they are cut down to size by the cool expediency of Grace: "each of you might be the man if the other were away. For you are reasonable creatures; you have understanding and discourse. And if fate send me an understanding husband, I have no fear at all but mine own manners shall make him a good one" (4.3.30–35). Thus driven into rationality, they display an absence of rivalry that is clearly meant to contrast not only with the romantic excesses of Palamon and Arcite but also with the excess of animal spirits in the puppet play's rendering of Damon and Pythias, each yelling Billingsgate abuse at the thought of the other possessing whore Hero. And yet, for all this modeling of rationality, Quarlous and Winwife only progress by totally irrational means. The centrality of Troubleall the madman in both the Grace and the Purecraft plots seems designed to make this point, and Purecraft's so-called reasons for loving Troubleall apply to the whole scenario: "Mad do they call him! The world is mad in error, but he is mad in truth. I love him o' the sudden" (4.6.157–58). We find ourselves in the fair in a world of unexpected and inexplicable events, of confusion and error, not unlike the magic wood in *A Midsummer Night's Dream,* where truth is simply another mode of imagination and where the irrational conviction that truth is present validates choice as well as anything else. "To buy a [ ] in a fair" is a common phrase for buying blind; and Jonson seems to use this idea to provide a context for courtship that puts rational judgment at its greatest disadvantage. As a containing structure Bartholomew Fair has obvious differences from the dukedom of Illyria, being as "low" as that is "high," as negative as that is positive, providing no support for the possibility that imagination will be fulfilled by truth; but the purpose it exercises, to make plans and purposes irrelevant, is very similar. Here, once again, time is abolished and the normal progressions are kept at bay while the *ethe* of the various characters flourish in the free space provided.

In its sealed-off, exclusive nature and its unprogressive quality the environment set up for *Bartholomew Fair* is clearly comparable to that of *Twelfth Night.* In some respects it has an even closer similarity to the Shakespeare play that Jonson specifically condemns—*The Tempest.* As I have noted above, *The Tempest* creates a a fictional world seemingly designed to show a future already planned and an intention only waiting to be fulfilled. But the power to control the future turns out to be a power that cannot be used, and Prospero has to settle for the world as it is, with all the uncontrollables present and flourishing in a magic isle no less than in Milan. The world of *Bartholomew Fair* is also, it has often been observed, a world in which the figures of authority (Busy, Waspe, Overdo) are set in the stocks and fooled out of their pretensions of control. The figure of Adam Overdo is particularly interesting in this context, since he (like Prospero) is given coherent oversight and proper power to accuse and punish all those genuine "enormities" he sees around him. But like Prospero, Overdo discovers that he is only the Adam who fell, "Adam flesh and blood," and that he is never going to be able to plot how the present can be turned into a future where hierarchy is universally revered and all enormities cut off. What is left to Overdo at the end of the play is only the power to forgive, to invite the whole cast home to dinner, puppets and all.

In the plays in the farce mode that I discussed earlier (including *The Alchemist*) the ending is difficult to achieve because the comedy has seemed to be dependent on the utter incompatibility of individual desires and social norms. Satisfactory endings are in fact achieved because it turns out that the opposites are both complex enough and flexible enough to make compromise believable. Kate can become a conservative instead of a radical shrew, Lovewit can accept trickery as a natural part of a respectable bourgeois life. In *The Tempest* on the other hand we do not register the presence of any such basic opposites. The island context is not set against Prospero. The only value system available is Prospero's, and the play seems to be moving toward a state in which everything present has been absorbed inside that system. The sense of challenge and of the possibility of loss is, however, preserved here as in other romance endings not only by the intransigence of Antonio and Caliban but, even more, by the spectacle of conflict and abrasion inside Prospero himself. If the end were simply the demonstration of Prospero's universal power, the ending would be flat and uninformative. But the perception that he is only Adam flesh and blood restores to Prospero the characteristically bittersweet conclusion of the romance mode. As at the end of *Twelfth Night* and of *Bartholomew Fair*, we see that freedom can be asserted only because the abrasive variety of its manifestations has also been allowed. The freedom of Caliban, of Antonio, of Ariel, and even of Prospero himself, is everywhere accompanied by a sense of the loss involved. The Milan voyage is a gesture of reconciliation that carries no more claim to permanency than Overdo's somewhat enforced love feast. It is a measure of will rather than nature and is therefore open to the willful rejection of the nonconformists—Edgworth the cutpurse, Antonio the younger brother, Malvolio the class warrior, or (to look forward a little) Loveit the cast mistress.

Etherege's *The Man of Mode* is a play whose social mode is very close to that of *The Country Wife,* and Dorimant, the hero of the former play, can easily be seen as an original for Horner. But a comparison of the methods by which the social worlds of these two plays are in fact developed may lead us to observe of these comedies that they are, however close in their content, quite distinct in their comic structures. *The Country Wife* begins with Horner setting up the pseudo-eunuch trap that will keep the action going for the rest of the play. *The Man of Mode* begins with Dorimant in company with his servants and hangers-on, with whom he develops nothing at all but the image of himself as a model for his society, a modish man who is also a man of action. Little sense is given in this opening of any necessary forward movement; and forward movement is indeed a dimension that the whole play seems careless about. Matters are of course planned, anticipated, and executed. In the main plot we see Mrs. Loveit set up for rejection and her counterplot unraveled; Bellinda's seduction is completed; Harriet (whose arrival in town is the new event of act 1) is found to be a worthy object, even if the cost be Hampshire and matrimony. The secondary plot shows us in a particularly illuminating way how Etherege handles such material. What we have in the scheme of Young Bellair to outwit his father is the classic farce plot of the young lover whose secret bride becomes the object of his father's marital intentions.[11] But *The Man of Mode* pays scant attention to the farcical mechanisms of mistake and near-discovery by which, traditionally, the son can outwit the father. Indeed, the mechanisms hardly seem to exist in this play, though it may be that Etherege assumes we know about the farcical possibilities. He prefers to occupy the space he has by particularizing the ethos of Old Bellair's country manners. The shadow of a different kind of treatment is thrown in front of us, but no substantial action is developed to interfere with the main focus on ethos. In the main plot we see the same shadow-play of action though without the same opportunity for generic comparison. Dorimant gives us a preview of the mechanisms Bellinda will use to anger Loveit:[12]

> She means insensibly to insinuate a discourse of me and artificially raise her jealousy to such a height that, transported with the first motions of her passion, she shall fly upon me with all the fury imaginable as soon as ever I enter. The quarrel being thus happily begun, I am to play my part: confess and justify all my roguery, swear her impertinence and ill humor makes her intolerable, tax her with the next fop that comes into my head and in a huff march away.

A number of points can be made about this speech as a preparative for action or a provocative to draw on interest in what will happen next. We note that the action to come is viewed less as behavior than as performance ("I am to play my part") and described as a consequence of ethos—in this case Loveit's passionate nature and Bellinda's malignity—rather than as an external event with consequences. Medley's comment marks out this focus: "This vizard [Bellinda] is a spark, and has a genius that makes her worthy of yourself, Dorimant" (1.232–33).

The pressure of ethos shows itself throughout the play and above all in the presentation of its actions less as individual histories than as representative events of the town. People here (from the shoemaker to the heiress) are bound by a common language of interests and valuations that are distinguished from one another less by separation of aims than by position on the common scale. All are playing the same game, and full freedom is simply the privilege of those who have the poise and wit to play the town game with detachment, with the knowledge that it is only a game. And such freedom is less the freedom to do this or that than (as so commonly in romance) the freedom to be oneself. This is a static rather than a dynamic quality, and the town game offers us an essentially static situation: the players come and go, but the new players must go through the same moves as the old players, for the rules stay the same. The rabble of fops, sparks, vizards, coxcombs, gallants, and whores fills every space in the landscape inside a perspective that carries us from the full-scale characters we are familiar with to a background of mere names—Lady Dealer and Lady Dapper, Lackwit, Wagfan, and Caperwell. The assumption made is of a consistency throughout the entire picture, so that if we got to know Dealer or Wagfan we would not find ourselves in a different world. Action by the characters we do know thus assumes a metonymic function: this intrigue succeeds or fails, that relationship is established or broken; but behind each of these individual motions toward change lies (we know) their repetition by other gallants and other ladies, so that eventually, we can see, nothing ever advances or changes, the short-term development being absorbed into the long-term stasis. In these terms it is easy to see how Dorimant differs from Horner. Horner makes his effect *against* the assumed norm of a gentleman and so frees himself from representativeness. Dorimant is less the servant of his appetite then of his looking glass. He shares many of the Man of Mode characteristics with his opposite, who is also his parodic double—Sir Fopling.

The "town" in Etherege is, I am suggesting, another of these enchanted spots where, in the mode of romance, ethos can flourish in freedom from desperate activity. But, of course, as a social context the town is as different from Jonson's fair as the fair is from Shakespeare's Illyria. One must note in particular that the town makes a specific claim to represent not simply a special theatrical place but an actual locale well known to members of the audience. This is a famous crux in the criticism of Restoration comedy; but we err if we do not notice that the reality of such a play as *The Man of Mode* (as also of *The Country Wife*) is the condition of its art, not an escape from its art. The artfully constructed world of *The Man of Mode* has the same function as do the worlds of *Bartholomew Fair* and *Twelfth Night*—to nourish the ethos of its particular world so long as the action stays inside that world. The play ends, as do other romances I have spoken about, with the idea of a departure from the enchanted place and with a hint that the balance achieved there *may* be able to survive in a less protected environment—but it may not, given the variety of freedoms allowed. At the end of *The Man of Mode* we may well ask if Harriet and Hampshire will in fact outweigh the charms of London with Bellinda and other victims yet unnamed. Dorimant himself seems to be looking to have his cake and eat it. And the structure supports the assumption of such a possibility; for the representative nature of the town action we have seen runs against any imagination of real change. In plays of the farce mode our relief at the end of the *moto perpetuo* of action allows us to think that the unification of opposites we are seeing does represent a permanent change. The four PP and the Church, Kate and Petruchio, Face and Lovewit, Falstaff and the Windsor bourgeoisie have been united in a manner that nowhere asks us to respond with further questions about the final arrangements. But in romance the ethos that declares itself by the freedom to choose is not canceled by the ending of the play. The only thing we can be sure of at the end of *The Man of Mode* is that Dorimant will continue to be Dorimant—and that puts everything else at risk.

I have spoken above of the space Shakespeare allows to exist around the persons of his plays in the romance mode (in *Twelfth Night* for example), so that the ethos engages our sympathy and attention as a static effect separable from the actions undertaken. In Jonson marginally and in Etherege very obviously (and in Congreve to an even greater extent) this space is provided by the detachment of the central characters from the actions they undertake (a detachment that is often called cruelty or coldness), by their gift of independence of mind, of style, or even by their controlled affectation. Horner also has something of this *sprezzatura*, but the intrigues of *The Country Wife* leave him too little space to develop it. Dorimant, on the other hand, is given little else to do but demonstrate his detached superiority, and the central distinction between Dorimant and Sir Fopling Flutter is phrased entirely in these terms, as is that between Harriet (tough and approved of) and Loveit (vulnerable and therefore contemptible). When we see Harriet set up with Young Bellair the mannerisms that will spell love to their watching but naive elders we are given a definition of ethical freedom as the power to hold and indicate valuations that socially required actions would seem to rule out of court. The plot (such as it is) can seem to be exacting the full conformity of the characters, but we are allowed to know that the conformities are performance only. Etherege plays with the realisms of social behavior to achieve a comedy in which, as in other romances, the power of the plot is distanced and reduced—in this case by the superiority of character to action. To compare *The Man of Mode* to *The Country Wife* in these terms is to see not only the obvious similarity in the life imitated but also the obvious dissimilarity in the methods by which imitation is achieved. It is open to us to describe the comedies of this period not only in terms of the life they present— the material that shapes the familiar landscape of literary history—but also in terms of their inner structures, showing the landscape more from a geologist's than a topographer's point of view, understanding the hills and valleys less as the kinds of places we live in and more as evidences of the hidden pressures that shaped them as they are.[13]

NOTES

1. The word *mongrel* is, of course, meant to recall Sir Philip Sidney's derogatory remarks about Elizabethan drama: "all their plays be neither right tragedies nor right comedies: mingling kings and clowns . . . so as neither the admiration and commiseration nor the right sportfulness is by their mongrel tragicomedy obtained" (*An Apology for Poetry*, ed G. Shepherd [London: Nelson, 1965] p. 135).

2. *Towards Standards of Criticism*, ed. F. R. Leavis (London: Wishart, 1933), p. 33. Rickword's elaborate chemical trope needs some elucidating. He says, "Only as precipitates from the memory are plot or character tangible; yet only in solution have either any emotive valency." *Valency* is the capacity of elements to combine with or displace hydrogen (or equivalent) atoms during chemical reactions. The word seems to be used in this passage to denote the power of the aesthetic experience to transform into a new vision all that we see or feel when we read (or spectate), and to do this at some level below our consciousness of distinction between the different artistic elements involved. "Emotive valency" may also mean "emotional power" (using a more root sense of *valency*). "In solution" presumably refers to that state in which the (chemical or artistic) reaction occurs, the moment of our transforming response, as against our subsequent thoughts about it. The *solution* is a homogeneous liquid and so is indivisible. But after the reaction has occurred new stable compounds are formed: these are precipitates—solid substances now separable from the solution in which their

elements were formerly dissolved, solidified memories of what the aesthetic moment was like in all its fluidity and wholeness, rationalizations of what happened.

3. Ibid, p. 31.

4. I should note that I am using the word *ethical* simply to represent the adjectival form of *ethos*, so that *ethical choice* (here and elsewhere) refers to a choice between different possible *ethe*, not to a choice concerned with moral right and wrong.

5. See G. K. Hunter, "The Idea of Comedy and Some Seventeenth Century Comedies," in *Poetry and Drama in the English Renaissance.*, ed. Koshi Nakanori and Yasuo Tamaizumi (Tokyo: Kinokuniya Bookstore Company, 1980), pp. 72–73.

6. Aristotle, *Poetics*, 5.1; 1449a34.

7. John Heywood, *The Four PP*, ll. 1166–74, in *Specimens of the Pre-Shakespearean Drama*, ed. John Manly, 2 vols. (Boston: Ginn and Company, 1897), 1:520; later citations of this edition appear parenthetically.

8. See *Times Literary Supplement* (5 March 1982), p. 252.

9. *Twelfth Night,* ed. J. M. Lothian and T. W. Craik (London: Methuen, 1975), 2.2.39–40.

10. Ben Jonson, *Bartholomew Fair,* ed. Eugene M. Waith (New Haven: Yale University Press, 1963), Induction, ll. 115–16. Later parenthetical citations refer to this edition.

11. Compare Plautus, *Mercator, Asinaria, Casina.*

12. George Etherege, *The Man of Mode,* ed. W. B. Carnochan (Lincoln: University of Nebraska Press, 1966), 1.222–30. Later parenthetical citations refer to this edition.

13. I am grateful to Marion Trousdale and Shelagh Hunter, whose dissatisfaction with an earlier version of this essay gave me the impetus to start again, correcting old mistakes into what, I fear, may only be new ones.

Comic Tradition and the European Context: The Testing of Love

Kenneth Muir

When Lysander and Hermia, doomed by Duke Theseus to everlasting separation, lament the various impediments to the course of true love—difference of class or age, parental opposition, sickness, mortality—they assume that their present predicament validates the genuineness of their love and is also a test of their fidelity. In their case, the test is not prolonged: it consists of a single unnerving night in the forest. The infidelity of Demetrius, the real cause of the trouble, is cured by supernatural means. Shakespeare's love comedies all end with the happiness of the lovers; and as the audience is as aware that the plays will end happily as readers of detective stories know that the sleuth will solve the mystery, the art of the dramatist consists in a plausible postponement of the final happiness. This he can achieve in a variety of ways: by the infidelity of one of the lovers (e.g., Proteus); by the lovers' ignorance of their own feelings (e.g., Benedick, Beatrice); by parental orders (Hermia, Portia); by the slander of the heroine (Hero, Imogen, Hermione); by the need of one or both the lovers to be reeducated (Katherine, Orsino, Bertram, and possibly Isabella); and by the confusions caused by disguise (Antipholus, Rosalind, Viola).

But the mere procrastination of happiness is not an adequate comic formula. The dramatists with whom we shall be concerned in this essay use the period of postponement in a more significant way: the lovers are under probation. In one of Shakespeare's early comedies, *Love's Labour's Lost*, the probation is extended for a year beyond the action of the play. The courtiers have to expiate not so much their broken vows as the motives that prompted the vows in the first place. Proteus has more to expiate. He is not merely unfaithful to Julia, he adopts the principle that all is fair in love: he betrays Valentine to the Duke and then tries to rape Silvia. He fails in whatever tests can be applied to love and friendship; and, despite his repentance and the forgiveness of Valentine and Julia, modern audiences do not regard the ending as a happy one. Shakespeare himself presumably realized, and perhaps relished, the absurdity of Valentine's offer to hand over Silvia to the thwarted rapist. He was parodying the Renaissance idea that friendship was superior to love:[1]

> . . . all thinges (friendship excepted) are subiect to fortune. . . . When aduersities flowe, then loue ebbes: but friendship standeth stifflie in stormes. Time

draweth wrinckles in a fayre face, but addeth fresh colours to a fast friende, which neither heate, nor colde, nor miseries, nor place, nor destiny can alter or diminish.

While writing *Two Gentlemen of Verona,* we may suppose, Shakespeare was treating the conflict between love and friendship in the *Sonnets,* with himself cast in the role of Valentine; but the only other time he treated the subject in drama is in *Much Ado about Nothing,* where Beatrice demands that Benedick prove the genuineness of his love by killing his bosom friend, Claudio. As the play is a comedy, Benedick does not have to implement his promise.

In *The Merchant of Venice* Bassanio's love undergoes a triple test. In the first place he has borrowed money from Antonio on the excuse that, by marrying a wealthy heiress, he can repay his previous debts. He runs the risk of being thought a fortune hunter—which a number of critics and directors have assumed to be his character—but his choice of the leaden casket frees him, according to the conventions of poetic drama, from this suspicion. If Portia is not his all, he is not hazarding all he hath in choosing. His second test comes when news of Antonio's danger reaches him. He confesses his responsibility to Portia and hurries back to Venice. The third test comes after the trial, when the disguised Portia asks as reward the ring with which he had vowed never to part. At first he refuses, but when Antonio begs him to give the ring to his savior, he realizes that if he refuses he will seem ungrateful both to the judge and to his friend who had signed the dangerous bond. But if he hands over the ring he will be breaking the first promise made to his wife. He decides rightly that ingratitude is worse than a broken promise, since what really matters is not the promise itself but the fidelity and love of which it is the symbol. Portia, indeed, recognizes this, even though she cannot resist giving Bassanio a bad quarter of an hour. The play recognizes that human motives are mixed, and there is some ambiguity in the treatment of the Christians; but there is no justification for the hostile treatment of Bassanio by some modern directors. He passes the three tests with which he is faced.

In *As You Like It* the testing of the hero is more subtle and more prolonged. He and Rosalind fall in love at first sight, but the element of absurdity in this romantic cliché is underlined by Phebe's love for Ganymede and by the sudden love of Celia and Oliver. Handsome wrestlers are not necessarily ideal husbands, and when the disguised Rosalind meets Orlando in the forest she puts him to the test. She wants to know if his love is merely "fancy," engendered in the eyes, as his verses might lead her to suspect, or something more substantial and lasting. She professes to cure him of his passion by satirizing her own sex, but her real motive is to have an excuse for being in his company and for discovering whether her satirical shafts have any effect. She enjoys her elaborate role playing—a woman, played by a boy, dressed as a boy, posing as a woman. In fact Orlando is captivated by the persona she assumes, as Orsino is unconsciously captivated by Cesario. The worthiness of the lover is tested not merely by the sincerity and steadfastness of his love. Orlando has already proved himself to be brave, dignified, modest, and compassionate. He succors Adam and rejects Jaques' cynicism. Before the end of the play he saves the life of the brother who has tried to kill him, and he practices the duty of forgiveness.

Orsino is not merely tested; he is reeducated in the course of the play in which he appears. As all critics have recognized, he is not so much in love with Olivia, who has refused him many times, as in love with the idea of love. Compared with her other suitors—Sir Andrew and Malvolio—he has a certain aristocratic grandeur. He "prizes not quantity of dirty lands." But he is much more concerned with his own feelings than with their object. Olivia, too, is a poseur. Although her love for her brother was doubtless genuine, it is also a convenient excuse for her rejection of Orsino. Although she proposes to weep once a day for seven years, she never sheds a tear in the course of the play. It is, of course, Viola who cures both Orsino and Olivia; and she knows that she has completed the reeducation of Orsino when, at the end, he shows that he is more jealous of Cesario, the lamb he loves, than the raven-hearted Olivia. He has for some time been in love with his page, despite his fashionably hopeless passion for Olivia.

In the comedies that followed the testing is more severe. Angelo is guilty of infidelity and cruelty to Mariana; he is corrupted by power; he blackmails Isabella to submit to his lust and then orders Claudio's execution. Isabella is persuaded to beg for Angelo's life before she knows that her brother has been saved—a fact that the Duke conceals from her, either to make her act of forgiveness more difficult and therefore more meritorious, or, as he puts it, "to make her heavenly comforts of despair," or to test whether she will make a worthy duchess, or, most likely, because Shakespeare wanted to have as exciting a finale as possible. In *All's Well that Ends Well* the nominal hero is contemptible. He is tested and exposed as inordinately proud, a hopeless judge of character, a lecherous and shifty liar, failing in every one of the tests imposed on him. But, as Mariana remarks of Angelo, "most men are moulded out of faults," and we are meant to suppose that Helena will make something of him. In *Troilus and Cressida* Shakespeare depicted for the first and only time in comedy—if indeed it can be regarded as a comedy—a woman guilty of infidelity. Compared with Chaucer's poem, the dramatic acceleration of the play's action makes Cressida succumb to Diomedes in a few hours; but this should not make us read into the early scenes our knowledge of what is to come. Cressida has loved Troilus, after her fashion, "for many weary months"; but she has held off because she is afraid of losing her power over him. She is more calculating than any other of Shakespeare's heroines, but when she vows to be faithful and when she refuses to leave Troy, we are not meant to doubt her sincerity. Her behavior in the next scene, which so shocks Ulysses, is no more than a reversion to that she had displayed in the second scene of the play—harmless in itself, but disturbingly juxtaposed with her apparently inconsolable grief. Alone among Shakespeare's heroines, she is tested and fails. Her failure enabled Bernard Shaw, who felt that Shakespeare's previous heroines were all idealized, to declare that Cressida was the playwright's "first real woman."

In the plays of the final period the heroines, though tested more severely than the earlier ones, all emerge triumphantly from their ordeals. Marina, "smiling extremity out of act," shows a patience that shames her father's lack of it.

Hermione forgives her erring husband as Imogen forgives hers. But both husbands do something to earn their forgiveness, Leontes by fourteen years of remorse and Posthumus by his admission that Imogen, whom he still believes guilty of adultery, is morally his superior. The younger generation also undergoes ordeals. Although Polixenes threatens Perdita with death and Florizel with disinheritance, both lovers remain true. Florizel proclaims that he is heir to his affection:[2]

> Not for Bohemia nor the pomp that may
> Be thereat gleaned, for all the sun sees, or
> The close earth wombs, or the profound seas hide
> In unknown fathoms, will I break my oath
> To this my fair beloved.

In *The Tempest* Ferdinand and Miranda are tested by Prospero, "lest too light winning / Make the prize seem light," and he warns them thrice not to forestall the marriage ceremony and "give dalliance too much the rein."

*   *   *

Most readers, with whatever reservations, will be in general agreement with the above account of the method of Shakespeare's comedies.[3] It will be the purpose of this essay to show that a number of other dramatists have used comedy for similar didactic purposes. Yet neither Calderón nor Marivaux seems to have been directly influenced by Shakespeare. Wycherley, to Macaulay's disgust, made use of the spotless heroine of *Twelfth Night* for the far from spotless purposes of *The Plain Dealer,* and, despite great social changes, Congreve owed as much to Shakespeare as he did to Jonson. Jonson's masterpieces are more about greed than love. Celia is a colorless creature in the world of *Volpone,* and the marriage that concludes *The Alchemist* is hardly a love match. Nor is there any testing of love in *Bartholomew Fair.* In most of his plays Jonson belonged to a rival tradition in which the function of comedy was seen to be the exposure of vice. In *Every Man Out of His Humour,* he proclaimed that on the stage[4]

> they shall see the times deformitie
> Anatomiz'd in euery nerue, and sinnew,
> With constant courage, and contempt of feare.

But the didactic function of Jonsonian comedy was somewhat blunted by the fact that most of his victims were not theatergoers.

Yet since one of the main themes of comedy has always been the relationship between the sexes—and, as Marx said, by that relationship one can judge how far mankind has become human—it is not surprising that dramatists should be independently concerned with the testing of love. In Middleton's citizen comedies what is tested is the ingenuity of the young in their plots against their elders; but one of his plays is concerned with the testing of hypocrisy in love. In *More Dissemblers Besides Women* the Cardinal keeps on reminding the Duchess of her promise to her dying husband never to remarry. The Cardinal acquires some reflected glory from her chastity, and he approves of his nephew Lactantio who professes to dislike women and to regard sex with aversion. All three characters are dissemblers. Lactantio has seduced scores of women by promising to marry them:

> If I should marry all those I have promised
> 'Twould make one vicar hoarse, ere he would dispatch us.

In the course of the play he is as promiscuous as Etherege's Dorimant: he has one cast-off pregnant mistress, a current mistress, Aurelia, and he hopes, a prospective wife, the Duchess. His hypocrisy results from his wish to inherit from the Cardinal, and his eventual downfall is caused by his ambition. He is exposed and compelled to marry the girl who has borne his bastard. She is the least guilty of the three women, for the Duchess has pretended to hate the man she loves and to love Lactantio, and Aurelia has exploited and been unfaithful to a man who sincerely loves her. The Cardinal is also a dissembler since he immediately changes his mind about second marriages when he has reason to believe that the Duchess wants to marry his nephew. The professed belief in the value of celibacy of the three main characters is put to the test, and in all three it is shown to be deliberately or unconsciously hypocritical.[5]

Another play concerned with second marriages is Chapman's masterpiece, *The Widow's Tears*. In this play there is an actual widow, Eudora, and a woman who believes (erroneously) that she is a widow; she has the chaste name of Cynthia. Eudora is persuaded to remarry by the exaggerated reports of Tharsalio's sexual prowess. The other plot is based on the famous story in Petronius's *Satiricon* about the widow of Ephesus. Chapman improves on the story with several alterations. Cynthia refuses to leave the vault in which she thinks her husband is buried; however, unknown to her—and this is Chapman's invention—Lysander is not dead but, because of his absurd jealousy, he has come back disguised to test Cynthia's fidelity. The more successful he is in seducing Cynthia, the more furious he becomes; but the tables are turned when Cynthia is informed in the nick of time that the soldier is her husband in disguise. She is therefore able to pretend that she had recognized him all along and that she is furious with him for presuming to doubt her fidelity and chastity. The wife, therefore, is tested and fails; but the husband never knows that she has failed. On the surface the play appears to be a satire on female frailty, especially on the voracious sexual appetites of widows. But the play, written about the same time as *The Duchess of Malfi*, can also be regarded as an attack on the contemporary prejudice against second marriages except those arranged for dynastic or financial motives and on the possessiveness of husbands. This point is brought out in the dialogue between Lysander and Tharsalio:[6]

> THARSALIO: Why, Brother; if you be sure of your wiues loialtie for terme of life: why should you be curious to search the Almanacks for aftertimes: whether some wandring *Aeneas* should enioy your reuersion; or whether your true Turtle would sit mourning on a wither'd branch, till *Atropos* cut her throat:

Beware of curiositie, for who can resolue you? youle say perhaps her vow.

LYSANDER: Perhaps I shall.

THARSALIO: Tush, her selfe knowes not what shee shall doe, when shee is transform'd into a Widdow. You are now a sober and staid Gentleman. But if *Diana* for your curiositie should translate you into a monckey; doe you know what gambolds you should play?

Chapman's other comedies, however amusing, are not concerned with the testing of love, even in this negative way.

No attempt has been made to survey all the Elizabethan and Jacobean plays that embody in one form or another an element of testing. Greene's wronged heroines are tested by the ill-treatment meted out to them by their atrocious heroes. (Shakespeare transformed Greene's *Pandosto* in *The Winter's Tale* and a Greene-type heroine in Hermione and Imogen.) In other plays it is chastity rather than love that is tested; in others there are foreshadowings of the comedy of manners. Before that flowered in England, the most interesting comedy was being written in Spain.

*   *   *

Calderón is the least appreciated of great writers of comedy for a variety of reasons. His output was enormous and his tragedies and tragicomedies are better known than his straightforward comedies; it is felt that the social customs of the society for which he wrote are completely alien to our own, and few of the comedies are available in satisfactory translations. Calderón was himself aware of the cruelty of the prevailing code of honor; and he was also aware of the wrongness of the double standard for men and women. As one of his most sympathetic characters expresses it:

> Woe to the first who made so harsh a law,
> A contract so unjust, a tie so impious,
> Which deals unequally to man and woman,
> And links our honour to another's whim.
> (*The Worst Is Not Always Certain*, 2.2)[7]

Here a man is complaining that the system is unfair to men; and in another play the hero complains that if a woman is unfaithful, one of the men with whom she is associated will die in a duel.[8] But Calderón was acutely conscious of the difficulties of women in a male-dominated society. Unmarried women, lest they be seduced, were kept in seclusion; and several of the comedies have as heroines women who circumvent these restrictions. One could hardly be a heroine without rebelling. Marcela in *A House with Two Doors Is Difficult to Guard* goes for a walk, chaperoned by her maid, so that she can encounter her brother's guest, whom she is not allowed to meet, although she is living in the same house. Angela in *The Phantom Lady* gains access to the guest's room through a concealed door. Clara in *Mornings of April and May*, forbidden to go to the royal park by Hipolito, nevertheless goes there in disguise, without being recognized by him. Lisarda in *From Bad to Worse* also ventures out in disguise and meets a potential suitor. Serafina in *The Advantages and Disadvantages of a Name* goes out to witness the carnival and narrowly escapes abduction and rape. Three of these five women marry the men they meet clandestinely. Clara wisely decides not to marry the lady-killer Hipolito, and Lisarda reluctantly marries the man chosen by her father.

All these women revolt, if not very fiercely, against the conventions of their society; rebellion is their only means of achieving the independence they need to feel more than sex objects. They have numerous obstacles to overcome before they can achieve their goals, including parental disapproval, fraternal conventionality, and the jealousy of lovers. Nor do the men they choose always come up to scratch. Even Bassanio, Orlando, and Orsino are often regarded as hopelessly inferior to their wives; but Angela, the gay and open-hearted heroine of *The Phantom Lady*, actually proposes to Don Manuel:

> It was for love of you that I became
> A phantom in my house; to honour you
> Became the living tomb of my own secret.
> Indeed, I could not tell you that I loved you,
> How much I honoured you, for such an avowal
> Would jeopardize your presence as our guest
> And make you quit the house. I sought your favour
> Because I loved you and I feared to lose you,
> Because I wished to cherish and obey you
> For term of life, and wed my soul with yours.

(3.4)

Manuel, however, does not respond to this avowal with enthusiasm. He is somewhat embarrassed, afraid of offending her brother; he thinks he would add to his sense of guilt by defending her; he is bound, as he thinks, to be either a false friend or a cad. In the end, on her brother's insistence, he agrees to marry her. The audience is bound to feel that Angela has obtained a poor bargain. Manuel is not a cad, like Bertram; but he does not rise to the opportunity. Indeed, all the young men of Calderón's comedies are far more conventional than the women, and many of them fail, at least in the eyes of a modern audience, in the tests they undergo.

Serafina in *The Advantages and Disadvantages of a Name* is an interesting example of a woman who is torn between contradictory impulses. On the one hand she is independent enough to take part in the carnival, despite the fact that she is the governor's daughter, and she is natural enough to be grateful to the man who rescues her from a rapist, even to fall in love with him. On the other hand, being a great lady, she wants to remain aloof from the carnival; and as a woman in a society that is riddled by literature (as the heroine of a sonnet-sequence, one might say), she wants to act the part of a disdainful beauty:

> FLORA *(her maid):*   Since you are grateful
> To Don Cesar for what he has done for you,
> Why do you show yourself offended, madam,
> That he should love you.
> SERAFINA: Because I have within me

> Two contradictory feelings, and that's why
> You'll see me play two different roles with him.
> In his presence, speaking to him, I wish
> To show him only coldness and disdain;
> But out of his sight, remembering he saved me
> Before he knew me, I want to render him
> A thousand services without his knowing
> From whom they came . . .
>   When he knows me,
> I'd have him love me for my beauty and,
> Not knowing me, to love me for my wit.
>
>   (2.2)

Another favorite situation in Calderónian comedy is for a heroine to be suspected of infidelity or unchastity on what seems to be overwhelming circumstantial evidence. Felix in *A House with Two Doors* finds that a stranger has been visiting Laura's house, and he naturally assumes that Laura is the object of the stranger's visits. Flerida in *From Bad to Worse* has been awaiting the arrival of the man she loves when another man imitates his signal and enters, closely followed by her lover who, of course, assumes that she is guilty. In *The Worst Is Not Always Certain* Don Carlos finds a man in Leonor's room and cannot believe in her innocence. In *The Advantages and Disadvantages of a Name* Cesar is attacked when he keeps an appointment with Violante, and he believes she has led him into a trap. All these women—Laura, Flerida, Leonor, and Violante—are perfectly innocent, but their innocence is not established until the last act. In these situations the men and women are both being tested; the men by their treatment of the women they believe to be guilty, and the women by their patience in adversity. Carlos in *The Worst Is Not Always Certain* is the most interesting case. He fights a duel with the intruder; he escorts Leonor to the house of a friend's sister, who befriends her; and he continues to love her, although he is ashamed of what he calls

> So base a passion, and a love so slavish!
> The more I'm wronged, the more I love; the more
> I'm outraged, I have greater tenderness;
> The more I am betrayed, the more I trust.
> Why should I be surprised? It can't be said
> He really loves a woman who does not love
> Even her very faults.
>
>   (2.4)

Leonor's would-be seducer, Diego, is loved by Beatriz in whose house Leonor has taken refuge; and there is a striking contrast between Beatriz's willingness to excuse Diego's infidelity to her and Carlos's inability to believe in Leonor's innocence. Yet Carlos is depicted as an honorable and sensitive man, whose feelings are more humane than the views he takes from society. He helps Leonor as much as possible; he even tries to arrange a marriage between her and Diego, though she still loves Carlos and Diego obviously loves Beatriz. In this play, as in others, characters are faced with a number of incompatible duties. Juan, Carlos's cousin, has a duty to Leonor because she is a woman in distress; he has a duty to Carlos because he is a friend; he has a duty to Leonor's father, because his liege lord has requested it; and he has a duty to himself, as all men do, to preserve his honor. At the climax of the play it seems that he cannot carry out any one of these duties without failing in the others.

The exoneration of the suspected heroines in these four plays throws some light on the ambiguous ending of *Mornings of April and May,* so ambiguous that it has been supposed that some lines are missing. In one of the two plots there is an inevitable breakdown of the engagement between Clara and Hipolito, partly because the lady's independent spirit will not consent to absolute submission and partly because Hipolito has proved to be excessively vain and a philanderer. Clara's devastating speech at the end of the second act is not merely a spirited defence of women's rights, it makes it clear that marriage between them is impossible. Arceo, a comic servant, is compelled to make an honest woman of the duenna, Lucia. But the future of the relationship between Juan and Ana is left uncertain. All depends on how the last five minutes of the play are staged. The same thing may be said of *Measure for Measure:* Isabella does not reply to the Duke's proposal of marriage. She can accept without speech or, as in several recent productions of the play, she can turn away in disgust, both as a natural celibate and because of the Duke's deception of her. Shakespeare, of course, could have made his intentions clear during rehearsals. In the same way Juan can finally refuse Ana's hand, or accept it.

Juan assumed that the man he killed some time before the opening of the play had obtained the key from Ana and that she had therefore been unfaithful. But it is Juan himself who reports that the man had exclaimed:

> "Whoever's here,
> I will discover him and kill him. None
> May enjoy the pleasures I have been denied."
>
> (1.1)

It is clear to the audience, and should have been clear to Juan, that Ana had not been the intruder's mistress and that he had doubtless entered the house uninvited. In the course of the play Juan has better reason to suspect that Ana, far from being an inconsolable recluse, has gone to the park in disguise and met Hipolito there; and, later, that she had made an assignation with him. Juan is finally convinced by Clara's confession that the letter to Hipolito was hers and that Ana is therefore innocent of these particular charges; but she is not cleared of betraying Juan with the man he killed. It is worthwhile to consider why Calderón left the matter unresolved and unexplained. When the heroine in *The Worst Is Not Always Certain* is cleared, we are provided with the moral: "Let no one distrust his lady, whatever the circumstances." Now *Mornings of April and May* has an exceptionally intricate plot, and Calderón could hardly have been guilty of carelessness in not providing an explanation of the intruder (e.g., that he had stolen the key or bribed Lucia).

In act 2 Ana tells Juan that a man who loved her would believe in her, and he retorts: "By such a reckoning I must love you ill" (2.3). In act 3 she tells him:

I would to God my truthful explanation
About that night could be convincing to you.
But if it cannot, there's a surer way:
Reminding you that I am who I am.
JUAN: If only that sufficed!
ANA: It would do so,
If you loved me truly.

(3.3)

She offers, merely as a hypothesis about the previous night—not about the
earlier occasion—that a man fleeing from officers of justice had taken refuge in
her house and had departed, "Moved by my tears, or of his own accord." In that
case, she says, Juan would have regarded her as guilty, although she was completely innocent. Juan retorts that the man he killed "that other time" "Was nobly
born, and entered with a key". Clara bears witness that Ana is innocent of the
later indiscretions, and Juan does not again raise the question of the man with
the key. He realizes that he has unjustly accused her in one case, and presumably
he tacitly admits that he has been wrong in the other. He can prove his love only
by trusting Ana: a proof of her innocence would not serve the same purpose.
Such an ending would be dramatically more satisfactory than to have both
couples declining marriage. It is significant, however, that both heroines are in
revolt against the double standard. Clara's rebellion is more vocal and emphatic;
but Ana is implicitly rejecting the right assumed by all gallants of Golden Age
drama to be suspicious of the conduct of the ladies they profess to love. Such
suspicions are an inevitable result of the way in which women are both idealized
and enslaved, and in which men are predators, jailers, and idolaters.

In Calderón's plays the rake always meets his comeuppance, and there can be
no doubt that in this matter at least he supported the woman's point of view.
Libertines violate the nobleman's code of manners and morals, not to mention
Calderón's code as a Christian. This is what gives an edge to Clara's denunciation
of Hipolito:

I thought it was small matter for acclaim
That one mere male should lord it over us,
And so I sought an opportunity
To snatch some laurels from him . . .
                            You imagined—vain
And foolish as you are—that in a trice
You had transfixed the hearts of all the beauties
Parading in the park. Not so, Sir Flirt.
Now learn your lesson; recognize the fact
That your behavior gives a bad impression
Of love which you profess. This healthy lesson
Leaves Phyllis now avenged for Fabio's scorn.

(2.3)

A different kind of test is imposed on the Duchess in *The Secret Spoken Aloud*.
Although she does not admit it, she is in love with Federico, her secretary; and all
through the play she is trying to discover which of her ladies-in-waiting Federico

loves. The lovers foil her for a time by the use of the code to which the title alludes. When at the end she finds out who the beloved is, she masters her jealousy with the help of the magnanimity and pride that a woman in her position ought to possess, and she agrees to marry the neighboring Duke who has wooed her as persistently as Orsino wooed Olivia.

There is a debate in act 1 on the question of what is the greatest pain in love, and the contributions of the main characters reveal their feelings and their situation. To the Duke of Mantua, whose suit Flerida has declined, the greatest pain is not to be beloved; to Federico, who sees little chance of consummating his love for Laura, it is lack of hope; to Flerida it is "To love and bear one's suffering in silence"; and to Laura, paradoxically, it is to have one's love returned. All four lovers are tested in the course of the play.

It has often been remarked that Restoration dramatists borrowed some of Calderón's plots. Wycherley's *Love in a Wood*, for example, is partly based on *Mananas de abril y mayo* and *The Gentleman Dancing-Master* on *El Maestro de Danzar;* but it is plot and situation that are borrowed rather than the tone or moral stance. In Calderón the libertine is deplored; in most Restoration comedies he is held up for our admiration. Calderón writes in verse, the English writers generally in prose.

*   *   *

In most of Molière's plays lovers are of minor interest. Who remembers even the names of the young lovers in *L'Avare, Le Bourgeois gentilhomme, Les Femmes savantes,* and *Le Malade imaginaire?* The heroine of *L'Ecole des femmes* is saved by her ignorance and innocence: neither she nor her lover is really tested. Even *Le Misanthrope* is not primarily concerned with love, Alceste's passion for Celimène being only one example of his failure in social relationships. Yet both Alceste and Celimène are tested and found wanting. She is beautiful, witty, high-spirited, and an inveterate coquette. She cannot help feeling that Alceste, much as she likes him, is absurdly extreme in his principles; and he, much as he dotes on her, cannot approve of her morals. When they quarrel about the love letter she has written to Oronte, Alceste arouses a good deal of sympathy, although in urging her to *pretend* to be true, he is advocating the hyprocrisy he attacks in everyone else.[9] In a later speech in the same scene, when Alceste declares that he wishes Celimène were poor and miserable—

> Afin que de mon coeur l'eclatant sacrifice
> Vous pût d'un pareil sort reparer l'injustice,
> Et que j'eusse la joie et la gloire, en ce jour
> De vous voir tenir tout des mains de mon amour—

it is obvious that his love is possessive, egotistical, and self-righteous.

Celimène's final test comes after she has been exposed and humiliated as a coquette, and Alceste offers to marry her nevertheless if she will consent to live in the country, far away from the corrupt Parisian society. Inevitably, and sensibly, she refuses; and immediately and ludicrously, Alceste proposes to Eliante. Both Alceste and Celimène have failed in the tests that the comedy imposes on them.

Molière's plays, like Calderón's, were quarried usefully for plots. Wycherley, for example, used *L'Ecole des femmes* and *L'Ecole des maris* in *The Country Wife* and the *Critique de l'école des femmes* as well as *Le Misanthrope* in *The Plain Dealer;* and there were close adaptations by other dramatists. All the same, the major influence on Restoration comedy was the English comedy written before the closing of the theaters. It could be maintained that the development of comedy was not really affected by the literary tastes acquired by the royalists, exiled during the interregnum. It would not be difficult to construct a genealogical tree from Jonson and Fletcher, through Shirley's *Hyde Park* and *The Lady of Pleasure,* to the early writers of the comedy of manners—which was always partly a comedy of humours. Even more than Elizabethan comedy, the comedy of manners is mainly concerned with the relation between the sexes, although it may be said that the tests applied to the lovers are generally cruder. Cressida's proverbial wisdom that "women are angels wooing" and that "men prize the thing ungained" is accepted as gospel:[10]

> Would you long preserve your Lover?
> Would you still his Goddess reign?
> Never let him all discover,
> Never let him much obtain.

The realization that desire fades with its satisfaction and that husbands, and perhaps wives too, are not naturally monogamous, provides the theme song at the beginning of *Marriage à la Mode:*[11]

> Why should a foolish Marriage Vow
> That long ago was made,
> Oblige us to each other now
> When Passion is decay'd?

This means that wives, as well as husbands, in the comedies of the period, are often adulterous, in thought if not in act; and the later wives who, in deference to Collier, do not actually succumb, are sorely tempted. The wives usually retain the sympathies of the audience because of the foolishness or unpleasantness of their husbands: Pinchwife, Sir Paul Plyant, Foresight, Squire Sullen, and Sir John Brute are men it is almost a duty to cuckold. Pinchwife, for example, marries a simple country girl because he could never keep a whore to himself; and all audiences, secretly or overtly, applaud Margery's revolt. Foresight is a superstitious fool and Sullen a drunken sot.

The gallants take advantage of the dissatisfied wives, as Horner does of Lady Fidget, Mrs. Dainty Fidget, and Mrs. Squeamish. They are revealed as hypocrites because they are always prating about honor and planning adultery. The innocence of Margery, with her open and avowed love for Horner, contrasts with this hyprocrisy. Horner's pretence of impotence is an effective test of the women of his acquaintance.

When gallants are attracted by unmarried women, their aim is usually seduction; but, if they succeed, they reject their lovers as possible brides. An archetypal figure is Dorimant in *The Man of Mode,* who throws over Mrs. Loveit who still loves him and it; takes up with Bellinda, who knows he cannot be trusted and yet agrees to be his mistress; and then is attracted by Harriet, who holds off until he agrees to undergo the marriage ceremony.

The gallants embarking on matrimony presumably hope that they will not tire of their wives as quickly as they have of their mistresses—a triumph of hope over experience. The women likewise hope that their husbands will not turn into Brutes or Sullens, or resume their promiscuous habits. It is plain that in the better comedies of the period both men and women are afraid of being disappointed and disillusioned by marriage. This is apparent in a play as early as *Marriage à la Mode* and in the later plays of Congreve. Cynthia in *The Double Dealer,* listening to the inane conversation of Lord and Lady Froth, remarks to Mellefont: "I'm thinking, though Marriage makes Man and Wife one flesh, it leaves them still Fools." She suggests that they break off their engagement, since one of them is bound to be a loser. Angelica in *Love for Love,* doubting whether Valentine's love will continue after they are married and wondering whether his real motive for marrying is her fortune, asks him:

> Wou'd any thing but a Madman complain of Uncertainty? Uncertainty and Expectation are the Joys of Life. Security is an insipid thing, and the overtaking and possessing of a wish discovers the Folly of the Chase. Never let us know one another better; for the Pleasure of a Masquerade is done, when we come to shew Faces. (4.1.785–90)

In *The Way of the World* Millamant, on the verge of matrimony, recites lines by Waller and Suckling on the disappointment attendant on "fruition." This is one of several bargain scenes in which lovers seek to put marriage on a strictly rational basis but avoid the realities of the situation by pretending that they can remain in a premarital stage of their relationship. So Celadon and Florimel in Dryden's *Secret Love* agree to various conditions: never to be jealous, to confess the truth when they cease to love, to have sexual intercourse only by mutual consent, and never to use the names of husband and wife. Whereas these characters seem to subscribe to a joint manifesto, the brilliance of the corresponding scene in *The Way of the World* depends on its apparently spontaneous overflow from the characters of Millamant and Mirabel. Its humor depends on the contrast between the apparent coolness and rationality of the lovers and the underlying violence of their passion, and also on the contrast of both with the plot, which is expressed in the Horatian epigraph: *Metuat doti deprensa* (She fears to lose her dowry). Millamant will get her entire dowry only if she marries with her aunt's consent. The scene, moreover, is neatly sandwiched between two abortive proposals—Sir Wilful's rustic attempt to broach the subject with Millamant, and the menopausal twittering of Lady Wishfort when "Sir Rowland" seeks her hand.

Mirabel and Millamant have good reason to be wary of each other and therefore to test each other. Mirabel has confessed in the first scene that he loves

Millamant "with all her faults, nay, like her for her faults." She has a string of foolish admirers, as long as Celimène's, and like Celimène she cannot contemplate life in the country; she professes to be glad that she gave Mirabel pain by refusing to see him; and she is full of affectations, such as the endearing one of never pinning up her hair with prose. What Mirabel has to find out or, failing that, to take on trust, is whether these affectations are inherent in her character or merely an armor she has put on to protect herself from the disillusionment that is the way of the world in the sphere of love and marriage. Millamant for her part wishes to be assured that Mirabel, whose former mistress is her friend, will prove to be a good and faithful husband. Otherwise, she confesses to Mrs. Fainall, she will be "a lost thing."

Angelica in *Love for Love* imposes a severer test on her lover. She is an heiress and Valentine, a bankrupt prodigal, may well be after her money. His father agrees to pay his debts if he will sign away any claim to the estate; he postpones signing by pretending to be mad, but when he hears that Angelica is going to marry his father, he agrees to sign. Whereupon Angelica tears the document and declares:

> Had I the World to give you, it cou'd not make me worthy of so generous and faithful a Passion: Here's my Hand, my Heart was always yours, and struggl'd very hard to make this utmost Tryal of your Virtue. (5.1.560–64)

Angelica is more easily satisfied than Congreve's critics who recall, for example, the brutality of Valentine's reference to his bastard (1.1.209–13). But a reformed rake must first be a rake and Valentine is more convincing than Charles Surface who never seems to be a rake at all.

Swift's Stella described the normal fate of women, with "no adornment but a face,"

> Before the thirtieth year of life
> A maid forlorn, or hated wife.

She thanks Swift for saving her from either fate:[12]

> You taught how I might youth prolong
> By knowing what is right and wrong;
> How from my heart to bring supplies
> Of lustre to my fading eyes;
> How soon a beauteous mind repairs
> The loss of changed or falling hairs;
> How wit and virtue from within
> Can spread a smoothness o'er the skin.

The Mrs. Sullens and the Lady Brutes have no such resources; and it is only in two of Congreve's heroines that we can discern the promise of intellectual or moral development. Lady Brute is saved from adultery by the fall of the curtain, Mrs. Sullen by a fortuitous burglary. But they are tested and they both undergo moral conflicts of a sort. Mrs. Sullen is relieved from the dreadful purgatory of marriage by the assumption that Milton's proposals on divorce had become law and that it was therefore possible to obtain a divorce on the grounds of temperamental incompatibility. Divorce, in fact, was virtually unobtainable in the seventeenth century, so that neither wives nor husbands had any legal method of redress if they were badly treated by their partners. Yet after reading a score of Restoration comedies one has to remind oneself that the picture they convey of marriage is one-sided; there were a number of contented marriages, even among the upper classes.

When we come to the attempted revival of the comedy of manners in the age of Sheridan, society was less permissive than it had been, and a writer of comedies could not allow his heroes to be Horners or Dorimants, or his heroines to be frail. Garrick's version of *The Country Wife* transformed Horner and Margery into paragons of chastity by reverting to *L'Ecole des femmes*.[13] Goldsmith's Marlow had presumably done more than flirt with girls who were beneath him socially and Charles Surface had done more than spend his money on stag parties, but the audience receives only hints. Lady Teazle, if she had been born a century earlier, would have cheerfully cuckolded her aged husband; but Sir Peter is made so sympathetic and Joseph so obviously hypocritical that the test of Lady Teazle's virtue is not very severe. The test applied to Charles has only sentimental significance. Sheridan, although he revolted against sentimental comedy, unwittingly enshrined some of its clichés.

*   *   *

Molière's followers are of minor importance, and the one French dramatist of the eighteenth century before Beaumarchais who must be considered in any account of the dramatic treatment of love is Marivaux. His plays were written between those of Congreve and Sheridan; they are unlike any that had been written before, and they owe more to the treatment of character in novels than in previous plays. He had no successful imitators, although Alfred de Musset aimed at some of the same effects, but he seems to have influenced French novelists. After a checkered reputation, Marivaux has come to be regarded in the present century as a dramatist who depicted women in love with great subtlety and understanding, and as the author of black comedies that conceal a deep pessimism beneath a gay and sparkling surface. This idea of his work is implied in Anouilh's *La Répétition*, in which *The Double Inconstancy* is being rehearsed by a group of aristocratic amateurs. Marivaux's play is described as "the elegant story of a crime."[14] The "crime" is the deliberate destruction of the innocent love of Silvia and Arlequin by the Prince, who wants to marry the country girl himself. She is kidnapped, and Arlequin sent for, because the Prince calculates that the girl will be more critical of her rustic lover when he is seen in a court environment. And so it proves. Silvia is advised by everyone to throw over Arlequin and marry the Prince. "What about fidelity, honesty, trust?" (2.1) she asks them. "They haven't the faintest idea what these words mean. I might as well be talking Greek".[15] She confesses nevertheless that she had been attracted by an officer in the Guards, "who's as handsome as anything. There's little chance that the Prince will be so attractive." The audience knows that this officer is the Prince. Silvia is informed that the ladies of the court assume that the Prince's love for her is only a temporary infatuation. Silvia, who has a touch of vanity, is piqued. She remarks "They're lucky that I love Arlequin so much, or I'd show them they were lying." In the end Silvia confesses her love for the handsome officer and he reveals his identity, while Arlequin marries the court lady who had engineered the plot. From one point of view, True Love has been corrupted and destroyed by Wealth and Class, using deceit and treachery. From another point of view, Silvia marries the Prince, who is greatly superior in sensitivity to the rather crude Arlequin; and Arlequin is consoled by the wealthy Flaminia who will keep him in affluence and contentment. Can this really be regarded as a crime? Silvia's love is tested, and it is destroyed; but it could also be said that the Prince was testing her and educating her to see whether she would be a suitable bride.

The Second Surprise of Love is a slighter work. Like many of Marivaux's comedies, it is concerned with the disparity between the conscious and unconscious feelings of the protagonists. The Marquise is devoted to the memory of her late husband who had loved her passionately and devotedly. She tells her maid that she has lost everything:

LISETTE: Everything? You make me tremble. Are all men dead?
MARQUISE: Oh! what does it matter to me that other men are still alive?
LISETTE: Ah! Madame, what are you saying? Let us never scorn our resources.

Although the Marquise's grief is perfectly genuine, there is a slight admixture of pose. Into the house of mourning comes the Chevalier, inconsolable because Angelique, whom he adores, has married another. The two mourners arrange to read serious books together. Everyone except the couple realizes that they are falling in love, but they both indignantly deny that their friendship is anything more. The Chevalier, however, becomes jealous when he hears that the Marquise is about to remarry; and she is equally jealous when she hears that the Chevalier is also on the verge of matrimony. The humor of the play derives from the self-deceptions of the two main characters, which are continued until the final scene. The conflicting emotions of the Marquise are neatly exhibited in a speech after she supposes that the Chevalier has rejected her:

Ah, sir, my widowhood will be for ever. Indeed, there's not a woman in the world who is less likely to marry than I am. As I've already told you, it is only the tone and manner which I blame; for if he had loved me, it would have been useless. But now he has refused me, he can boast of being constant to Angelique. (2.5)

In *The Indiscreet Vows* there is a similar conflict between love and pride. Lucile overhears Damis swearing that he is marrying her only to please his parents and that he will never love her. It is not until the last act, after Damis has been absurdly betrothed to Lucile's sister, that the couple admit their love for each other. Before this Lucile had answered her maid's question, "Am I to understand that you love him?" with some irritation:

Yes, girl, I do love him since you force me to utter a word which is disagreeable to me, and which I use only through necessity. (5.2)

She is driven to declare:

Our vanity and our coquetry—these are the greatest sources of our passions; from them men most often obtain all they value. Whoever would strip our heart of its foibles would leave us with hardly any estimable qualities. (5.2)

These words are unfair to herself, whose fault is rather a reluctance caused by pride to confess that she has been mistaken.

The Game of Love and Chance is based on a double deception. Dorante disguises himself as his servant, and Silvia as her maid, so that they can discover what their betrotheds are really like. Neither knows of the other's deception: they each fall in love with the supposed servant. Silvia tells Dorante that she does not hate him, that he does not displease her, and that she would love him if he were her social equal. He thereupon confesses who he is; but she does not make a similar confession because she wants to test whether his love is strong enough to overcome the class barrier and marry beneath him. When her brother says that he is sorry for Dorante, Silvia replies:

The cost he pays in deciding makes him more worthy in my eyes; he thinks he will grieve his father in marrying me, and that he is betraying his fortune and his birth. Those are great considerations to give him pause. I'll be delighted to triumph. But I must seize my victory and not be handed it. I want a combat between love and reason. (3.4)

Not surprisingly, her father speaks of her insatiable vanity. Before Dorante finally proposes to her, Silvia is sufficiently sure of victory to warn him of the disadvantages of loving her:

You love me, but your love is not a very serious matter for you. How many things there are to make you give it up! the distance between us, a thousand objects you'll encounter on your path, the desire of other women to attract you, the amusements of a man in your position—all these things will remorselessly take away your love for me. (3.8)

Then she cunningly provokes a proposal by pretending to hide her feelings:

Do you realize that if I loved you, all the greatest things in the world would not touch me? So judge the state I'm in. Have the generosity to hide your love. I myself would scruple to say I love you while you're in your present mood; the avowal of my feelings would threaten your reason, and so you see that I hide them from you. (3.8)

In this play, therefore, it is the man's love that is put to the severest test; and Silvia is probably right to think that each time Dorante remembers that his love overcame so many obstacles, he will love her afresh, and that she will never be able to think of it without loving him. Nevertheless Dorante is somewhat relieved when he finds that he is marrying someone of his own class.

False Confessions is concerned with an ingenious—a positively Machiavellian—series of tricks by which another Dorante wins the love of a wealthy widow, Araminte. He gets a post as her steward and by refusing a bribe that would have prejudiced her interests he convinces her of his loyalty and integrity. Then his former valet reveals to Araminte that Dorante had applied for his post as her steward because he was desperately in love with her. Then he has delivered to the house a portrait of Araminte painted by himself, making certain that she gets to hear of it. He also makes her know that he has refused marriage with a wealthy woman. But when Araminte asks him about this, he tells her he loves a widow, still pretending that she does not know of his love for her:

ARAMINTE: And will you not marry her? She loves you, I presume.
DORANTE: Alas, madame, she is not even aware that I adore her.
ARAMINTE: It is nothing but my astonishment that makes me ask these questions. You say that she does not know that you love her? And yet you have sacrificed your fortune for her sake. That's incredible. How have you managed to remain silent? It seems to me that it would have been natural and pardonable to try to get her to return your love.
DORANTE: Heaven forbid that I should dare to conceive the faintest hope. Love me? No, madame, her station is far above mine. My respect for her condemns me to silence; and at least I shall die without having suffered the torment of causing her displeasure.
ARAMINTE: I cannot imagine any woman worthy of inspiring such an extraordinary passion. I cannot believe that such a woman exists.

(2.15)

After several further incidents, Dorante comes to say good-bye and asks for the return of his portrait of his mistress. Araminte says:

Give you my portrait? Don't you realise that that would be to admit that I love you?
DORANTE: Love me, madame? What an idea! Who could imagine any such thing?
ARAMINTE: Nevertheless, that is what I have come to.

(3.12)

Only then, when he has extracted this confession, does Dorante confess to the tricks he has employed. Araminte admits that if anyone else had informed her of his deceptions, she would have hated Dorante, but "since your love is genuine, what you have done in order to win me is not worthy of blame." Nevertheless Araminte has been manipulated and Marivaux shows here, as in several of his plays, that love can coexist with Machiavellian scheming; and, since this is so, one is driven to ask whether deceit and manipulation are really compatible with genuine love, since to treat the beloved as an object is a denial of the equality that should be the basis of love in a civilized society.

This is a question that arises again with *The Proof,* a play written near the end of Marivaux's career, which imposes the severest test on a woman. The proof sought by Lucidor is that a country girl, Angelique, loves him for himself alone and not because he is wealthy. To this end he employs a battery of tests. He pretends that he wants to arrange a wealthy marriage for her, either to his valet disguised as a gentleman, or to a well-to-do farmer. In both cases, despite his offer of a large dowry, she refuses. Then he cruelly pretends that the miniature portrait he carries in his pocket is that of a woman he intends to marry. (It is really that of his sister.) In the end, after Angelique has sent her suitors packing, Lucidor finds her in tears:

> LUCIDOR: Will you leave me with the grief of not being able to make you happy?
> ANGELIQUE: Oh, that's all over. I want nothing of a man who has given me the reputation of loving him without return.
> LUCIDOR: That wasn't my idea.
> ANGELIQUE: I would never have boasted that you loved me, though I might have thought you did after all the friendship you have shown me since you came here. Yet I've never presumed on that; you have never gone further; and I've been duped by my simplicity.
> LUCIDOR: When you thought I loved you, you would not have been deceived. To be quite frank, I confess that I adore you, Angelique.
> ANGELIQUE: I don't know about that. But if ever I were to love anyone, I wouldn't hunt for girls for him to marry. I would rather he died a bachelor.
>
> (sc. 21)

Angelique has undergone a cruel ordeal; and, although she passes all Lucidor's tests, an audience is bound to feel that she has been treated abominably. He himself has failed in all the tests. Critics have suggested that he is a foolish young man who prides himself on his knowledge of women, whereas he is completely baffled by the simple sincerity of Angelique. Others regard him as a basically insecure person who finds it difficult to believe that he can be loved for himself. Others again brand him as proud, wicked, savage, atrocious, and sadistic, one who will prove to be an impossible husband. These conflicting views of Lucidor illustrate Marivaux's subtle ambiguity. The original audience—at least its male members—may not have realized quite how selfish and cruel Lucidor's actions are; but Marivaux himself must have known. It is apparent from this play, and from his other portraits of women in love, that he has every sympathy with Angelique. Like many sophisticated writers, Marivaux believed, or half believed, or would have liked to believe, in the pastoral dream—that dream which is a standing reproach to the corruptions and sophistications of civilization.

*　　*　　*

Robert B. Heilman in his wide-ranging book on comedy makes no mention of Marivaux and refers only to the most famous of Calderón's plays, *Life's a Dream*.[16] I have concentrated on these two dramatists not to redress the balance but because they exemplify, with Shakespeare, the kind of comic writing with which we are concerned in this essay. I have omitted other important dramatists, either because my knowledge of them is superficial or because they do not use comedy for the purposes I have described. Goldoni, for example, is an excellent playwright; but when we read *La locandiera* we are interested primarily in the way Mirandolina wheedles her aristocratic guests, persuading even the misogynist Baron Ripafratta to fall in love with her, and then marries her servant. Similarly in *La vedova scaltra* we admire Rosaura's cleverness in securing a husband. But in neither play is there a test of the quality of love.[17]

The corrective idea of comedy, derived largely from the commentators on Plautus and Terence, has been followed by many dramatists since the Renaissance. But side by side with such satirical plays there have been many more in which what satire there is is subordinated to other concerns, especially to the treatment of love. The mutual happiness of lovers, expected by the audience at the end of the last act, may be postponed by quarrels, misunderstandings, separations, disguises, and accidents. But the most interesting comedies are those in which the plot is not merely a device to postpone happiness, but those in which one or both lovers are rigorously tested, emerging more worthy of their partners in the process. As Milton said: "That which purifies us is triall, and triall is by what is contrary."[18]

NOTES

1. John Lyly, *Endymion*, 3.4.122–23, 132–34, cited from R. W. Bond, ed., *The Complete Works of John Lyly*, 3 vols. (Oxford: Clarendon Press, 1902), vol.3.

2. *The Winter's Tale*, 4.4.481–85, cited from William Shakespeare, *The Complete Works*, gen. ed. Alfred Harbage, Pelican Shakespeare rev. ed. (New York: Viking Press, 1969).

3. Many of the same points are made in Kenneth Muir, *Shakespeare's Comic Sequence* (Liverpool: University of Liverpool Press, 1979) and others by John Russell Brown in *Shakespeare and his Comedies* (London: Methuen, 1957).

4. *Every Man Out of His Humour*, Prologue, ll. 120–22; see C. H. Herford and P. and E. Simpson, eds., *Ben Jonson*, 11 vols. (Oxford: Clarendon Press, 1925–52), 3:432.

5. See "Two Middleton Plays," in *Accompaninge the Players*, ed. Kenneth Friedenreich (New York: AMS Press, 1983), in which I develop my views on *More Dissemblers Besides Women*.

6. *The Widow's Tears*, 2.1.18–28, cited from Allan Holaday, gen. ed., *The Plays of George Chapman: The Comedies* (Urbana: University of Illinois Press, 1970).

7. See Pedro Calderón de la Barca, *Four Comedies*, trans. Kenneth Muir (Lexington: University Press of Kentucky, 1980), p. 170. All subsequent quotations of Calderón's plays are cited by act and scene number and refer to *Four Comedies* (for *From Bad to Worse, The Secret Spoken Aloud, The Worst Is Not Always Certain, The Advantages and Disadvantages of a Name*), and to versions of *A House with Two Doors Is Difficult to Guard* and *Mornings of April and May*, trans. Kenneth Muir and Ann L. Mackenzie (Lexington: University Press of Kentucky, 1985).

8. *Mornings of April and May*, 2.3 (see n.7).

9. *Le Misanthrope*, 4.3; see Molière, *Oeuvres complètes*, ed. Robert Jouanny, 2 vols. (Paris: Garnier, 1960); subsequent quotations of Molière's plays are cited by act and scene.

10. William Congreve, *The Old Bachelor*, 2.2.192–95, cited from Herbert Davis, ed., Congreve, *The Complete Plays*, Curtain Playwrights (Chicago: University of Chicago Press, 1967); subsequent quotations of Congreve's plays refer to this edition.

11. John Dryden, *Marriage à la Mode*, 1.1.4–7, cited from L. A. Beaurline and Fredson Bowers, eds., *John Dryden: Four Comedies*, Curtain Playwrights (Chicago: University of Chicago Press, 1967).

12. "To Dr. Swift on his birthday, November 30, 1721," ll. 33–40, cited from *The Poems of Jonathan Swift*, ed. Harold Williams, 3 vols. (1937, reprint, Oxford: Clarendon Press, 1958), 2:737–38.

13. This was the version used by the Lena Ashwell Players in the boroughs of South London, c. 1926.

14. Jean Anouilh, *La Répétition, ou l'amour puni* (1950), 1.1, my translation.

15. Pierre Marivaux, *The Double Inconstancy*, 2.1, my translation from *Théâtre Complet*, ed. Bernard Dort (Paris: Editions du Seuil, 1964); subsequent quotations of Marivaux's plays are cited by act and scene.

16. Robert B. Heilman, *The Ways of the World* (Seattle: University of Washington Press, 1978).

17. The same things may be said of another important dramatist, Lope de Vega, if *El perro del hortelano* is characteristic of his comedies. The Countess Diana is tested in a somewhat superficial way and is saved from having to choose between love and pride of birth by a trick ending. On learning that her secretary Teodora is in love with Marcela, she becomes wildly jealous. Throughout the play she oscillates between love and pride; and Teodora deserts Marcela when he thinks Diana will marry him and reverts to Marcela when the Countess decides to marry a man of her own class. At the end a servant arranges for Teodora to be accepted as the lost son of a nobleman so that Diana can marry him without losing face.

18. John Milton, *Areopagitica;* see *Complete Prose Works,* gen. ed. Don M. Wolfe, 7 vols. (New Haven: Yale University Press, 1953–74), 2:515.

Tragicomedy and Comic Form

R. A. Foakes

PLAYER:	. . . . We've played to bigger, of course, but quality counts for something. I recognised you at once—
ROSENCRANTZ:	And who are we?
PLAYER:	—as fellow artists.
ROSENCRANTZ:	I thought we were gentlemen.
PLAYER:	For some of us it is performance, for others, patronage. They are two sides of the same coin . . .

Tom Stoppard,
Rosencrantz and Guildenstern Are Dead, act 1

In his account of tragicomedy, in 1599, Giambattista Guarini emphasized that whatever dangers it presented, it displayed "above all the comic order." By this phrase, he seems to have meant that the ordering or shape (*ordonnance*) of the action should lead to a resolution appropriate to comedy, but this view also presumably implies that the audience should expect such an order from the beginning of the play. Tragicomedy, in other words, is controlled by a comic order and is, in effect, a subspecies of the genre comedy. This is not the way in which critics often respond to the tragicomedies of Beaumont and Fletcher and Shakespeare; so, reading them, one remarks of *The Winter's Tale* that the play gives "no hint in the first half that the second will be comic,"[1] and another says of *Measure for Measure,* "The power of *Measure for Measure* is in the dramatization of the felt experience of characters caught up in potentially tragic situations."[2] These are familiar responses of critics reading the text in thematic terms, but Norman Rabkin's comment on *The Winter's Tale* is worth pursuing, since he rejects a thematic approach, stressing the way the play calls attention to "the artifice of his [Shakespeare's] art,"[3] and claiming that the meaning of this play is contained in the plot structure and in the continual probing of "the question of the nature of art"; but still he sees the last part of the play as a "mitigation of the tragedy we have witnessed."[4] It is as if he is disappointed that the play does not end tragically, reflecting a common bias that finds tragedy superior to comedy in a hierarchy of forms.

74

Recent criticism of Shakespeare's late plays has moved away from a primary concern with themes or with a symbolic reading, and toward a concentration on their self-conscious theatricality, but this shift has not noticeably affected our understanding of the "comic order," if *The Winter's Tale* can still be read as *Othello* giving way in act 3 to *Mucedorus*. It seems to me rather that there are indications from the start of romantic tragicomedies like *The Winter's Tale* or *Philaster* which prevent an audience from ever supposing that the outcome might be tragic or that they are at any point engaged with a tragic world, a kind of *Othello*. I say "audience" to emphasize that a proper answer to this question relates less to themes, the nature of art, or a reader's response, than to the dramatic conventions, and presentation of an unfolding action as experienced in the theater.[5] In reading a play it is tempting to treat it more or less like a novel, to pass quickly by much of the dialogue and ignore the staging and stage directions in order to focus on the characters as psychologically real, and on the most intense or serious passages of poetry. In this process the jealousy of Leontes and the dignified patience of Hermione under trial are justly celebrated, but the pointers that for an audience may establish a comic order are overlooked.

Some kinds of comic pointer are nevertheless familiar enough from our experience of romantic comedies, in which there is often a threat of death or violence in the opening scenes, but we know from the mode of narrative (as in *The Comedy of Errors,* where Egeon's fantastic tale of coincidences, shipwrecks, and identical pairs of twins does not allow us to take seriously his threatened death), from the tone of the dialogue, or sometimes from other indications, like the Induction to Marston's *Antonio and Mellida,* in which actors mock the roles they are to play, that we can expect comedy. In Shakespeare's romantic comedies death persists as an underpresence, distanced in various ways from the main action but never forgotten entirely. From one perspective there is no clock in the forest of Arden, or in Illyria, or in the woods near Athens, as these are all countries of the mind, liberated from the ordinary world of cool reason, the world of work and daily responsibilities. Most of the lovers in these plays are also free from parental authority or social obligations so that the pleasures, confusions, and mistakes of courtship become their prime occupation. From another perspective, the threat of death—or, to put it another way, the pressure of time— is felt again and again. In *A Midsummer Night's Dream* the threat to Hermia at the beginning, and the violence of the lover's quarrel in act 3, relate to the tragical mirth of Pyramus and Thisby, which distances and turns into farce a lovers' tale that ends unhappily, while at the same time presenting, however comically, their deaths on stage. In *Much Ado*, Claudio and Don Pedro hang an epitaph for Hero on her tomb in her family's "monument" (5.3), and sing a dirge with the refrain

> Graves yawn, and yield your dead
> Till death be uttered,
> Heavily, heavily.
>
> (5.3.19–21)

"Uttered" meant both "expressed" and "made manifest, revealed," and although the audience know Hero lives, the scene sharply reminds us, in setting and words, of death and time: "Yearly will I do this rite." Feste's songs help to establish the underpresence of time and death in *Twelfth Night* with their reminder that youth's a stuff will not endure, the conceit of the lover slain by "a fair cruel maid" in "Come away, come away, Death," and his final song, a compressed version of Jaques' speech on the ages of man to old age and the grave. As marriages return the lovers to the world of time, so Feste's song ends this play with a poignant reminder that the play is returning the audience to their world in which "The rain it raineth everyday"—rain which is in one respect a rain of tears for the decay of all things, *lacrimae rerum,* the touch of death.

Tragicomedy also has to establish its comic credentials, crudely as in *Mucedorus,* which has an Induction and Epilogue in which Comedy is challenged by Envy with threats of "treble death," but Envy is put down and finally overwhelmed (Epilogue, line 6); or in more sophisticated ways, as in Beaumont and Fletcher's *A King and No King,* which establishes a comic tone at the start in the initial dialogue involving the braggart soldier Bessus. In relation to the pressures of time and potential deaths or violence in romantic comedy, however, Guarini's definition of tragicomedy as taking from tragedy "its danger but not its death," and Fletcher's version, that tragicomedy brings some near death, "which is enough to make it no comedy,"[6] do not adequately differentiate what is specific to tragicomedy, or at any rate the tragicomedy of Shakespeare and Beaumont and Fletcher. Tragicomedy is a complex mode of drama, and its specific qualities can only be identified as emerging from a number of shifts and developments that took place in the early years of the seventeenth century. In seeking to identify these qualities, I shall be concerned with how tragicomedy was affected by various factors. One, the increasing self-consciousness of dramatists in their plays, has been touched on and will be discussed further. Others include the growth of satire, with its emphasis on sexuality rather than love, the impact of the private theaters and the court masque, and changes in theatrical presentation and in audiences that led to an increasing preoccupation with artifice on the stage and in life. Each factor may perhaps in itself be familiar, but the effect of their combined influence upon the growth of an important and innovative group of plays has not been sufficiently noticed, as I shall try to illustrate in a reassessment of *Philaster.*

To take satire first, it is significant that tragicomedy came into prominence in the wake of the satire that flourished toward the ends of the reign of Queen Elizabeth. Arthur Kirsch has drawn an analogy between Guarini and Ben Jonson, with special reference to theatrical self-consciousness, pointing out that satire in drama tends in the early plays of Jonson to be articulated through moral commentators who stand outside the action and whose "eventual effect is to italicize the audience's distance from the action and characters."[7] Even when the satiric commentator is absorbed into the play as agent, he remains at the same time a critical observer detaching himself from the action to mediate in a self-conscious way between the action and the audience; this can be seen in, for example, Vindice in *The Revenger's Tragedy* and Malevole in *The Malcontent.* Both these plays were performed by Shakespeare's company at the Globe; but *The Malcontent* was written for the private theaters that flourished for some years after 1600, and the companies of boy actors who performed in them probably contributed to the development of highly self-conscious modes of drama insofar as their style of acting necessarily drew attention to or exploited its artifice in marking the discrepancies between the actors and the characters they impersonated, as notably in such plays as *Antonio's Revenge,* where Pandulpho cries "Why, all this time I ha' but play'd a part/Like to a boy that acts a tragedy" (4.2.70–71).[8]

The growth of satirical drama fed into the development of tragicomedy, another mode that could exploit theatrical self-consciousness. Shakespeare, indeed, may have adapted Jonsonian types for his first essays in tragicomedy. In *Every Man Out of His Humour* Jonson created three satiric personae ranging across the spectrum from envious malice (Macilente) to irresponsible jesting (Carlo Buffone), with the just commentator (Asper) in the middle. Macilente, the poor but honest intellectual, a sketch for a malcontent, knows how to prize virtue but envies those more fortunate than himself, and his criticism of others is tainted by his own selfishness. In the end, purged of envy, he becomes Asper, as Jonson exposes the difficulty in keeping his free and independent judge separate from the critic within the action who is involved in the vices he castigates. Marston's clever solution in *The Malcontent* was to use disguise much more directly in the action of the play, with Malevole (a kind of Macilente) able to reveal himself at will as Altofronto (Asper). Shakespeare appears to have been influenced by the new developments in satirical drama in his early tragicomedies, which are related to forms of what Jonson called "comical satire"; so each of the dark comedies has its relative of Carlo Buffone, a railer, or man of words, a scurrilous or irresponsible jester—Thersites, Parolles, Lucio; and each has a version of the just commentator, whose involvement in the action raises questions about his status, in Ulysses, Lafeu, and the Duke.

The partial detachment of the critical observer, marked especially in the fantastical Duke of dark corners manipulating affairs, and the voyeuristic Thersites relishing the stupidity of his betters, gives to these plays a degree of self-consciousness derived from satire. This is an important link between satire and tragicomedy, which notably affects its form, structure, and tonality; but satire also had a more fundamental effect on content. For in directing its attack on folly and vice, and exposing the gap between things as they were and things as they might be, satire inevitably laid open to ridicule the extravagances of romantic love. This is one of Jonson's targets in *Every Man Out of His Humour* in the absurd posturings of Puntarvolo, and Marston makes fun of the conventions of romantic comedy in *Antonio and Mellida.* In the latter, comic confusions arising because the hero is initially disguised as a woman, an Amazon, and the heroine then appears disguised more conventionally as a man, are resolved when they recognize one another in an extraordinary burst of dialogue in Italian. This episode has been explained as the equivalent of an aria in grand opera, but it is difficult to see how it could be played as anything but burlesque, especially as a page remains on stage after the departure of the lovers to point to the absurdity of their "Babel of tongues," incomprehensible to the audience.

From the perspective of the satirist who is concerned with human behavior as it is, the worlds of romantic fiction, Illyria or Arden, are artificial and even silly.

And yet satirical drama emphasizes "the audience's distance from the action and characters" through the detachment of its moral commentators and so reinforces theatrical self-consciousness, drawing attention to the artifice of the play. For in his romantic comedies Shakespeare delights in the artifices of his dramaturgy, as shown by the complicated variations he plays on the nature of illusion in *A Midsummer Night's Dream,* and the tricks played by what Theseus calls "strong imagination." Indeed, Shakespeare was always conscious of his art, and in his romantic comedies he relies upon and exploits the ability of the audience to believe anything while knowing that all they see is make-believe.[9] The theatrical self-consciousness of the late plays is not in itself an innovation, but it differs in kind and degree from the conscious artifice of the earlier comedies. Satire introduced a much stronger sense of critical detachment, and it also shifted attention away from romantic love toward lust; the city comedies of the early seventeenth century may focus on a relationship with a whore, as in *The Dutch Courtesan,* in which Malheureux discovers "He that lust rules cannot be virtuous," or make a hero of a rake, as in *A Trick to Catch the Old One.* In other words, satire brought into drama what romantic comedy had kept out: sexuality. But satire could deal with sexuality only as vice, condemning those who gave in to lust, or as folly, allowing the keeping of a whore as a minor peccadillo in relation to the greed of a usurer, a favorite target of city comedy. Jacobean tragicomedy, like satire, concerns itself centrally with sexuality rather than with romantic love and might almost be differentiated as a mode of drama in which the world of romantic comedy is invaded by the forces of sexuality.[10]

This is in effect what gives rise to the "problems" of Shakespeare's "dark" or "problem" comedies. For in these plays Shakespeare treats sexuality not as something to be either condemned or lightly dismissed but as a central aspect of human experience. In this sense, like satire, the plays confront things as they are rather than show the course of true love ending in happy marriage, which is the stuff of romantic comedy. The difficulty was to find a way of acknowledging and absorbing sexuality into a mode of drama that would allow its power and importance, and yet end in reconciliation or harmony. For in the dramatic world of these plays the law that would condemn and not allow sex is shown to be an ass, as Pompey demonstrates to Escalus:

> POMPEY: Does your worship mean to geld and splay all the youth of the city?
> ESCALUS: No, Pompey.
> POMPEY: Truly, sir, in my poor opinion they will to't then.
> $\qquad\qquad\qquad\qquad\qquad\qquad\qquad\qquad\qquad$ (2.1.230–34)

It is arguable whether Shakespeare found a satisfactory way of both coping with sexuality in these plays and maintaining a "comic order" in them, but to treat them as the dramatization of characters "helplessly caught up in potentially tragic situations" is to misread them. *Measure for Measure* and *All's Well that Ends Well* dramatize the "mingled yarn" of life, in which "our virtues would be proud, if our faults whipt them not, and our crimes would despair, if they were not cherish'd by our virtues" (*All's Well,* 4.3.71–74), and in the end they offer not moral truths or comments on justice, chastity, or holiness but, rather, the triumph of the instinct to survive and mate and reproduce over all that the rigors of law, social distinctions, plots, or accidents can do to thwart it. Claudio, Juliet, Angelo, Helena, and Bertram are all, like the Clown in *All's Well,* "driven on by the flesh" (1.2.29) to lose their virginity or have issue of their body; and Isabella's repressed sexuality, which she would initially put under "strict restraint" in a nunnery, is brought to consciousness through her confrontations with Angelo and Claudio, and acknowledged vicariously through her acceptance of the bed trick and, at the end, in her kneeling to plead for the "virgin-violator," Angelo, so that her yielding to the Duke's proposition by accepting his hand for the final exit is appropriate, a fitting completion of the comic measure (or dance). Moral and thematic readings of these plays often seem to miss the dramatic experience in their efforts to squeeze out a meaning. The dark comedies' dramatic energy comes to a focus in characters whose very presence points to comedy and whose irrepressible vitality symbolizes what in the end prevails, the instinct for life,[11] characters like Pompey Bum, or Barnardine, who survives in drink by never being prepared to die, and Parolles, whose "simply the thing I am shall make me live" remains the most memorable line in *All's Well.*

Once sexuality had taken firm root in the drama, it was there to stay in the three main forms of drama that could accommodate it: satirical comedy; tragedy increasingly concerned with lust's dominion in which women take the central roles, from *Antony and Cleopatra* to *'Tis Pity She's a Whore;* and tragicomedy. If satirical drama had encouraged theatrical self-consciousness in plays that included critical commentators on the action or drew attention to various kinds of artifice, tragicomedy developed subtler ways of establishing its artificiality and creating a special relation with its audience. As it came to a flowering in the late plays of Shakespeare and the early works of Beaumont and Fletcher, tragicomedy seems to have catered more and more to the refined and courtly spectators of the Blackfriars theater, and it may be seen as developing in tandem with the masque, another factor that affected the growth of tragicomedy. Guarini had recommended tragicomedy as the best kind of play because it did not offend against "the modesty and decorum of a well-bred man,"[12] and its main appeal was no doubt to the sophisticated audiences of the small indoor winter theater of the King's Men, which steadily gained in prestige over the Globe during the reign of James I.[13]

The relationship of tragicomedy to the masque is relevant here: not in terms of masques in plays or the use of masque elements but, rather, with reference to the interchange of role playing between masquers and audience.[14] For the masque has been seen as expressing the baroque in art and in life, and characterized as a preoccupation with "the immense importance of cutting a figure in the world, of projecting an image," so that the idea of the world as a stage or theater could "be elaborated into a full and valid view of life";[15] in going so far, Peter Skrine had in mind a German play, von Lohenstein's *Sophonisbe,* first performed in 1666, but the court masque in England had also been concerned with man as "caught up in his role and act, yet always more or less aware that he is only acting his role."[16] The masque has been described more precisely by D. J.

Gordon as a form in which "the audience is required to be aware, consciously, all the time, of the performer beneath the role; to know that the king is king, and to take his various impersonations as translations of that basic, true identity. The roles he takes are real—as real as the role of king—because they are ways of defining his identity within the society; every role is true, in the sense that it is an abstraction, a personification of his qualities."[17] So in Jonson's *Masque of Queens* (1609), which he published with an elaborate commentary describing the performance, an antimasque of witches vizarded was suddenly dispelled by the revelation of the House of Fame, where sat twelve symbolic figures, representing legendary queens famous for their virtue. These mounted into three chariots and were drawn in by heraldic beasts with the witches bound before them; the last of the chariots, drawn by lions, contained Queen Anne, figured as Bel-Anna. The masquers descended from the chariots and "took out the men," including presumably the king, who was watching; among their dances was one that disposed the dancers into letters honoring the name of Prince Charles, then eight years old. This masque thus symbolized in make-believe an image of the divinely appointed role of the monarch as virtue, light, and order, overthrowing malice, darkness, and disorder. The witches, perhaps played by professional actors, were masked, but the court masquers did not wear vizards. Their "disguises" were transparent, and everyone knew who they were; their roles mirrored the nobility of mind monarchy might be expected to aspire to or embody, and for a brief while they carried over these roles into the world of the audience in the general dancing that wound up the masque.

A third factor is the nature of the new private theaters, especially the Blackfriars. In the theaters at this time the practice of members of the audience sitting on the stage during a performance was growing.[18] If this practice originated in the public playhouses before the turn of the century, it grew notably with the coming of the private theaters after 1600 and became particularly associated with the Blackfriars stage.[19] Here the wealthier patrons of the drama, no longer using the now unfashionable "Lord's rooms,"[20] came to see and be seen:

> When I first enter, you shall have a murmure in the house, every one that does not knowe, cries what Noble man is that; all the Gallants on the Stage rise, vayle to me, kisse their hand, offer mee their places. (*The Woman Hater,* 1.3.65ff.)[21]

This is a character, Count Valore, speaking in a play performed by the children of Paul's in 1606, but other references bear out what this image suggests. In *The Knight of the Burning Pestle*, the Citizen, his wife and Rafe come from the audience to join the "gentlemen" on the stage and command "a cupple stooles," thus mingling actors with spectators. Although the stools on stage seem to have been occupied by wits or gallants, whose object was partly to display themselves, Jonson brings on "4 Gentlewomen LADY-like attyred" as dour gossips to sit on the stage in *The Staple of News* (1625[?], printed 1631), where they "come to see, and to be seene" (Prologue, ll. 9–10). In Jonson's *The Devil Is An Ass* (1616; printed 1631), Fitzdottrell speaks of going to the Blackfriars to

Sit i' the view, salute all my acquaintence,
Rise up between the *Acts,* let fall my cloake,
Publish a handsome man, and a rich suite
(As that's a speciall end, why we goe thither,
All that pretend, to stand for't o' the *Stage*)
The Ladies aske who's that? (For, they doe come
To see us, *Love,* as we doe to see them) . . .

(1.6.32–38)[22]

The Prologue to this play complains that the "Grandee's" on the stage do not allow the actors enough space, but interfere among them, "thruste and spurne," knock them on the elbows, and bid them "turne." Which way were the actors to "turn" or face?—either north or south was liable to give offence, this Prologue seems to imply.

It appears, then, that the gentlemen who paid high prices to sit on stools on the stage might assume the license to interfere in the action and interrupt the actors, and were concerned as much to display themselves as to see the performance. The custom of sitting on the stage is related to the private theater practice of observing act intervals, and during these the gallants might "Rise up between the *Acts*" or, indeed, "censure the whole play."[23] In these conditions the spectators in the main body of the theater were involved in two performances, one by the actors and another by the group of auditors sitting on the stage, who were there to provide a show or display of themselves and to make their presence felt by acting as critics and commentators. The effect of all this on the self-consciousness of players and audience in a small theater like the Blackfriars can only be guessed at, but it may well help to account for some aspects of the development of tragicomedy and the drama of Beaumont and Fletcher in particular. For in a theater where gallants sat on the stage to be seen, to criticize and to unmask the players for the benefit, perhaps, of masked women in the audience, the players were no longer the only performers, and the audience had a show from life to watch on stage in addition to the play.

The heightened sense of artifice and new level of theatrical self-consciousness in the tragicomedies of the years after 1608, when the King's Men began to use Blackfriars, may be partly a response to changing theater circumstances. The characters in these plays embody passions or ideas, and strike attitudes in accordance with these, to the extent that a recent editor of *A King and No King* describes the play as "a conflict. . . between Reason and Will, stimulated in this case by the passion lust."[24] This may be less a "stress upon artifice for its own sake"[25] than a way of achieving a distancing from the audiences on and off stage, while reflecting something of their preoccupation with "cutting a figure in the world" and "projecting an image." In this respect the masque and tragicomedy seem to have a fundamental connection. As satire and tragicomedy parted company, one obvious means of establishing comic form—that is, through a satirical spokesman or commentator—was lost to tragicomedy. The abstraction of characterization, the conscious artifice, and posing of the new tragicomedies in vogue after 1608 provided one way of contriving a theatricality that ensured the action could not be taken too seriously. Passions might be "raised to that excellent

pitch" and "excellently wrought"[26] in the easy but (precisely the word) highly
"wrought" style of Beaumont and Fletcher, but all for the moment, to create a
theatrical event, a virtuoso projection of a particular stance to be enjoyed for
itself. Such events, moreover, take place in a world characterized by Eugene
Waith as one of "pseudo-history and romance," where, he says, fantastic happen-
ings "have the deceptive appearance of actuality."[27] Romance and pseudo-history, locating actions in remote times and places, and permitting any kind of
coincidence or extravagance, contribute to the sense of artifice, and such hap-
penings deceive no one.

The artifice and theatricality of such plays established a sense of comic form,
and "a god is lawful" in them (as Fletcher said in the preface to *The Faithful
Shepherdess*) because a miracle, or the dramatic equivalent, is the normal way in
such plays of resolving the apparently insoluble. As in the masque, the appearance of evil and misfortune is transformed by revelation into an appearance
of good and harmony, and this transformation always requires a palpably theatrical maneuver, even if at its highest it can also symbolize something larger,
such as "the workings of Providence,"[28] and be seen as an epiphany. In fact, this
maneuver is part of the usual convention, the characteristic form of the tragicomedies of this period, and part of the pleasure such plays gave was no doubt
derived from the skill with which the dramatist extricated himself from a plot
seemingly impossible to resolve except in disaster. So much might be said of the
plays of Beaumont and Fletcher and of Shakespeare's late tragicomedies; but
most think of Beaumont and Fletcher as lacking seriousness, and as "morally
shabby"[29] in contrast to Shakespeare. So Eugene Waith complains that *A King
and No King* "says nothing about incest, pride, jealousy, or wrath, but it presents
an arrangement of dramatic moments in which these passions are displayed," [30]
so that although moments in the play may have a meaning, the whole does not.

I think there is more to it than this. Waith's list of the eight characteristics of
the pattern of tragicomedy in Beaumont and Fletcher does not include what is
the most notable feature of their plays, the treatment of sexuality. If from the
moralizing critic's point of view these plays are preoccupied "with the exhibition
of the foolish and the foul,"[31] from another point of view they discovered a new
way of accommodating sexuality in comic form. However remote the worlds of
these plays, they deal with matters excluded from romantic comedy, the darker
possibilities within family relationships and relations between men and women,
lust in its most outrageous forms (incest, for example), and love in its more
perverse forms where it is hard to distinguish from lust. These things are real
enough, and a mode of drama that could expose sexual fantasies and suppressed
desires within a framework providing the overall control of comic restoration
had its own importance and originality. Beaumont and Fletcher may "say
nothing *about* incest," but what is there to say? These plays concern the experience, not an extractable meaning or moral. So, for example, *Philaster* at once
establishes a court in which the promiscuous Megra, who "has destroyed the
worth of her own body, by making experiment upon it," flourishes, and it is
inevitable that she should prefer the lecherous Prince Pharamond to the "worth-
iest" Philaster. In the splendid night scene (2.4), the King, alerted by Arethusa,

knocks at Pharamond's door; Pharamond, entering "above," is summoned down by the King, who then sends his guard in to search while Pharamond tries to prevent them, and the climax comes when Megra herself appears "above," visually emphasizing both his and her "loosenesse." Megra carries it bravely, diverting accusations onto Arethusa:

> I know her, and her haunts,
> Her layes, leaps, and outlayes, and will discover all;
> Nay will dishonor her. I know the boy
> She keepes, a handsome boy, about eighteene:
> Know what she does with him, where and when.
>
> (2.4.157–61)

So the ground is prepared for Philaster to mistake Arethusa's eager defense of her "boy," Bellario—Euphrasia in disguise—for sexual passion, and then, after a tirade against women, to turn misogynist and abandon the court; and for Arethusa, in reaction, to banish Bellario.

The scenes in the woods in act 4 form the centerpiece of the play. The setting offers no escape to a pastoral and generally healing and improving Arcadia, like Arden in *As You Like It*, but is, rather, a place where inhibitions lose their power. Philaster, finding Arethusa and Bellario together, flies into a passion of jealousy; once calmed, he seeks his own death but ends by wounding Arethusa in the breast, calling the act "a peece of Justice" (4.5.70). The woodcut frontispiece to the 1620 quarto of the play shows this most spectacular moment in the action, depicting Arethusa as costumed in a fashion of the period, with her very full breasts exposed. Evidently the wound bled visibly, as the Country Fellow points out:

> h'as hurt her in the breast, looke else.
> PHARAMOND: O sacred spring of innocent blood!
>
> (4.5.115–16)

The country fellow who sees Philaster wound Arethusa and intervenes to wound him in turn, is reproved by Arethusa: "What ill-bred men art thou, to intrude thy selfe/Upon our private sports, our recreations?" (4.5.59–60). This bravery the country fellow cannot appreciate, but her acceptance of the wounding as sport might be understood by the sophisticates in the audience as a surrogate for sexual penetration, a kind of symbolic deflowering. A little later Philaster stumbles on Bellario and believing him (really her, the disguised Euphrasia) to have been "taken with" Arethusa in lust (3.1.100) wounds him too. Arethusa and Bellario were played by boys, and we do not know how Arethusa's "breast" bled on stage, but the effect, marked in the subtitle "Love lies a Bleeding," must have been sensational.

The forest is no place of virtue; the country fellow tries to embrace the bleeding Arethusa, and Philaster, having wounded Bellario, creeps into bushes (how was this staged?) like a coward leaving Bellario to be taken as the attacker of Arethusa. Bellario's lies on his behalf provoke Philaster to reveal himself, and he in turn is arrested and doomed to death. In the last act Arethusa marries

Philaster, and they make a masquelike entry led by Bellario "in a Robe and Garland." Were Philaster to be executed, both Arethusa and Bellario determine on suicide; Bellario says, "Should I outlive you, I should then outlive/Vertue and Honour" (5.2.15). Philaster's "virtue and honour" are reestablished when he rescues the King from the rebels led by Pharamond, who is shown to be a coward as opposed to Philaster, a "*Mars* of men" to the citizens, the "King of Curtesia" (5.4.141). The citizens threaten to geld Pharamond, but he is shipped off home, and the revelation that Bellario is really a girl ends all jealousy, exposes Megra's accusations as false, and brings about the final comic resolution and harmony.

This play was very successful on stage and in print, and, like other tragicomedies of Beaumont and Fletcher, offered many "dramatic moments" for the display of passion and for grand gestures. Its success was not, however, merely a result of its brilliant sequence of theatrical moments. In act 5, Bellario, presenting the newly married Philaster and Arethusa to the King, describes them as "two faire Cedar branches," which had been free and quiet,

> Till never pleased Fortune, shot up shrubs,
> Base underbrambles to divorse those branches;
> And for a while they did so, and did reigne
> Over the Mountaine, and choke up his beauty
> With Brakes, rude Thornes, and Thistles. . .
>
> (5.3.34–38)

The "divorce" of Philaster and Arethusa was displayed in the forest scenes of act 4, where jealousy and anger led to the wounding of both; the "virtue and honour" of Philaster, then, are not stable aspects of character but more like a veneer that can be stripped off by the "thorns and thistles" of passions. If the masque offered symbolic images of the order and virtue royalty should aspire to, it could also be seen as flattering the king with illusions of power.[32] A play like *Philaster* offered its audience symbolic images of the virtue, honor, and courtesy of a soldier prince, but also exposed the fragility of such terms when challenged by the passions generated by sexuality. By comparison with Pharamond and Megra, Philaster seems virtuous, but their frank lust is in a way paralleled by the shocking events of act 4, where Philaster wounds Arethusa in a vicarious act of sexual violation.

Such an account is a far cry from those readings that find this play contains "serious concerns" with contemporary politics,[33] or deals with love and honor, culminating in "the marriage of Arethusa's patience to Philaster's magnanimity";[34] these are more superficial aspects of the play, and the subtitle points to its real concern. It seems to me mistaken to think that Beaumont and Fletcher's central concern was with honor and personal gentlemanly conduct in love and politics. Philaster offers no model, any more than Arbaces does in *A King and No King;* within a comic pattern these plays reveal powerful sexual drives that lie just beneath the surface of courtly appearances, of civilized stances of honor and love, and that can emerge in jealous madness, in the stabbing of his mistress by a prince, or in an admission of incestuous lust. The conscious theatricality of the plays makes possible the presentation of such shocking images and at the same time holds them in check by arresting them as gesture. Arethusa's wound is quickly forgotten, and Arbaces discovers Panthea is not his sister.

In such plays character is not stable, but can change with circumstance; passions explode and evaporate with equal suddenness, and moral stances may be revealed as skin-deep, especially when they are exposed to the shock of sexual drives. All this relates to what seems to have been a major shift in awareness; perhaps London was expanding and social groupings were diversifying to the point where it was no longer easy to relate to the court or city as a coherent community marked by traditional social distinctions. In modern urban societies, we are familiar with the way groups or classes preserve or establish their own identity through style in behavior, appearance, and so on, and tend to become conscious presenters of themselves. Something analogous happened at the Blackfriars and the second Globe, when presenting an image of oneself, or staging an event in an appropriately theatrical manner, came to seem of prime importance (as when Philaster twice threatens to stab himself in the final scene of the play, or as the stage directions put it, "offers to kill himself," an offer he knows will be denied by someone begging him not to, or staying his hand). "The ending end of all earthly knowledge," said Sir Philip Sidney, "is vertuous action," and such a moral attitude informs the world of most of the major drama up to Shakespeare's central tragedies, in which to act in the sense of doing is to be (even for *Hamlet,* who seizes on the players, or on speculations whether to be or not to be, as tactics for evading or postponing doing the deed he is driven toward); but in the world of these later tragicomedies, to be is to act in the sense of performing. The conscious theatricality of these plays relates to life at the time and allowed the drama to deal on the stage with the most shocking and therefore normally repressed human drives and instincts; and theatricality could work only by creating a mode, tragicomedy, in which the "comic form," in Guarini's phrase, was in control from the start.

Finally, let me add a word about Shakespeare's late tragicomedies; these share many of the characteristics of the plays of Beaumont and Fletcher, notably their conscious theatricality, but also differ significantly. Criticism has tended to concentrate on the differences, and certainly Shakespeare uses conscious artifice to larger effect by making a series of unexpected twists in the plot seem to embody the workings of providence in *Cymbeline,* and by going further in *The Winter's Tale* and *The Tempest,* incorporating presenter or artist figures in the action, Paulina and Prospero, whose art or magic in directing their productions turns theatricality into ritual and tricks us into accepting the final disclosures and reconciliations in these plays as "holy" or the work of "immortal Providence." At the same time, these plays start from a similar basis in sexuality. *Pericles* begins with incest in Antioch and takes Marina into a brothel in Mytilene in the most spectacular episode in the play. In *Cymbeline* the visual rape of Imogen by Iachimo and the obscene revulsion of Posthumus in act 2, scene 5 are paralleled comically by the quasi-incestuous and adulterous threats of Cloten to possess Imogen. The absurd, obscene jealousy of Leontes in *The Winter's Tale* releases fantasies of sexual horror, while in *The Tempest,* Caliban embodies, among other forces, sexuality, the libido unrestrained by morality, which is a part of everyone, as Prospero concedes in the end in turning to Caliban with "This thing of darkness/I acknowledge mine" (5.1.275–76). In these plays, too, a sense of comic form is established by their conscious artifice, their treatment of character and presentation of events; even in *The Winter's Tale*, the jealousy of Leontes, however vividly registered as a "revulsion against his own sexuality" in "images of great physical intensity,"[35] springs from nothing and, indeed, is rendered absurd in relation to the spectacularly pregnant Hermione, whose adultery would have had to take place nearly nine months previously for their "issue" to be a bastard. So jealousy is detached from cause and is staged by Leontes as a performance, using Mamillius as his uncomprehending audience within the play, while the great curve of his passion is seen by others as a madness, an affliction of the heavens, a disease, or an absurdity that will raise "laughter" when the "good truth" is known. As in *Philaster*, character is not stable but can change with circumstance, or even with costume, as Perdita finds her robes as a goddess seem to change her disposition, and the Shepherd and his son are transformed in act 5, scene 2 by a change of clothes into "gentlemen born." Despite differences, Shakespeare's late plays, like the central tragicomedies of Beaumont and Fletcher, relate to a world in which performance and patronage were, in the words of the Player in Tom Stoppard's *Rosencrantz and Guildenstern Are Dead*, "two sides of the same coin."[36]

NOTES

1. Norman Rabkin, *Shakespeare and the Common Understanding* (New York: Free Press, 1967), p. 220; cf. also Robert W. Uphaus, *Beyond Tragedy* (Lexington: University Press of Kentucky, 1982), p. 71: "Few if any will argue that the first three acts of *The Winter's Tale* are something other than tragic." My parenthetical citations of Shakespeare refer to *The Riverside Shakespeare*, ed. G. Blakemore Evans et al. (Boston: Houghton Mifflin, 1974).

2. Richard P. Wheeler, *Shakespeare's Development and the Problem Comedies: Turn and Counter-Turn* (Berkeley and Los Angeles: University of California Press, 1981), p. 151.

3. Rabkin, *Shakespeare and the Common Understanding*, p. 215.

4. Ibid., pp. 214, 220.

5. Rabkin skillfully attacked the search for meanings in plays in "Meaning and Shakespeare," *Shakespeare 1971*, ed. Clifford Leech and J.M.R. Margeson (Toronto: University of Toronto Press, 1972), observing that the more sharply criticism is "focussed on explaining what plays are about, the farther it gets from the actuality of our experience in responding to them" (p. 89). See also Richard Levin, *New Readings vs. Old Plays* (Chicago: University of Chicago Press, 1979). pp. 11ff.

6. Giambattista Guarini, "The Compendium of Tragicomic Poetry" (1599), translated by A. H. Gilbert in *Literary Criticism from Plato to Dryden* (New York: American Book Co., 1940), p. 511; John Fletcher, "To the Reader," Preface to *The Faithful Shepherdess* (c. 1609).

7. Arthur Kirsch, *Jacobean Dramatic Perspectives* (Charlottesville: University Press of Virginia, 1972), p. 19. Eugene Waith was among the first to appreciate the connection between satire and tragicomedy; see his important discussion, "Characterization in John Fletcher's Tragicomedies," *Review of English Studies* 19 (1943): 144–53.

8. *Antonio's Revenge*, ed. G. K. Hunter (Lincoln: University of Nebraska Press, 1965).

9. See R. A. Foakes, "'Forms to his Conceit': Shakespeare and the Uses of Stage Illusion," *Proceedings of the British Academy* 66 (1982): 112, 115–19.

10. *Sexuality* is, in fact, a modern concept, and as this term came into use in the nineteenth century, so the word *sexual* was itself differentiated in the seventeenth century and is first recorded by OED in 1651. Perhaps this differentiation can be related to the "advent of the great prohibitions, the imperatives of decency, the obligatory concealment of the body, the reduction to silence and

mandatory reticences of language" that Michel Foucault claims occurred during the seventeenth century; see his *History of Sexuality* (1976), vol. 1, trans. Robert Hurley (New York: Pantheon, 1979), p. 115 (*La Volonté de Savoir,* p. 152).

11. See Arthur Kirsch's fine analysis of the way *Measure for Measure* translates "our awareness of theatrical artifice into a consciousness of transcendent forces in human life" in *Shakespeare and the Energies of Love* (Cambridge: Cambridge University Press, 1981), pp. 92–105.

12. Guarini, "The Compendium of Tragicomic Poetry," p. 512.

13. See G. E. Bentley, *The Jacobean and Caroline Stage,* 7 vols. (Oxford: Clarendon, 1941–68), 6 : 12–13.

14. The masque, as Eugene Waith has recently argued, has formal links with comedy, and these links are relevant to my general argument; see his "The English Masque and the Functions of Comedy," *The Elizabethan Theatre* VIII, ed. George Hibbard (Port Credit, Ontario: Meany, 1982), pp. 144–63.

15. Peter N. Skrine, *The Baroque* (London: Methuen, 1978), p. 8. The plays of Beaumont and Fletcher have been associated with baroque art by several critics but usually in aesthetic terms of "distortion" (as by M. C. Bradbrook, in her introduction to Beaumont and Fletcher, *Select Plays* [London: Dent, 1962], p. vi), or "dislocation" (as by Clifford Leech, in *The John Fletcher Plays* [London: Chatto and Windus, 1962], p. 32). The idea of role playing is perhaps less obviously "baroque" in artistic terms but is certainly a feature of the period, and is related to that displacement "from a stable, inherited social world" detected by Stephen Greenblatt as a feature of sixteenth-century authors in *Renaissance Self-Fashioning* (Chicago: University of Chicago Press, 1980), pp. 7–8.

16. Skrine, *Baroque,* p. 9.

17. D. J. Gordon, "Roles and Mysteries," in *The Renaissance Imagination* (Berkeley and Los Angeles: University of California Press, 1975), p. 21.

18. See E. K. Chambers, *The Elizabethan Stage,* 4 vols. (Oxford: Oxford University Press, 1923), 2 : 535–37.

19. Bentley, *Jacobean and Caroline Stage,* 6 : 7.

20. Thomas Dekker, *The Gull's Hornbook* (1609), referred to the Lord's rooms as "now but the Stage's Suburbs"; see A. M. Nagler, *A Source Book in Theatrical History* (New York: Dover, 1959), p. 134.

21. *The Dramatic Works in the Beaumont and Fletcher Canon,* ed. Fredson Bowers, vol. 1 (Cambridge: Cambridge University Press, 1966). All subsequent quotations of Beaumont and Fletcher are from this edition.

22. All quotations of Jonson's plays refer to *Ben Jonson,* ed. C. H. Herford, Percy Simpson, and Evelyn Simpson, 11 vols. (Oxford: Clarendon Press, 1925–52).

23. The phrase is Francis Beaumont's, from his commendatory verses written for the first edition of *The Faithful Shepherdess* (c.1609).

24. Robert K. Turner, Jr., in the Introduction to the Regents Renaissance Drama edition (Lincoln: University of Nebraska Press, 1964), p. xviii.

25. Arthur Kirsch, *Jacobean Dramatic Perspectives,* p. 39.

26. James Shirley, Preface to the first folio edition of the *Comedies and Tragedies* of Beaumont and Fletcher (London, 1647).

27. E. M. Waith, *The Pattern of Tragicomedy in Beaumont and Fletcher* (New Haven: Yale University Press, 1952), p. 18.

28. Arthur Kirsch, *Jacobean Dramatic Perspectives,* p. 59.

29. Robert K. Turner, Jr., ed., *A King and No King,* p. xvii.

30. Waith, *The Pattern of Tragicomedy in Beaumont and Fletcher,* p. 41.

31. Alfred Harbage, *Shakespeare and the Rival Traditions* (New York: Macmillan, 1952), p. 71.

32. See Stephen Orgel, *The Illusion of Power* (Berkeley and Los Angeles: University of California Press, 1975).

33. See, for example, Peter H. Davison, "The Serious Concerns of *Philaster,*" *ELH* 30 (1963):1–15. If I am right in seeing the convention of the play as essentially comic, then it relates to romance rather than to politics, and to look for serious political concerns or to complain of their absence, as Margot Heinemann does, is beside the point—even if she is correct in her argument that "serious political historical drama was becoming impracticable" in the reign of James I; see her *Puritanism and Theatre* (Cambridge: Cambridge University Press, 1980), p. 46.

34. A. J. Gurr, ed., *Philaster* (London: Methuen, 1969), pp. lxvi–lxvii.

35. L. C. Knights, " 'Integration' in *The Winter's Tale,*" *Sewanee Review* 84 (1976): 602.

36. This is, I am aware, a "modern" reading that necessarily reflects the preoccupations of our time, and the reason these plays seem peculiarly sympathetic now may well be that our age too is

preoccupied by what Richard Poirier called *The Performing Self* in his book on fiction (New York: Oxford University Press, 1971). A concern with performance and the presentation of the self is also a feature not only of much modern drama (hence the quotation from *Rosencrantz and Guildenstern Are Dead* at the head of this essay), but also of our society at large, which has been categorized in the title of Christopher Lasch's book (New York: Norton, 1978) as *The Culture of Narcissism.*

Shakespearian Comedy

Shakespearian Comedy and Its Courtly Audience

Alvin B. Kernan

Reputation, Ulysses explains to Achilles, is not the inalienable possession of a great warrior, "though in and of him there be much consisting," for he cannot know what he and his deeds are,

> Till he behold them formed in th'applause
> Where they're extended; who, like an arch, reverb'rate
> The voice again, or, like a gate of steel
> Fronting the sun, receives and renders back
> His figure and his heat.
>
> *(Troilus and Cressida, 3.3.119–23)*[1]

The "applause" image implicates the playwright and his plays, along with the soldier and his actions, in a condition in which being depends on perceiving, and directs attention to those many scenes in Shakespeare where the audience forms the meaning of the scene it watches. In *Troilus*, for example, Ulysses' reception theory is enacted and complicated when Troilus, Ulysses, and Thersites "reverb'rate" different meanings for the scene between Diomed and Cressida; similarly, we see the "gate of steel Fronting the sun" when Othello observes and misinterprets Cassio boasting of his familiarity with Bianca. Shakespeare's self-consciousness about audience control of the meaning of a play is recorded, however, most formally and extensively in the several plays-within-the-play—in *Love's Labour's Lost, A Midsummer Night's Dream, The Taming of the Shrew, Hamlet*, and *The Tempest*—where a theatrical performance on stage is watched and commented on by a stage audience. In every case, to put the argument bluntly, the audience plays its part badly and misinterprets the play. Possible exceptions such as Ferdinand and Miranda at *The Masque of Juno and Ceres* staged by Prospero in *The Tempest* are always qualified by a failure of some kind, when the mere approach of such groundlings as Caliban, Trinculo, and Stephano is enough to break off the illusion. Quite obviously, Shakespeare was not only aware that a play was not real and complete until it was reverberated by the audience but that the process was more than likely to be a distorting one in which the personal attitudes of the members of the audience reshaped the image projected at them from the stage. *The Murder of Gonzago* in *Hamlet*, to take the extreme example, is interpreted differently, or not interpreted at all, by every member of the audience, and misinterpreted in every case because it is understood in the context

91

of immediate, particular interests rather than in the timeless context of the internal play itself.

The various audience-response scenes in Shakespeare, however, do more than merely register the sensitivity of the playwright to the realities of his situation in the theater and the vulnerability of his plays to their spectators. At the same time that he images his theatrical circumstances, he attempts to control them. In a distinguished essay, "The Writer's Audience Is Always a Fiction,"[2] Walter J. Ong tells us that every writer, in an attempt to shape interpretation, builds a specific role for his audience into his work and attempts by various strategies to manipulate the actual reader or auditor into assuming that role. The "Dear Reader" of Victorian fiction is probably the simplest and most familiar form of audience creation.

To define the audience is to control, at least to some extent, interpretation, and, as the long history of the Shakespearian audience shows, critics and scholars as well as authors play this game. In Shakespeare's own time, Puritan polemicists tried to discredit the theater by manufacturing an audience made up entirely of whores, cutpurses, swaggerers, and idle apprentices. These nutcracking Elizabethans hovered about the plays for centuries and still do to some extent, but in the scholarly world, if not in popular mythology, historical research has replaced the audience of the idle and the wicked with a superior audience of several thousand London citizens of all kinds who went daily to the Globe and other theaters in or near the great city. This audience reinforces the felt greatness of Shakespearian theater by supplying it with an appropriate auditory of true English folk, learned in theology, sensitive to language, and interested in history, a cross section of Elizabethan society of whom Alfred Harbage could write, "It thrived for a time, it passed quickly, and its like has never existed since. It must be given much of the credit for the greatness of Shakespeare's plays."[3] To validate its own definition of literature, modern criticism has silently constructed a universal audience for Shakespeare, man as he always was and always will be, looking at the retold myths of being, at images of the eternal self in all its hopes, disappointments, and mysteries, at the power of art to shape life and confer meaning on it. At the moment, reception theory is proposing still another audience made up of a number of isolated individuals, each enclosed in his own solipsistic self and interpreting the plays out of his own subjectivity, which brings us back to the situation that so deeply concerned Shakespeare in the first place.

None of these audiences created by criticism and scholarship is exactly the audience Shakespeare seems to have had in mind for himself. Whenever he constructs an objective image of the audience he was trying to shape, it is not a vulgar audience in the public theater, like that Beaumont mocks in *The Knight of the Burning Pestle*, nor a universal spectator like Revenge in *The Spanish Tragedy*, but a courtly audience. Sly may be only made to believe that he is part of a noble household while watching the performance of the internal play in *The Taming of the Shrew*, but in *Love's Labour's Lost*, *A Midsummer Night's Dream*, *Hamlet*, and *The Tempest*, where plays-within-the-play are played, the stage audience consists of kings, queens, princes, dukes, noble peers, and lords and ladies of the court. This was the ideal audience that Renaissance humanism conceived for its arts, desiring no less than Hamlet, one of its chief spokesmen, to use its plays to catch the consciences of kings. This was the audience that the arts, including theater, did in fact have for the most part across Europe in the sixteenth and seventeenth centuries; and, although Shakespeare may have spent most of his time and made most of his money in the public theater, this was the audience that "fronted" his company at least 245 times between 1594 and 1612 at Whitehall, Hampton Court, the Queen's House, and other aristocratic settings. After an exhaustive study of the English theater from 1300 to 1660, Glynne Wickham has concluded that "the roofed hall, candlelight and ceremonial occasions" of the palace or noble house were "the alpha and omega of the professional actor's status and environment in England from the middle of the fifteenth century to the Civil War, notwithstanding notable and extensive sallies into less sophisticated places of public recreation."[4] It was from the court that Shakespeare's playing companies derived their names—the Lord Chamberlain's Men, the King's Men—their legal status as members of an aristocratic or the royal household, and the very real protection and favors that went with such service. It was also this court whose lives and concerns the Shakespearian plays reflect—his is not citizen theater—showing his noble audience their own social world engaged in dynastic matters, playing out fashionable games of verbal wit, concerned endlessly with love and the relationship of the sexes, and attending plays in the great halls of palaces and country houses.

In presenting his fictional audience as a courtly group, Shakespeare realizes theatrically the dream of humanism and its ambitious writers to play a part in the affairs of the great world of state. But he was also trying to control that audience and the understanding of his plays in an unusual and risky way. Unlike other court dramatists such as John Lyly and the Ben Jonson of the masques who showed their noble spectators idealized, positive images of themselves as an audience, instructing them by showing them what they might be, Shakespeare showed the court negative images of itself in the theater, hoping, presumably, to make its members into what the playwright wanted them to be by provoking their ironic scorn for and laughter at stage audiences who talk away during performances, interrupt the actors, comment loudly and foolishly on the play, and regularly miss the dramatic point because they are so supremely self-centered and certain of their own courtly reality. No doubt he was trying to improve theater manners, which contemporary reports suggest left a great deal to be desired; but the latter issue, the danger that the play will not be understood because the audience cannot or will not project their understandings outside the circle of their own subjective reality, was the most important in all the plays-within-the-play, and in all the internal playlets as well, as when Prince Hal rejects Falstaff's playing of the king, or Cleopatra disdains the crude way the common players will present her and Antony. There is clearly some tension between Shakespeare and the courtly audience. But what, his built-in perspective on courtly performance forces us to ask, would a group of aristocrats seated in the great hall of a palace have seen when they looked at Shakespeare's plays? And what would he have wanted them to see? It may be possible to at least approach this question in the context of Shakespearian comedy—a topic that Eugene

Waith has explored profoundly in his teaching and writing, in ways from which the present writer has gratefully benefited.

The normative structure of Shakespearian comedy has been established so firmly by a collective critical enterprise in this century, that Sherman Hawkins can succinctly define it as "the juxtaposition of two strongly contrasted locales, representing two different orders of reality, and the movement of the action from one to the other."[5] C. L. Barber in *Shakespeare's Festive Comedy* calls the two locales "everyday" and "holiday," and defines them in the context of ancient folk rituals of social release, still celebrated by the Elizabethans, such as Maying or the Feast of Misrule. Northrop Frye places the Shakespearian comic locales in the context of a universal comic myth, man's most fundamental story of hope, in which a condition of restraint of pleasure by an overly strict authority leads to a period of freedom and license, which in turn provides the basis for the formation of a new society controlled by the young and celebrated with marriage, feasting, and dancing. The city and the " green world," the place of reason and the place of folly, order and topsy-turvydom; these locales have many names. They mark the two places through which the plot of Shakespearian comedy moves in a timeless rhythm of human life: one generation gives way to the next, energy and pleasure break through social constraints, and "the full stream of the world" flows onward. But the most immediate and literal names for the two places are the court and the country.

No doubt Shakespeare's courtly audience, like the men and women in criticism's more universal audience, felt the power of the full stream of the world as it flowed through Shakespearian comedy, but the terms *court* and *country* had intense significance for a group of English courtiers in the sixteenth and seventeenth centuries. Historians searching for explanations of the English rebellion of the 1640s and 1650s have in recent years begun to see the English civil war as part of a broad pattern of long continuing revolts that broke out throughout Europe, not only in England, but in Spain, France, Sweden, the Ukraine, Germany, and the Low Countries. The details differ in each country, but as Perez Zagorin says in his summary book, *The Court and the Country,*

one broad feature nevertheless characterized in some degree the context of nearly all the mid-century rebellions. Most of them were directed against a monarchical power which, however vulnerable at the moment of revolt because of war or other difficulties, had grown during the preceding decades more centralized, more capable of imposing its will, more uniform in controlling and disciplining all ranks of its subjects. . . . in the foremost states of Europe the progress of royal authority had been in full career for more than a hundred and fifty years. Despite intervals of retrogression, that authority was increasing in all the attributes which could make its rule over its subjects an untrammelled reality. Everywhere there were groups, orders, and whole regions upon whom regal sovereignty fell as a vexation and a burden. The inherited and prescriptive privileges of assemblies of estates, the liberties of provinces and of degrees of men, were pared down, became thin and emaciated, or were rendered lifeless at the feet of the all-conquering Leviathan. And at the same time the administrative apparatus of the crowns expanded, the costs of their government rose, and expenditure for the maintenance of courts and the support of wars became more prodigal. To finance government, war, and courts, the princes challenged or obtained a taxing power that invaded their subjects' security of property. It was inevitable that so far-reaching an application of royal power among peoples not yet fully habituated to bear the yoke should give rise to popular and aristocratic reaction.[6]

In England this ongoing struggle between an increasingly powerful court and resisting subjects took a number of different forms, all of which appear in Shakespeare's plays. Resistance by the remnants of the old feudal nobility to the strong centralized monarchy established by the Tudors and later intensified by the Stuart kings gradually died out in the sixteenth century, ending with the last rebellion in the north in 1569. Open rebellion was immediately replaced with struggles between court factions that intensified in the 1590s, the period when Shakespeare's plays began to be presented at court. The most famous of these factional struggles was that between the Cecil and the Essex groups, and it is at least interesting to note that the one aristocrat, Henry Wriothesley, the third Earl of Southampton, with whom William Shakespeare can be definitely connected through the dedications of his poems, was deeply involved with Essex, being in the earl's London house during the brief revolt in 1601, an occasion on which Shakespeare's company was persuaded to perform one of their old plays, *Richard II*, showing the deposition of a legitimate but weak king. The Lord Chamberlain's Men managed to get out of this trouble with some difficulty and sharp questioning, and shortly afterwards became the King's Men. Southampton escaped the axe and was restored to favor by James, but he soon found his way into the opposition out-group again and shortly before his death wrote disingenuously, "I have been wholy a country man and seldom seen either the Court or London."[7]

By 1623, when Shakespeare's plays were published in folio and Southampton wrote these words, the term *country* referred not only to the pastoral life of "quiet and content" of which he speaks later in the same letter, but to a political proto-party made up of

a loose collaboration or alliance of men in the governing class, peers and gentlemen of assured position and often of substantial fortune, alienated for a variety of reasons from the Court. Principles counted for it more than persons. It found its main focus of action in parliament, and to a lesser extent in local government, in both of which it eventually secured an ascendancy beyond the monarch's ability to control.[8]

The country was not a revolutionary group, quite the reverse. Its members were upper class, and in their struggle against the king's prerogative and the increasingly autocratic power of the court, "they conceived themselves defenders of an immemorial legal order of rights and liberties against which the king was the transgressor."[9] The ancient liberties they claimed for themselves were the now-familiar rights of protection of property, freedom of speech and association, due process and, in general, the limitation of the power of the king to act outside what the country considered to be the ancient natural law. Revolution and the seeds of license were in the country's position, but they would have themselves been surprised by where their views were eventually to lead in the 1640s.

The third symbolic place in the political map of England in the sixteenth and seventeenth centuries was the city, and there was only one city in England, London, many times as large and important as its nearest competitors. Traditional views have seen London because of its commercial interests, puritanism, and ancient town privileges as the consistent antagonist of a court that interfered with business and civic freedom. In this understanding it is not at all surprising that London should take the parliamentary side and drive Charles from his palace in 1642. But recent historians have constructed quite a different picture of city politics. Valerie Pearl in her *London and the Outbreak of the Puritan Revolution* (1961) has shown that the city fathers consistently identified with the crown, and that it took a minor revolution to bring London over to the parliamentary side, a view that has been only slightly modified by Robert Ashton, *The City and the Court, 1603–1643* (1979), who shows that the interests of city and court began to diverge sharply in the 1630s. Court and city were, it now appears, in alliance during Shakespeare's lifetime, and this accords with the relationship of the two in his plays where court and city are usually conjoined in opposition to country.

Thomas Hobbes remarked that "the poets have lodg'd themselves in the three regions of mankinde, *Court, City,* and *Country,* correspondent in some proportion to those three Regions of the World."[10] These are indeed "the three regions of mankinde," the universally symbolic places where, as books like Raymond Williams's *The Country and the City* demonstrate, the poets have always set their stories; in the sixteenth century, from Skelton to Spenser and Sidney, the contrast of court and country became a literary staple. But during the sixteenth and seventeenth centuries these poetic places also corresponded in more than a little proportion to the three regions of the social and political world: a court that exercised increasing but still unaccepted power over the lives and property of the people; the country, which, particularly after the 1590s, opposed the court in defense of freedom and ancient, natural rights; and the city of London, which, according to the most recent historians, found for a time that its commercial interests were best served by an alliance with the court but eventually broke away to join the country.

However familiar these places—court, city, country—may have been in quest romance, comedy, and carnival, audiences at the courts of Elizabeth and James when they watched a Shakespearian comedy were not only often looking at a stage audience that fronted them with their own reality but also at a theatrical arrangement of the places that were the symbolic centers of their social and political lives. Many of them were present in the court, as Lawrence Stone has shown in his *The Crisis of the Aristocracy, 1558–1641,* because the monarch forced them to leave their country seats and live at court—a very expensive matter— where they could be watched, controlled, and in some cases even purposely bankrupted to limit their power. We expect that Shakespeare showed his great patrons pretty much what they wanted to see, as Lyly did in his court plays and Jonson in his masques, or as Van Dyck painted them in the desired heroic style; but, as always, Shakespeare both satisfies and surprises, and by looking at what he does in his comedies we can at least glimpse something of the way he managed the patronage relationship.

His comedies sometimes begin in the city—Ephesus, Padua in the play within *The Taming of the Shrew,* or Shylock's more realistic Venice—but most often they begin in the court—of Navarre, Athens, Illyria, Vienna, Sicilia—and even those comedies that begin in the city often center the civic scene on a duke or ruler, as in *The Comedy of Errors,* which opens in Ephesus with the duke of the city dispensing justice. The court as regularly occupies the place of primacy in Shakespeare's comedies as it did in England, and, to generalize boldly, the court is regularly shown exercising power and affecting its citizens, often by applying the law in a way that is harmful to the property rights, freedom, happiness, and lives of various courtiers. Occasionally the lower orders also feel the power of the court, like the humble folk of *Love's Labour's Lost* or the underworld element of Vienna, though commoners are nearly as unimportant in Shakespeare's comedy as they were in Whitehall. Sometimes the court is openly tyrannical—the usurping duke in *As You Like It* or Leontes in *The Winter's Tale*—sometimes, like Theseus, reluctantly applying the strict law of the state that gives fathers absolute authority over children; sometimes the court has lost control of the state, like the Duke of *Measure for Measure,* thus opening the way for Angelo's tyranny; sometimes it has lost its potency—witness Orsino's self-indulgence; or sometimes it tries to impose unrealistically high ideals on the state, as Navarre does in forming his academy, banishing women, and forbidding sex on pain of death. The details are interestingly various, but in all cases the court and its ruler are being criticized in a perceptive and tactful way. The court thwarts the wills of its subjects not because it is essentially evil even in cases of outright tyranny, but because its great power tends to push its civil virtues and rightful political functions toward excess: too strict application of the law, too refined sensitivity, too idealistic a conception of reality, too much mercy or too much justice. Shakespeare, unlike Marlowe, is not presenting a revolutionary view of the court and its monarchs. He is, in the best tradition of humanist art, responsibly advising the governor, constantly reminding the court that its enormous power, wealth, refinement, and responsibility for administration of the law and the welfare of the kingdom—all the things that make it the center and the ideal expression of the national life—tend toward their own forms of excess, which may defeat the very values the court embodies. In Venice the duke must deliver Antonio to death in order to uphold the laws of contract on which the prosperity of his commercial state depends; in Vienna and in Milan moral refinement in the first case, and intellectual refinement in the second, put the state in the hands of insensitive, tyrannical powers, Angelo and Antonio; in Illyria leisure and overly cultivated sentiments leave the Duke reveling in the pleasurable intricacies of a love turned inward on itself, while its supposed object, the Lady Olivia, sits immured in her house behind a dark veil of mourning; and in Sicilia, the superheated atmosphere of courtly manners, courtesy, and intrigue pushes a king to paranoia and destroys his family and court. All this is lightly done in a comic manner in each individual play, and no one need take it too seriously, but as a whole Shakespearian comedy reveals a sense of ever-present danger in the court.

Threatened and thwarted in the city and the court, life, particularly young life, flees to the country in "green world" comedies such as *Two Gentlemen, The Merchant of Venice, As You Like It,* and the play that defines the Shakespearian comic pattern in its full perfection, *A Midsummer Night's Dream.* In the major variant form of Shakespearian comedy, "the characters," as Hawkins says, "stay put, but they are visited by outsiders, who upset the routine of the community into which they come."[11] These outsiders usually have the "green world" experience in some form behind them, as do Viola and Sebastian, the survivors of storm and wreck in *Twelfth Night,* coming to a too sophisticated Illyria. Both the major Shakespearian comic patterns have the same result of exposing the courtly world to the country, to nature, and to the larger experience of reality that these words represent in Shakespearian comedy. Sometimes the exposure is managed satirically, as when Touchstone in the Forest of Arden parodies the formal way in which quarrels are managed, and real danger escaped, by fashionable young courtiers; more subtly in *The Merchant of Venice* where the various nobles who come to win Portia's hand in Belmont are amusingly revealed as blinded by their own sense of self-importance. But the criticism of courtly values in Shakespearian comedy more often proceeds by exposing the traveling courtiers to a series of very fundamental human and natural realities that have been concealed or forgotten in the court but are known and felt with great force in the country. As the particular type of courtly excesses varies, so the range of basic human experiences in the country is again very broad. Natural reality may be as immediate and inevitable as the foul weather, hunger, and curbs upon the will that Kate is forced to endure in Petruchio's country house, or it may verge on the supernatural like the unstrained quality of mercy that in Belmont "droppeth as the gentle rain from heaven/Upon the place beneath." The natural powers at work in Shakespeare's second place may be as crudely known and expressed as Pompey's underworld awareness that the enforcement of Angelo's laws against extra-marital sex is going to require some very strong measures: "Does your worship mean to geld and splay all the youth of the city?" (*Measure,* 2.1.228–29); or they may be as imperiously elegant as the fairy king and queen, Oberon and Titania, who jealously govern a fertile sexual world "where the wild thyme blows,/Where oxlips and the nodding violet grows" (*Dream,* 2.1.249–50). "Blood, thou art blood" (*Measure,* 2.4.15), says Angelo, discovering that it is Isabella's chastity that has inflamed him, not wantonness; and the Shakespearian second place always provides some such startling discoveries of unexpected turns of the human mind. Love and cruelty, pleasure and pain are not so far apart as the young lovers in *A Midsummer Night's Dream* had thought; rural idiocy has its own truths as different clowns reveal, paranoia its own satisfactions in *The Winter's Tale;* and every magical island comes with a Caliban to match its Ariel.

A generation of criticism has thoroughly worked out the primary conditions of the Shakespearian green world—female dominance, disguise and loss of identity, the triumph of fools and folly, playfulness and release of imagination—but for our purposes it is perhaps enough to remark that it is the place where home-truths, the basic realities of human life, are made known. Perhaps the sharpest image of what is ultimately experienced in the country comes in *Love's Labour's Lost* where the messenger Marcade suddenly appears in the midst of the comic proceedings with the news of the death of the king of France. News about what men and women basically are like sometimes comes from lower-class city dwellers like Bottom and his artisan friends of Athens, or the watch of Messina, or a tapster of Vienna like Pompey; but most often it comes from the country, from the Forest of Arden, or an aristocratic country house like Belmont, or the sheep farm of pastoral Bohemia, or, at the extreme, a violent storm at sea that tells Viola in *Twelfth Night* or Alonso and his party in *The Tempest* something of human helplessness faced with the awesome forces of nature. Shakespeare associates the country, and the wide range of natural experience this term represents for him, with fundamental realities that form the given basis and background of human life but that get forgotten and lost from time to time in the court, the chief emblem of the socially constructed world.

But it is to the court in Athens, Illyria, Sicilia, Milan, that life eventually returns in Shakespearian comedy, with only rare exceptions like *The Merchant of Venice* where the play ends in Belmont, but Belmont is an aristocratic great house, partaking of both courtly and country values of the most rarefied kind. The return to court is not always plotted very carefully: in *As You Like It* the usurping Duke experiences a miraculous conversion and retires to a monastery to repent his wicked ways, and the courtiers troop back from the country to the court singing the praises of "Hymen, god of every town." In most of the comedies, however, the freedom and exhilarating encounter with the forces of nature experienced in the country have a dangerous tendency toward license that eventually complicates and confuses life in ways which make a satisfactory human outcome impossible. In the carnival atmosphere of *Twelfth Night* the rioting of Sir Toby and his friends nears disaster, and the love of Olivia for the disguised Viola has no possibility of a satisfactory outcome. The summary image of the impossibility of a natural life of complete freedom appears, however, in the forest of *A Midsummer Night's Dream* where the lovers, after brushing against a both terribly attractive and frighteningly inhuman nature and chasing each other in hatred through the dark, lie exhausted in darkness and sleep, a few feet apart but incapable of enjoying one another. The country frees and invigorates, but its powers are finally too much for the courtiers, and so they must return to the social world made by men, usually to a court and town where a duke or king straightens things out, joins the right people, and celebrates the happy outcome with civil rituals of marriage, feasting, dance, and high ceremony.

"The ancient and undoubted right to debate freely," liberty of speech, "redress of mischiefs and grievances," a return to the old ways and values of the nation— these were the leading political principles of the country party in the seventeenth century, and they sound at least something like a program of the activities in the second place of Shakespearian comedy. And the eventual return of the exiles to a renewed court in that comedy accords well with the royalism of the gentlemen who were associated with the country, never considering that there was any right of rebellion against the king and a monarchical form of government. They simply wanted reform and a restoration of what they conceived to be natural rights and freedoms, which is exactly what the Shakespearian comic plot provides.

My argument is not that Shakespearian comedy was an exact allegory of late Tudor and Stuart politics. What I would like to suggest is that in times such as the late sixteenth and the seventeenth century when the established order is pulling apart under strong tensions, men—politicians, poets, theologians—try to construct new orders that will put the pieces together in a way that defines and resolves those tensions in some satisfactory manner. The pieces to be manipulated are usually symbols, and in late Tudor and Stuart England the primary symbols, partly drawn from poetry, but, as Hobbes saw, "correspondent in some proportion to . . . the World," were the court, the city, and the country. Using these symbols, Shakespeare constructed comedy that provided amusement and delight, dances, clowns, songs, wit, and love stories with a happy ending, which the court audience required, and, to judge from his success, applauded, rewarded, and called for again and again. At the same time this comedy commented in a profound way on the central political issues of the day, issues that were vitally important to the monarchs and to the many aristocrats who had left their country estates and gathered in the court to participate in its excitement, fashion, and fortune. The image that Shakespeare showed them of themselves was radical in some ways but conservative in its final implications. In the end the return is always to the court, because only in the court can human affairs be satisfactorily ordered and human needs satisfied. But the court itself always has its danger, an excess of its own virtues; it tends to throttle life and thus engender defiance and revolt. But revolt, though satisfying for a time and renewing, cannot be sustained for long and leads back to court.

How much of this the courtly audience understood, Shakespeare leaves in profound doubt. Ben Jonson's masques with their magical triumphs by omnipotent divine monarchs over the forces of chaos may well have better suited the beliefs and understanding of a royal patron than comedies in which the court and the king are legitimated not by God Almighty but by a human need for both nature and nurture that cannot finally comprehend the farther ranges of the natural world and human experience. But there is no doubt about which of these two types of royal entertainment more accurately forecasts future events when a corrupt and tyrannical court would be left behind, and after a period of wandering not in a wood outside Athens but in a Kingdom of the Saints—encountering not fairies but such stranger creatures as Praise-God Barebones, Oliver Cromwell, and the Diggers, the Levellers, and the Family of Love—the nation would joyfully return to the kingdom again, ruled by a new, jolly, tolerant monarch, leaving behind not a Jaques "for other than for dancing measures," but the author of *Paradise Lost*.

NOTES

1. All citations of Shakespeare are to the *Signet Classic Shakespeare*, ed. Sylvan Barnet (New York: Harcourt Brace Jovanovich, 1963).

2. Walter J. Ong, *Interfaces of the Word* (Ithaca: Cornell University Press, 1977), pp. 53–81.

3. Alfred Harbage, *Shakespeare's Audience* (New York: Columbia University Press, 1941), p. 159. Recently this audience has been further upgraded by Ann Jennalie Cook who has shown us that they

were a "privileged" group. The term *privileged* is complex, but the total effect of her powerfully reasoned argument is to make the Shakespearian audience a distinctly intellectual upper-class group, which corresponds, it might be pointed out, to the actual audience for Shakespeare in our own time. *The Privileged Playgoers of Shakespeare's London, 1576–1642* (Princeton: Princeton University Press, 1981).

4. Glynne Wickham, *Early English Stages, 1300–1600* (London: Routledge and Kegan Paul, 1972), 2.2, p. 150.

5. Sherman Hawkins, "The Two Worlds of Shakespearean Comedy," in *Shakespeare Studies III*, ed. J. Leeds Barroll (New York: Center for Shakespeare Studies, 1967), p. 65.

6. Perez Zagorin, *The Court and the Country, The Beginning of the English Revolution* (London: Routledge and Kegan Paul, 1969), pp. 4–5.

7. Ibid., p. 34.

8. Ibid., p. 75.

9. Ibid., p. 83.

10. Thomas Hobbes, "Answer to Davenant's Preface to Gondibert" (1650) in *Critical Essays of the 17th Century*, ed. J. E. Spingarn, 3 vols. (Oxford: Oxford University Press, 1908), 2:54–55.

11. Hawkins, "Two Worlds," p. 65.

The Education of Orlando

Marjorie Garber

When Rosalind learns from Celia that Orlando is in the Forest of Arden, she cries out in mingled joy and consternation, "Alas the day, what shall I do with my doublet and hose?" (3.2.219–20).[1] Members of the audience might perhaps be pardoned were they to answer her, not in the "one word" she demands, but with the familiar chant of the burlesque house, "Take it off!"—either literally (if she has been provident enough to bring a change of clothing with her to Arden) or figuratively, by identifying herself to him at once as Rosalind, rather than continuing the fiction that she is a youth named Ganymede, a native of the forest. Indeed Celia makes a suggestion along these lines, when she hears Rosalind—as Ganymede—abusing the reputations of women when she talks to Orlando about the nature of love. "You have simply misus'd our sex in your love-prate," says Celia. "We must have your doublet and hose pluck'd over your head, and show the world what the bird hath done to her own nest" (4.1.201–4). There is in fact very little risk to her should she do so, except perhaps from a blast of the "winter wind" about which Amiens sings so feelingly (2.7.174). She is perfectly safe. Clearly there are no outlaws in the forest, or other predatory men; they have all been left behind at court. Moreover, she is assured of Orlando's love for her, since both she and Celia have read the poems with which he has festooned Arden's otherwise blameless trees. In short, there is apparently no reason for her to remain clad as a boy. Why then does she do so?

In other Shakespearian comedies, women dressed as men have compelling reasons for remaining in disguise. Julia in *The Two Gentlemen of Verona* is trapped in her male attire because of the perfidy of her erstwhile lover, Proteus. She initially disguises herself for the same reason Rosalind gives: "for I would prevent/The loose encounters of lascivious men" (2.7.40–41), but she fully intends to reveal herself once she reaches her "loving Proteus" (7). When to her chagrin she finds him in the act of offering his love to Silvia instead, she retains her male guise, enlists herself in Proteus's service, carries his love tokens to Silvia, and only reveals her true identity in the final scene, when she fears that Valentine will make good on his extraordinary promise to give Proteus "all that was mine in Silvia" (5.4.83). At this point Julia swoons (or pretends to swoon), produces a ring given her by Proteus, and acknowledges that her "immodest raiment" is a "disguise of love" (106–7). Her costume is essential to the working out of the plot.

The same is true in *Twelfth Night*. Shipwrecked in Illyria, Viola initially wishes to gain employment with the Countess Olivia in her own shape as a woman, though without disclosing her name and station. "O that I serv'd that lady," she tells the sea captain who rescues her, "And might not be delivered to the world/Till I had made mine own occasion mellow,/What my estate is" (*Twelfth Night*, 1.2.41–44). It is only because Olivia's mourning makes a suit to her impossible that Viola determines to "conceal me what J am" (53) and seek service with Duke Orsino in the guise of the youth Cesario. Like Julia she is then trapped in her disguise when she falls in love with the man she serves and is sent by him to plead his love to Olivia. Here the disguise is even more central to the plot than in *Two Gentlemen*, since it is the means by which Olivia meets and marries Sebastian, and Orsino discovers his own love for Viola.

Portia is not trapped in her role as the wise young judge Balthasar, but it is essential that she should be dressed as a man in order to free Antonio, confound Shylock, and—ultimately—teach her husband a lesson about the nature of generosity and love. And Imogen, too, is forced by circumstance to retain her male disguise. Dressed as a boy, and fleeing like Julia after her departed lover, she thinks she has found him dead and therefore enlists as "Fidele" in the service of the Roman general. Her disguise and subsequent adventures lead directly to the restoration of Cymbeline's sons, as well as to her reunion with her beloved Posthumus.

All these women must retain their disguises because of exigencies of the plot. But what is Rosalind's rationale? What if she were to step forward in act 3, scene 2, not like a "saucy lackey" (296) but like herself, and declare that she is the "Heavenly Rosalind" Orlando has been seeking? There would of course be one unfortunate repercussion, since the play would effectively come to an end in the middle of the third act (as would have occurred if Cordelia had answered at once when Lear asked her how much she loved him). But beyond that, would anything be lost? Can Shakespeare be keeping Rosalind in disguise merely to prolong his play, or is there another purpose in her decision not to unmask herself?

Many reasons have been advanced for the continued existence of Ganymede after Orlando comes on the scene. G. L. Kittredge quotes one Lady Martin, writing in *Blackwood's Magazine* for October, 1884, who offers the opinion that "surely it was the finest and boldest of all devices, one of which only a Shakespeare could have ventured, to put his heroine into such a position that she could, without revealing her own secret, probe the heart of her lover to the very bottom, and so assure herself that the love which possessed her own being was as completely the master of his." In a rather ungentlemanly fashion Kittredge then goes on to demolish Lady Martin: "This amiable and eloquent observation," he notes, "is typical of many that have been mistakenly made upon details of Shakespeare's plots. The 'device' is not Shakespeare's, but Lodge's."[2] Subsequent critics have been willing to recognize that Shakespeare was capable of changing what he did not wish to retain from his sources and have tended to theorize somewhat along Lady Martin's lines. C. L. Barber, for example, remarks that when disguised "Rosalind is not committed to the conventional language and attitudes of love, loaded as these inevitably are with sentimentality,"[3] and Anne

Barton suggests that as Ganymede "she learns a great deal about herself, about Orlando, and about love itself which she could not have done within the normal conventions of society."[4] A recent feminist critic, Clara Claiborne Park, carries the argument for Rosalind's independence and self-knowledge a step further, pointing out that "male garments immensely broaden the sphere in which female energy can manifest itself. Dressed as a man, a nubile woman can go places and do things she couldn't do otherwise, thus getting the play out of the court and the closet and into interesting places like forests or Welsh mountains. Once Rosalind is disguised as a man, she can be as saucy and self-assertive as she likes."[5] Those critics interested in the question seem in general to agree that disguise is a freeing action for Rosalind and that her double role allows her to be at once caustic and caring, tender and tough.

I do not wish to quarrel with these sensible observations, but I would like to suggest a slight change of emphasis. As the lessons she gives to Orlando immediately testify, Rosalind does not have to learn much, if anything, about love, or about the quality and depth of her own feelings. Nor, as I have already mentioned, does she really need assurance (*pace* Lady Martin) that Orlando loves her. What she does need, and what the play needs, is an Orlando who knows "what 'tis to love" (5.2.83). He is the one who has immersed himself in a pseudo-Petrarchan fantasy world, hanging "tongues . . . on every tree" (3.2.127) in unconscious fulfillment of Duke Senior's attitudinizing ("tongues in trees, books in the running brooks,/ Sermons in stones, and good in every thing" [2.1.16–17]). What Barber calls the "conventional language and attitudes of love," with their attendant "sentimentality," are pitfalls for Orlando much more than for Rosalind.

H. B. Charlton comments that "Rosalind, disguised as Ganymede, pretends to be herself in order to teach Orlando to woo."[6] This is certainly true, but it is not, I think, the whole truth. For what Rosalind is teaching is not so much technique as substance. Her disguise as Ganymede permits her to educate him about himself, about her, and about the nature of love. It is for Orlando, not for Rosalind, that the masquerade is required; indeed the play could fittingly, I believe, be subtitled "The Education of Orlando." Whether we agree with Ms. Park that "she is twice the person he is" or not,[7] it seems clear that in *As You Like It*, as in so many of Shakespeare's comedies, the woman is superior to her man in self-knowledge and in her knowledge of human nature. The degree to which Orlando is successfully educated, and the limits of his final understanding, can be seen by examining their various encounters in the court and in the forest and by considering what happens as a result of those encounters.

In act 1, scene 2 Rosalind and Orlando meet at the wrestling match and fall in love at first sight. The following scene, which begins with Rosalind's acknowledgment of her passion to Celia, ends with her banishment, and Celia's resolution to accompany her to the Forest of Arden. The two events are psychologically related; Rosalind's advancement toward maturity by falling in love is in a sense the same act as her banishment from the palace of Duke Frederick. Banishment is a rite of passage here, a threshold moment that leads both lovers to the forest. The whole scene is beautifully modulated, as the young women's discussion of

Orlando leads naturally into some playful observations on the paternal generation and the relationship between his father and theirs.

ROSALIND:	The Duke my father lov'd his father dearly.
CELIA:	Doth it therefore ensue that you should love his son dearly? By this kind of chase, I should hate him, for my father hated his father dearly; yet I hate not Orlando.
ROSALIND:	No, faith, hate him not, for my sake.
CELIA:	Why should I not? Doth he not deserve well?
	Enter DUKE [FREDERICK] *with* LORDS.
ROSALIND:	Let me love him for that, and do you love him because I do. Look, here comes the Duke.
CELIA:	With his eyes full of anger.
DUKE FREDERICK:	Mistress, dispatch you with your safest haste, And get you from our court.

(1.3.29–43)

The shift from prose to verse with Duke Frederick's first speech underscores the
sudden change from intimacy to formality. Rosalind's act of falling in love is itself
a rebellion against patriarchal domination and the filial bond. Since she is living
under the foster care of her jealous and unloving uncle, her sundering from his
protection is abrupt and harsh, but some such separation would have been
inevitable. Her love, as much as his hatred, banishes her to Arden.

Meanwhile Orlando, who has also fallen in love, is likewise banished from
home. His tyrannical older brother, Oliver, has usurped his patrimony and
stands in a relationship to him that is structurally analogous to that between
Duke Frederick and Rosalind. Although he is the youngest son, Orlando bears
his father's name ("Rowland de Boys" translates readily as "Orlando of the
forest"), and in the play's opening scene he asserts that "the spirit of my father,
which I think is within me, begins to mutiny against this servitude" (1.1.22–24).
Orlando's banishment, like Rosalind's, is a step toward independence and maturity. It is interesting to note that in the first scene he complains about the quality
of his upbringing; Oliver, he says, "mines my gentility with my education"(21).
The education he does not receive at home he will find in the forest, with
"Ganymede" for his teacher. Carrying old Adam on his shoulders like Aeneas
bearing his father Anchises, Orlando enters the forest (where, as he matures, the
father-figure Adam disappears from the plot), and shortly begins to post his love
poems on the trees.

When she learns that it is indeed Orlando who has written these poems in her
praise, Rosalind asks Celia a crucial question: "But doth he know that I am in this
forest and in man's apparel?" (3.2. 229–30). Deception is already in her mind. If
he does not know who she is, she will not at this time reveal herself to him.
Instead she declares her intention to "speak to him like a saucy lackey, and under
that habit play the knave with him" (295–97).

What is her motivation for doing so? In seeking to answer this question, we
should note that there are three distinct stages in Orlando's development as a
lover. When he first meets Rosalind after the wrestling match he is tongue-tied,

unable to speak. She has presented him with a chain, but he can find no words to acknowledge her gift: "Can I not say, 'I thank you'? My better parts / Are all thrown down, and that which here stands up / Is but a quintain, a mere lifeless block" (1.2.249–51). Rosalind abandons maidenly modesty to approach him ("Did you call, sir?" [253]), but he remains speechless, struck dumb by love: "What passion hangs these weights upon my tongue? / I cannot speak to her, yet she urged conference" (257–58). This is the first stage, that of ineffability; for the match to succeed he must somehow learn to communicate his feelings.

He does this initially through the medium of his love poems, but while the poems are an advance upon total speechlessness, they do not constitute a wholly satisfactory mode of communication. For one thing, they are one-sided, mono-vocal; Orlando has no reason to expect that Rosalind will ever see or hear of them. For another thing, as Touchstone drily points out, they are simply not very good poems. "The very false gallop of verses" (3.2.112) is his sardonic verdict, and even Rosalind acknowledges that they offer a "tedious homily of love" (155–56) with "more feet than the verses would bear" (165–66), and lame ones at that. Hackneyed, conventional, derivative, ineloquent, Orlando's poems announce an emotion but fail to go further than that; they do not attain the condition of discourse. One of Rosalind's tasks, therefore, will be to make him speak to her in the natural language of men and women. The method she adopts to do so—remaining in a disguise that will make him less ill at ease than he was at their first meeting—is somewhat comparable to the plot of Goldsmith's *She Stoops to Conquer,* in which the bashful young Marlow is able to make love to Miss Hardcastle because he thinks she is a servant in a country inn, not the well-bred daughter of a wealthy man. Rosalind, too, stoops to conquer, by retaining her doublet and hose.

Orlando's love poems also suggest a psychological state of self-absorption that accords with Erik Erikson's description of adolescent love: "an attempt to arrive at a definition of one's identity by projecting one's diffused self-image on another and by seeing it thus reflected and gradually clarified."[8] The first time Rosalind sees him in the forest he is deep in conversation with Jaques, the play's epitome of self-love, and there are resemblances between them, despite their mutual antipathy (and perhaps contributing to it). Both are obsessed with their own feelings. Orlando successfully teases Jaques with the old joke of the fool in the brook, but there is a sense in which he himself is also a Narcissus, seeking his own reflection. His mock-Petrarchan poetry, like that of the lords in *Love's Labour's Lost,* indicates a lack of maturity and a failure of other-directedness. Like Phebe, he is in love with love and with the image of himself as a lover. Rosalind seems to sense this when, in the character of Ganymede, she points out that he is not dressed in the true lover's traditional disarray: "you are no such man; you are rather point-device in your accoutrements, as loving yourself, than seeming the lover of any other" (3.2.381-84). Orlando needs time—time to grow from an infatuated youth to a man who knows the real nature of love, from a boy who pins poems on trees to a man whose love token is a "bloody napkin" (4.3.138). By not revealing her true identity Rosalind gives him that time. From their first encounter in the forest she becomes his teacher.

Time is, indeed, the first subject that they touch upon in the course of that encounter—time and its relativity. Pretending she does not know who he is, Rosalind is able to mention the hypothetical presence of a "true lover in the forest" (3.2.302) and to comment upon the eagerness of "a young maid between the contract of her marriage and the day it is solemniz'd" (313–15). She thus usurps and desentimentalizes the topic of love that Orlando has elaborately established as his own. Jaques had addressed him contemptuously as "Signior Love," and I think we may see his insistence on playing the part of the lover as an aspect of his adolescent posturing. He will now be required to prove his love by acts of constancy and by the quick use of his wits—very different from the self-glorifying practice of posting love poems for all to see. Dialogue and interplay have already begun to replace the sterile and stereotypical intercourse between a man and his pen. Orlando is no longer in command of the love theme—if, indeed, he ever was. The focus and the creative energy are instead to be found in "Ganymede"—or rather, in "Ganymede" as "he" will take up the part of "Rosalind."

It is a convention of Shakespearian comedy that husbands and lovers do not recognize their ladies when those ladies are dressed in male attire. Bassanio fails to see through Portia's disguise, and Posthumus cannot recognize Imogen. But both of these men are distracted by important events taking place concurrently. Bassanio is overwhelmed with gratitude by the salvation of Antonio, and Posthumus is convinced that his wife is dead and that he has found her murderer. Orlando, by contrast has his mind wholly on Rosalind, yet he does not see her as she stands before him. "Let no face be kept in mind," he wrote, "But the fair of Rosalind" (3.2.94–95). He is now gazing into that face and does not recognize it. This is particularly striking because of the nature of the dialogue that takes place between them. Consider some of the peculiarities of diction in the following exchange:

ORLANDO: Where dwell you, *pretty* youth?
ROSALIND: With this shepherdess, my sister; here in the *skirts* of the forest, like fringe upon a *petticoat*.
ORLANDO: Are you native of this place?
ROSALIND: As the *cony* that you see dwell where *she* is kindled.
                                   (334–340; emphasis mine)

Given the dramatic situation, such a collection of sex-linked words is bound to call attention to itself. Orlando's word "pretty" probably carries the primary meaning, now obsolete, of "clever, skillful, apt" (OED II.2a), referring to the witty conversation that has just taken place. But the word *pretty* in Shakespeare is almost always used to describe either women or children; it is interesting to note that the only reference to a "pretty youth" in any of Shakespeare's other plays is addressed to Julia in *Two Gentlemen* when she is masquerading as a boy (4.2.58). Moreover, a few scenes later in *As You Like It* the infatuated shepherdess Phebe also uses the phrase "pretty youth" (3.5.113). She is cataloguing "Ganymede's" verbal and physical charms, and her word "pretty" could refer to either, though she will shortly speak of "a pretty redness in his lip" (120). The phrase "pretty youth" is not conclusive evidence that Orlando somehow senses the woman beneath the doublet and hose, but it is suggestive, especially in view of what follows. For Rosalind's key words in this exchange are unambiguously female: "skirts" and "petticoat"—both garments she is not wearing but should be—and the image of a female rabbit rather than a male one with whom to compare herself. "Skirts" meaning "borders" is a word in common usage, appearing both later in this play (5.4.159) and in *Hamlet* (1.1.97), as well as in the works of many of Shakespeare's contemporaries, but in combination with "petticoat" it is plainly mischievous, a witty and pointed literalizing of the implicit metaphor. "Petticoat" itself is often a synonym for woman, as in Rosalind's own earlier exclamation as the travelers entered the Forest of Arden: "I could find it in my heart to disgrace my man's apparel and to cry like a woman; but I must comfort the weaker vessel, as doublet and hose ought to show itself courageous to petticoat" (2.4.4–7). As to "cony," which in the forest context means "rabbit," in Shakespeare's time it was also a term of endearment for a woman. For Orlando as well as for the audience these words are clues to her real identity, though clues he is too dense to follow up. This part of the scene should, I think, be extremely funny on the stage—but funny at Orlando's expense.

Since the Elizabethan actor playing Rosalind would of course have been a boy, presenting the Chinese box syndrome of a boy playing a girl playing a boy playing a girl (actor-Rosalind-"Ganymede"-"Rosalind"), some periodic hints or asides would have been dramaturgically helpful in keeping the audience cognizant of what they were supposed to be seeing. *As You Like It* is particularly playful in this regard, ringing the changes on these changes throughout the play and especially in the epilogue. But the proliferation of such sly hints in the first conversation between Orlando and the disguised Rosalind is of considerable interest. "I thank God I am not a woman," she remarks (347–48), and again there is a broad wink to the audience—but perhaps also a small nudge in the ribs to Orlando. Yet he is so determined to be lovesick that he does not recognize the object of his love.

> ORLANDO: Fair youth, I would I could make thee believe I love.
> ROSALIND: Me believe it? You may as soon make her that you love believe it, which I warrant she is apter to do than to confess she does: that is one of the points in the which women still give the lie to their consciences.
>
> (385–91)

Here Rosalind is wrestling with the same maidenly dilemma that troubled Juliet and Cressida—what are the social risks for a woman who tells her love? But like those women, she is in a sense telling her love now—if only Orlando had the wit to listen. Yet by the end of the scene he is still addressing her as "good youth" (433). "Nay," she replies, "you must call me Rosalind" (434).

Their fictive courtship, with its badinage, wooing lessons, and play-acted "marriage," threatens to go on forever in the timelessness of Arden. Under the guise of Ganymede, Rosalind teaches Orlando not only the rules of love and its nature, but the uses of language—and even, to her everlasting credit, the gentle arts of irony and self-deprecation. But two events intervene to bring the fiction to an end: Orlando's rescue of his brother Oliver from a lioness, and the instant mutual passion of Oliver and Celia.

I have elsewhere discussed at length the incident of the lioness and the "bloody napkin" Orlando sends as a love token "unto the shepherd youth/That he in sport doth call his Rosalind" (4.3.155–56).[9] Let me merely say briefly here that I regard this as an initiation ritual, both in martial and in sexual terms, and that I see the gift of the bloody napkin as a curiously but appropriately displaced version of the ceremonial "showing of the sheets" by which in some cultures a newly married woman demonstrates her virginity and fidelity to her husband. The napkin is thus a love token of a very different kind from the superficial love poems Orlando has earlier sent to Rosalind in testimony of his love. For the education of Orlando, however, the love match between his brother and Celia is even more germane, because it brings an end to the fictional world in which Orlando has lived with his "Rosalind." "O, how bitter a thing it is to look into happiness through another man's eyes!" he exclaims (5.2.43–45), and Rosalind asks, "Why then, tomorrow I cannot serve your turn for Rosalind?" (48–49). Orlando's reply is the single most important turning point in his development: "I can live no longer by thinking" (50). In the language of education we have been using, this is both a graduation and a commencement, a change and a new beginning. Imagination and play, which have brought him to this point, are no longer enough to sustain him. And as if he has said the magic words—as indeed he has—Rosalind now promises to produce his true beloved, "to set her before your eyes to-morrow, human as she is, and without any danger" (66–68). The significant phrase here is "human as she is." The real Rosalind is not the paper paragon of Orlando's halting sonnets but a woman of complexity, wit, and passion. This will be Orlando's final lesson.

Readers of the play are occasionally as nonplussed as Orlando by the rapidity with which Oliver and Celia fall in love.[10] "Is't possible that on so little acquaintance you should like her? that but seeing, you should love her? and loving, woo? and wooing, she should grant? And will you persever to enjoy her?" (5.2.1–4). Our amazement is the more because all of this wooing takes place offstage, between acts 4 and 5. Compared with the protracted courtship of Orlando and Rosalind, which has constituted virtually the entire action of the play, this manifestation of betrothal-at-first-sight is potentially unsettling, especially because we have no particular reason to like Oliver before he appears in the forest and because we have been led by Rosalind to believe that some extended education is necessary to develop a true and enduring love. Orlando, too, liked and loved at first sight, but he is still learning "what 'tis to woo," and is—or so he thinks—very far from having his lady grant his suit.

Oliver describes his transformation from tyrant to lover as a "conversion." "I do not shame/To tell you what I was," he explains to Celia, "Since my conversion/So sweetly tastes, being the thing I am" (4.3.135–37). His is the alternative path to Rosalind's gradualist mode of education, an instantaneous Pauline reversal that fills the erstwhile nay-sayer with the spirit of love. Oliver's "conversion" accords with the Christian doctrine of salvation; like the late-arriving laborers in the vineyard (Matt. 20:1–16) his reward is made equal to that of his apparently more deserving brother, and the two courtships, one so lengthy and the other so swift, are, in Hymen's words, "earthly things made even" (5.4.109).

Conversion is in fact a recurrent theme in the final scene of the play. We learn that Duke Frederick, advancing on the forest with malign intent, has encountered "an old religious man" and "after some question with him, was converted/Both from his enterprise and from the world" (5.4.160–62). Like Oliver he offers to abdicate his lands and position in favor of the brother he had formerly sought to kill. At this point Jaques decides to join him, observing that "Out of these convertites/There is much matter to be heard and learn'd" (184–85). The emphasis upon instruction and discourse here is significant, offering a pertinent analogy to the love lessons Rosalind has been giving Orlando. But while Duke Frederick's conversion removes him from society, Oliver's socializes him. Learning to love his brother, he finds himself, more or less in consequence, capable of falling in love with Celia.

As we have seen, the lightning love affair of Oliver and Celia acts as a catalyst for Orlando, moving him to make the crucial transition from play acting to reality. His declaration, "I can live no longer by thinking," makes possible Rosalind's change of roles, from teacher to "human" lover. The lessons, and the need for them, are over. But how much has Orlando really learned? Throughout the play Rosalind has offered clues to her real identity, double-edged hints that she is in fact the very woman she is pretending to be. Orlando's failure to take those hints was, for the audience as well as Rosalind, an indication that he was not yet prepared to have the truth thrust upon him. When he finally feels ready to choose the real, despite its inherent dangers, over the make-believe, we have some reason to think that he has profited from the unsentimental education he has received. Yet even after "Ganymede" promises to set Rosalind before his eyes, Orlando makes one significant error in interpretation that makes it clear he is, in one sense at least, no match for Rosalind. The issue is subtle—some might say finical—but it is also, as is Rosalind's way, instructive, for the audience in the theater if not for Orlando.

In the course of that same first conversation in the forest with which we have been so much concerned, Orlando inquiries as to whether the "youth" he addresses is native to the forest. "Your accent," he observes, "is something finer than you could purchase in so remov'd a dwelling" (3.2.341–42). Once again he hovers on the brink of discovery. But Rosalind has a ready reply, one that touches on "Ganymede's" own education. "An old religious uncle of mine taught me to speak, who was in his youth an inland man; one that knew courtship too well, for there he fell in love" (345–47). The former courtier who finds purity and peace in the countryside is a commonplace of pastoral literature; Spenser's Melibee is only one member of a hoary and numerous tribe, who, had they all inhabited England's forests in Elizabeth's time, would have jostled one another uncomfortably for lack of room. Rosalind's invention thus has just the right degree of verisimilitude to take in Orlando, and just the right degree of triteness to amuse the listening audience. Orlando readily accepts this explanation, moving eagerly on to the more tempting topic of love, and the matter is dropped. Or so it seems.

Much later in the play, when the spectacle of Celia and Oliver in love has incited him to abjure "thinking" for action, Orlando is vouchsafed another item of information about the supposed education of "Ganymede." "Believe then if you please," the disguised Rosalind tells him,

> that I can do strange things. I have, since I was three years old, convers'd with a magician, most profound and yet not damnable. If you do love Rosalind so near the heart as your gesture cries it out, when your brother marries Aliena, shall you marry her. I know into what straits of fortune she is driven, and it is not impossible to me, if it appear not inconvenient to you, to set her before your eyes tomorrow, human as she is, and without any danger.
>
> ORLANDO: Speak'st thou in sober meanings?
> ROSALIND: By my life, I do, which I tender dearly, though I say I am a magician.
>
> (5.2.58–71)

Orlando accepts this windfall without question and confides his good luck to Duke Senior, who willingly agrees to give Rosalind to him in marriage. On the following day "Ganymede" approaches both Orlando and the Duke to make sure their minds are constant. Receiving the appropriate assurances, "he" exits the stage, and the Duke turns immediately to Orlando to offer one of those observations that so often herald the clearing of the skies at the close of Shakespearian comedy: "I do remember in this shepherd boy/Some lively touches of my daughter's favor" (5.3.26–27). We are very close to the truth here. Yet Orlando, characteristically, confuses rather than clarifies the matter, so sure is he that he is in possession of the facts.

> My lord, the first time that I ever saw him
> Methought he was a brother to your daughter.
> But, my good lord, this boy is forest-born,
> And hath been tutor'd in the rudiments
> Of many desperate studies by his uncle,
> Whom he reports to be a great magician,
> Obscured in the circle of the forest.
>
> (28–34)

It is Orlando himself who is obscured here, in the circle of the forest. For notice what he has done. He has conflated the two tales Rosalind told him, identifying the "old religious uncle" who ostensibly taught young Ganymede to speak, with the profound magician with whom Ganymede has conversed from the age of three. This inference makes perfect sense, but it is wrong, and wrong in an important way. "I am a magician," she told him, plainly. And plainly the magician with whom Rosalind has conversed from the voluble age of three is no one but Rosalind herself, the only begetter of the magic that will produce Orlando's beloved before his eyes and reveal to the Duke and all the lovers her true identity, and their true partners.

Rosalind's role as a magician is emphasized in the epilogue, when she announces to the audience "My way is to conjure you" (Epilogue, 10–11). As she herself remarks, "It is not the fashion to see the lady the epilogue" (1–2), but in this play the lady has earned her place. Hand in hand with Orlando she danced in celebration of her wedding, and then, with the other couples, departed the stage. But she returns, and she returns alone. Her reappearance underscores the degree to which she has directed events in Arden from her first encounter with Orlando to the successful performance of four marriages. "Human as she is" she has played two parts throughout the play and, in the process, transformed Orlando from a tongue-tied boy to an articulate and (relatively) self-knowledge-able husband. If he is not entirely her equal, it is hard to fault him for that. For Rosalind stands alone among Shakespeare's comic heroines as clearly as she stands alone on the stage for the Epilogue. Like Prospero, whom in many ways she prefigures, she tempers her magic with humanity, and were she to divest herself of her doublet and hose, she might justifiably address them as Prospero addresses his "magic garment": "Lie there, my art" *(Tempest,* 1.2.24).

NOTES

1. References are to *The Riverside Shakespeare*, ed. G. Blakemore Evans et. al. (Boston: Houghton Mifflin, 1974).

2. *As You Like It*, ed. George Lyman Kittredge (Boston: Ginn and Co., 1939), pp. 149–50.

3. C. L. Barber, *Shakespeare's Festive Comedy* (Princeton: Princeton University Press, 1959), p. 233.

4. Anne Barton, Introduction to *As You Like It*, in *The Riverside Shakespeare*, ed. Evans, p. 366.

5. Clara Claiborne Park, "As We Like It: How a Girl Can Be Smart and Still Popular," in *The Woman's Part: Feminist Criticism of Shakespeare* (Urbana: University of Illinois Press, 1980), p. 108.

6. *Shakespearian Comedy* (1938: reprint, London: Methuen, 1973), p. 282.

7. Ibid., p. 109.

8. Erik Erikson, *Identity: Youth and Crisis* (New York: W. W. Norton, 1968), p. 132.

9. Marjorie Garber, *Coming of Age in Shakespeare* (London: Methuen, 1981), pp. 145–48.

10. I say "readers" because audiences in the theater tend to be so swept up by the energies of the plot that they do not stop to analyze the improbability here. My students, however, have occasionally been perturbed by it.

The Difficulties of Closure: An Approach to the Problematic in Shakespearian Comedy

Jean E. Howard

For those of us schooled on the work of C. L. Barber and Northrop Frye, the phrase "Shakespearian comedy" is probably forever linked in our minds with "green worlds," "idiotes figures," and "transformed societies."[1] Frye and Barber taught an entire generation of Shakespearian critics a way of comprehending Shakespeare's comic practice, and it was with an immediate sense of understanding that I recently read an article by Charles Sugnet that began with the author's assertion that he found it comparatively easy to teach Shakespearian comedy because its generic features had been so well defined by prior critics such as Frye, Barber, and Kott, whereas he did not feel that so clear a map had ever been provided for Shakespeare's handling of the tragic genre.[2]

Most readers of the present essay, I am sure, are familiar with the specific theories of Frye and Barber. What I propose to do here is neither to rehash nor to refute those theories but, rather, to reflect on some of the implications of their large-scale adoption as a frame through which to see individual plays. In particular, I want to consider how reliance on certain premises of Frye and Barber can lead us to minimize some aspects of the comedies, most notably the degree of unresolved turbulence and contradiction present in these plays and present in the audience's aesthetic experience of them.

Of course, the work of Barber and Frye differs in many ways, and to group these critics together can be misleading; nevertheless, it does seem to me that they both share an inherently conservative and relatively unproblematic view of the comedies. For both, these plays are primarily vehicles for testing and confirming social order and sexual difference by a purely temporary confounding of both.[3] Turbulence, misrule, and Saturnalian confusion erupt within the plays only to give way before the reimposition of order and traditional values. Barber quite explicitly suggests that the social stability of Shakespeare's Elizabethan rural background—a stability profound enough to tolerate temporary disruptions in the form of holiday inversions of order—was the origin of the balanced aesthetic vision he sees in the festive plays, an equilibrium disturbed only in the problem comedies of the early Jacobean period.[4] Frye, by contrast, emphasizes the mythic and universal dimensions of the comedies, not their relationship to a specific culture, and he tends to homogenize the entire comic canon, finding more similarities than differences among the early comedies, the problem comedies, and the romances, while privileging the romances as Shakespeare's highest achievement in the genre.[5] Both Barber, however, in studying the festive comedies, and Frye, in considering Shakespeare's entire comic oeuvre, treat the plays as a mechanism for containing the eruption of the chaotic and the disorderly within a social and aesthetic system. Not only do characters move from confusion to clarification, but so does the audience, as challenges to traditional modes of thought and belief are played out and defused before its very eyes.

What I would like to question is the adequacy of this serene view of Shakespearian comedy, even of the so-called festive plays. Without wishing to suggest that all comedies are uniformly problematic, I do think that criticism of the comedies has not sufficiently acknowledged their problematic dimensions, that is, the presence within them of conflicting generic codes and cultural norms that resist easy harmonization. Some of the most interesting recent work on the comedies has shown, for example, that these plays are not solely concerned with the mythic realm of man's timeless and collective existence, as Frye has suggested; nor, as Barber has argued, are they related to the larger culture simply as dramatic transformations of the rituals of Elizabethan holiday; rather, they are inextricably bound up with the contradictions and discontinuities of the Elizabethan cultural matrix, sometimes mediating or harmonizing conflicts and sometimes merely reflecting them.[6] Consequently, rather than problem-solving mechanisms that express turbulence only to tame it, even the festive comedies frequently function as problem-posing structures that produce aesthetic experiences marked as much by rupture and discontinuity as by the serene harmonization of contradictory elements. It is with the problematic dimensions of the viewer's experience of the comedies that I wish chiefly to deal in this paper, in part by making use of the work of Wolfgang Iser on the way texts are assimilated by readers. It is my contention that the wrong kind of reliance upon generic approaches to Shakespearian comedy, such as those developed by Frye and Barber, can result in our projecting upon these plays an image of harmony that masks their discontinuites and the instability of the viewer's imaginative closure of them. To support this contention I wish in particular to look at the endings of several comedies and evaluate the difficulties they present a viewer attempting to assimilate all of the final elements of a particular work into a satisfying gestalt.

Before turning to specific plays, let me say a word about Iser, whose theories concerning the assimilation of texts by readers seem to me of interest to Shakespearians, even though Iser writes primarily about novels and not about drama. For Iser, all aesthetic objects have only a virtual existence and are the products of the controlled interaction between text and reader.[7] He argues, correctly I believe, that rich texts, as opposed to those that are trivial or propagandistic, require readers to complete the aesthetic object by themselves supplying what is unsaid within the work itself. In constructing meaning, the reader is guided by the strategies of the text in his attempts to create a consistent and coherent image from the welter of literary norms and cultural perspectives present in the work. All rich texts involve the reader in the process of producing a sequence of new images or gestalts as the reading of each new textual segment reveals information that alters the significance of what has come before. The reader is driven along in the reading process by the desire to "close the gestalt," to bring all the pieces of the text into a satisfying configuration in his mind. If closing the gestalt is too easy, that is, if the text is too explicit in laying down instructions for the production of meaning, the reader feels cheated, uninvolved, or bored. If, on the other hand, the text strongly resists closure, the result may also be boredom or frustration or, ironically, the production of rigid interpretations that block out the intrusion of new and disturbing information. Iser most often cites modernist texts, such as those by Joyce and Beckett, as works which resist closure, but he acknowledges that such texts can exist in any era; and he does not assume that "good" literary works necessarily produce in the reader a state of equilibrium and harmony. For him the only literature that is deficient is that which leaves the reader with little to do and which leaves open no possibilities for change in the reader. Such change, Iser argues, occurs when the reader confronts the literary and cultural norms of his own or another culture "depragmatized" by their inclusion in a literary work, that is, removed from the everyday context in which their validity is assumed, so that they can be held up for interrogation. The result may be a change in the reader's attitude toward or relationship to these norms.[8]

While I doubt that there are many Shakespearian dramas that are unsatisfactory in the sense that they are too easy to assimilate, I do believe that a good number of the comedies are more difficult to reduce to a satisfying coherency than has generally been acknowledged. By way of example, consider *The Taming of the Shrew*, a very early play, but one that reveals in a relatively simple fashion how difficult it is to establish a single interpretative perspective from which to master the turbulence of the text. Initially *The Taming of the Shrew* sets for the audience the task of examining, by way of ongoing juxtaposition, two women who seem to sum up two competing cultural conceptions of the female. The fair Bianca is described by all as everyman's dream of Petrarchan perfection; the shrewish Kate as everyman's image of the female harpy. The genius of the play is to make the audience progressively more aware of the insufficiencies of these conceptions of the female to accommodate the reality of either woman (Kate finding it in her heart, for example, to protest the wanton abuse of servants, and Bianca finding in her gentle heart the capacity to deceive her father and flout her husband's wishes); gradually, the audience reverses its initial assumptions about the relative value of the two women. One need only experience, in sequence, the initial wooing of Kate in act 2, scene 1 and the wooing of Bianca in act 3, scene 1 to realize that Kate, even in her untransformed shrewish condition, summons up the wit and energy of the male, while Bianca evokes supine obeisance and contrived love rhetoric. In short, the shrews of the world may be worth the winning and the "good" girls may not. To use Iser's terms, contemporary cultural conceptions of the female have been brought into the literary work in order to depragmatize them and open them to the audience's reexamination.

But, of course, the destabilization of the audience's easy assumptions about shrews and princesses, and about Kate and Bianca as examples of these types, is only one of the play's strategies. If the shrew in this work clearly becomes the more vital and interesting character, nonetheless, the middle portion of the play prevents the audience from a reverse romanticization of the shrew, as it is forced to assimilate, through Petruchio's instructive assumption of the traits of the shrew, the pernicious consequences of the unbridled exercise of selfish willfulness. Though the farcical tone of Petruchio's actions in his country estate mitigates our sense of their brutality, certainly they are meant to show Kate—and to show us—how unsatisfactory is a relationship based on the perpetual assertion of personal will and the reflexive defiance of others. As Petruchio exclaims in frustration: "Evermore cross'd and cross'd, nothing but cross'd!" (4.5.10).[9] Nothing can come of a relationship based solely on personal willfulness. The task for the audience is to imagine, and for Kate and Petruchio to embody, a more perfect male/female relationship than that based either on shrewish combat or the artificial and deceptive posturings of Petrarchan courtship. The last actions of the play tentatively help the audience construct such an image as we see Kate and Petruchio playfully exercising their wits *together* upon the hapless Vincentio, negotiating *together* in the streets of Padua for the mutual fulfillment of their desires (he gets the kiss he seeks; she the chance to follow the Vincentio party to her father's house and to her wedding feast); and teaming up *together* to win a match against the world in the play's closing moments. Watching these actions, we begin to sense that two strong-willed people can play *with* and not *against* one another in the fulfillment of separate, but mutually accommodated, desires.

As everyone knows, however, the last events of act 5, particularly Kate's final speech, raise disturbing questions about the exact nature and the exact value of this new image of mutuality. It is as if this last speech deliberately foregrounds contradictions that are inherent in the play from the beginning but that are repeatedly displaced from the center of the audience's attention: for example, the inherent contradiction between comedy's typical emphasis on conformity and this play's emphasis on individuality, and the potential conflict between personal sincerity in the presentation of self and this play's emphasis on the social mastery to be gained through successful role playing and disguise. These contradictions come to the fore as one realizes that there are, and traditionally have been, two quite contradictory ways to interpret and deliver Kate's last speech. Each implies a different way of synthesizing all the divergent perspectives of the play into a final gestalt. To use Richard Lanham's suggestive terminology, in part what is at issue is whether the speech is a reflection of a serious or a rhetorical being—that is, whether it is a straightforward expression of belief by a stable, unitary self speaking with sincerity—or whether it is a playful manifesto delivered by a woman whose true self is unknowable or a fiction, being no more than the sum of those roles assumed in different circumstances.[10] By examining in some detail the function of the speech in the audience's imaginative closure of the drama, we can see how Shakespeare makes difficult an all-inclusive harmonization of the play's diverse materials.

Certainly the speech *can* be delivered "straight," as Kate's unironic summation of what she has come to believe about men and women. Frye and Barber have argued, for example, that in comedy the highest wisdom is found in the eschewal of idiosyncracies and the embrace, on a heightened level of awareness, of communal norms. By such reasoning, when Kate's antisocial humor has been exorcised, her unironic acceptance of a socially approved, hierarchically subservient relationship to Petruchio simply signals her increased maturity and her ultimate difference from Bianca, who never really accepted such a role but only appeared to do so.[11] Such a reading, however, is unsatisfying in so far as it forces us to ignore or suppress aspects of the play that previously received great weight. In short, we close the gestalt by surpressing what will not fit. For example, a sincere and straightforward delivery of the speech makes of the vital and energetic Kate a simple reciter of truisms. Embedded in the speech is a dense tissue of Renaissance commonplaces about proper hierarchy in family and state and about the mutual duties, within that hierarchical relationship, of husband and wife. In a play that so richly debunks conventional perspectives on experience, this speech propounds conventional wisdom, cultural clichés.[12] Delivered straight, it suggests that even the least conventional of couples—and Kate and Petruchio have surely seemed that—finally finds fulfillment by embracing the common wisdom of socially inscribed roles: he the benevolent prince/husband and she the adoring subject/wife. Further, the speech thus delivered suddenly short-circuits the audience's meaning-making activities. We are handed a "message," rather than being invited, as elsewhere in the play, to create meaning from partially rendered perspectives. Perhaps most significant, such a delivery ignores the enormous emphasis the work has heretofore placed on self-conscious role playing as an aspect of maturity and an expression of self-mastery.[13] From this perspective, it is only if Kate is now the playful mistress of her public role and of the power that successful manipulation of it brings that her growth is complete and she becomes the normative figure her centrality implies she is intended to be.

The alternative reading of the speech, of course, stresses just its ironic or playful potential. It *can* be delivered to the stage audience in a tone of triumphant comic vengeance. If a playful and exultant Kate speaks the lines to onstage beholders who are miffed and amazed by turns, we infer that she who was once the self-destructive prisoner of the role of shrew has learned how to discomfort old enemies by the ostentatious manipulation of a new role, that of obedient and subservient wife. She has become playful and self-conscious about roles as Petruchio has been playful throughout the drama. Such a reading draws together different strands of the drama than does the "straight" reading, but it, too, must ignore or beg certain issues to achieve coherence. First, such a delivery leaves Kate's "real views" opaque. We simply cannot know how great or how small is the distance she places between her private views and those she publicly espouses. Second, a playful reading of the speech blurs the distinction between Kate and Bianca that the play has heretofore so carefully maintained. Bianca is, after all, the play's great mistress of self-serving disguise whose sincerity is ever in question. Such considerations argue for a Kate sincere, at least, in her love for Petruchio and her willingness to undertake the accommodations that would make a marriage work. But if sincere in these regards, why not in all?

While I myself feel that what I have called the "playful" reading of the speech is more interesting and more ideologically acceptable to me than the "straight" reading of it, I nonetheless am forced to admit that neither reading allows me to synthesize in perfect harmony all elements of the aesthetic experience; and I am less concerned to argue that one view is more correct than the other than to highlight the way the speech functions to complicate the play's entire exploration of the relationship of men to women, individuals to social roles, and of role playing to sincerity. The interpretive crux is deceptively simple to state: at the play's end the audience must come to terms with a perplexing foray into commonplaces and preachiness by a heroine previously noted for neither in a play that heretofore has undermined the sufficiency of simplifying schemata. The difficulty arises as we attempt to assimilate these anomalies, which requires a conscious interpretive act, an attempt to make the speech consistent with what we expect from comedy and with what this play has previously revealed to us about Kate and Petruchio, about conventional perspectives on reality, about the benefits of role playing, and about the dangers of seeming. That neither directors nor critics have ever been able to agree about whether the play is best closed by an ironic or a straight rendition of the speech is only surprising if one subscribes to the view that Shakespearian comedy is primarily a vehicle for problem solving and that the ending of such a comedy should leave the audience serenely in possession of simple truth. Choose we must, but the very act of choice with which Kate's speech confronts us is one that makes us self-conscious about the contradictions that are embedded in the play: for example, the inherent tension between comic expectations concerning conformity to socially prescribed roles and this play's emphasis upon the human impulse to play with roles and to assert individuality through their subversion or self-interested manipulation. It is, I think, difficult to link Kate's last words to the rest of the play in a way that lets the Kate-Pertruchio relationship take shape in our minds as a happy harmonization of *all* competing perspectives and desires. As we wrestle with the speech, trying to tame its potential to disrupt our desire for a perfectly harmonious conclusion, we are led—not away from the problematic—but into it.

Now what I wish to argue is that the local difficulty we experience in assimilating Kate's final speech, which challenges our consistency-making strategies and makes us self-conscious about the difficulty of creating a final synthetic gestalt from materials that are partially opaque and potentially contradictory, is writ large in many of the comedies and not just in this early play and not just in the problem comedies. Often the very conventions so well mapped by Frye and Barber that invite us to approach the comedies with a strong set of interpretive expectations are the very features undermined or challenged within the plays themselves, resulting in a troubling and open-ended theatrical experience for the audience. By way of demonstration, I wish to compare the meaning-making tasks facing the audiences of *The Merchant of Venice* and *Measure for Measure,* the former grouped by Barber among the festive plays and the latter a text generally agreed to be problematic both in terms of its handling of certain psychological and thematic issues and in terms of the aesthetic experience it evokes. My point will be to underline for *both* works those elements of discontinuity or rupture in the audience's assimilation of the theatrical event that make it hard for us to interpret it solely in terms of a single generic code and that make the experience of both works something infinitely more troubling than a serene march toward clarification.

Measure for Measure is a problem for readers and audiences in large part because it repeatedly evokes comic expectations only to make us aware of a gap between those expectations and features of the play (structure, characterization, and even style) that refuse to fit within the comic frame. Invited to assimilate the play's action in terms of a dominant generic code and yet unable to do so without strain, critics have handled the resulting tension in various ways. Some have denied that the play *is* problematic and have argued that it is a straightforward comedy if properly viewed; others have complained that it is a botched comedy; others, finding their attempts to read the play by comic codes meeting strong resistance, have argued that the play best fits into yet another generic category, such as tragicomedy.[14] Who is "right" seems to me a less important question than asking why this text evokes such divergent responses and what relevance our critical struggles with the play may have for the study of Shakespearian comedy in general.

I feel that *Measure for Measure* deliberately toys with our expectations about comedy in order, in part, to make us aware of our desire for an interpretive framework with which we can in some fashion master the intractable aspects of the text. In this regard, *Measure for Measure* puts the audience in an analogous position to those great seekers of ordering systems within the text: the Duke, Isabella, and Angelo, each of whom wants life to be tidier and more tractable to human design than it proves. In the end what the audience may be forced to recognize is that truth and rigid formulas seldom keep company and that vital art refuses to yield the truth of its turbulence to a reified schema.[15] *Measure for Measure* thus constitutes a perfect opportunity for considering whether our rage for a totalized textual meaning and a harmonious aesthetic experience does violence both to the Shakespearian artifact and to the theory of art implied by it.

The assimilation of *Measure for Measure* by the audience is from the start conditioned by comic expectations. As Michael Goldman has argued, *Measure for Measure* at first looks very much like a comedy.[16] A city is diseased; lawlessness and unrestrained sexual appetite run rampant; and the legalistic surrogate ruler installed to quell disorder is himself suspected by the real Duke to be a seemer. What we expect is that, vice having run its course and the surrogate ruler having been exposed as a hypocrite, the benevolent father figure, Vincentio, will step in to redeem Vienna from disorder. And in a certain broad sense, that is what happens. The last scene of the play returns Vincentio to power, unmasks the hypocrite Angelo, redeems the city from lawlessness by calling the guilty to account, while tempering legal excess by mercy and redeeming sexuality from lust through marriage. However, time and again critics have found the last scene false and unsatisfying. As I hope briefly to show, this response results from the fact that here, as elsewhere in the play, a gap opens between our comic expectations and the textual details that should confirm those expectations, leaving us unable to trust the sufficiency of the comic gestalt we have been invited to construct.

To take but a few examples from early in the play, consider the characterizations of Angelo and Isabella—characterizations that have struck many readers as somewhat discontinuous. On the one hand, Angelo appears at first simply to be

the antisocial idiotes figure: legalistic, puritanical, and self-righteous. But his is
not the comic folly of a Malvolio but, rather, a monstrous vice that leads him to
the threshold of rape and to the supposed execution of Claudio for sleeping with
a woman out of wedlock, though this is exactly what Angelo intends to do with
Isabella. In the middle sections of the play, under the pressure of Angelo's
tyrannous lust, both Claudio and Isabella face decisions and must cope with
emotions of genuinely tragic scope. But just as their situations are at their most
intense, in comes the disguised Duke, deus ex machina fashion, and begins his
abortive series of attempts to fix what is disordered, in the process halting the
psychological dynamics unfolding within and among Angelo, Isabella, and
Claudio. Quite justly one might ask: What am I watching? Is this a comedy, a
tragedy, or neither? Are Isabella and Angelo primarily to be regarded as full-
fledged psychological portraits of repressive personalities or simply as two-
dimensional counters in the Duke's chess game? It is as if the comic situation had
grown beyond predictable proportions and then had been abruptly and self-
consciously returned to a comic course by means of the Duke's intervention, an
intervention stylistically signaled by a sudden descent into prose and even into
doggerel. But the very abruptness of the transition, the emergence of the Duke
as comic dramatist, and the subsequent marginalization of the psychic traumas
we have been watching unfold merely serve, in Iser's terms, to depragmatize the
very norms of comedy and make them conscious objects of examination. Are
they, for example, sufficiently inclusive to handle the psychological turbulence
that we have glimpsed in the fictive world of Vienna? What truths of experience
can they not capture? When are they formula and not vision?

A further feature of the play that stands in the way of an unself-conscious
imaginative realization of it according to comic codes is its insistent polarizations.
Richard Fly has called it a play of failed mediation in which no figure emerges to
bridge, in true comic fashion, the divides that separate the social community and
the psyches of individuals.[17] Characters, for example, who speak the wordless
language of the body, such as Juliet, are rendered nearly speechless in the play's
action or deal in lies (Lucio) or gibberish (Elbow and Froth); those whose tongues
are eloquent, such as Isabella and even Angelo, either do not understand the
language of the body or speak it only in the idiom of lust. Characters either
brook no restraint or are hamstrung by a neurotic inner system of prohibitions.
Either utter lawlessness or tyrannical legalism holds sway in Vienna. And the
character Vincentio, upon whom, much more than upon Isabella, devolves the
task of synthesis and healing, remains, as Richard Wheeler has recently argued,
inadequate to the task.[18] That audience and critics *need* to have him serve as the
play's regenerative healer is signaled by the elaborate defenses for his actions
assembled in the literature on the play, but the fact remains that as a comic
redeemer he all too often replicates in his failed schemes the rigidity and the lack
of human understanding characteristic of Angelo, that as a merciful dispenser of
justice he overreacts to the jibes of Lucio, and that as a promulgator of marriage
his professed disinclination for women makes perplexing his own unanswered
marriage proposals and his very view of marriage, since it seems as often a
punishment as a celebration in his hands.[19] In the end, the audience is prevented

from seeing embodied in any one character a convincing norm of behavior, that comic synthesis of divergent perspectives so richly embodied, for example, in Rosalind of *As You Like It.*

The last scene of the play is simply the final example of both the constant reflexivity of this play and the problems it poses for its harmonious assimilation by the viewer. I would argue that in the last scene the marriages and marriage proposals, the doffing of disguises, and the apparent mingling of justice and mercy, passion and the legal institutionalization of passion in marriage, are gestures toward a comic conclusion evoked, not for our uncritical assent, but for examination. Persistently, details and omissions disturb or call in question our hope that the intractable human problems broached in the work have been solved: Isabella has spoken eloquently for mercy for Angelo, but she has not embraced marriage and the life of the body that implies; Angelo has confessed his great crimes, but he, too, seems unenthralled by his rapid marriage and pleads, self-punishingly, for death, rather than life; the Duke, open now to marriage and actively "staging himself" in the people's eyes, still cannot rise above his anger at the lying, but insightful, Lucio; and the low-life characters of the work give no evidence of a repentance that will make unnecessary the subsequent reimposition of the law's full rigor or another descent into moral chaos. Such details make the comic ending seem half a lie, a wish, more than a fact; and they force the audience to recognize how hard it is to reconcile the great polarities of this work: body and soul, mercy and justice, scope and restraint, passion and its control.

This conclusion does not necessarily mean an artistic failure on Shakespeare's part, but it does force the audience into a self-conscious examination of the generic codes it relies upon for its meaning-making activities and of its need for art to provide a tidier world than experience generally affords. Form and matter are at war throughout the play in a way that forces the audience to participate in the struggles of the characters to reconcile, usually unsuccessfully or unconvincingly, the discontinuities of their own natures. The gaps between scope and restraint, chaotic passion and the rigid codification of experience by moral and legal codes, are mirrored in the theatrical experience by the gap between the harmonizing comic perspective and the intrusive details—such as Isabella's speechless silence in the face of the Duke's unanticipated marriage proposals—which undermine that comic perspective. The work remains resistant to harmonious totalization with the viewer's imagination much more profoundly than does *The Taming of the Shrew.* It invites the audience to feel a tough-minded skepticism about the tractability of our deepest social and psychic dilemmas, but also to feel a heightened awareness of the potential gap between the coherent paradigms we seek to impose upon art and the untidy challenges to those paradigms that art can pose.

Many readers would agree with what I have been saying about the play and about the difficulties that face an audience attempting to harmonize the literary codes and the thematic polarities deployed within it. But what about one of the truly festive comedies, one of the plays written between *A Midsummer Night's Dream* and *Twelfth Night?* In order to talk about what is problematic in the assimilation of these texts, I have somewhat arbitrarily decided to focus on *The Merchant of Venice*, though others, certainly *Much Ado about Nothing*, also bear special examination. At first glance *The Merchant of Venice* certainly appears much more congruent with Barber's notion of a coherent festive comedy than does *Measure for Measure*. It has, for example, in Belmont a "green world" lacking in *Measure for Measure*, unless one counts the misty unreality of Marianna's moated grange, and in Portia the typical wise and accomplished heroine we are accustomed to encountering in the early comedies and whose function is largely usurped in *Measure for Measure* by the enigmatic Duke. In fact, the most recent full-scale study of *The Merchant of Venice*, Lawrence Danson's *The Harmonies of "The Merchant of Venice"*, indicates by its very title the congruence of his approach with that of Barber.[20] Both read the play as an indictment of legalism and greed and a celebration of the riches of love and Christian mercy as they receive their fullest embodiment in Portia and her estate at Belmont.

On the other hand, not all responses to the play have been so certain of its moral vision. Danson begins his book by discussing at length what he calls the Janus-faced criticism the play has evoked, especially since the arrival on the nineteenth-century stage of not a grotesque and comic Shylock but of a tragic Jew, victim of Christian oppression.[21] Critics who find Shylock's victimization at the heart of the play focus on the flaws and hypocrisy of the Christians and on the pathetic plight of an alien abused by an intolerant majority, stripped of his identity, and tricked by a woman most notable for her arrogant delight in controlling others. The difference between the two readings is that one emphasizes every instance of Christian goodness (such as the mercy granted Shylock, Portia's reverence for her father's will, the generosity of both her and Antonio) and every instance of Jewish evil (such as the blood bond, Shylock's confusion of his daughter with his ducats, his vengeance), while the other emphasizes every instance of Christian cruelty or hypocrisy (such as Gratiano's responses at the trial, Antonio's spitting upon Shylock, Bassanio's fortune-hunting instincts) and every instance of Jewish victimization and nobility (such as Shylock's "I am a Jew" speech, his emotion at the sale of Leah's ring, his forced conversion).

Of course, neither approach to the play—the celebratory or the cynical—necessarily casts all issues in the black-and-white terms I have been suggesting. Those who see the play celebrating Christian virtues often acknowledge that many Christians in the play are flawed, as does Danson himself, and those who stress Shylock's victimization frequently acknowledge the monstrosity of the emotions that emerge in him as a result of his ill treatment. Nonetheless, both approaches to the play save the audience from the anxiety of incoherence by establishing a dominant interpretive perspective from which to view the play's action. Neither approach is on the face of it absurd; each reveals above all, however, the truth of Iser's assertion that the audience's desire to build a consistent perspective upon the textual action can lead inevitably to the disregard or distortion of elements that do not fit neatly into the developing gestalt which the audience constructs during the theatrical experience. And, as Iser has noted, a text strongly resistant to harmonious totalization leads often to the imposition of the rigid formulas of allegory such as we find, for example, in Barbara Lewalski's

reading of the play in terms of Old Testament Law and New Testament Grace.[22]
Indeed, there is about much interpretation of the play a strangely defensive or
strained cast, as when Danson, in arguing for the harmony of the play, asserts
that there is absolutely no reason to believe that Portia and Antonio are rivals for
Bassanio's love, or when he asserts that to believe that Portia "tips off" Bassanio in
the casket scene is simply to make nonsense of the play's comic structure.[23]
Certainly Danson is right to assert that the play's status as comedy creates the
expectation of the noble heroine and a selfless Antonio, though Danson himself
argues that Antonio is intolerant and lacking in Christian charity toward Shylock
until the trial scene. But to argue that because the play is listed among the
comedies means that all local cruxes in the play can be resolved by recourse to
comic theory is false unless one assumes that individual comedies are simply
particular embodiments of a Platonic ideal comedy and that Shakespeare's master idea of comedy precludes the possibility of contradition and discontinuity
within the aesthetic structure. I prefer to see the evocation of comic conventions
in the work as one important textual element feeding into the reader's actualization of the aesthetic object, but not the only element; and with James Kincaid I
would argue that the generic approach to literature, obviously of immense value
in the interpretation of texts, too often founders on the assumption that any
work is an unmixed manifestation of any genre and that the function of literary
criticism is the ferreting out of the true generic code and the suppression or
marginalization of conflicting codes.[24]

Clearly the dominant generic code in *The Merchant of Venice* is comedy, but as in
Measure for Measure, it is not always easy to assimilate all the action of the play in
terms of that code. The two plays, however, do not cause identical problems for
the viewer or reader. What is striking about *The Merchant of Venice,* considered as
comedy, is how difficult it makes the establishment of definitive *differences* between characters, locales, and motives—differences upon which the creating of
harmonious comic perspective must rest. If *Measure for Measure* is an example of
a play that lacks mediation, *The Merchant of Venice* is overly mediated in the sense
that apparent differences continually reveal an underlying sameness. In the
Vienna of Duke Vincentio warring elements in the human condition are never
successfully bridged by a higher synthesis. In *The Merchant of Venice* everything
turns into its opposite at some point so that meaningful differences are obliter-
ated. As a result, the reader's efforts to create satisfying distinctions between Jew
and Christian, the selfish and the generous, the harsh bonds of law and the
gentle bonds of love, are repeatedly thwarted in ways that stymie those consist-
ency-building strategies which are based on the expectation that comedy celebrates the triumph of redeemed mankind over the pernicious and antisocial
impulses which divide and debase it. If, in the simplest terms, Christian and Jew
remain largely indistinguishable throughout the play, then the reader at the very
least may be driven to conclude that the harmonies of heaven are impossible to
achieve with the deformed instruments of earth, or, put more archly, that the
notions of difference upon which societies and audiences base their categories of
good and evil and their codes of exclusive privilege, can be simply defensive
fictions created to mask a frightening sameness. The experience of the text thus

becomes problematic in that it confronts the reader with the inadequacy of strategies of meaning-making based on pervasive notions of differences within the fictive world of the play and hallowed by the comic conventions so often evoked to explain away the puzzling aspects of this particular text.

Take, for example, the play's distinctions concerning money's worth and value. At first view, Christians give and Jews hoard; Christians value people over money and Jews do not. Hence Antonio hazards his very life to supply the needs of his friend and Shylock ruins widows and orphans to increase his wealth. But, as the play unfolds, overt Christian generosity begins to appear as a disguised manifestation of selfishness. Antonio gives Bassanio money in order to bind the young man to him. Witness the guilt-inducing note he sends to Bassanio at Belmont and his martyr-like behavior at the trial where he quite explicitly establishes a love triangle with Portia for Bassanio's affection: "Say how I lov'd you, speak me fair in death;/And when the tale is told, bid her be judge/Whether Bassanio had not once a love" (4.2.275–77). Portia, in her turn, having been pursued by Bassanio to recoup his fortunes, reminds him after the casket scene that he has been "dear bought" (3.2.313) and then uses her bounty to bind him and others to her.[25] At the play's end, having stripped Shylock of half his gold and determined the ultimate disposition of the rest, she feeds Jessica and Lorenzo the "manna" (5.1.294) of gold and gives Antonio "life and living" (5.1.286) with the return of his wealth. Shylock, though he would not give Leah's ring "for a wilderness of monkeys" (3.1.122–23), remains the play's most overtly avaricious figure, but gold is Christian sustenance as well, and a mighty source of power and obligation.

Take, too, the play's crucial distinction between Christian mercy and Old Testament legalism. In the trial, Portia fittingly shows Shylock the pernicious consequences of legalism untempered by humility and then evokes mercy from the Christians. What they offer feels very like vengeance disguised as its opposite. The Duke grants Shylock his life but calls attention to the fact that he does so to show the difference between Jewish and Christian spirits. A pardon so self-righteously granted seems more a gesture of pride than of spontaneous mercy arising from a sense of man's universal folly in the eyes of God; and a minute later the Duke's pardon is made conditional upon Shylock's conversion to Christianity. That conversion, technically effected for the salvation of Shylock's soul, strips the Jew both of his identity and of the opportunity to embrace willingly the promise of grace. Shylock is *compelled* to convert, to forfeit half his wealth, and to lose ultimate control of the rest. That he "deserves" such torment may be true, but if every man is treated as he deserves, who would escape whipping? Christian charity should drop more sweetly upon the court of justice.[26]

Finally, consider the play's distinction between fallen Venice and the graced Belmont. That Venice is degraded by mercantilism and legalism is clear; that Belmont is different becomes more difficult to believe as the reader moves toward the play's final act. Not only does money figure prominently in Belmont's life, but so do bonds. Portia's father has bound her to observe the terms of his will, and she binds Bassanio to the terms of his pledge with rings. Shylock's merry bond was meant by him in deadly earnest, and so is Portia's sport in act 5, for by it she confirms that her dearly bought husband will be hers and not

Antonio's. Her mercy and bounty can flow when the literal import of the ring pledge—thou shalt have no other Gods before me—has been insisted upon and confirmed.

Repeatedly this play offers distinctions that upon examination turn out not to constitute differences. The play's structure, with its insistent alternations between Venice and Belmont, implies differences between these locales. The play's generic codes imply differences between antisocial forces of disorder and comic forces of order. The play's language is studded with oppositions: Christian/Jew, mercy/law, bounty/greed. But the experience of reading the play confounds these categories and expectations of difference, making it hard for the reader to achieve a perspective on the play by which either the liberal or purist concretizations of the action can be maintained without strain. In the end, it is the ironies and not the harmonies of the play that are its most striking feature.

Not all Shakespearian comedies, of course, make the task of closure so difficult for the audience as the particular plays I have chosen to discuss. And yet there are a number of comedies, both written early in Shakespeare's career and written late, that yield readily to the kind of analysis I have undertaken in this essay. I think, for example, of the anti-comic entrance of Marcade and the deferred marriages of *Love's Labour's Lost* that prevent the viewer from enjoying the expected satisfactions of seeing each Jack with his Jill and invite us to reflect on the gap between desire and fulfillment so familiar both in the world as we live it and as it is so often represented in Shakespeare's comic creations. Or I think of the more severe disjunctions of *Pericles,* a play that simultaneously invites the audience to interpret its events as a confirmation of a benevolent providential order and as a revelation of the fictiveness of such an order. Or I think of *Much Ado* with its unstable intermingling of romance and realism, which invites actualization in terms of competing conventions and expectations. To deal in detail with these or other plays is beyond the scope of this essay, but I suggest that there is still much work needing to be done before we understand fully the complex nature of the aesthetic experience Shakespearian comedy affords.

By indirection I have also been arguing that it is not sufficient to use a reified conception of how the comic genre typically works to explain away anomalies that contradict our expectations. In my view Shakespeare frequently uses comic conventions in order to problematize them, that is, to test their efficacy to embody convincingly the full range of human situations he wished to dramatize and to make his viewers aware of the dangers of relying upon any formula to interpret material that feels like a vision of truth precisely because it resists schematization. When we experience most of Shakespeare's comedies, what we experience are aesthetic objects that resist our desire to domesticate their energies by a too easy synthesis of their fundamental discontinuities and contradictions, whether those discontinuities are expressed, as in *The Taming of the Shrew,* as a gap between man conceived of as a serious or as a rhetorical being; or, as in *Measure for Measure,* as a gap between an idealized notion of order and concrete manifestations of continuing disorder; or, as in *The Merchant of Venice,* between abstract systems of difference and concrete manifestations of sameness. As the reader tries to bridge the discontinuities, he can fall back upon an ordering perspective that suppresses incoherence through an act of will bolstered most often by recourse to arguments about how comedy *must* work, or he can confront with heightened awareness his own need for such coherence and perhaps transcend it. In any case, for me the challenge afforded by these, as by all great texts, is their ability, not to solve problems, but to make us live with a heightened sense that the problematic is the inescapable element in which we live and move, even in the theater.

NOTES

1. The fullest statement of each man's views is contained, respectively, in Barber's *Shakespeare's Festive Comedy: A Study of Dramatic Form and Its Relation to Social Custom* (Princeton: Princeton University Press, 1959) and Frye's *A Natural Perspective: The Development of Shakespearean Comedy and Romance* (New York: Harcourt, 1965).

2. Charles Sugnet, "Exaltation at the Close: A Model for Shakespearean Tragedy," *Modern Language Quarterly* 38 (1977):323–35.

3. While Barber quite explicitly sees Shakespearian comedy, like Elizabethan holidays, as serving the social function of releasing and exploring chaotic impulses in order to clarify, by contrast, the value of traditional order *(Shakespeare's Festive Comedy,* pp. 3–15), Frye severs Shakespearian comedy and romance from a specific social context and purpose. He is concerned with the way the events of comedy serve a dramatic end: enact a story. Yet for Frye, too, though he denies that comedy is either didactic or even very concerned with "the real world," comedy serves to reveal and affirm an irrational desire for a world in harmony with nature and desire, and triumphant over the forces that threaten its realization (see *A Natural Perspective*, esp. pp. 121–24).

4. Only in the character of Falstaff does Barber see a threat to the old verities too profound to be exorcised easily. He argues that Falstaff's banishment is a failure precisely because the sophisticated London world of *Henry IV, Part II* is too far removed from the values of the countryside and too permeated by the opportunism Falstaff represents for the reconstitution of traditional values magically to be effected by his banishment. See *Shakespeare's Festive Comedy,* pp. 213–21.

5. Frye, *A Natural Perspective*, p. viii.

6. I am thinking, for example, of such studies as Robert Weimann's *Shakespeare and the Popular Tradition in the Theater: Studies in the Social Dimensions of Dramatic Form and Function*, ed. Robert Schwartz (Baltimore: Johns Hopkins University Press, 1978), which argues that the Shakespearian public theater was an arena for the negotiation of complex conflicts arising from a society in rapid transition. His book was first published as *Shakespeare und die Tradition des Volkstheaters; Soziologie, Dramaturgie, Gestaltung* (Berlin: Henschelverlag, 1967). Pursuing similar ideas are Louis Montrose, " 'The Place of a Brother' in *As You Like It:* Social Process and Comic Form," *Shakespeare Quarterly* 32 (1981):28–54 and Leonard Tennenhouse, "The Counterfeit Order of *The Merchant of Venice*," an essay included in *Representing Shakespeare: New Psychoanalytic Essays*, ed. Murray M. Schwartz and Coppélia Kahn (Baltimore: Johns Hopkins University Press, 1980), pp. 54–69. Montrose and Tennenhouse see in plays such as *As You Like It* and *Merchant of Venice* reflections of Elizabethan uneasiness about primogeniture, patron-artist relations, the relationship of court to country, and the place of wealth in a society based on venture capitalism *and* on Christian ethics. Similarly, contemporary feminist and psychoanalytical criticism of the comedies has seen in them reflections of the age's contradictory attitudes toward women. See *The Woman's Part: Feminist Criticism of Shakespeare*, ed. Carolyn Ruth Swift Lenz, Gayle Greene, and Carol Thomas Neely (Urbana: University of Illinois Press, 1980) and *Representing Shakespeare*, ed. Murray M. Schwartz and Coppélia Kahn. Such studies represent a convincing challenge to the notion that the relationship between the plays and Elizabethan culture is either unimportant or simple.

7. For the fullest statement of Iser's views see *The Act of Reading: A Theory of Aesthetic Response* (Baltimore: John Hopkins University Press, 1978), first published as *Der Akt Des Lesens: Theorie ästhetischer Wirkung (Munich: Wilhelm Frank, 1976)*, and also his subsequent article, "The Current Situation of Literary Theory: Key Concepts and the Imaginary," *New Literary History* 11 (1979):1–20.

8. For a discussion of how extratextual systems of thought or paradigms are incorporated in a literary work in a state of suspended validity so that their premises can be examined, see Iser, *The Act of Reading*, pp. 68–79.

9. All quotations from Shakespeare's plays are taken from *The Riverside Shakespeare,* ed. G. Blakemore Evans et al. (Boston: Houghton Mifflin, 1974).

10. For his extremely interesting discussion of the ongoing tension in the Western literary tradition between "serious" and "rhetorical" conceptions of the self see Richard A. Lanham's *The Motives of Eloquence: Literary Rhetoric in the Renaissance* (New Haven: Yale University Press, 1976).

11. Irene G. Dash, in *Wooing, Wedding, and Power: Women in Shakespeare's Plays* (New York: Columbia University Press, 1981), pp. 33–64, discusses how the play has been repeatedly adapted for the stage in ways that make of Kate simply a boisterous and unsympathetic shrew whom we wish to see tamed and whose final speech thus requires presentation as a sincere reflection of a fundamental and necessary change of attitude. It is not, however, only pre-twentieth-century productions that present the speech in this fashion. In Joseph Papp's 1978 version in the Delacort Theater in Central Park, Meryl Streep, who played the role of Kate, also delivered these lines "straight," attesting to the continuance of this particular theatrical tradition in our own time.

12. For an insightful discussion of the way in which this play mocks convention, see Alexander Leggatt's *Shakespeare's Comedy of Love* (London: Methuen, 1974), pp. 41–62.

13. In *Shakespeare's Comedies of Play* (New York: Columbia University Press, 1981), pp. 58–93, J. Dennis Huston argues that the drama is a celebration of "the power of play" and that Petruchio liberates Kate from her humor by teaching her to play.

14. Roy Battenhouse in "*Measure for Measure* and Christian Doctrine of the Atonement," *PMLA* 61 (1946):1029–59, and Robert Hunter in *Shakespeare and the Comedy of Forgiveness* (New York: Columbia University Press, 1965), are two critics who stress the play's unifying Christian themes and really do not see it as a "problem." Harriet Hawkins in "'The Devil's Party': Virtues and Vices in *Measure for Measure*," *Shakespeare Survey* 31 (1978):105–13, sees the play as a failure because the second half of the work does not resolve the sexual and psychological issues broached in the first half. Arthur Kirsch in "The Integrity of *Measure for Measure*," *Shakespeare Survey* 28 (1975):89–105, sees the play as a tragicomedy enacting the happy fall in which tragic experience leads to comic salvation. The differences among these critics are indicative of the continuing debate over both the play's success and its generic status.

15. For a fuller exploration of the metadramatic aspects of the play and of the Duke as a schematic dramatist who is the object of considerable irony in the play see my article, "*Measure for Measure* and the Restraints of Convention," *Essays in Literature* 10 (1983):149–58.

16. Michael Goldman, *Shakespeare and the Energies of Drama* (Princeton: Princeton University Press, 1972), esp. pp. 164–65.

17. Richard Fly, *Shakespeare's Mediated World* (Amherst: University of Massachusetts Press, 1976), esp. pp. 63–74.

18. See Richard Wheeler's *Shakespeare's Development and the Problem Comedies: Turn and Counter-Turn* (Berkeley and Los Angeles: University of California Press, 1981), pp. 122–24. Having indicated a number of interpretations offered of the Duke, Wheeler argues that each view "seeks an order of inner coherence in Vincentio as the dramatic center of *Measure for Measure* that is not fully realized in the play's comic movement" (p. 123).

19. Clifford Leech in "The 'Meaning' of *Measure for Measure*," *Shakespeare Survey* 3 (1950):66–73, argues at length the case against Vincentio as Godlike redeemer. Both Battenhouse, "*Measure for Measure* and Christian Doctrine of the Atonement," and Hunter, *Shakespeare and the Comedy of Forgiveness,* muster defenses in his behalf, arguing that his role as Duke, and therefore as God's agent on earth, justifies both his assumption of the disguise of Friar and his persistent meddling in the lives of Isabella, Angelo, Claudio, and Marianna. Donna B. Hamilton in "The Duke in *Measure for Measure*: 'I Find an Apt Remission in Myself',", *Shakespeare Studies* 6 (1970):175–83, argues that Vincentio is a flawed character who must and does come to terms with his limitations in the course of the drama, an argument in some ways analogous to that of Louise Schleiner in "Providential Improvisation in *Measure for Measure*," *PMLA* 97 (1982):227–36. Schleiner argues that the Duke is fallible but well-meaning in his quixotic attempts to imitate Providence.

20. Danson, *The Harmonies of "The Merchant of Venice"* (New Haven: Yale University Press, 1978).

21. Ibid., pp. 1–18.

22. Barbara Lewalski, "Biblical Allusion and Allegory in *The Merchant of Venice*," *Shakespeare Quarterly* 13 (1962):327–43.

23. Seeking to discredit the notion that Antonio and Bassanio's love for one another is of a homosexual nature and to discredit the idea that Antonio and Portia are in competition for Bassanio, Danson writes: "Now *The Merchant of Venice* is a play in which harmonies are discovered where only discord had seemed possible, and its dominant figure (whether in details of imagery or in the implied shape of the fable as a whole) is the circle, ring, or round. The love of Antonio and Bassanio chimes

in that harmonious round, as does the love of Bassanio and Portia. But to suppose a competition between Antonio and Portia introduces a discord more intractable to resolution than that of Skylock, the unmusical man, himself. So it is not the realism nor the humanness, but the consequent introduction of this irreconcilable competition, that leads me to reject the psychosexual explanation for Antonio's sadness" (*Harmonies*, pp. 38–39). In other words, such possibilities are impossible because they would destroy the harmony Danson postulates as a given of the play. Again, in arguing that the song sung as Bassanio chooses is not a deliberate clue to the choice he should make, Danson writes: "if the play is to remain a romantic comedy rather than a farce or a neatly disguised satire, then the idea that Portia tips off Bassanio has got to be dismissed. It is an idea contrary to the expectations properly aroused by the dramatic and literary conventions the play exploits" (p. 118). Again, the appeal to the dictates of an overarching comic intention is used to explain away details that do not fit.

24. James Kincaid, "Coherent Readers, Incoherent Texts," *Critical Inquiry* 3 (1977):781–802, esp. p. 784.

25. Harry Berger in "Marriage and Mercifixion in *The Merchant of Venice:* The Casket Scene Revisited," *Shakespeare Quarterly* 32 (1981):155–62, argues that Portia constantly strives to gain power in this play by showering others with gifts that put them under obligation to her.

26. R. Chris Hassel, Jr., in *Faith and Folly in Shakespeare's Romantic Comedies* (Athens: University of Georgia Press, 1980), argues that *The Merchant of Venice* is anomalous among the romantic comedies in that its chief characters are remarkably lacking in humility and in the true Christian charity that comes from the recognition of man's universal folly. See esp. his chapter "'I Stand for Sacrifice': Frustrated Communion in *The Merchant of Venice*," pp. 176–207.

Stuart and Caroline Comedy

"Make odde discoveries!" Disguises, Masques, and Jonsonian Romance

John Lemly

Ile strip the ragged follies of the time,
Naked, as at their birth . . . .

Every Man Out of His Humour, Induction, 17–18

If there bee never a *Servant-monster* i' the *Fayre;* who can
help it? he sayes; nor a nest of *Antiques?* Hee is loth to
make Nature afraid in his *Playes,* like those that beget
Tales, Tempests, and such like *Drolleries,* to mix his head
with other mens heeles, let the concupisence of *Jigges*
and *Dances,* raigne as strong as it will amongst you: yet if
the *Puppets* will please any body, they shall be entreated
to come in.

Bartholomew Fair, Induction, 127–34

Whither? oh whither will this Tire-man growe?
His name is Σκευοποιός wee all knowe,
The maker of ye Properties! in summe
The Scene! the Engyne!
. . . .
How would he firke? lyke Adam overdooe,
Up & about? Dyve into Cellars too
Disguisd? and thence drag forth Enormity?
Discover Vice? Commit Absurdity?
Under ye Morall?

"An Expostulation with Inigo Jones," 59–62, 79–83

Affinities abound between romance and the masque. Each is emblematic, tending toward allegory. Schematic conflicts between polarized characters—extremes
of good and evil—get resolved through sudden reversals, recognitions, and
revelations brought about by the intervention of the gods or their agent, the
author. The three classical unities of action, time, and place are conspicuously
compromised by extreme improbabilities that, in the theater, require and allow

131

for spectacular effects. The comic romances of the Jacobean theater obviously drew upon features of the court masque, which, not coincidentally, flourished at the same time. Both forms developed common dramatic resources to satisfy their audiences' similar tastes.[1]

A modest but telling example of this resemblance appears in comparable incidents near the end of both *The Winter's Tale* and *The Tempest*. Abruptly, frighteningly, Polixenes throws off his disguise at the sheepshearing to shatter Florizel's nuptial plans and sports. So, too, Prospero, having broken off Miranda's betrothal masque, abjures his own "rough magic," disrobes, and resumes his former guise.

> Not one of them
> That yet looks on me or would know me. Ariel,
> Fetch me the hat and rapier in my cell.
> I will discase me, and myself present
> As I was sometime Milan.
>
> (5.1.82–86)

These acts of undisguising, like the unmasking at the end of court revels, reveal the sovereign in his own person and power. Such startling revelations hasten the romances toward conclusions that "invariably contain a strong anti-romantic dimension,"[2] inherent limits on the genre's escapist, unrealistic tendencies. For all their violations of realism, neither the masque nor romance can sustain their extraordinary illusions, a concession that most works in each genre inevitably make evident.

Such strikingly theatrical devices are less usual in earlier Shakespearian plays. Although disguises are common enough, they rarely come off suddenly onstage.[3] These exceptional instances, like the removal of the Duke's cowl in *Measure for Measure*, signal an unequivocal assertion of royal authority. Usually such characters as Portia, Rosalind, Viola, or Edgar's Tom 'o Bedlam shed their disguises more discreetly and gradually, often offstage. Even Bottom as an ass and Henry V as a private soldier are changed back into their rightful selves without exploiting the spectacular effects of sudden theatrical metamorphosis.

Not so in Ben Jonson's plays. Although he repeatedly scorns the excesses of romance and masque alike, in his use of disguise and sudden disclosure, as in many other respects, he adapts from both traditions elements to serve his comic drama. And although his caustic comments about Shakespeare and Inigo Jones are notorious, Jonson never closed his mind to possible influences by these chief rivals in the theaters and at court. From *Cynthia's Revels* to the last extant scene of *The Sad Shepherd*, Jonson's plots often turn upon a disturbing, unexpected stripping away of disguise, not to manifest a masquelike triumph of the ideal or divine—as do the theophanies central to each Shakespearian romance[4]—but rather to reveal a fradulent impersonator in the trappings of nobility and virtue. His earlier plays do so with a satiric vengeance foreign to the redemptive ethos of romance and masque. Only in the later plays, from *Bartholomew Fair* on, are such exposures of vice and folly matched with more genial unveilings of essentially beneficent authority—Adam Overdo, Peniboy Canter, Host Goodstock, Canon

Hugh.[5] In these plays, Jonson's closest approximations to romantic comedy, he manipulates their final festive reconciliations with a mechanical ingenuity informed by working two decades with and against Inigo Jones.

In *Cynthia's Revels* the monarch herself appears only in act 5 to preside over a final masque in her honor. When commanded to unmask, the masquers are exposed as unworthy courtiers unable in

> their unmeasurable vanitie [to]
> Dance truely in a measure.
> . . . .
> So many follies will confusion prove,
> And like a sort of jarring instruments,
> All out of tune . . . .
>
> (5.5.7–12)

Their indecorum clashes with a true masque's ethical assumption—confirmed at its conclusion—that the "masquer's disguise is a representation of the courtier beneath."[6] Here in Jonson's comedy, as in his later masque *Love Restored*, those who improperly impersonate the noble masquers are actually antimasquers, grotesque figures threatening the final harmonious vision. Their performance at Cynthia's court becomes a satire rather than a celebration, until Cynthia's grace reforms them.

Volpone is full of scenes akin to interrupted antimasques: the Pythagorean entertainment by Nano, Androgyno, and Castrone (1.2); the Mountebank's show stopped by Corvino (2.2); Bonario's rescue of Celia from an undisguised seducer promising her endless performances.

> and my dwarfe shall dance,
> My eunuch sing, my foole make up the antique.
> Whil'st we, in changed shapes, act *Ovids* tales.
> . . . .
> Then will I have thee in more moderne formes,
> Attired like some sprightly dame of *France*
> . . . .
> Or some quick *Negro*,[7] or cold *Russian;*
> And I will meet thee, in as many shapes.
>
> (3.7.219–33)

But instead of these promised revels, the final act presents a frenzy of harsh unmaskings: Mosca disguised as heir; Sir Politick in the "ingine" of a tortoiseshell; Mosca as clarissimo and Volpone as commandatore, who, caught at last, "must be resolute/The *Foxe* shall, here, uncase" (5.12.84–85). Such grotesqueries are not answered by any final redemption of this "world in which virtue is inoperative, drained of energy, unable to infect the infected world of vice, saved only by accident."[8] A very different sort of court from Cynthia's or James's at Whitehall, the Venetian tribunal presiding over this finale lacks splendor and honor, itself feebly impersonating the just authority that could convincingly triumph over evil. The sole masquelike glimpse of transcendent transformation lies outside the play itself, in Jonson's dedication to "The Two Famous Universities":

> If my *Muses* be true to me, I shall raise the despis'd head of *poetrie* againe, and stripping her out of those rotten and base rags, wherewith the Times have adulterated her form, restore her to her primitive habit, feature, and majesty, and render her worthy to be imbraced, and kist, of all the great and master-*spirits* of our world. (128–34)

Characteristically, though, even the dedicatory epistle refuses to end here but returns for one last outraged assault upon the "vile, and slothfull."

Jonson's gentlest exposé of the vile and slothful is *Bartholomew Fair,* which, as William Blissett provocatively argues, is entirely antimasque in its performance at Whitehall where "the presence of the court itself must, if it can, serve as its own masque to dispel this antimasque."[9] To Smithfield everyone comes with license to masquerade. At the end the masks come off, but not quite as Adam Overdo promises, "to reveale my selfe, wherein cloud-like, I will breake out in raine, and haile, lightning, and thunder, upon the head of enormity" (5.2.4–6). Rather, simpler and less sublime revelations occur: Leatherhead's puppet is sexless; Mrs. Littlewit, Mrs. Overdo, and Quarlous give up their low-life disguises; and Overdo himself is "but *Adam,* Flesh, and blood! you have your frailty, forget your other name of *Overdoo,* and invite us all to supper. There you and I [Quarlous] will compare our *discoveries*" (5.6.96–99). Or, as he says just after the stage direction, *"The Justice discovers himselfe":* "I have discover'd enough" (5.5.126).

This prevalent use of climactic discoveries is not limited to Jonson's comedies. *Sejanus,* a false claimant to royal power, is himself undone in an almost instantaneous turn of events, a literal revolution. The tyrant's fall is presaged by an antitheophany, a violated oblation before the goddess Fortune, whose statue Sejanus angrily overthrows even as his own public statues are about to be desecrated. And then in another sacred place, the Temple of Apollo, Sejanus, who "this morne rose proudly, as the sunne," is suddenly exposed and then eclipsed by the whims of Tiberius, the people, and Fortune—a mechanical reversal that turns the medieval *de casibus* pattern into a masque's *machina versatilis.*

> LEPIDUS: O, violent change,
> And whirle of mens affections! ARRUNTIUS: Like, as both
> Their bulkes and soules were bound on fortunes wheele,
> And must act onely with her motion!
>
>   (5.709,701–4)

Dramaturgically this uprising unleashes in Rome a corrective force like the almost arbitrary reassertions of rightful power at the end of masques or satiric comedies. But in this tragedy, as in much of his drama for the theater and even for the court, Jonson doubts whether history or art can teach the truths necessary to sustain a vision of goodness and happiness.

Such pessimism about human progress pervades Jonson's work, even at its most affirmative moments. Gruesome though the analogy is, something like the mob's dismembering of Sejanus echoes in Jonson's preface to his first masque some two years later. Presumptuously preserving the texts of these most short-lived phenomena, he alludes to the audience's rifling the elaborate scenery at the end of the evening.[10]

> The honor, and splendor of these *spectacles* was such in the performance, as could those houres have lasted, this of mine, now, had been a most unprofit-able worke. But (when it is the fate, even of the greatest, and most absolute births, to need, and borrow a life of posteritie) little had beene done to the studie of *magnificence* in these, if presently with the rage of the people, who (as a part of greatnesse) are priviledged by custome, to deface their *carkasses*, the *spirits* had also perished. (*The Masque of Blackness*, 1–9)

At the inception of the masque's brief flourishing as a literary form, Jonson speaks with some irony to its essential paradox: this most ephemeral, occasional art attempts to preserve the most permanent values. For Jonson that paradox becomes increasingly true and troubling, apposite not only to his masques but to everything he wrote.

*   *   *

Twenty years later the vagaries of fortune seemed to be turning against Jonson himself. After a decade that had seen Jonson made unofficial laureate, monopo-lize the writing of masques for James, publish his monumental folio, and offer but one comedy on the public stage,[11] Charles became king and proved to be unlike his father in many respects, including his persistent coolness toward the aging poet. Largely because of this indifference at court, Jonson turned back to the theaters, his lifelong irascibility toward that audience heightened perhaps by a need to recoup his former successes under James. These late comedies are not the "dotages" Dryden called them, but few would argue with Thomas Carew's opinion that Jonson's "comique Muse from the exalted line/Toucht by thy Al-chymist, doth since decline" (H&S, 11:335). Jonson's Caroline comedies imply a similar concession of his own, as if the old playwright was actually not so self-assured as his familiar artistic pronouncements sound. Indeed, the problems posed by these late plays are attributable less to waning senility than to confusion about what sorts of drama would suit both the dramatist and his audience. Until his death in 1637, Jonson's uncertain experiments in several dramatic modes often suggest an ambivalence toward both romance and masque. Frequently he condemns these theatrical kinds, "wherein, now, the Concupiscence of Daunces, and Antickes so raigneth, as to runne away from Nature, and be afraid of her" (*The Alchemist*, Preface, 5–7). At the same time he borrows their least naturalistic elements: allegory, nostalgic movement toward a pastoral landscape, deliberate archaism, sudden revelations, music and dance, and incredible, convoluted plots.

That ambivalence about genre characterizes *The Staple of News*, with which Jonson resumed writing for the public theater. Such realistic materials as allu-sions to current events, newfangled journalism, and low-comic characters mix unevenly in an allegorical fable about prodigality and prudence. The very same materials, on the other hand, had well served the antimasques of entertainments for James's court, especially *News from the New World Discovered in the Moon* and *Neptune's Triumph for the Return of Albion*. The latter masque was never actually performed but was intended to celebrate Prince Charles's safe return from wooing the Spanish Infanta, Isabella Clara Eugenia, an unpopular, thwarted courtship that *The Staple of News* alludes to in Peniboy Junior's infatuation with the Infanta of the Mines, Aurelia Clara Pecunia. Presumed dead, the father— Peniboy Canter—turns out to be very much alive and sets straight his son's misguided amours and misused inheritance.

The play appeared just after Charles's coronation (2 February 1625/26) at Shrovetide, the season—except for Christmas—most celebrated with royal masques (H&S, 2:169). Like *Bartholomew Fair*, it too was repeated at Whitehall, "fitted for your *Majesties* disport,/And writ to the *Meridian* of your *Court*" (Prologue for the Court, 2–3). One wonders how this image of filial follies struck the austere, twenty-five-year-old king, newly crowned and newly married to a different Catholic princess, Henrietta Maria. As far as history records, the play did not harm Jonson's favor at court, but it did not help him either. Nearly five years would pass before any work of his was again played before Charles. His career making masques was effectively over.[12]

Nevertheless, *The Staple of News* both borrows heavily from recent masques and generally reflects Jonson's long preoccupation with the form's sudden transformations, antithetical abstractions, and emblematic costumes. Act 4, the comedy's high point, takes place under the mock aegis of Apollo at the dining room of the Devil Tavern, where Peniboy Junior and his cronies—like Perdita and Florizel, Prospero, Henry VIII—"make a masque."[13] Like Polixenes, a disguised Peniboy Canter observes his son's mindless antics; but unlike *The Winter's Tale*, *The Staple of News* verifies the father's fury against these youthful frolics.

> They are a kinde of dancing engines all!
> And set, by nature, thus, to runne alone
> To every sound! All things within, without 'hem,
> Move, but their braine, and that stands still! mere monsters,
> Here, in a chamber, of most subtill feet!
> And make their legs in tune, passing the streetes!
> These are the gallant spirits o' the age!
> The miracles o' the time!
>
> (4.2.134–41)

Peniboy Canter's aside reverberates with Jonson's own hearty disdain of Shakespeare's romances and Inigo's masques. He argues so irrefutably against their excess that the play tends to discredit its own most entertaining moment. As often in *Volpone* or *The Alchemist*, the masquers' vice is theatrically far more alive and compelling than is the father's virtue. Characteristically, Jonson here gives with one hand and takes with the other; inventing a wildly enjoyable fantasy, he immediately rebukes his characters and audience for enjoying it. The ethical point holds, but it spoils a good party; or, as one of the onstage Gossips remarks,

"It was spitefully done o' the *Poet*" (Intermean, 4.22). Another makes the even more crucial observation: Peniboy Canter is "a kin to the *Poet*" (4–5), and such an authorial surrogate—present also in his next two plays—tends to shatter the drama's naturalistic pretensions.

Just as Peniboy Junior's entertainment threatens to invert the "good, and vertuous" (4.4.135), "his *father* discovers himselfe" (116 s.d.) by throwing off his ragged cloak for the profligate son to inherit. His charges against the prodigal's parasitic entourage stress their violation of the courtly ideals they impersonate.

> A worthy *Courtier,* is the ornament
> Of a *Kings Palace,* his great *Masters* honour.
> . . . .
>   So, a *true Souldier,*
> He is his *Countryes strength,* his *Soveraignes safety*
> . . . .
> 'Cause he's an *Asse,* doe not I love a *Herald?*
> Who is the pure *preserver of descents,*
> The keeper faire of all *Nobility,*
> Without which all would runne into confusion?
>   (140–45, 151–54)

These lines explicitly convey the poet's own sentiments, lecturing a court that in the years ahead would largely ignore such prudent, conservative advice. But Peniboy Junior learns this lesson, while the Staple he would project dissolves, leaving not a rack behind.

> Our *Emissaries, Register, Examiner,*
> Flew into vapor: our grave *Governour*
> Into a subt'ler ayer. . . .
> . . . .
> I, and my fellow melted into butter,
> And spoyl'd our Inke, and so the *Office* vanish'd.
>   (5.1.45–50)[14]

He proves himself to his father, who invites him finally to "Put off your ragges, and be your selfe againe,/This *Act* of piety, and good affection,/Hath partly reconcil'd me to you" (5.3.22–24). Having tried on and been tried by extremes of dress, Peniboy Junior reverts to a true appearance at one with his underlying nature. Although anticipated in the endings of *Every Man in His Humour* and *Bartholomew Fair,* the masquelike theatrics of *The Staple of News* highlight a further shift from satiric exposé toward comic transmutation, a redemptive alchemy or metamorphosis travestied in earlier plays. Here Jonson first dramatizes what Anne Barton has termed the "Shakespearean premise" of the later plays: "the possibility that people may actually learn from experience, that they can metamorphose themselves and change."[15]

In *The New Inn,* his next play, these motifs of disguise, discovery, and familial reconciliation are so overwrought and "the action is so manipulated that it betrays Jonson's illusionist principles."[16] For twenty years Jonson scoffed at Jones as a pretentious puppeteer—"a Master of motions" (*Bartholomew Fair,* 5.1.8 s.d.)—

but in this romantic comedy he pulls such obvious strings as to be guilty himself
of "running away from Nature." (Notably, the Inn's Host, who in many ways
stands for the playwright, has been "Puppet-master" and traveled with "*Yong
Goose,* the Motion-man" [1.5.61–62].) Although Jonson's invective "Ode to Himself" may sneer at "some mouldy tale,/Like *Pericles*" (21–22), he is not above
using devices Shakespeare exploited in his romance. His hero's long-lost daughter has not been sold to a bawd; even more fantastically, she has been stolen by
her own mother—disguised as an Irish beggar—and sold as a boy to her own
father, disguised as the Host Goodstock. The Light Heart in Barnet is no brothel
in Mytilene but, rather, a suburban rendezvous for afternoon liaisons (4.3.71–
72n),[17] and Frank—"Suppos'd a boy"—dresses as the girl she actually is to join in
harmless amatory interludes.

The New Inn is a sort of anti-Penshurst, the City's bourgeois analogue to the
great houses Jonson so loved to visit and entertain. The Host early suggests how
fallen off are "these nourceries of nobility":

> I [aye] that was, when the nourceries selfe, was noble,
> And only vertue made it, not the mercate,
> That titles were not vented at the drum,
> Or common out-cry; goodnesse gave the greatnesse,
> And greatnesse worship: Every house became
> An Academy of honour, and those parts—
> We see departed, in the practise, now,
> Quite from the institution.
>
> (1.3.51–59)

Throughout the play such nostalgia for nobler times calls into question the
possibility of present greatness. The characters' aspirations are tarnished and
qualified; high ideals that a masque or romance would represent unequivocally
are here sketched not on a grand scale but, rather, as epic miniatures. Yet
however slight, these glimpses of human excellence accumulate and demand to
be taken seriously. Hardly a satire on recently fashionable Neoplatonism, Jonson's comedy earnestly pursues realistic, limited definitions of love and valor
commensurate with an unheroic age. The mock-heroic "*Militia* below stayres"
serves as an antimasque to the main action, an uncouth counterpoint that is
omitted from the last act lest they "offend" either the playwright or the audience
(Epilogue, 18). Before its disastrous public performance, Jonson intended to
present this play—like *Bartholomew Fair* and *The Staple of News*—at court, and in
some key respects it resembles a masque: noble abstractions are debated and
ultimately enacted; ignoble alternatives get transformed or banished; a harmonious finale is celebrated with unmaskings and song; and even Jonson's bitterly
mundane ode ends with a fleeting apotheosis, a triumphant image of "raysing
Charles his chariot, 'bove his *Waine*" (60).

The New Inn's Court of Love offers as extensive a study of virtue as Jonson ever
wrote. Despite the surrounding triviality and frenzy, Lovel's Neoplatonic addresses achieve an ethereal transcendence that, however protracted and hyper-
bolic, is no satiric parody.

> In what calme he speakes,
> After this noise, and tumult, so unmov'd,
> With that serenity of countenance,
> As if his thoughts did acquiesce in that
> Which is the object of the second houre,
> And nothing else.
>
>   (4.4.18–23)

L. A. Beaurline finds in Lovel's romantic melancholy and "old-fashioned aristo-cratic values" a persuasive analogy to Jonson's accomplished patron, Sir Kenelm Digby, "A Gentleman absolute in all Numbers," who "doth excell/In honour, courtesie, and all the parts/Court can call hers, or Man could call his Arts" (H&S, 8:272, 262).[18] An even more self-conscious resemblance exists between Lovel and William Cavendish, Earl of Newcastle, whose horsemanship and fencing Jonson was praising in poems contemporary with *The New Inn*. Alluding to Sidney's *Arcadia*, Bevis of Hampton, Virgil, Seneca, and Hercules, these two fine epigrams evoke the earl's "true/Valour" (H&S, 8:233, 228) in heroic phrases also applied to Lovel (1.3.60–62; 4.3.11–20; 4.4). Preferring Homer's and Virgil's "examples/Of the *Heroick* vertue" (1.6.132–33), Lovel early expresses a Jonsonian distaste for chivalric romances. Similarly, Newcastle embodies an ancient nobility now almost extinct. The Earl of Newcastle would later lavishly underwrite Jon-son's last entertainments for Charles at Welbeck and Bolsover (in 1633 and 1634); seemingly only under the auspices of such a courtier could the bedridden poet still attempt to address a court no longer open to his instructions in courtesy.

Unlike the epigrams in tribute to Newcastle and Digby, however, the play cannot sustain its lofty visions of heroism. As in Shakespeare's romances, these unreal moments of sublime art give way before more common human impulses. Lovel's exquisite, concentrated meditations are undercut not only by his own ennui and Lady Frampul's pretenses but also by bizarre impostors akin to Stephano and Trinculo "in stolen apparel" or Autolycus, that trafficker in sheets who "cannot be but a great courtier." Pinnacia Stuff, their direct descendant, storms into the Light Heart wearing a gown ordered for the court's festive sovereign. Before Lovel can resume his definition of valor, this interloper must be stripped and driven off. Her expulsion soon leads to a more crucial disrobing when the maid Prudence, for whom the gown is intended, tries to teach her mistress Lady Frampul to leave off dissembling and own her love for Lovel. Lady Frampul explains that

> frowardnesse sometime
> Becomes a beauty, being but a visor
> Put on. You'l let a Lady weare her masque, *Pru*.
> . . . .
> PRUDENCE: I sweare, I thought you had dissembled, Madam,
> And doubt, you do so yet. LADY: Dull, stupid, wench!
> Stay i' thy state of ignorance still, be damn'd,
> An idiot Chambermayd! Hath all my care,
> My breeding thee in fashion, thy rich clothes,
> Honours, and titles wrought no brighter effects
> On thy darke soule, then thus? Well! go thy wayes,

Were not the Tailors wife, to be demolish'd,
Ruin'd, uncas'd, thou shouldst be she, I vow.
PRUDENCE: Why, take your spangled properties, your gown,
And scarfes. LADY: *Pru, Pru,* what doest thou meane?
PRUDENCE: I will not buy this play-boyes bravery,
At such a price, to be upbraided for it,
Thus, every minute.

                                              (4.4.293–95, 310–23)

Unhesitatingly, the maid meets this test of her mettle, demonstrating an instinctive valor such as Lovel has just been discoursing upon. "Pinnacia and Pru
are parallel figures: both put on the clothes of someone above them in station.
When Pru does this, like Shakespeare's Perdita, her unusual dress serves to
reveal her innate aristocracy and intelligence; by play-acting, she uncovers the
person she really is."[19] Instead of the splendor of costume or rhetoric, hers is a
self-possessed bravery of a sort Jonson always admired in others and attributed
to himself. Pru's defiance here anticipates Jonson's later claim that his own
"clothes shall never be the best thing about him . . . humane letters, or severe
honesty, shall speak him a man though he went naked" (*Magnetic Lady,* Chorus,
2.54–47). An unmistakable spiritual kinship links the playwright and the maid:
impatient with this hypocrisy of their superiors, each oversteps social rank to
claim equality with them. By divesting herself, Pru precludes her mistress's
threat and exemplifies the initiative, frankness, and vitality conspicuously muted
in Lady Frampul and the other jaded aristocrats, Goodstock and Lovel. Like
Brainworm or Molière's Dorine, but more upwardly mobile than the traditional
"tricky servant," she intuits the uses and limits of pretense, when to affect and
when to avoid disguise. To remove one's own mask voluntarily is an ennobling
self-assertion unlike those dehumanizing instances when one is stripped by
accident or by another's authority.

   Her undaunted, vigorous action sets in motion a welter of happy discoveries.
Reconciled and reclothed in their finery, both ladies preside over the plot's
unraveling, punctuated by repeated revelations that climax with Goodstock.

                      Fly, take away mine host,
         My beard, and cap here, from me, and fetch my Lord. . . .
                              I am Lord *Frampull,*
         The cause of all this trouble; I am he
         Have measur'd all the Shires of *England* over
         . . . .
         To search their natures, and make odde discoveries!
         . . . .
                      Take heart, and breath, recover,
         Thou hast recover'd me, who here had coffin'd
         My selfe alive, in a poore hostelry,
         In pennance of my wrongs done unto thee,
         Whom I long since gave lost.

                                              (5.5.86–108)

Enacted by an actual change of costume like Prospero's, Lord Frampul's idiom of
uncovering and recovering leads to a joyous exit "with a *Song,*" a finale like the

"final dance of the masquers, known as the 'going off,' or 'the last dance.'"[20] Having rediscovered himself, his family, and his rightful robes, Lord Frampul at last becomes the true Master of Revels he has ineffectually pretended to be.

A Tale of a Tub also ends with a masque, but one not so eloquently redemptive. Indeed, if these late plays suggest "something of the pattern of antimasque and masque"[21] and if the structure of the masque is like that of romance, then this rustic Valentine's Day might well be dubbed a mock- or anti-romance. Jonson's earlier ambivalence toward both romance and masque largely gives way to a simpler, less experimental form of parody. But even as *The New Inn* nostalgically recalls outmoded norms of nobility, so this period comedy—set in Queen Mary's reign almost a century before (H&S, 9:270)—cherishes native virtues and bonds of a yeomanry now similarly old-fashioned. Repeatedly and self-consciously it subjects the materials of Elizabethan pastoral romance and comedy to gentle, appreciative mockery, while the interpolated scenes about In-and-In Medlay— "The onely man at a disguize in *Midlesex*" (5.2.33)—poke more heavy-handed fun at Inigo Jones's masques. This essay is no place to resume the long and in-conclusive debate over the dating of the play. That it was the last play Jonson readied for performance (in 1634) suffices to include it in a discussion of developments in his later drama.[22] For all its unevenness, moreover, the satire on Jones gets subsumed in the entire action's unfrivolous urgency to satisfy spring-time's primitive drives. As much as Jonson's comedy burlesques romance and the masque, it shares their purposes—and often their techniques—to affirm an essential human spirit, at once playful and serious, escapist and pragmatic. Although in *A Tale of a Tub* the powers that make all end well are more domestic than Olympian, this rural setting, like those of *The New Inn* and *The Sad Shepherd*, seems surprisingly congenial to the former master of city comedy. In this homely world, as in Smithfield, Jonson laughs both at and with the clowns and their games.

The unlikely object of their prevernal mating ritual is Awdrey Turfe, "probably the extremest example of this anti-romantic type to be found in the Elizabethan drama" (H&S, 1:300). But her very lack of Rosalind's—or even Phebe's—charms stresses the simple-minded ineluctability of the quest "to have her married / To day by any meanes" (1.1.49–50). Shakespeare's later youthful heroines embody idealized purity vulnerable to a sordid, imperfect world. Cordelia, Octavia even, Marina, Perdita, Miranda, all like the Virgin of the medieval carol, are "make-less," troubled or forestalled in their matchmaking because they are too good, matchless. Awdrey, by contrast, is merely a maiden who needs a mate, a need unknown to her two days before: "I care not who it be, so I have one" (3.6.44). She has little patience for foolery, pretensions, and idle talk.

> No Mistris, Sir, my name is *Awdrey*. . . .
> But hee's [Squire Tub] too fine for me . . . .
> I have heard much o' your words, but not o' your deeds.
> (2.3.63, 69; 2.4.68)

Despite herself, she gets pursued by almost every eligible man in the play, and at the hands of her last, successful suitor is transformed, like Pru in *The New Inn*, into the fine lady she earlier refuses to mimic. Her no-nonsense nature remains skeptical of romantic artifice, especially flattering words, while pragmatically accepting whatever will serve her purpose: "Can you make me / A Lady, would I ha' you?" (4.5.92–93). Later when she does marry her surprise couturier-lover, "She was so brave. . . . so disguis'd, so Lady-like; / I thinke she did not know her selfe the while" (5.4.21–24). What she lacks in wit is offset by her resolute, resilient energy. Awdrey's Valentine escapades typify what Susanne Langer has called comedy's quintessential "image of human vitality holding its own in the world amid the surprises of unplanned coincidence."[23]

With such a heroine and other mock echoes of romance—an errant knight in disguise, a burlesque herald "made a Purs'yvant against my will" (2.6.27), relentless archaisms and proverbial lore, allusions to medieval legend (Virginia, Awdrey's antitype), and romance heroes (St. George, Bevis, Guy, even Pericles)[24]—A Tale of a Tub is Jonson most like Cervantes, but more in the vein of Sancho Panza than of Quixote. Such a pastiche serves as a fit context for the closing wooden spoof of Jones: "A Masque, what's that? Scriben. A mumming, or a shew. / With vizards, and fine clothes" (5.2.29–30). Appropriately, it is Scriben, "the great Writer," who offers this reductionist definition.

As his own late masques and country-house entertainments tended to do, Jonson here conflates the ideal—what little there is—and the real; Medlay's final grand show and the day's rambling quest are one in their banality.[25] The play's action and its triumphant festival become indistinguishable, species of dumb shows. What Jonas Barish has observed about the later country-house masques is germane as well to Jonson's most country comedy.

> And in country divertissements like Pan's Anniversary or The Masque of Gypsies, where stage machinery must have been almost nonexistent and elaborate transformation scenes out of the question, Jonson can make the masque and antimasque virtually coextensive, mingling them and overlapping them at pleasure, so as to disguise the dualism inherent in the genre.[26]

In Finsbury Hundred, the world of A Tale, "elaborate transformation" is even less possible, except for Hilts's and Canon Hugh's foolish disguises and Awdrey's modest dressing up to be a lady. In turn, though the Prologue boasts "to shew what different things / The Cotes of Clownes, are from the Courts of Kings," that inherent dualism gets called into question by a burlesque of the court's chief entertainer. Performed at court with its satire of Jones censored, the play was "not likt" (Office Book of the Master of the Revels, in H&S, 9:163). Significantly, in the same month (January 1634), performances that were "likt" included Cymbeline, The Winter's Tale, Fletcher's The Faithful Shepherdess, and Jones and James Shirley's lavish masque, The Triumph of Peace, with its procession through the city streets and some dozen antimasques, presented by the Inns of Court to show their support of Charles and Henrietta Maria, whose liking for spectacle Prynne's Histriomastix had attacked the year before. In Percy Simpson's witty words, "Jonson was both out of favour and out of fashion."[27] Without the compliments of masque or the refinements of romance, A Tale of a Tub both flouted the court's tastes and implicitly impugned its integrity. The play's unexpurgated text reflects Jonson's disappointment that courtly entertainment derived from old-fashioned country mumming has, in substance, reverted to its origins: a wordless interlude, an excuse for frivolous spectacle.[28] Or, as "An Expostulation" had put it more bitterly, "Oh, to make Boardes to speake! There is a taske" (H&S, 8:404, line 49).

*   *   *

Jonson was never one to avoid contradictions. Although *A Tale of a Tub* most openly suggests a contempt for current trends in masque and romance, his final play, *The Sad Shepherd*, most favorably resembles both kinds of drama. Like the great fourth-act entertainments in Shakespeare's last two romances, this very native *"Tale"*—"such wooll,/As from meere *English* Flocks his *Muse* can pull" (Prologue, 15,9–10)—is literally broken off, left incomplete at his death. But in the pastoral fragment culminate artistic developments evident in the previous comedies. The opening page of the 1640 Folio reveals its debts to masques. "The Persons of the Play" are headed by Robin Hood and Marian, "Master of the Feast" and "His Lady, the Mistris," then listed in formal groups—"Their Family," "The Guests invited," "The troubles unexpected"—with each "guest" and each "Trouble" given an abstract epithet, for example, "the Sad," "the Kind," "the Envious." Even more than in the Caroline comedies, "the characters have strong allegorical tendencies."[29] Despite its realistic depictions of rustic woodlore and the psychology of love, the play suggests a stylized conflict between good and evil. Maudlin, the embodiment of evil, like the Dame of witches in *The Masque of Queens*, whom Jonson glossed as "the person of *Atè*, or *mischiefe*,"[30] disrupts the feast through baneful transformations that "make *Nature* fight/Within her selfe" (*Queens*, 147–48).

"The Scene is *Sher-wood*." This opening description, unique in all of Jonson's plays, recalls the idealized setting of *Chloridia*, his last masque at Whitehall, where the figure of Spring is assaulted by mute antimasquers from Hell who "raise Tempest, Windes, Lightnings, Thunder, Rayne, and Snow" (159–60). Only slightly less allegorical is the abduction of Earine, "mistress of the spring" (H&S, 10:363n), whom the Sad Shepherd fears drowned but whom Maudlin has imprisoned, like Ariel, in a tree. Though comically clumsy in his "new breikes [breeches] . . . and thy duiblet" (2.3.22), the witch's swineherd son has the same rapist's intentions toward Earine as has Sycorax's son toward Miranda. And like Caliban, he threatens the day's festivities, a sheepshearing celebrated oddly enough in a forest. Jonson's Sherwood is such a place, expansive, easily able to include both native woodlore and classical pastoral, Shakespearian comedy and Whitehall masque. The setting, like the play itself, evokes a generosity of spirit, a hospitality evident in Robin's welcome to the visiting shepherds.[31]

> Why should, or you, or wee so much forget
> The season in our selves: as not to make
> Use of our youth, and spirits, to awake
> The nimble Horne-pipe, and the Timburine,

> And mixe our Songs, and Dances in the Wood,
> And each of us cut downe a Triumph-bough?
> Such are the Rites, the youthfull *June* allow.
>
> (1.4.11–17)

It is a genial, emphatically youthful world the old poet imagines, one at odds with his own invalid condition and the kingdom's general malaise on the eve of revolution.

The fragment offers few clues to the outcome, but it is surely prefigured in Robin's third-act discovery of Maudlin disguised as Marian. Just as the fragment ends, he exercises the perennial Jonsonian power to strip away her deceptive charms and expose the impostor beneath. If she is the least equivocal personification of vice in Jonson's comedies, he is the most potent, attractive figure of virtue. Whatever the details of the two missing acts, the forces of good are destined to win out over Maudlin's witchcraft, a comic triumph with more precedent in Jonson's masques than in his Jacobean drama.

The pastoral's reminiscences of Shakespeare's plays a quarter century before imply neither intentional, if belated, imitation of the "Sweet Swan of Avon," nor some "biographical allegory" in which even Jonson at the end converts to romance.[32] They do show, however, the versatility and inventiveness of a playwright too often still considered wooden, mechanical, "humourous." His devoted Oxford editors grudgingly noted the exceptions to this static caricature: "That the least lyrical personality among all the poets of his time should pass away with such a swan-song [*The Sad Shepherd*] is no doubt startling" (1:115). The full wonders and range of his achievement will become less startling to those readers who avoid two ancient fallacies: faulting Jonson for not being Shakespeare, and judging his plays and verse too literally, simplistically in terms of his own criticism. Sixty years after Eliot's call for "intelligent saturation in his work as a whole,"[33] we still read Jonson piecemeal—plays, poetry, masques—informed by select passages culled from his diverse, sometimes inconsistent critical remarks. His work is not all of a piece, but it all supplies a necessary context for appreciating any part. Although my term "Jonsonian romance" is overstated and polemical, outmoded notions of Jonson's art and temperament should no longer make of it an oxymoron. There are many facets to Jonson yet to be discovered, some more genial, lyrical, and unJonsonian than once thought. He rejected a monopolistic and monochromatic poetics with only "one Character:/In which what were not written, were not right"; the true poet or true critic is not like those "*Painters* who can only make a *Rose*" (*Sad Shepherd*, Prologue, 56–57, 62). Or to reverse the Horatian anecdote: in Jonson's case, at times, less typically he *did* make roses, and they seem most to flower toward the end of his life.

NOTES

1. See especially Northrop Frye, "Romance as Masque," and Clifford Leech, "Masking and Unmasking in the Late Plays," in *Shakespeare's Romances Reconsidered*, ed. Carol McGinnis Kay and Henry E. Jacobs (Lincoln: University of Nebraska Press, 1978), pp. 11–59; also, M. C. Bradbrook,

"Social Change and the Evolution of Ben Jonson's Court Masques," *Studies in the Literary Imagination* 6, no. 1 (April 1973): 101–2; Inga-Stina Ewbank, "'These pretty devices': A Study of Masques in Plays," in *A Book of Masques: Essays in Honour of Allardyce Nicoll*, ed. T. J. B. Spencer and Stanley Wells (Cambridge: Cambridge University Press, 1967), pp. 407–9, 426–29. Sarah Sutherland's *Masques in Jacobean Tragedy* (New York: AMS Press, 1983), pp. 1–26, begins with succinct surveys of "The Critical Heritage" and of the mutual influences between the London theaters and the court masques.

Quotations of Jonson are from *Ben Jonson*, ed. C. H. Herford, Percy and Evelyn Simpson, 11 vols. (Oxford: Clarendon Press, 1925–52); this edition cited throughout as "H&S," with "i/j" and "u/v" spellings normalized. References to Shakespeare are taken from the Pelican edition, ed. Alfred Harbage et al. (Baltimore: Penguin Books, 1969).

2. Howard Felperin, *Shakespearean Romance* (Princeton: Princeton University Press, 1972), p. 50. Northrop Frye, in "Romance as Masque," argues that "the interruption is a part of the sense of the transient quality of the masque" (p. 38).

3. See David William's sensible discussion of costume, "*The Tempest* on the Stage," in *Jacobean Theatre*, ed. John Russell Brown and Bernard Harris (London: Edward Arnold, 1960; New York: Capricorn Books, 1967), pp. 150–51.

4. Felperin, *Shakespearean Romance*, 27–28. See also Kenneth Muir, "Theophanies in the Last Plays," in *Shakespeare's Late Plays: Essays in Honor of Charles Crow*, ed. Richard Tobias and Paul Zolbrod (Athens: Ohio University Press, 1974), pp. 32–43.

5. Such a survey could consider almost all Jonson's plays. Further instances would include *Epicoene, The Devil Is an Ass, The Magnetic Lady*, and Brainworm's "day of my *metamorphosis*" in *Every Man in His Humour* (5.3.83).

6. Stephen Orgel, *The Jonsonian Masque* (Cambridge, Mass.: Harvard University Press, 1965), p. 117. Ever suggestive, Northrop Frye makes a similar point about the endings of romance, in *The Secular Scripture* (Cambridge, Mass.: Harvard University Press, 1976), p. 155: "we have statues coming to life, as in the concluding scene of *The Winter's Tale;* we have stories of snow maidens thawed out and sleeping beauties awakened. The familiar Classical version is the story of Pygmalion . . . . One very significant image of this type is the conclusion of a masque, where, as in *Comus*, the actors come out of their dramatic frame and revert to the people they actually are."

7. Earlier that same year the queen herself had realized Volpone's fantasy in *The Masque of Blackness*. Stephen Orgel recounts the bizarre consequences in his edition of *The Complete Masques* (New Haven: Yale University Press, 1969), p. 4.

8. George A. E. Parfitt, "Virtue and Pessimism in Three Plays by Ben Jonson," *Studies in the Literary Imagination* 6, no. 1 (April 1973):25.

9. "Your Majesty Is Welcome to a Fair," in *The Elizabethan Theatre IV*, ed. George Hibbard (Hamden, Conn.: Archon Books, 1974), p. 105.

10. Bradbrook, "Jonson's Court Masques," p. 122, describes the typical anarchy at court during the performance of a masque. See also H&S, 10:449.

11. Eugene Waith, "Things as They Are and the World of Absolutes in Jonson's Plays and Masques," in *The Elizabethan Theatre IV*, pp. 106–26, discusses the final decade of James's reign, 1616–25.

12. The Oxford editors list no further court perfomances of any Jonson play until November 1630 (H&S, 9:196); that same winter saw Jonson's only Caroline masques at Whitehall, *Love's Triumph through Callipolis* and *Chloridia* (H&S, 1:96). Herford and Simpson suggest that this modest resurgence of favor may have been in response to Jonson's recent misfortunes: a stroke and the fiasco of *The New Inn*. When he published the two masques, however, Jonson slighted his collaborator Jones enough to rekindle their feud and to squelch any prospects of further royal commissions.

13. D. F. McKenzie, "*The Staple of News* and the Late Plays," in *A Celebration of Ben Jonson*, ed. William Blissett, Julian Patrick, and R. W. Van Fossen (Toronto: University of Toronto Press, 1973), p. 98. Although my study came to my attention after this essay was completed, Alexander Leggatt makes a similar point in discussing "the most masque-like of the late plays," in *Ben Jonson: His Vision and His Art* (London: Methuen, 1981), pp. 186–87.

14. Waith, "Things as They Are," p. 117, considers the resemblances to masques in this crucial moment when the "lives of most of the principal characters are instantly transformed . . . [a scene] which cries out for a visual transformation."

15. "*The New Inn* and the Problem of Jonson's Late Style," *English Literary Renaissance* 9 (1979):399. Later (p. 411), she cites the passage concerning alchemical transmutation (3.2.171–77) from which I have taken my image. I am everywhere indebted to her splendid reevaluation of the late plays.

16. Northrop Frye, *A Natural Perspective: The Development of Shakespearean Comedy and Romance* (New York: Columbia University Press, 1955; reprint, New York: Harcourt, Brace and World, 1965), p. 17.

17. Win Littlewit and Dame Overdo are promised such a rendezvous in *Bartholomew Fair* (4.5.38).

L. A. Beaurline, *Jonson and Elizabethan Comedy: Essays in Dramatic Rhetoric* (San Marino: Huntington Library, 1978), p. 259, notes that even Tottenham Court—the setting of *A Tale of a Tub*—offered such lascivious escape.

18. Beaurline, *Elizabethan Comedy*, p. 261. See also Richard Peterson, *Imitation and Praise in the Poems of Ben Jonson* (New Haven: Yale University Press, 1981), pp. 82–87, 106–10, for a lucid reading of Jonson's poems on the Digbys.

19. Anne Barton, "Jonson's Late Style," p. 404.

20. Enid Welsford, *The Court Masque* (Cambridge: Cambridge University Press, 1927), p. 167; quoted in Orgel, *The Jonsonian Masque*, p. 5. Calvin Thayer, *Ben Jonson: Studies in the Plays* (Norman: University of Oklahoma Press, 1963), p. 230, likens Goodstock to Prospero.

21. Waith, "Things as They Are," p. 118, citing Thayer, *Ben Jonson*, p. 160. Beaurline, *Elizabethan Comedy*, examines clearly the "anti-romantic strategy of the play" (p. 278).

22. John Enck, *Jonson and the Comic Truth* (Madison: University of Wisconsin Press, 1957), p. 271, summarized the debate, concluding that the play appears to be late in Jonson's canon. More recently, Barton, "Jonson's Late Style," p. 398, and Beaurline, *Elizabethan Comedy*, p. 275, support such an opinion. J. A. Bryant, *The Compassionate Satirist: Ben Jonson and His Imperfect World* (Athens: University of Georgia Press, 1972), p. 175, speculates that it may date from the time of *Bartholomew Fair*.

23. Susanne Langer, *Feeling and Form* (New York: Charles Scribner's Sons, 1953), p. 331.

24. See especially 3.6 and 3.9.51–52 and 52n. Elsewhere, Jonson had little use for the stock romances, as he exclaims in "An Execration Upon Vulcan" (H&S, 8:203–5):

> Had I compil'd from *Amadis de Gaule,*
> Th'*Esplandians, Arthurs, Palmerins,* and all
> The learned Librarie of *Don Quixote;*
> And so some goodlier monster had begot:
> . . . .
> Thou then hadst had some colour for thy flames,
> On such my serious follies . . . .
>
> (29–41)

If he had only known Vulcan's intentions ahead of time, he would have, in place of his own work, offered up

> pieces of the *Legend;* The whole summe
> Of errant Knight-hood, with their Dames, and Dwarfes,
> Their charmed Boates, and their inchanted Wharfes;
> The *Tristrams, Lanc'lots, Turpins,* and the *Peers,*
> All the madde *Rolands,* and sweet *Oliveers* . . . .
>
> (66–70)

His next poem, "A Speech according to Horace" (p. 215), more bitterly ridicules pretentious, unfounded claims to heroic heritage and satirizes those who can buy a pedigree, "Descended in a rope of Titles, be / From *Guys,* or *Bevis, Arthur,* or from whom/The Herald will" (80–82).

25. Waith, "Things as They Are," p. 118, examines corresponding changes in the late Jacobean masques and comedies that intermingle "the ideal" and "the familiar." Among the most important late masques are those country-house entertainments based largely on materials drawn from the surrounding area. Examples include *The Masque of Owls, The Gypsies Metamorphosed, The King's Entertainment at Welbeck,* and *Love's Welcome at Bolsover.* The latter two, performed for Charles's progresses in 1633 and 1634, resemble these late plays. Jones is soundly mocked in *Bolsover; Welbeck* depicts the king—like Peniboy Canter, Goodstock, Lady Tub, and Awdrey's parents—looking forward to his children's children and back to his own roots:

> To see his Native *Countrey,* and his Cradle,
> And find those manners there, which he suck'd in
> With Nurses Milke, and Parents pietie!
>
> (311–13)

26. *Ben Jonson and the Language of Prose Comedy* (Cambridge, Mass.: Harvard University Press, 1960), p. 269.

27. H&S, 9:163. See also Clifford Leech's introduction to *The Triumph of Peace,* in *A Book of Masques,* pp. 277–80; and D. F. McKenzie's trenchant discussion of Jonson, Prynne, Shirley's masque, and censorship, in *A Celebration of Ben Jonson,* pp. 107–11. Christopher Hill, *Milton and the English Revolution* (New York: Penguin Books, 1979), pp. 19–21, argues that cultural insularity accompanied

the growing political and religious isolation of Charles's court: "Ben Jonson represents the last attempt to infuse moral commitment into court art; and he was first absorbed into the court and then ultimately squeezed out" (p. 20).

28. Orgel, *The Jonsonian Masque*, pp. 19–21.

29. Enck, *Comic Truth*, p. 230. *Love's Triumph through Callipolis* (pp. 107ff.) presents similar epithetical characters.

30. Ben Jonson, *Masque of Queens*, line 95 (Jonson's note). Significantly, it is in this masque that Jonson first develops the antimasque as a crucial component of the overall form. Felperin, *Shakespearean Romance*, p. 24, includes Maudlin in a discussion of "the Atè figures who stalk the boards of Elizabethan romance."

31. Thomas M. Greene discusses the "openness of Jonson's last dramatic home—the bower of Robin Hood and Marian" and *The Sad Shepherd's* "fresh urge to venture out," in "Ben Jonson and the Centered Self," *Studies in English Literature* 10 (1970): 347–48.

32. Felperin, *Shakespearean Romance*, pp. 304–5.

33. "Ben Jonson," from *Selected Essays 1917–32;* reprinted in *Ben Jonson: A Collection of Critical Essays,* ed. Jonas Barish (Englewood Cliffs, N.J.: Prentice-Hall, 1963), p. 15. My exhortation has been anticipated by the recent fine work of such critics as those cited above and others, especially Ian Donaldson.

Tragicomic Romance for the King's Men, 1609–1611: Shakespeare, Beaumont, and Fletcher

Lee Bliss

> To remark the folly of the fiction, the absurdity of the conduct, . . . and the impossibility of the events in any system of life, were to waste criticism upon unresisting imbecility, upon faults too evident for detection, and too gross for aggravation.
>
> General Observation on *Cymbeline*, *The Plays of Shakespeare*, ed. Samuel Johnson, 1765

Until the twentieth century's reassessment of romance, Dr. Johnson's dismissal of *Cymbeline* might have summed up a widespread response to Shakespeare's last plays. With the possible exception of *The Tempest*, redeemed by its otherworldy charm and tantalizing autobiographical potential, here was a sad falling off indeed after the tragic heights of *Lear* and *Antony and Cleopatra*, even *Coriolanus*. Despite the recent critical exaltation of Shakespeare's romances, Dr. Johnson's evaluation still describes, for most critics, Beaumont and Fletcher's contemporary ventures in the same mode. Condemned in their own right, they are also seen as initiating a period of general decadence: they ape Shakespeare while missing the essential point of those last Olympian summations of an entire moral as well as dramatic career. Posterity has rendered its judgment, but it might be well to remember that the seventeenth century favored *Pericles*, *Philaster*, and *A King and No King*.

For their contemporaries, Shakespeare and Beaumont and Fletcher successfully met the same social and theatrical challenge: the expanded audience provided by the King's Men's acquisition of a private theater in addition to the Globe, and the new vogue for dramatic romance. Arguments over whether *Cymbeline* influenced *Philaster*, or vice versa, are perhaps not only inconclusive but beside the point, for interest in romance may have stemmed from the reprinting and perhaps revival of *Mucedorus* in 1606, the 1605 edition of *The Arcadia*, or such Sidney-derived comedies for the children's companies as Day's

Isle of Gulls and *Humour out of Breath*. Moreover, Beaumont and Fletcher as well
as Shakespeare seem to have undertaken encouragingly successful trial efforts at
romance that might themselves explain the more characteristic *Philaster* and
Cymbeline: *Cupid's Revenge*, an "Arcadian tragedy" fashioned out of Sidney for the
boys of the Queen's Revels; and *Pericles*, Shakespeare's probably collaborative
and certainly more archaic first romance. Ashley Thorndike's argument for
Beaumont and Fletcher's priority has been largely rejected (more on grounds of
"Bardolatry" than logic), but his description of this new type of play suggests how
similar, in very general terms, the plays are, how explicable their appeal to the
same audience. With the exception of *The Maid's Tragedy*, all these largely "non-
historical heroic plays" are tragicomic, and all mix "tragic and idyllic events, a
series of highly improbable events, heroic and sentimental characters, foreign
scenes, happy dénouements."[1] Later commentators stress another shared feature: the literary self-consciousness distinguishing this return to older, non-
dramatic sources of inspiration. Naive, popular, and so-called escapist subject
matter is handled with great technical sophistication, and the art that seeks to
transform romance into drama is not a self-effacing one. The plays' own
awareness of themselves as art and evident enjoyment of the "technical brilliance" of their dramatic solutions appeal—and are intended to appeal—to a no-
longer naive audience.[2] As a type of romance, then, these plays mark a distinct
departure from prevalent earlier dramatic forms, both for their authors and, in
their enormous popularity, for Jacobean theatrical taste. Earlier experiments in
romance and tragicomedy—in *Twelfth Night* or the problem plays, in *The Knight
of the Burning Pestle* or *The Faithful Shepherdess*—hardly predict the common
elements in Shakespeare's astonishing turn from tragedy and in the major works
of Beaumont and Fletcher's brief but immensely influential partnership.

Ignoring such similarities obscures the larger importance of these plays as a
group, written for the period's most influential theatrical company and popular
well into the Restoration. Echoes of Shakespeare mark all Beaumont and
Fletcher's plays and further support at least an appearance of superficial resemblance, if not downright déjà vu.[3] Still, the plays capping the career of the
most famous Elizabethan dramatist and inaugurating that of his principal successor reveal differences as well as resemblance, and with such differences this
essay will be concerned. Considering the plays together helps distinguish the
structural and thematic features that allow *Cymbeline, Winter's Tale*, and *Tempest*,
on the one hand, and *Philaster, Maid's Tragedy*, and *King and No King*, on the
other, to epitomize the passing of one order and establishment of the next.[4]
Generically, *The Maid's Tragedy* seems the odd woman out (though in the Restoration Edmund Waller turned it, too, to tragicomedy), yet it is one of Beaumont
and Fletcher's most interesting plays and central to understanding the evolution
of a dramaturgy that then served Fletcher, and his numerous collaborators, for
another fifteen years. *The Maid's Tragedy* also deals most clearly with the young
playwrights' attitude toward art and so helps illuminate their divergence from
Shakespeare as well as the development of their own tragicomic form. The
comparison aims to be descriptive rather than evaluative; if discussion is

weighted, it will be toward Beaumont and Fletcher, allowing Shakespeare's better-known plays to clarify the technique and attitudes of his now infamous younger colleagues.

Initial selection of material suggests some pertinent differences in taste. However Shakespeare came upon *Pericles,* he accepted its terms and completed the old "mouldy tale" as his own. His first romance reaches back to this genre's archetypes, and an archaic flavor is maintained not only in the episodic sweep of its fabulous events, in its tone and flat characterization, but in Gower's insistent intrusiveness as chorus and in the old-fashioned language and apparent naiveté with which he mediates between his ancient auctors and the immediacy of his tale's physical representation. Shakespeare moves toward more modern sources with the wager story for *Cymbeline,* with Greene's *Pandosto* for *The Winter's Tale,* and with the original collocation of Carribean adventure reports for *The Tempest;* he also begins to set his romance stories within more sharply defined political frameworks. He never relinquishes an essential predilection for the marvelous in event or for the ways in which supernatural forces unexpectedly interpenetrate human affairs. Strange potions and doctors with astonishing powers mix comfortably with tales of long-lost children, "miraculous" preservation from death, oracular riddles, and implied or staged theophany. Unconstrained by a narrative source, *The Tempest* uses the most modern political complications to enclose the most fabulous romance setting, and with the shipwrecked tourists we experience an Alice-in-Wonderland sojourn into a parallel world beyond normal time and space.

If Shakespeare takes us back, in Bishop Hurd's phrase, to "fine fabling" at its most imaginative, Beaumont and Fletcher turn first to the great Renaissance romancers, Montemayor, Spenser, and especially Sidney. Given Beaumont's treatment in *The Knight of the Burning Pestle* of popular tales of peripatetic love-and-adventure, as well as Fletcher's delicately pastoral *Faithful Shepherdess,* the choice of sophisticated, philosophical, and aristocratic romance—with its emphasis on love and honor and princely education—seems deliberate. Indeed, taking his cue for the early tragicomedies from a red-handed plundering of *The Arcadia* in *Cupid's Revenge,* Andrew Gurr asserts that Beaumont and Fletcher's tragicomedy dramatizes not particular stories but a genre, the traditional prose romance. Beaumont and Fletcher are "literary gentry" writing "to a bookish rather than a theatrical specification" and attempting to translate "the high literary and educational designs of Sidney's *Arcadia* into commercial drama."[5] Gurr helpfully points to the kind of tale and characters the young playwrights favored, though he misses another major "source" and interest: contemporary drama, particularly Marston and, above all, Shakespeare. Beaumont and Fletcher's borrowing of lines, scenes, and situations from Shakespeare (especially *Hamlet*) begins with *The Woman Hater* and *The Faithful Shepherdess;* more important, after the aesthetic confusion of *Cupid's Revenge,* they discover a coherent tragicomic structure for *Philaster* through a rather more self-conscious fusion of *Hamlet* and *Othello* with Shakespeare's most romantic comedy, *Twelfth Night.*[6]

Yet the dramatists are moving in different directions. Despite Sidney and Shakespeare, Illyria is largely excluded from Beaumont and Fletcher's early plays. After *Cupid's Revenge* and *The Faithful Shepherdess,* gods and miraculous landscapes disappear. Locales are remote but not particularly exotic; they do not open out in adventurous excursions or offer pastoral interludes rich in alternative possibilities. Indeed, the tragicomedies' world nearly matches that of *The Maid's Tragedy* in claustrophobic intensity. The wood in *Philaster* provides merely a locus for the full efflorescence of personal despair; although in *A King and No King* the interspersed scenes of Gobrius, Penthea, and Arane tantalizingly hint at the nearness of resolution, they take place in the court and ostensibly complicate and heighten an increasingly unbearable tension. Subplots offer no sense of openness or mysterious potential, in man or nature.

Stories and their working out, possibilities seized or rejected, display both convergence and contrast in fundamental interests and attitudes. In all these romances political concerns remain subordinate, and their resolution awaits the exploration and untangling of the personal difficulties that constitute the dramatists' primary focus. All reflect a Jacobean interest in psychology, frequently those abnormal states in which the mind bows under extreme contradictions among desire, fear, and fact; though emphasis varies, all probe the subjective effects of illusion and delusion. Characters try to supplant or deny reality in favor of their own private truth. *A King and No King* and *The Tempest* both subordinate other interests to this attempt, though the protagonists' degree of success differs. In his martial boasting and response to Panthea, Arbaces seeks to impose his desired reality on his court. To his subjects, his assertions of "fact" are astonishing and ridiculous (albeit frightening). His words lack the godlike force he claims, and his effort collapses; he is saved, in good tragicomic fashion, by a reality that more truly satisfies his wishes. An older and now wiser Prospero succeeds where Arbaces (and Leontes) fail. His vision extends beyond himself, to a moral life in which men can effect some compromise between Gonzalo's wistful ideal and Antonio's harsh opportunism. Prospero spends his play attempting to impose his dream on a group of men that for twelve-odd years has ignored the dream's existence, and the dreamer's. With the aid of a magic that can apparently transform the external world, and some good luck in the matter of Ferdinand's natural virtue and unforced attraction to Miranda, Prospero triumphs, at least in the crucial instances.

The plays all involve, and usually resolve into, questions of romantic love; from romance they take love's confrontation with friendship, honor, and public life. *Cymbeline* and *The Winter's Tale, The Maid's Tragedy* and *Philaster* center on love's faith. All explore the way inconstancy dissolves the lover's sense of self, destroys his world's goodness and rationality, and even threatens the possibility of trust on which the larger community is founded. Posthumus and Philaster respond to apparent infidelity with analogous denunciations of all womanhood. Philaster wishes to die himself as well as punish Arethusa and Bellario, while Posthumus plots his wife's death, razes his identity, and as a mean soldier seeks annihilation in war. In *The Maid's Tragedy,* desertion pushes Aspatia into psychological as well as physical isolation, and, in disguise, she provokes a real love-death in place of the marital one denied her by Amintor's inconstancy. Amintor is in turn devastated by Evadne's horrible truth, and from the "dream" he resists believing he wakes to a nightmare reality in which the shattered self plays fragmentary and contradictory parts—happy bridegroom, loyal subject, irate revenger, repentant deserter of true love, murderer, suicide. The first half of *The Winter's Tale* deepens Philaster's response to double betrayal and pursues its terrible, logical consequences. Initially, the whole Sicilian court seems to lie in the level of Leontes's dreams, as with royal power he proceeds to exterminate in literal-minded fashion all badges of his former identity: wife, baby, friend; his idyllic childhood, now retrospectively poisoned; his own and Sicily's hope of succession; the gods' favor. Apparent success leaves him with nothing; he awakens to the life-in-death of a hermit dedicated to perpetual mourning.

The story of Posthumus's or Leontes's jealousy and its consequences hardly accounts for the plays in which they appear, however, and this fact points to a distinguishing characteristic of Shakespeare's last works: scope. In physical sweep, the lure of these mouldy old tales builds on a lifetime of theatrical wanderlust. The stark narrative leaps of *Pericles* modulate into Imogen's flight and adventures as Fidele, the shifts from Britain to Rome, court to Welsh camp, battlefield or prison. The later plays may be less episodically constructed, but *The Winter's Tale* offers well-defined, opposed locales, sea voyages and storms, surprise appearances by Time and an ursine stage-clearer; *The Tempest,* at least in report, encompasses a known Italy and contemporary political intrigue, quasi-classical Carthage, and a fantastic island among whose spirits, magician, and princess Ulysses would have felt at home. Geographical expanse is complemented by temporal depth: all Shakespeare's late romances work their resolutions through the cycles of human generation, and final harmony depends both on the healing effects of time and the vital optimism of youth. In *Cymbeline* this theme appears in most muted form, but if the Posthumus-Imogen plot closely resembles *Philaster*'s, the story of the kidnapped princes provides a sudden sense of history and duration even as it recalls the fabulous losses and restorations of *Pericles* and looks forward to the final plays. Multiple plots, interspersed or sequentially developed through time (plus healthy chunks of narrative exposition!), allow Shakespeare to dramatize both generations, combine romance wonders with modern intrigue, and generally project a world both rich in character types and classes and open to the possibilities for renewal offered by chance, the operations of time, and youth's natural innocence.

Beaumont and Fletcher have been condemned for narrowing the scope of Renaissance drama, contracting its issues while presenting—and appealing to—only a small segment of its richly diversified audience. That their plots are generally single and developed logically and sequentially, in a relatively short though unspecified time, is true, as is the general impression of a cast of characters seldom ranging beneath the gentry. If we recall the sophisticated multiple plotting of *The Woman Hater* and *Knight of the Burning Pestle,* and the adequate if not inspired mixtures of the *The Captain* and *The Coxcomb* (comedies c. 1609–12, the latter for a children's company), the restriction seems intentional. Beaumont and Fletcher forgo the advantages of diffuseness to gain those of concentration.

For them the interaction between generations holds no interest. *Philaster*'s

King exists only as political tyrant and blocking father figure for Arethusa's intended romantic comedy; in *A King and No King,* Gobrius's paternal function consists of providing the crucial fact that transforms his distraught son into happy consort for the natural queen. Playwrights persistently accused of constructing plots as mere scaffolds for emotional confrontations turn their backs, in *The Maid's Tragedy,* on some very promising sentimental material in the Calianax-Aspatia relation. The wronged and desperate daughter never meets her father on stage; Calianax never expands beyond blustering coward and comic foil to Melantius. Beaumont and Fletcher's subject is idealistic adolescence, trembling on the brink of adult commitment and decisive action, and youth's first confrontation with experience and disillusionment. They are obsessed with the "Hamlet dilemma," but it is *Hamlet* without act 5 and transposed from a predominately political situation into a largely private and subjective one. The shift in emphasis makes echoes of Othello and Troilus appropriate but also dilutes the action's scope and the protagonists' tragic stature. Assertions of an undramatized nobility and courage produce characters who resemble Shakespeare's Bertram, Claudio, and the Posthumus of *Cymbeline's* first two acts, or Marston's Antonio.

Though we will return to their qualification, two points might be made here about these vacillating, self-obsessed young men, so popular in their own time and so remarkably repellent to modern eyes. First, dramatic allusions to *Hamlet* obscure crucial differences. However idealized by despair, the heroic past by which Hamlet measures his world offers a locus, a reality, to the values condemning present kingship, marriage, friendship, trust. Beaumont and Fletcher's young men have no fathers, their world no past. The vision with which they confront the world is an altogether more literary one, a grafting of the bright highmindedness and ready-made goals of romance onto childhood's fantasies of security and omnipotence. They wrap themselves in a dream, try to shape their lives by the "plot" of an earlier age's fictionalized golden world, and they attempt to maintain the role of ideal lover or warrior in the face of all contrary evidence. Second, the plays' reality, however artificial it may seem to us, refuses to conform to romance conventions: the tests of love and friendship do not appear in recognizable or acceptable form. Both internal and external imperatives shatter the dream—and dream self—and provoke psychic crisis.

The component of human existence for which romance offers perhaps the least useful program of conduct is mature sexuality, and this inherently sensational subject matter, so prominent a thread in Shakespeare's problem plays as well as his romances, becomes the central test in Beaumont and Fletcher's more restrictedly private focus. By manipulating conventional romance *topoi,* Beaumont and Fletcher force upon their heroes the inadequacy of the traditional moralized split between Petrarchan worship and inherently perverse sexual desire. Philaster is faced not with a situation in which he and his friend adore the same woman and can exercise their nobility in deciding who will choose friendship over love, but with the accusation that his betrothed and treasured page are already secret lovers. Amintor confronts an Evadne who shockingly admits her sexual eagerness and then informs him that as husband he must remain the chaste cover for her adultery with the king. Love at first sight in *King and No King* is immediately discovered to be sexual, violent, and, for Arbaces and Panthea, apparently incestuous. The witty inversion of Petrarchan conceits, which both shocks and appeals to our literary sophistication,[7] is not the only point of these scenes, nor are unusual sexual predicaments presented solely for extradramatic thrills. The force and range of sexual desire highlights one of romance's limitations; it also conveniently marks off adulthood's ambiguous complexity, our participation in human frailty and fall from childhood innocence. Shakespeare's Leontes recognizes its implications: from the position of king, husband, and father he tries to deny the "imposition . . . Hereditary ours" and regain the integrity and purity of Mamillius's "play" by wiping out the evidence of a manhood now seen as inherently corrupt.

The vacillation of Beaumont and Fletcher's heroes, their refusal or inability to act, and their recurrent death wishes, all suggest a refusal to cross the threshold on which they stand. They face sexual betrayal where they sought confirmation, broken commitment where they expected idealized love and marriage. And it is not simply their world that refuses to meet the dream's terms, for by their own complicity they betray themselves. As Philaster tempts Bellario to reveal Arethusa's physical charms or Amintor anticipates losing his "lusty youth" in Evadne's royally prescribed embraces, the desire they deny or ignore in themselves peeps through their language. All women may be tainted, but so are they and the existence to which they are asked to commit themselves. The rationalization of behavior, the attempt to deny contradiction by being all things to all people, the schizophrenic "splitting," all desperately attempt to salvage at least part of the dream. Retreat seems the better part of valor. Though Arethusa, the more dangerous the more desired, has passed beyond the bounds of idealization, romance's absolute friendship can perhaps be asserted. To Bellario, Philaster declares that "a love from me to thee/Is firm, whate'er thou dost," though it requires trusting honest looks "though I know 'em false" (3.1.285–86, 281). Amintor begs Evadne to deny her words, make her truth a bad dream from which he can wake to his earlier fantasied fulfillment. He grasps at the doctrine of the king's immunity partly to rationalize his abhorrence of his own situation and, in immediate terms, of any act that would bind him to it, signal his acceptance, and define publicly an Amintor wholly incompatible with his idealized self-image. Melantius knows better than to trust women (his own mistress's heart is "stone, no better"). He maintains absolute dedication, for "The name of friend is more than family,/Or all the world besides," and to him the bewildered Amintor retreats: "ay, thy love, Melantius—/Why, I have nothing else" (3.2.169–70, 258–59). Despite all the talk of honor, the code no longer fits, and the protagonists (at least intermittently) know it. There is no way to make the dream real; passivity offers no more satisfactory a solution than action, as the careers of Euphrasia, Aspatia, and Panthea demonstrate. Finally, the only "honor" lies in more complete retreat, in the death that refuses the world's conditions and atones for one's own failings.

If we are appalled by the lengths to which these adolescents will go to refuse reality's claims, the lives they will sacrifice to maintain their own conviction of innocence, and the self-indulgence with which they wrap themselves in their tormented emotions, we must also recognize a truth, however narrow and unattractive, in their presentation. They may have appealed to a proto-Cavalier taste for "adolescent intensities," a crumbling political order hankering for just such ideals and absolutes,[8] but beneath the contemporary trappings and code words lies a human predicament of universal applicability. The characters may be abstractions from the full human personality, but they are not wholly unreal or without the power to elicit our self-recognition. This psychological fidelity explains some of the sympathy that is necessary if plays centering on such protagonists are to work dramatically,[9] and, to be fair, Beaumont and Fletcher develop their characters' predicament to its natural end. The despair, self-absorption, and pointless suicides of *The Maid's Tragedy* merely complete a process arrested by the tragicomedies' fortunate resolutions. With the exception of Tigranes, the subplot prince of *King and No King,* and possibly of Philaster, who sees (though he cannot maintain) the kind of active faith needed to safe-guard love in marriage, Beaumont and Fletcher's characters are rescued in spite of their unchanged selves. Arbaces repents, but only after a long, quite humor-ous exchange in which his father and "mother" try with great difficulty to tell him the saving news of his true identity. The tragicomedies provide generically appropriate happy endings, but their resolutions remain provocatively in-complete, self-consciously aware of their own inadequacy.

Audience sympathy, and the protagonists' despair, also stems from the nature of the plays' social and political settings. Discovering sexuality may be the sensa-tional and immediate personal spur to confusion, but these young men also face a thoroughly disillusioned, complacently self-interested court. As petty and venal as other men, Beaumont and Fletcher's kings lack any redeeming regal features; they are colorless, frequently anonymous tyrants whose embrace of sin is often more comically inept than frightening. More important, the courts are peopled with smuttily knowing, cynical and "sophisticated" gentlemen who, despite their satiric comments and revolutionary talk, will not themselves act against the royalty they criticize. At best, *Philaster's* Dion, willing to second Megra's falsehood to gain a political end even though his lie devastates the man he would have king; at worst, *The Maid's Tragedy's* gentlemen of the king's chamber who would "have a snap" at Evadne "one of these nights as she goes from him," or the toady braggart Bessus, who will happily arrange the incest that so shocks his king, Arbaces.

A world of apparently casual betrayal and impenetrable pretense, it fosters doubt of even the closest friends and loved ones. The young women become victims of slander or arbitrary edicts, the young men hopelessly confused by contradictory imperatives and a world in which, as Philaster bewails of his page, "the face you [gods] let him wear/When he was innocent is still the same,/Not blasted; is this justice?" (3.1.153–55). Given the contradictions between Evadne's admitted nature and her sound sleeps and breath as "sweet as April," how can Amintor trust that Melantius too is not "by the course/Of nature . . . dissembling as the sea" (3.1.40, 58–60)? Indeed, when charged by Calianax, Melantius suc-cessfully transposes appearances and reality and convinces the king of his inno-cence. Such guiltfree inversions baffle moral judgment, and Calianax might well join in Amintor's cry: "I'll be guilty too/If these be the effects" (3.1.40–41). In *Philaster*, Arethusa and Bellario are in fact as innocent as they look, but the courtiers and king easily believe their guilt (and Ligones leaps to the same conclusion about his daughter in *King and No King*). Since Dion willingly corroborates Megra's charge and Arethusa lacks tangible "means . . . To clear myself," she finds, like Hermione on trial, that her constancy "lies in your belief" (5.5.42–43). Yet how can faith persist in an age all agree "We dare not trust our wills to" (1.1.317)?

In Shakespeare's romance worlds disastrous misjudgments in love—like those of Posthumus and Leontes—are countered by the intuitive rightness of attraction elsewhere: Guiderius's and Arviragus's for Fidele, Florizel's for Perdita, Ferdinand's for Prospero and Miranda. Good counsellors balance bad, and faith between men can be maintained in spite of slander and threats, as Pisanio, Camillo, and Gonzalo demonstrate. In Beaumont and Fletcher, *A King and No King*'s Spaconia rightly distrusts Tigranes' constancy, and good men, like Mardonius, can neither cure nor circumvent their erring king's folly. This world discounts grandeur as well as goodness. The continual eruption of low comedy—the buffoons like Calianax and Bessus who serve as grotesque foils and parallels for their plays' protagonists—keep "the scale of things small" and return us frequently to the gross and petty.[10]

Attitudes toward human potential reflect more general schemes of value. In Shakespeare love can mend as well as destroy, effect the beneficent loss of self that transports the youthful Florizel out of childhood's narcissism and into loving care and the proper valuation of power and rank. Loss repeatedly proves the gateway to self-knowledge and spontaneous repentance. And human events mirror larger natural patterns: rough seas can prove kind; a missed chance can be redeemed by golden opportunity; what was carefully destroyed may yet prove to have been saved. In short, the benevolent coincidences that provide the occasion for final resolution—*Cymbeline*'s fifth-act conjunction of all the principal characters (and the queen's convenient suicide), Camillo's fortuitous presence and advice at the moment of the lovers' flight or Autolycus's meeting with the one source of Perdita's history, the voyage that brings the men of sin within the orbit of Prospero's magic—all seem part and parcel of a providence that has operated throughout.

Beaumont and Fletcher's world is one of apparently certain betrayal and hostility on all fronts. Aspatia's comments on the embroidered tale of Ariadne abandoned by Theseus suggest that Amintor merely reenacts an old story. The standard of virtue by which characters condemn each other is not a "natural" one. Beyond the court lies neither moral nor physical comfort, only bestial sexuality or the primitive, virtuous but ugly, peasant life to which both Mardonius and Philaster consider fleeing. Despite their happy resolutions, the tragicomedies do not imply a world order fundamentally different from that of *The Maid's Tragedy*. There, seas can only be unkind, "Tempting the merchant" and then "destroying all/'A carries on him" (3.1.62–65); they allow Theseus to escape because they represent a power equally amoral: "Could the gods know this/And none of all their number raise a storm?/But they are all as ill" (2.2.49–51). The initial wedding masque captures this world perfectly and provides the opposite of Prospero's idealistic vision. The containment of Boreas fails, as it does within the play proper. No more than the human king he supposedly "flatters" can Neptune order reality to obey his words; envy and ambition work everywhere to invert order, and even Night covets to "hold" her place "and outshine the Day" (1.2.135).[11] In such a world the tragicomedies' happy endings must seem improbable. Although individual characters may express gratitude for heaven's aid, the plays' events have not validated these verbal ascriptions; plot resolutions stress their unmiraculous and very human origin.

Whatever destructive force Shakespeare's natural world reveals, it is held in check, ultimately negated, by powers of goodness with which man can learn to harmonize himself. Shakespeare's characters, however erring, can thus recover themselves in a way Beaumont and Fletcher's cannot. Posthumus and even Iachimo spontaneously repent their unnatural behavior, while Mamillius's death shows Leontes his mistake; imitating nature's justice, the sinners exile themselves from the human community they feel they have violated. Alonso's loss awakens a conscience that now can hear the billows speak to tell him of his "trespass." There is no world elsewhere in Beaumont and Fletcher, no countryside where natural virtue can flower untainted while biding the proper time for its saving reintegration into "civilized" society. Moreover, guilt is seldom re-creative. In Beaumont and Fletcher the shock of disillusionment is all; men do not progress, through healing time, to the second half of Shakespeare's romances. Beaumont and Fletcher's young protagonists lose themselves in the gap separating the code of morality embodied in their dream romance from their discovery of things as they are. Such discovery threatens to unravel an entire system of belief and instead confirm man's participation in a nature inimical to civilization: the possibility of their own involvement—such as Amintor's consideration that "the king first mov'd me to 't, but he/Has not my will in keeping" (2.1.126–27)—must be rejected. These protagonists swing disjunctively from denial to extravagant, despairing acceptance because they have lost their own moorings. Both disaster and final good fortune come to seem equally dreamlike and unreal. For these characters, their sense of alienation is not self-punishment but a solitude thrust upon them, a betrayal by others that cannot be fit to any intelligible or just order. With the bewildered Evadne (and Middleton's later tragic heroines) they might well cry out, "Gods, where have I been all this time? How friended,/That I should lose myself thus desperately,/And none for pity show me how I wander'd?" (4.1.179–81).

Shakespeare's last plays encompass the slow growth of repentance and forgiveness over time; they move through human cycles toward genuine integration of the individual—with himself, with those he betrayed, with nature—and, with evil converted or contained, toward a consensus of values. Physical restorations—of people, of the proper political order—come only with the re-creation of personal meanings, and the sequence of action suggests cause and effect connections. The individual recovers his sons, wife, daughter, realm because he himself has changed and now treasures the relationships he once spurned. Banished values, as well as people, have been reestablished. The sense of loss touching these conclusions makes the victory seem hard-won and therefore durable. The marvelous and the naturalistic meet: astonishing coincidence is paid for with permanent deprivation, with characters who cannot be restored, and with the time—even a lifetime—that has passed unlived.

In Beaumont and Fletcher's conclusions the gods remain offstage and uninvolved, and events are more fully explicable by rational means. Yet these plays seem anything but "realistic"; they stress the disjunction between a character and the event his actions have brought about. The concentration on one psychological moment, protracted through numerous recapitulations, the indifference to time, and, in the tragicomedies, the ostentatiously tidy avoidance of disaster all sever potential links between the play's world and the audience's. Rather tightly developed plot sequences, working out at double-time the "logical" consequences of some initial premise, and more satiric court milieus accentuate the effect of withheld or only hinted information: the resolutions seem less wondrous than arbitrary and wittily surprising. Even in tragedy this effect persists. *The Maid's Tragedy*'s principal characters may be marked for death from the beginning, but the conjunction of a disguised Aspatia, Amintor, and the bloody Evadne is as unpredictable as the way in which they neatly execute a complex triple suicide.

Beaumont and Fletcher's characteristic emphasis on fragmentation is of course clearest in the tragedy. Having secured his revenge and forced a pardon from the new king, Melantius returns to find his success baffled by Amintor's unexpected suicide. More important, the one value that had promised to withstand pressure and enable action suddenly appears as hollow and self-contradictory as the various meanings of honor into which that concept finally dissolves. The absolute friendship that claims Amintor as "sister, father, brother, son,/All that I had" proves to be self-regarding egotism (5.3.268–69). Melantius easily sacrifices his sister in his own and Amintor's interests, but his actions also trample his friend's wishes, and, in persevering, Melantius helps destroy the life he sought to redeem. Amintor can face neither his own deeds nor Evadne's. Melantius's revenge solves nothing; his plan drives Evadne mad and pushes Amintor into a final confrontation with Aspatia to which Melantius and his "honor" and love are all irrelevant. The play ends anticlimactically: the successful Melantius is left stunned, confused, and suicidal, while the largely unchanged court blandly asserts the traditional values whose disintegration we have witnessed. *The Maid's Tragedy* self-destructs, leaving only the shell of a conventional shape and moral, and in more muted form this pattern underlies the tragicomedies as well.

While Shakespeare's last three plays look back to the very roots of romance, and to *Pericles* and the unearthly tone of its conclusion, Beaumont and Fletcher's Sidneian choreography of movement and speech remains detached and frequently satiric. Their plays are already at a double remove: they refer to rather than re-create romance's special world; they allude to—sometimes extensively crib from—earlier Jacobean plays. Beaumont and Fletcher's plays work toward surprise, not wonder; and teasing hints of solution, such as Gobrius's as early as act 2, scene 1 of *King and No King*, focus our attention on the means by which the dramatists will manage to save their characters rather than on the resolution itself—on, that is, an aesthetic and technical rather than a primarily emotional response. Action is repeatedly rationalized, even overexplained. It is not allowed to evoke our participation in mysteries beyond full comprehension. *A King and No King* comes closest to full resolution and some sense of wondrous completion: Tigranes is reunited with Spaconia, Arbaces is repentant and now a worthy husband. Yet the absoluteness of passion's sway throughout, the reiterated bewilderment at sins thrust "Helpless upon me," work against the celebratory conclusion and our belief that Arbaces has truly learned, with Tigranes, what it means to have the "passions of a man" (5.4.64; 5.2.88). In *Philaster* and *The Maid's Tragedy* our sense of dislocation survives the ending. The surprise revelation of Bellario's true identity stabilizes a situation about to dissolve into recapitulating the play we have seen; it also leaves Bellario-Euphrasia as a barely assimilable loose end, an image of frustrated love and devotion that can never win its proper reward. Beaumont and Fletcher concentrate on the pathos of her circumstances at the end of *Philaster,* just as they force *The Maid's Tragedy* to its anticlimactic ending and to the despair with which Melantius confronts his "success."

Because of man's propensity to betray self and others and to retreat to wholly self-referential meanings, romance's ideal fidelity can be maintained only in death. This potentially tragic knowledge underlies the tragicomedies' uneasy resolutions. Beaumont and Fletcher leave us with reunited lovers but with no convincing affirmation of man's ability to win through guilt to any other-directed awareness on which trust could securely base itself. Because the challenge to romance's fabric of belief implies such a horrifyingly complete reduction of man to beast, the challenge itself must be denied. The Calibans and Antonios of this world, or in oneself, cannot be accepted and thus forgiven and transcended. Beaumont and Fletcher's characters are thrust into glimpsing Lear's world, but they retreat as quickly as possible from metaphysical significance and seek comfort in surface meanings, in reputation and in the social codes that prescribe choice.

Structurally as well as thematically, Shakespeare gradually submerges us in romance. We may start with the relatively probable and contemporary, but we soon move into another world, one in which long-lost royal children prove themselves buds of nobler race, where two boys, an old man, and a shabby soldier defeat the Roman army, and unmapped islands produce strange noises and stranger inhabitants. Dreamlike unreality proves true and supplants the old known world; boundaries of belief as well as situation dissolve, and things monstrous to human reason come wondrously to pass. Self-conscious primitivism in technique expresses Shakespeare's sophistication—in theatrical practice, in literary experience, in a lifetime's verbal and dramatic experimentation. Revealing the influence of a younger Shakespeare and the satiric plays of 1600–1605, Beaumont and Fletcher's dramaturgy is altogether more conventional, their form closed to any sense of unforeseen human potential. Instead of invoking romance and its conventions directly, they continue to play its assumptions off against a satirically conceived dramatic world. Traditional heroic and amatory *topoi* are present but in inverted or grotesquely comic form. Juxtaposed scenes and minor characters—like Megra, Calianax, and Bessus—throw love and honor into question; major figures like Evadne and even Arbaces and Panthea make conventional ideals seem fairy-tale impossibilities. Until the very end, dream and reality do not—cannot—coalesce, and the plays move on two levels: a private world of anguished soliloquy and desperate, subjective assertion, and a public world of ugly and seemingly immutable fact. Although especially evident in Arbaces's claims for the royal fiat, in all the plays language tries repeatedly and unsuccessfully to dictate and transform unassimilable truths. Beaumont and Fletcher's plays, like their characters, remain stuck where they began, endlessly reenacting their initial scenes of bewildered disillusionment. Neither literally nor metaphorically do they move us to any new realm in which men might be tested but also freed.

Beaumont and Fletcher's structure does not fully resolve ironies of character or presentation, and a note of mockery—of the characters, of the ending itself—remains. The disbelief and dawning joy with which Philaster greets the news of Bellario's sex—the repeated "It is a woman!"—provoke our laughter, and the extended, even parodied, father-child recognition scene here, or in *A King and No King,* draws our attention to its artifice and to the playwrights' amused elaboration of a generic *topos.* Narrative jumps and scenes introducing new characters from beyond the court further reinforce a detachment only intermittently challenged by an emotionally charged soliloquy or duet. Even *Philaster,* the play most Shakespearian in tone and resolution as well as structure, uses interspersed scenes to undercut the heroic plot's concerns and provide a pattern of commentary-through-juxtaposition typical of earlier Jacobean satiric drama. The Country Fellow's cheerful goodwill and bumptious naiveté about court matters explode our acceptance of Philaster's attempt to kill Arethusa (after she has refused him the same fatal solace). What had seemed the inexorable, tragic result of court intrigue on exquisitely refined sensibilities suddenly enters a new context: "I know not your rhetoric, but I can lay it on if you touch the woman" (4.5.97–98). A rustic clod whose language betrays him to our laughter as well as to the protagonists' aristocratic scorn, the Country Fellow also introduces a new standard by which we see, momentarily, the lovers' hyperbole as rant, their emotional fluidity as hysteria, their code of honor and manners as sophistical and mad. In *A King and No King,* act 2, scene 2, the hilarious interchange between citizens and artisans, and their comments on Arbace's triumphal public address, serve a similar function.

The playing with aesthetic distance, the moment-to-moment manipulation of the audience's engagement, of course belongs to tragicomedy, not merely to Beaumont and Fletcher. It distinguishes each of Shakespeare's structurally varied final experiments. In Shakespeare, as in Beaumont and Fletcher, characters move out of, and then back into, generic stereotypes and abstract moralizing; our immediate involvement with them and their story is intermittent, "disciplined and calculatedly occasional."[12] Comic ironies can surround even the most sympathetic characters. In a particularly Beaumont-and-Fletcher scene, Imogen mistakes the unspeakable Cloten's headless body for her husband's, not merely by the borrowed "meanest garments" but because she recognizes "the shape of 's leg . . . His foot Mercurial: his Martial thigh" (4.2.309–10). With its multiple revelations, presented at double-time pace, the ending of *Cymbeline,* too, has an archly self-conscious theatricality like that of Beaumont and Fletcher and the earlier problem plays from which they learned so much. Yet even in *Cymbeline* Shakespeare organizes his techniques—his blending of old-fashioned devices into a new, "open form" dramaturgy[13]—toward a thematic resolution characteristic of all his last plays. Disjunctive presentation and the late introduction of new characters look toward final synthesis, and disparate plot threads at last merge into harmony. With Cloten and the calculatingly ambitious queen gone, revelations and self-confessions provide a stable new political and social order; intuitive understanding welcomes this mysterious restoration and issues in a gratuitous gesture toward renewed community with Rome and universal peace.

Oscillation of tones, multiple perspectives, and the varying level of our involvement in Shakespeare's romances thus enhance the final revelation that transforms discord into wonder, nature into art. The romances build toward these visionary moments: the dream-appearance of Jupiter; the enshrined statue of "dead" Hermione; the illusions and masque by which Prospero turns fragmented human lives toward harmony and a vision of perfected life. Shakespeare's art in his last plays is, finally, inseparable from that of the world he dramatizes. If the play's self-conscious theatricality keeps us aware of it as "play" and invites us to share the godlike view of Time, Prospero, or Shakespeare himself, the characters too become aware of their own artfulness, their unconscious participation in a drama scripted by powers that direct all earthly existence. Aesthetic distance collapses into identity, the carefully graded perspective defining our privileged status flexes suddenly into a circle where all actors, all playwrights, all spectators stand equidistant from one controlling center. The art that so calls attention to itself finally denies its own craft; like Hermione's statue, it asks us to look through artifice to nature, the reality that is itself a supreme art. Theophanies revealing man's place in the natural order erase the traditional oppositions between art and nature, appearance and reality, dream and waking. The contradictions that make existence intolerable at last become the paradoxes of religious transcendence, intuitive understanding, and acceptance, just as the bewildered faith that moved Pisanio and Camillo to be false in order to be true leads toward the living statue of Hermione, or the gracious guilt of Leontes and Alonso, or the freedom in submission of Ferdinand and, ultimately, Prospero.

In Beaumont and Fletcher, verbal and situational paradoxes repel rather than require identification; they remain obtrusive and wittily self-regarding. Like the permutations of "honor" in *The Maid's Tragedy,* they may challenge our intellect and force us to reconsider the "validity of received opinion";[14] or they may merely tease our attention, like the central conundrum of being king and no king. Paradox's sense of tension, of checkmate, captures in little Beaumont and Fletcher's dramatic world, for their plays portray the fundamental opposition of destructive and chaotic forces to man's fragile imposition of order. Human art cannot align itself with great creating nature's, for the gods are not benevolent, and, except as the means to a tragicomic denouement, there are no fortunate coincidences on which men can build. In *The Maid's Tragedy,* the set pieces of man's artistry come early and forebode disaster: the Masque of Night and Aspatia's embroidery of the abandoned Ariadne copy a nature in every way inimical to human desire. In *Philaster,* the brief wedding masque—in which Bellario tries to emblematize the lovers as "fair cedar branches" that now "meet and twine together,/Never to be divided" (5.3.25, 40–41)—fails to convert the king. He disowns his daughter and orders immediate execution. The "art" of Gobrius's long-term scheming does bring about *A King and No King's* happy ending, but it is fundamentally different from Camillo's or Paulina's or Prospero's. Gobrius's plan stems from his own ambition for his son. Any sense that spontaneous love between Arbaces and Panthea demonstrates the marvelous conjunction of human plotting with providential design is lost in the general horror at apparent incest.

Beaumont and Fletcher work to enforce a double perspective throughout, and their plays' concerns, as well as their characters, remain both serious and devalued at the same time.[15] By never allowing sympathetic engagement wholly to dissolve our separation from character and situation, they also enforce the disparity between life and art. Instead of collapsing distance, Beaumont and Fletcher appeal to us to share their own godlike detachment from the entire enterprise; they offer us the very satisfactions their characters seek. In this sense the plays are opaque: we do not look through them to life—or rather, we glimpse only briefly and intermittently, with the characters, life's essential hostility. Instead, we are returned to the polished surface and to the human ingenuity which so artfully reorders and controls that implicit abyss. Beaumont and Fletcher's "play" is not re-creative like Paulina's or Camillo's or Prospero's—though it is recreative in a narrower sense. They offer no ideology to bridge the gap between things as they are and as we would have them be, only a sudden reversal that denies the contradiction. They allow us, too, to "play" with the painful and destructive elements that lead "naturally" to despair and, through art, permit us to triumph briefly over life.

Both the consolations and limits of their art are worked out in the career of Aspatia, which initially seems so tangential to *The Maid's Tragedy.* Cut off from life and happiness, "the lost Aspatia" in private emblematizes herself as "Sorrow's monument," the living picture of a psychological exile that her women will eternalize in their embroidery (2.2.66, 74). Her handmaids' command of their medium allows not only Aspatia's self-transformation into art, her own lineaments copied for Ariadne's, but also her revenge on the life that has condemned her to a similar fate. Although the "story" recounts Theseus's escape from Naxos, in her reworking he "shall not go so"; instead, she adds a quicksand, deceptive "smiling water," and "a Fear" done "to the life" (2.2.53–57). As moral artist she recasts the legend "wrong'd by wanton poets" to satisfy a human demand for justice (2.2.58). Yet her art cannot coerce nature's; unsatisfied, she leaves her static isolation to seek death on Amintor's sword.

Like Aspatia's embroidery, Beaumont and Fletcher's tragicomedies in the end offer us an image of our desires; in their structure and presentation, however, they acknowledge a world that mocks our ability to tell life that it "shall not go so." Theirs is not an art irrelevent to life or incapable of tragic vision. At base, their early plays depict a frighteningly Ovidian world where overmastering passion links us to an amoral nature, and where man and his institutions prove incapable of facing or mastering this "fate."[16] Beaumont and Fletcher lack Shakespeare's humanistic faith—even the circumscribed faith of *The Tempest*—in the ultimate goodness and purposefulness of creation, in human potential, in the power of art to heal the wound in nature and guide man's realization of desire. For them, art and nature remain separate and irreconcilable. *Philaster* and *The Maid's Tragedy* are the more powerful because they allow, with differing generic emphasis, each realm its due. With *A King and No King*, Beaumont and Fletcher move toward a more thorough taming of nature to the pattern of human will. The playwrights' art and our awareness of its shaping control become paramount; plotting becomes more self-consciously intricate. In reworking the entire tapestry to acknowledge yet vanquish contradiction, they pleased their audience but, by exaggeration, trivialized both the dangers and the triumph.

NOTES

1. Ashley H. Thorndike, *The Influence of Beaumont and Fletcher on Shakspere* (Worcester, Mass.: Oliver B. Wood, 1901), p. 107.

2. "Technical brilliance" is a term frequently used to condemn Beaumont and Fletcher's reputedly empty dramaturgy, but the phrase need not be pejorative. I have quoted it here from J. M. Nosworthy's description of the cascade of revelations in *Cymbeline*'s last act (Arden edition [London: Methuen, 1955], p. xlii); equally striking examples could be found in the insistent use of theatrical metaphor or medial chorus of *The Winter's Tale*, or in *The Tempest*'s smug reminders of its classical time scheme.

3. Further discussion of Shakespeare's influence on his younger contemporaries' work, as well as interesting observations on the rest of the King's Men's repertoire at this time, can be found in Richard Proudfoot's "Shakespeare and the New Dramatists of the King's Men, 1606–1613," *Later Shakespeare*, Stratford-Upon-Avon Studies 8, ed. J. R. Brown and B. Harris (London: Edward Arnold, 1966), pp. 235–61. For an extensive, though not complete, listing of Beaumont and Fletcher's Shakespearian borrowings, see D. M. McKeithan, *The Debt to Shakespeare in the Beaumont-and-Fletcher Plays* (1938; reprint, Folcroft, Pa.: Folcroft Press, 1969).

4. Beaumont and Fletcher are here treated as equal collaborators, irrespective of the shares apportioned to each by various scholars; editions cited in this paper will be Andrew Gurr's Revels Plays edition of *Philaster* (London: Methuen, 1969) and the Regents Renaissance Drama editions of *The Maid's Tragedy*, ed. Howard B. Norland (Lincoln: University of Nebraska Press, 1968), and *A King and No King*, ed. Robert K. Turner, Jr. (Lincoln: University of Nebraska Press, 1963). References to Shakespeare's romances will all be to Arden editions: *Cymbeline*, cited in n. 2 above, *The Winter's Tale*, ed. J. H. P. Pafford (London: Methuen, 1963), and *The Tempest*, ed. Frank Kermode (London: Methuen, 1961), respectively. Although precise dating of these plays remains impossible, and various suggestions differ slightly or overlap the years given here, the approximate dates and order generally assumed are: *Cymbeline* and *Philaster*, 1609; *The Winter's Tale* and *The Maid's Tragedy*, 1610; *The Tempest* and *A King and No King*, 1611. Problems of manageability curtail treatment of both, very interesting, natural *termini: Cupid's Revenge* and *Pericles* as well as the later Shakespeare-Fletcher collaborations.

5. Gurr, introduction to *Philaster*, pp. lxvii, xxv.

6. *Cupid's Revenge* is only technically a tragedy. As Eugene M. Waith notes in *The Pattern of Tragicomedy in Beaumont and Fletcher* (New Haven: Yale University Press, 1952), "If all the characters were saved from death and if the play ended in repentance and reconciliation, its total effect would be very little different. Even as it stands, with five deaths, *Cupid's Revenge* is more like tragicomedy than tragedy" (p. 14).

7. See John F. Danby's brilliant discussion of this metaphysical aspect of Beaumont and Fletcher's dramaturgy, their staging of moral puns, in *Poets on Fortune's Hill: Studies in Sidney, Shakespeare, Beaumont and Fletcher* (1952; reprint, Port Washington, N. Y.: Kennikat Press, 1966).

8. The phrase is from Danby's argument of this point, ibid., p. 165. Aesthetic distance created by exaggeration and by the Sidneian verbal and dramatic patterning also, of course, encouraged contemporary enjoyment of the plays' emotional and rhetorical displays; these are offered with a generosity excessive for modern taste, but to their popularity the many prefatory verses to the 1647

Folio bear enthusiastic witness. Full discussion of this rhetorical aspect and its influence on larger matters of story and structure can be found in Waith, *Pattern of Tragicomedy*, pp. 86–98, 178–201; for an account of Fletcher's influence and the audience he helped create, see Michael Neill, "'Wits most accomplished Senate': The Audience of the Caroline Private Theaters," *Studies in English Literature* 18 (Spring 1978): 341–60.

9. In "Beaumont, Fletcher, and 'Beaumont & Fletcher': Some Distinctions," *English Literary Renaissance* 1 (Spring 1971), Philip J. Finkelpearl finds the early collaborations to be withering satires on James's court and courtiers in which Beaumont's "satiric realism" balances—even predominates over—Fletcher's "stagey romanticism" (p. 153). Although this reading may be attractive to skeptical modern sensibilities, both the plays' dramaturgy and the kinds of response indicated by the 1647 Folio's prefatory verses suggest this was not the contemporary reaction. Beaumont and Fletcher's popularity had little to do with politically challenging material, though this was noted, and everything to do with a brilliant accommodation of seemingly opposite demands. To suggest that *Philaster* as well as *A King and No King* can best be described as a "comedy about intemperance and vanity" (p. 158) is to overweight the ironic elements and disturb an essentially tragicomic balance.

10. The quoted phrase is Clifford Leech's, from his description of Bessus's effect on *King and No King;* see *The John Fletcher Plays* (London: Chatto and Windus, 1962), p. 99.

11. For further discussion of the masque and its relation to the play, see William Shullenberger, "'This For the Most Wrong'd of Women': A Reappraisal of *The Maid's Tragedy*," *Renaissance Drama*, new series 13 (1982), esp. pp. 134–40.

12. R. J. Kaufmann, review of F. Kermode's *Shakespeare: The Final Plays*, in *Essays in Criticism* 13 (October 1963): 396.

13. An interesting discussion of the "tactics" and "strategies" of the late plays can be found in the chapters so named in Barbara Mowat's *The Dramaturgy of Shakespeare's Romances* (Athens: University of Georgia Press, 1976).

14. This phrase, and the distinction between uses of paradox, is drawn from Rosalie Colie's *Paradoxia Epidemica: The Renaissance Tradition of Paradox* (Princeton: Princeton University Press, 1966), p. 481.

15. Jacqueline Pearson comments helpfully on this "teasing double vision" and the way in which the plays question without entirely negating the appeal of their own highly colored rhetoric and apparent social ideals; see *Tragedy and Tragicomedy in the Plays of John Webster* (Manchester: Manchester University Press, 1980), esp. pp. 33–38. See also Leech, *The John Fletcher Plays*, pp. 89–94; and, for an attack on linguistic corruption that links Beaumont, at least, with Marston and Jonson, see Finkelpearl, "Beaumont, Fletcher, and 'Beaumont & Fletcher,'" p. 149.

16. Analyzing the play from a different standpoint in "The Defence of Contraries: Skeptical Paradox in *A King and No King*," *Studies in English Literature* 21 (Spring 1981), Michael Neill reaches a conclusion more strongly worded than, but related to, my own: "for language proves to be not the projection of a divinely inspired reason, but a mere decoration on the surface of reality. Men finally *are* nothing more than sophistical beasts; and their happiness consists rather in giving way to their beastliness, than in striving to be lords of creation. . . . Beaumont and Fletcher, however, skirt delicately around the edge of that fallen wilderness and maintain at least the illusion that they occupy a paradise of wit" (p. 332).

Quomodo, Sir Giles, and Triangular Desire: Social Aspiration in Middleton and Massinger

Gail Kern Paster

The rapid emergence of city comedy as a major genre soon after the accession of James I indicates how quickly popular theater may incorporate accelerating social and economic changes, however imperfectly it may understand them. Ever since L. C. Knights's classic *Drama and Society in the Age of Jonson,* the critical tradition has also reflected the social content of city comedy, encouraged to do so by the obsessive feuding between merchant and gallant that is the genre's staple plot.[1] The comedies do, of course, provide abundant if indirect evidence of contemporary reaction to changes in the traditional social hierarchy.[2] But the specific relations among the plays—as one play influences another in the explosive development of dramatic genres in the period—may be even more revealing of the social intuition of Jacobean playwrights. One case in point, it seems to me, is the contrasting portraits of social ambition in Middleton's *Michaelmas Term* and Massinger's *A New Way to Pay Old Debts.* Massinger himself invites the comparison with Middleton by borrowing from him so often. Welborne's plot to trick Overreach in *A New Way* is almost certainly based on Witgood's successful hoax of his uncle Lucre in Middleton's *A Trick to Catch the Old One,* and there can be little doubt of Massinger's familiarity with other Middleton comedies.[3] The comparison yields the additional convenience of significant chronology, with Middleton's play (1605–6) coming near the beginning of James's reign and Massinger's written just after its close.[4] There is a much greater complexity in the nature and portrayal of Sir Giles's social ambitions in *A New Way* compared to those of Ephestian Quomodo in *Michaelmas Term.* And it may result not only from Massinger's social conservatism and characteristic sobriety of outlook, but also from the unconscious wisdom born of twenty years' experience of social change under James.

The overall stability of the English aristocracy, Lawrence Stone has argued, derived from its willingness to let invaders from below purchase status—for their descendents, if not for themselves. By thus accommodating itself to the most successful members of the trading class, the Stuart aristocracy ensured its own continuing participation in the control of capital and political rule.[5] The city comedies, however, rarely highlight such accommodations, perhaps because social compromise is inherently less dramatic than social conflict or perhaps because the playwrights felt that some things—like land or women—cannot

165

easily be shared. It is one thing for a merchant to aspire to the social ideal embodied in the landed gentleman, quite another to aspire to the land itself. A significant feature of the contrast between *Michaelmas Term* and *A New Way* is that the differences in situation between Quomodo and Overreach neatly represent the beginning and end of the process of acquiring status. Middleton quickly establishes Quomodo as a rising member of the merchant class: he is wealthy, apparently from having long practiced the city art of gulling younger gentry through the usual commodity swindles. Though he has married within his own class, he nevertheless displays social ambitions by placing son Sim at Cambridge and the Inns of Court and by marking out daughter Susan for an advantageous match. Most important, Middleton times the action of the play at a crucial turning point in the merchant's social development. At the beginning of the play he has returned to the city at term-time having seen "what I desire": "Land, fair neat land" (1.1.98, 101). The action occurs precisely at the point when Quomodo decides to lay claim to the essential possession of the ruling class. Sir Giles, on the other hand, is already a substantial landowner, having risen above his city origins by making an extramural marriage to a country gentlewoman and by taking his nephew Welborne's ancestral estates through means similar to Quomodo's. (If Overreach does not actually entice Welborne into debauchery, as Quomodo does Easy, he has taken advantage of it: he "On foolish mortgages, statutes, and bonds,/For a while suppli'd your loosenesse, and then left you" [1.1.50–51].) Possessing Welborne's estates has not, of course, sufficed for Sir Giles. Bothered by the "foule blemish" to his own holdings by a neighbor's land lying in their midst, he plans to go after it by harassment: "These Trespasses draw on Suites, and Suites expences,/Which I can spare, but will soon begger Him" (2.1.38–39). Sir Giles is thus several steps beyond Quomodo not only in his methods and status, but in social attitudes as well. Unlike Quomodo, eager to acquire land for the first time, Sir Giles is willing to wait for these additional holdings "two, or three yeare" (40). Indeed, he is even beyond aspiring to the distinction of county office, understanding that the leverage of owning a justice of the peace may be greater than that of actually being one:

> In being out of Office I am out of danger,
> Where if I were a *Justice*, besides the trouble,
> I might, or out of wilfulnesse, or error,
> Run my selfe finely into a *Praemunire*,
> And so become a prey to the Informer.
>
> (2.1.14–18)

Sir Giles's social distance from citizen Quomodo is further demonstrated by *A New Way*'s Nottinghamshire setting. Massinger's unusual choice of location may well suggest that the original production occurred in the provinces when London theaters were closed by the plague,[6] but it also works thematically to suggest how far on the road to aristocratic station Sir Giles has already traveled.[7] Since class rivalry occurs, predictably enough, between those classes nearest one another in the social hierarchy, Quomodo aims at untitled gentry like Easy, and the higher reaches of aristocracy never appear in his dramatic world, even by way of reference. He is still so much a citizen of London that the announcement of plans to take possession of Easy's land is framed as a celebration not of the upper class way of life but of the capitalist ethos:

> Give me the man
> Who out of recreation culls advantage,
> Dives into seasons, never walks but thinks,
> Ne rides but plots.
>
> (1.1.94–97)

His eagerness is ungentlemanly. Even his rapt daydreams of being master of Easy's Essex estate take London as their point of departure and return. Thinking "now shall I be divulg'd a landed man/Throughout the Livery" (3.4.5–6), Quomodo turns himself into the focus of an imaginary London conversation:

> —Whither is the worshipful Master Quomodo and his fair bedfellow rid forth?—To his land in Essex!—Whence comes those goodly load of logs?—From his land in Essex!—Where grows this pleasant fruit? says one citizen's wife in the Row.—At Master Quomodo's orchard in Essex. (3.4.13–17)

Sir Giles, who employs poor Lady Downefalne as a maidservant while her husband languishes in debtors' prison, has already conquered the class that is Quomodo's target and aspires to the higher reaches of titled aristocracy represented by Lady Alworth and Lord Lovell.

Of the two, Quomodo is the sharper student of class behavior. Middleton has endowed him with a thorough sociological understanding of the upper-class psychology of conspicuous consumption and competitive debauchery. In plotting to trap Easy into a dangerous intimacy with his disguised accomplice Shortyard, Quomodo instructs Shortyard to "Keep foot by foot with him, out-dare his expenses,/Flatter, dice, and brothel to him" (1.1.120–21).[8] Such insight makes Quomodo an especially shrewd representative of his class in a play dominated by class consciousness. It is particularly apparent in the thinking of Quomodo and that of his wife Thomasine. Not her virtue but her class pride is wounded by the upstart Lethe's epistolary advances: "'tis for his betters to have opportunity of me, and that he shall well know . . . for all his cleansing, pruning, and paring, he's not worthy a broker's daughter" (2.3.7–8, 15–17). Much less, of course, a merchant's wife. Quomodo's habitual pronouncements on class behavior have the formulaic quality of social axiom, the collective wisdom of his class. He explains to Shortyard about the "deadly enmity" between citizen and gentry "which thus stands:/They're busy 'bout our wives, we 'bout their lands" (1.1.106–7). He tells Shortyard to "dispatch!/Gentry is the chief fish we tradesmen catch" (131–32) and, dispensing with couplets reminds Thomasine, "he's often first a gentleman that's last a beggar" (2.3.51). Typically, such apothegms favor the class of the speaker, though both Shortyard and Quomodo recognize the double edge of class rivalry. Like Mosca with Volpone, Shortyard enjoys taunting his master with sly suggestions of a sexual impotence that he associates with economic aggressiveness: "to get riches and children too, 'tis more than one man can do" (4.1.34–35).[9] And there is a hilarious casuistry in the reasoning behind his assurance to Quomodo:

> Your revenge is more glorious:
> To be a cuckold is but for one life,
> When land remains to you, your heir, or wife.
>
> (1.1.108–10)

As Thomasine's later interest in Easy makes clear, land left to such a wife is hardly land left safely within class lines.

Such speech tags and couplets are so frequent in *Michaelmas Term* that Middleton gives them to characters as minor as Shortyard's Boy (see 3.2.19–22). And of course their subject matter—the inevitable cuckoldry jokes, or city versus country—is original neither to Middleton in particular nor to city comedy in general. These tags and couplets do, however, have the special effect of reducing individuality—even that of Quomodo himself—and emphasizing instead the ready identification of characters with their social status. Such an emphasis on representativeness is partly a result of the influence of the moralities: Brian Gibbons has described the plot as a "modernised, urbanised version of *Everyman*," while George E. Rowe, Jr. has recently noted Middleton's frequent borrowings from the prodigal son plays, especially in *Michaelmas Term* and *A Trick to Catch the Old One*.[10] But Middleton makes the sense of class representativeness part of his characters' thinking about themselves and others. And this, combined with their habit of proverbial utterance, gives the characters of *Michaelmas Term* a predictability only slightly less than that of automatons. To call these characters predictable is, of course, merely to recognize their conventionality: the gallants Salewood, Rearage, and Easy could appear in any number of Jacobean city comedies, as could the foolish son Sim Quomodo, the lusty widow, or the conycatching Shortyard.[11] Here, however, their conventionality becomes less an implicit dramatic condition arising from genre than a more or less explicit social fact that the playwright allows us to regard critically. As the Country Wench says of her father, "How can he know me, when I scarce know myself?" (3.1.30–31).

The high reliability of social axiom in *Michaelmas Term* makes the nature and collision of appetites as predictable as the characters. Country wants city; merchants want land; gallants want pleasure; city wives want sexual satisfaction. Though such predictability does not make the urban world less disorderly, it does make its disorder explicable. Characters like the Country Wench and her father, or Andrew Lethe and his mother, may have difficulty recognizing one another, but we have no difficulty recognizing them or the part they play in the urban game. Even the surprise of Quomodo's decision to counterfeit death is mitigated by our inference that Quomodo, too, has overestimated himself. His ultimate self-defeat is the common destiny of almost all cony-catchers in Jacobean comedy. The guller gulled is normally self-gulled. Here, however, the revelation of Quomodo's foolishness underscores Middleton's refusal to credit the social hierarchy—at least insofar as it distinguishes between merchant and gentry in social worth—with any real validity except as the mental furniture of conventional characters or as a reliable index of specific behaviors. While the possession of land marks gentry off from the merchant class, Middleton gives the landowners and former landowners no particular moral distinction to justify their claim. Easy ought to have his land returned by right, though hardly by merit. And it is the landless Londoner Quomodo who most appreciates the natural world:

> Oh, that sweet, neat, comely, proper, delicate parcel of land, like a fine gentlewoman i'th' waist, not so great as pretty, pretty; the trees in summer whistling, the silver waters by the banks harmoniously gliding. I should have been a scholar. (2.3.82-86)

An even more radical critique of social hierarchy appears in the ease with which a character like Shortyard impersonates his betters, or arrivistes like Lethe and the Country Wench disguise their origins from other characters and even from their parents. The pander Dick Hellgill arouses Lethe's appetite for the Country Wench by convincing him of her great rank and thus her greater humiliation in becoming his "plain pung" (3.1.74). Lethe's grotesqueness is best captured in the contrast between his "foul neck" and his white satin suit, which makes Thomasine Quomodo call him a "maggot crept out of a nutshell" (2.3.13). But the Country Wench in a *"new fashion gown, dress'd gentlewoman-like"* provokes in Dick Hellgill a disavowal of social distinctions that the play's action does not completely discount:

> You talk of an alteration; here's the thing itself. What base birth does not raiment make glorious? And what glorious births do not rags make infamous? Why should not a woman confess what she is now, since the finest are but deluding shadows, begot between tirewomen and tailors? (3.1.1–5)

Thus Quomodo, otherwise pretty astute, mistakes the fashionable-looking Lethe. And the Country Wench's father, whom Middleton uses as a spokesman for traditional morality, never achieves recognition of his debauched offspring, even after he learns the gentlewoman he serves is a bawd. Shortyard carries off his impersonation of Master Blastfield so successfully that we see him initiating Easy in the minutiae of fashionable behavior, and Easy himself understands the truth only after Thomasine Quomodo tells him. As their names indicate, the "real" gallant Salewood and the impostor Blastfield have similarly disastrous effects on the land. Shortyard's ultimate cowardice in the face of Easy's fury diminishes but does not completely wipe out his stunning record of accomplishment as the most effectual character in the play, defeated not by his own presumption but by the love of Thomasine for Easy.

The judgment scene at the end restores the characters to their social status quo ante, with Lethe recognized by his mother and engaged to his punk, Susan promised to Rearage, and Thomasine returned unhappily to a resurrected but landless Quomodo. Quomodo's comeuppance, however, can hardly be called climactic: if as a cuckold he is truly his "own affliction" (5.3.164), his and Shortyard's temporary acquisition of Easy's land has come about as the result of the prodigality and slavish conformity to fashionable behavior that are the afflictions of the class above him. As Easy tells Quomodo about the bond he has cosigned, "You know my entrance was but for fashion sake" (3.4.49). The exchange of women and estates back and forth between the two classes, which seems to be the essential social dynamic of the plot, is one that redounds to the credit of neither and hardly promises to cease with Quomodo's defeat here. The end of *Michaelmas Term* imposes a severer judgment on Quomodo than on Easy, but the unresolved ambiguities suggest that the traditional social hierarchy so much a part of the characters' thinking has little real value or substantiality except as a specious justification for appetitive behavior and mutually self-destructive class rivalry.

However detached in tone, Middleton's satiric attack on the social pretensions of merchant and gallant is devastating: in Quomodo he denies the merchant class any permanent strategic superiority in the acquisition of land or money; in Easy he denies the lower gentry their traditional claim to moral consequence. In all the representatives of either class, he denies the capacity for effective self-management and self-restraint. Those values that the play affirms—such as the relative innocence of country over city, the greater value of land than money—remain unattached to any characters in the play. Of course, it is also important to acknowledge just how narrow Middleton's social range in *Michaelmas Term* really is, especially in comparison to *A New Way to Pay Old Debts*. Unlike Massinger, Middleton leaves the aristocracy out of his comedy and safely reserves his jaundiced treatment of ruling class behavior for the Italianate world of revenge tragedy.

In *A New Way to Pay Old Debts*, by contrast, Massinger broadens his social panorama, despite the limitations imposed by his provincial setting. In the country-house world of this play, for instance, the tapster Tapwell and his wife Froth look like transplanted Londoners, while the reformation plot that takes up half of the play's action occurs normally in an urban setting. Massinger may have felt that the affirmation of traditional values, his clear didactic intent in *A New Way*, made the rural locus classicus of those values a far more appropriate setting than London. In any case, the provincial world of Lady Alworth and Lord Lovell is one in which long-standing class divisions remain firmly in place, despite the land holdings of Sir Giles and the two decades that separate this play from Middleton's. The intensity of Welborne's fury at Tapwell in the opening scene springs not from having been refused a drink and tobacco on credit but—more nobly—from having been refused by an ingrate, "Borne on my fathers land, and proud to bee/A drudge in his house" (1.1.28–29). While Welborne has indulged spectacularly in the vices that Middleton teaches us to associate with the lower gentry, his desire to reform is generated by a residual class pride to which Massinger gives full approval. Thus Welborne angrily spurns Tom Alworth's offer of charity and gains Lady Alworth's support out of her gratitude for the very sort of past generosity of which Tapwell is so forgetful. In Massinger's reformed rake, as in those of the eighteenth-century sentimentalists, prodigality and generosity go hand in hand. Furthermore, like Middleton, Massinger sees class continuity as a function of cultural memory, but, unlike Middleton, he is able to find it in some members of his dramatic world. Even affection can be transmitted by inheritance in this play, as when Welborne tells young Alworth he is bound to give him good counsel: "Thy father was my friend, and that affection/I bore to him, in right descends to thee" (1.1.117–18).

There is no need here to demonstrate yet again the traditional underpinnings of Massinger's social vision, since even a reader with little historical background can recognize a celebration of social hierarchy in Massinger's simple idealization of Lady Alworth and Lord Lovell. But it is precisely the high importance that Massinger insists on awarding to inherited station in the play that gives his portrait of Sir Giles Overreach its peculiar power and, paradoxically, its modernity. Traditional readings of the play tend to regard Sir Giles rather as the play's aristocrats do—as a despicable upstart who acts out of monumental self-regard and ambition and thus more or less deserves whatever revenge the higher orders can wreak on him. For Patricia Thomson, Sir Giles becomes a particularly powerful portrait of the Jacobean New Man, cut off from his class (as Quomodo certainly is not). Alan Gerald Gross, comparing him to Lady Frugal in *The City Madam*, describes him as "steeped in evil of a more serious sort" and considers him an example of Massinger's tendency to analyze impersonal economic forces in terms of individual moral perversion.[12] There have been more sympathetic responses: Robert Fothergill, for instance, finds Sir Giles to be "a positive human presence with a special sensibility," motivated less by personal ambition than by an ambitious, if misdirected, love for Margaret. More important, both Fothergill and Michael Neill understand that Massinger writes—probably unawares—out of a significant identification with the feelings of his villain.[13] But it is René Girard, not writing about Massinger at all, who provides the most help in comprehending Overreach and thus in appreciating Massinger's perhaps involuntary achievement. Girard's *Deceit, Desire, and the Novel* explains the aspiration to higher social rank as a version of the imitation of Another that unites the behavior of characters such as Don Quixote or Julien Sorel. Each has surrendered the right to choose his own objects of desire for that which is desired, possessed, or represented by the perceived rival. Desire is mediated, critically, by the presence of a third party—in the creation of triangular desire.[14] Applying Girard's theory of desire to Jacobean social comedy enables us to realize that Overreach's actions in *A New Way* spring not from self-love but from self-hatred. The person he really loves is neither himself nor his daughter, but Lord Lovell, whom he wishes secretly to become. Furthermore, the relevance of Girard's discussion of Stendhal and Proust to Massinger's protagonist—however improbable—goes a long way toward explaining the remarkable fascination Overreach had for the nineteenth-century audiences in England and America.[15]

Sir Giles's apparent obsession concerns his efforts to marry his only daughter Margaret to "the gallant minded, popular Lord *Lovell;*/The minion of the peoples love" (2.1.69–70). On the face of it, Lovell seems to be only a convenient vehicle for the achievement of Overreach's desire to have a "right honorable daughter":

> I will have her well attended, there are Ladies
> Of errant Knights decay'd, and brought so low,
> That for cast clothes, and meate, will gladly serve her.

>And 'tis my glory, though I come from the Cittie,
>To have their issue, whom I have undone,
>To kneele to mine, as bond-slaves.

>   (2.1.78–83)

The note of apparent contempt discernible in Overreach's reference to Lovell, as he sets himself apart from feeling as the people do about the nobleman, is even stronger in his reference to other aristocrats. He will not only have Lady Downefalne serve Meg, but she will serve her without repining or be packed off to the Counter to howl with her husband. Moreover, Overreach is just as ostentatious in his scorn for the self-abnegation of Christian morality:

>I would be worldly wise, for the other wisdome
>That does prescribe us a well-govern'd life,
>And to doe right to others, as our selves,
>I value not an Atome.

>   (2.1.23–26)

What he does seem to value is the meaning of his own upward rise, rebuking Meg for imagining that her birth makes her fitter to be the servant of Lady Downefalne than her mistress: "In birth? Why, art thou not my daughter?/The blest child of my industrie, and wealth?" (3.2.52–53). And, like the comparably industrious Quomodo, Overreach seems to accept class warfare between citizen and gentry as thoroughly natural, justifying his efforts to debase the upper classes by the "strange Antipathie/Betweene us, and true Gentry" (2.1.88–89).

His last phrase, however, is telling and suggests a crucial difference between Overreach and Quomodo—and the reason to use Girard in comparing them. In Quomodo's language, there is nothing like the hint of wistfulness that there is in Sir Giles's "between us, and *true* Gentry" (emphasis mine). Quomodo's is an example of what Girard calls linear desire: "there is no mediator, there is only the subject and the object."[16] Quomodo wants Easy's land because of the value he and everyone else place on it; Easy himself is truly unimportant except, accidentally, as the possessor of that land and, later, as an attraction apart from land for Thomasine Quomodo. For Quomodo, the desire to possess Easy's land does not conceal a desire to become Easy's rival in any larger sense, to become Easy himself. Such foolish desires are reserved in *Michaelmas Term* for provincial upstarts like Lethe who imitate the manners of gentry apparently because they do not know any better: they lack the self-assurance of the London citizenry as represented by Quomodo and Shortyard. Even for Shortyard, as we have seen, the successful impersonation of gentry has no greater social potential than that of taking over for his master when Quomodo seems to die, becoming another Quomodo as Mosca becomes another Volpone.

This all makes good sense in *Michaelmas Term*: Middleton's refusal to idealize the significance of gentry means that Quomodo has no reason to want to be anyone other than a successful Quomodo. His ambitions are entirely material. We can begin to suspect the existence of a far more complicated desire in Sir Giles, however, once we investigate the obvious contradiction between his professed scorn for the aristocracy and the intensity of his desire to marry Margaret into it. In such a case, Girard tells us to look for the presence of a mediator, a third party whose rivalry or interference in the pursuit of desire may illuminate its secret nature.[17] In the context of his obsession with Margaret's marriage to Lovell, Sir Giles's vanity and apparent self-love crumble. The ostentation with which he separates himself from allegiance to the Christian morality and customary social sanctions he has violated begins closely to resemble Girard's protagonist of internal mediation who belittles the objects of his emulation in order to conceal the admiration he feels from them and himself. Sir Giles tells Marrall, "I must have all men sellers,/And I the only Purchaser" (2.1.32–33) and professes himself unmoved by the curses of which he knows himself to be the object:

> with mine owne sword
> If call'd into the field, I can make that right,
> Which fearefull enemies murmur'd at as wrong.
> Now, for these other pidling complaints
> Breath'd out in bitternesse, as when they call me
> Extortioner, Tyrant, Cormorant, or Intruder
> On my poore Neighbours right, or grand incloser
> Of what was common, to my private use;
> . . . .
> I only thinke what 'tis to have my daughter
> Right honorable; and 'tis a powerfull charme
> Makes me insensible of remorse, or pitty,
> Or the least sting of Conscience.
>
> (4.1.118–31)

But in speeches like these, there is reason to suspect that the city knight protests too much. The care he takes to assure whoever is listening that he does not mind curses hailed down on him; that he enjoys "these darke,/And crooked wayes" of getting wealth more than possessing it; that he condemns report "as a meere sound" (4.1.93) sounds very much like a man trying hard to convince himself and not quite succeeding. His moral ugliness is obvious to everyone, but to himself not least of all. Viewed in this light, Sir Giles's desire to marry Margaret to Lovell is not an attempt to use Lovell as a vehicle for Margaret's promotion but an attempt to use Margaret as a vehicle for his own redemption in a vicarious union with a secretly beloved alter ego. Reading the play this way makes much more sense than accusing Massinger or his protagonist of being unaware of the contradiction inherent in the highest social ambitions. Instead we get a play that is an early example of full-blown snobbery, with its built-in contradiction along Groucho Marx's line—Sir Giles not wanting to belong to any club that would have him (and thus needing to become somebody else). He asks us to regard his fawning before Lovell as merely hypocritical, telling himself: "Roughnesse a while leave me,/For fawning now, a stranger to my nature,/Must make way for mee" (3.2.159–61). But to see himself as hypocritical is comparable to professing indifference to what others say or think about him—a strategy that tries to conceal from himself and others the full extent of his hatred for himself and his admiration for Lovell. After all, an ambitious Jacobean father really interested in the social transformation of his daughter rather than in the power of the person who will transform her would have some shred of concern for her virginity. But because Overreach's real goal—to unite with Lovell through Margaret—requires Margaret's loss of virginity, he encourages her to get about it as quickly as possible: "Virgin me no Virgins./I must have you lose that name, or you lose me" (3.2.112–13). As his last phrase suggests, his investment in the match is total. Even Quomodo's impatience for land dwarfs in comparison with Overreach's desire to have Margaret married and pregnant. He is uninterested in the manner of her wedding—"So my Lord have you/What do I care who gives you?" (4.3.106–7)—because he is interested only in its results for him. He even fears her peevishness will "lose a night/In which perhaps he might get two boyes on thee" (4.3.101–2). Here, finally, is where Margaret's status as vehicle is clearest, in her father's passionate desire to be grandfather to a young Lord Lovell. He tells the astonished prospective father: "And might I live to dance upon my knee/A young Lord *Lovell*, borne by her unto you,/I write *nil ultra* to my proudest hopes" (4.1.101–3).

This fantasy of being a grandfather is perhaps the most revealing of the nature of Sir Giles's desire. In a young Lord Lovell, the ugly existence and name of Overreach would be extinguished—replaced and legitimized as it could not be, for instance, were Sir Giles's only offspring male instead of female. Because his son could never qualify as true gentry, Sir Giles would find it hard to love such an extension of himself the way he can an extension in Lord Lovell, senior or junior. That he would like to see himself in Lovell may also explain why Massinger makes Lovell so much closer in age to father than daughter: Lovell is not an appropriate mate for Margaret, chronologically, as Lovell himself explains to Lady Alworth, but his age does make him a more numinous object of Sir Giles's admiration than a younger, if equally exalted nobleman. Furthermore, the image of young Lord Lovell dancing upon Overreach's grandfatherly knee may conceal a desire not only to have a Lovell dwarfed physically and socially by the larger adult, and in his control, but also to have the elder Lovell dead, as he would have to be were Sir Giles actually to dance Lord Lovell on his knee. Thus there is something deeper and more complicated than either hypocrisy or simple fatherly ambition animating Sir Giles's speeches to Lovell offering all his worldly goods with Margaret or assuring the nobleman that he runs no hazard in marrying an Overreach:

> I still will be so tender
> Of what concernes you in all points of Honour,
> That the immaculate whitenesse of your Fame,
> Nor your unquestion'd integrity
> Shall e're be sullied with one taint, or spot
> That may take from your innocence, and candor.
>
> (4.1.93–98)

The apparent comic point of this exchange is to reveal Sir Giles so blinded by ambition that he cannot see the impossibility of Lovell's purity surviving its contact with ill-gotten wealth or recognize how Lovell must react to his eager overtures. He cannot even hear the irony in Lovell's response to his disavowal of conscience: "I admire/The toughnesse of your nature" (4.1.131–32). We ought also to perceive here, however, the presence of obsessive love, self-protectively disguised from both its subject and object as conventional social ambition. Sir Giles is more interested in Lovell's virginity—his immaculate whiteness—than Margaret's!

The eagerness with which Sir Giles offers himself and his possessions up to Lovell, ostensibly for Margaret's sake, thus represents a truer reflection of his real feelings of admiration and respect than Sir Giles clearly can afford to admit. If he seems to make an exception of himself as smarter and stronger than the rest of his world, he makes an even larger exception of Lovell. Lovell personifies everything that Sir Giles would be and cannot. They are the play's two patriarchal figures, Sir Giles as actual progenitor, Lovell as the paternal authority figure for the orphaned Tom Alworth in particular and the larger social order in general. In a play filled with military references, Lovell is the legitimate soldier, leader of a regiment that Welborne joins at the end to complete his reformation. But Sir Giles also represents himself in quasi-military terms, imagining himself and Lovell in single combat over the question of Margaret's honor:

> How? forsake thee?
> Doe I weare a sword for fashion? or is this arme
> Shrunke up? or wither'd? does there live a man
> Of that large list I have encounter'd with,
> Can truly say I e're gave inch of ground,
> Not purchas'd with his blood, that did oppose me?
> Forsake thee when the thing is done? he dares not.
>
> (3.2.139–45)

Even by making Lovell his opponent in single combat, Sir Giles can approach him more closely, make him engage in an exclusive relationship—which is the real object of his efforts in the play. Lovell's age, moreover, means that Sir Giles can regard him not only as a suitor for Margaret but, potentially, as one for Lady Alworth—and thus as his own romantic rival. He refuses at first to believe that Lady Alworth would receive Marrall and Welborne at her table, having refused to entertain him. Later he is upset that she seems to prefer Welborne to both him and Lovell, feeling torn between his outrage at her affront to decorum in apparently loving the debased Welborne and his hopes to gain her estates through Welborne in order to give them to Lovell:

> Shee's caught! O woemen! she neglects my Lord,
> And all her complements appli'd to *Welborne!*
> The garments of her widdowhood lay'd by,
> She now appeares as glorious as the spring.
> Her eyes fix'd on him; in the wine shee drinkes,
> He being her pledge, she sends him burning kisses,
> And sitts on thornes, till she be private with him.
> She leaves my meate to feed upon his lookes;
> And if in our discourse he be but nam'd
> From her a deepe sigh followes; but why grieve I
> At this? it makes for me, if she proves his.
>
> (3.3.1–11)

Most important, Sir Giles shares with Lovell the nobleman's sense of his own exaltedness, unaware that Lovell's sublime self-esteem is exactly what makes marriage with Margaret so unthinkable. While Sir Giles wants to extinguish his own name in a Lovell grandson, Lovell himself would rather have his name die out than allow his blood to mingle with a lesser line:

> I would not so adulterate my blood
> By marrying *Margaret,* and so leave my issue
> Made up of severall peeces, one part skarlet
> And the other *London*-blew. In my owne tombe
> I will interre my name first.
>
> (4.1.223–27)

The absoluteness of Lovell's argument here finally reveals the pathos that surrounds Sir Giles for modern readers of the play and the complexity of Massinger's portrayal of him. Sir Giles cannot help but confirm the social distinctions by which Lord Lovell and Lady Alworth set such store, for the reality of class lines is what validates his strenuous efforts to connect with the aristocracy. Herein lies the humor of his outrage that Lady Alworth would feed Marrall and pretend to favor Welborne. His sense of his own moral ugliness and the concealed sense of identification with Lovell hint at a repressed awareness of the self-contradiction of his being—that the very successes which bring him close enough to Lovell to identify with him at all make the gap between them impossible to close. But the deepest irony in the inflexible social structure which Massinger has built into this play is that even if Overreach's wealth had been gotten legitimately, it would not affect Lovell's attitude toward marrying Margaret. What counts in this world is expressed in the career and name of Welborne—that reformation is only possible for those lucky enough to be born into the right families and metamorphosis is not possible at all. Even Margaret's marriage with Alworth does not contradict this basic social premise of *A New Way to Pay Old Debts,* for Margaret's elevation is bestowed on her by a well-born husband almost as a reward for not aiming higher, not by a father working hard on her behalf. If, as Robert Fothergill has argued, Massinger's social recommendation to the lower orders is to respect and imitate those above them without actually claiming their prerogatives, to do as the humble Margaret does,[18] the madness of Sir Giles Overreach at the end reveals Massinger's perhaps unconscious understanding of the psychological impossibility of successfully doing so.

Ultimately then, the meaning of Overreach's love for and desire to be Lovell has little to do with the existence of a traditional social hierarchy (which was increasingly eroding during Massinger's lifetime anyway). The unbridgeable gap that Lovell posits between himself and Overreach as a matter of birthright collapses in the face of Jacobean social reality, which saw a great deal of movement up and down the social ladder, even at the uppermost rungs.[19] Faced with the choice between dying out or marrying a rich City heiress, most Jacobean noble families were less masochistic than Lord Lovell, more interested in progeny—even of a hybrid kind. While Massinger may well have dramatized an unrealistically rigid social situation in *A New Way* as an example of conservative wishful thinking, the expressive longing of Sir Giles Overreach has less to do with class dynamics at a specific historical moment than with the permanent human fantasies about self-transformation that manifest themselves here in terms of class division. Again, a comparison with Quomodo seems apt: Quomodo's final humiliation is far less severe than Sir Giles's because his fall results in large part from Middleton's interest in completing a circle, in making sure that every major participant in the action demonstrates the universality and circularity of appetitive behavior. Middleton refuses to allow us comfortably to identify with anyone in his play—or, perhaps, makes us uncomfortably identify with all of them. Massinger, however, offers us a variety of characters who seem to command admiration at different levels and who serve ostensibly to affirm the rightness of traditional class boundaries. But he also creates a villain whose extreme ambivalence about himself is easy for a modern audience to sympathize with and comprehend. The play's appeal after its time and—who knows?— perhaps in it has always lain not in its old-fashioned celebration of the birthright gentry but in its subversive recognition of what it feels like to be excluded for the wrong reasons. Sir Giles's appetites, unlike Quomodo's, are metaphysical: he longs for a transformation denied him not so much by his own self-hatred but by the intractability of circumstances and the ironies of birth. He can never be Another, he can only be himself. And in his world, being himself is condemnation enough.

NOTES

1. L. C. Knights, *Drama and Society in the Age of Jonson* (1937; reprint, New York: Norton, 1968). Two standard treatments of city comedy are Brian Gibbons, *Jacobean City Comedy: A Study of Satiric Plays by Jonson, Marston, and Middleton* (Cambridge, Mass.: Harvard University Press, 1968) and Alexander Leggatt, *Citizen Comedy in the Age of Shakespeare* (Toronto: University of Toronto Press, 1973). Representative critical discussions of Massinger include Michael Neill, "Massinger's Patriarchy: The Social Vision of *A New Way to Pay Old Debts*," *Renaissance Drama*, new series 10 (1979):185–213. Also, Patricia Thomson, "The New Way and the Old Way in Dekker and Massinger," *Modern Language Review* 51 (1956): 168–78, and Alan Gerald Gross, "Social Change and Philip Massinger," *Studies in English Literature* 7 (1967): 329–42.

2. I am thinking particularly of Lawrence Stone's now classic *The Crisis of the Aristocracy 1558–1641* (Oxford: Clarendon, 1965). There is a handy summary of developments, particularly as they affected London, in Margot Heinemann, *Puritanism and Theatre: Thomas Middleton and Opposition Drama under the Early Stuarts* (Cambridge: Cambridge University Press, 1980), pp. 1–17.

3. On this source, see the Introduction to *A New Way to Pay Old Debts*, in *The Plays and Poems of Philip Massinger*, ed. Philip Edwards and Colin Gibson, 5 vols. (Oxford: Clarendon, 1976), 2:279; for Massinger's familiarity with Middleton, 4:3. All quotations from Massinger refer to this edition and will be incorporated in the text with silent modernization of i, j, u, and v.

4. I have used Richard Levin's edition of *Michaelmas Term* for the Regents Renaissance Drama series (Lincoln: University of Nebraska Press, 1966); for the date, see pp. x–xi. For the date of *A New Way,* see Edwards and Gibson, *Massinger*, 2:275–76.

5. See Stone, *Crisis*, pp. 52–53. He also convincingly demonstrates the continuing supremacy of land as status symbol, p. 41.

6. Edwards and Gibson, *Massinger*, 2:276.

7. Patricia Thomson has pointed out how much closer Sir Giles is to Lionel Cranfield, the Londoner who became Earl of Middlesex, than to Sir Giles Mompesson, whose Wiltshire origins were far from obscure; see "The New Way," pp. 170–71.

8. On the relation between status and lavish expenditure, see Stone, *Crisis*, p. 50.

9. Cf. *Volpone* (1.1.16–17) when the Magnifico elevates gold above "all stile of joy" in children.

10. Gibbons, *City Comedy,* p. 129; Rowe, *Thomas Middleton and the New Comedy Tradition* (Lincoln: University of Nebraska Press, 1979), pp. 53–92. Rowe's discussion of *Michaelmas Term* seems to me especially noteworthy.

11. The point has been made often, most recently by Rowe, *New Comedy Tradition,* p. 62.

12. Thomson, "The New Way," p. 169; Gross, "Social Change," pp. 329–36.

13. Robert Fothergill, "The Dramatic Experience of Massinger's *The City Madam* and *A New Way to Pay Old Debts,*" *University of Toronto Quarterly* 13 (1973): 78–79; Neill, "Massinger's Patriarchy," p. 207.

14. René Girard, *Deceit, Desire and the Novel,* trans. Yvonne Freccero (Baltimore: Johns Hopkins University Press, 1965); see the first chapter, "Triangular Desire," esp. pp. 11–14.

15. See R. H. Ball, *The Amazing Career of Sir Giles Overreach* (1939; reprint, New York: Octagon Books, 1968).

16. Girard, *Deceit,* p. 2.

17. Ibid., pp. 10–11.

18. Fothergill, "The Dramatic Experience," p. 73.

19. See Stone, *Crisis,* pp. 51–53.

Philip Massinger: Comedy and Comical History

Philip Edwards

It is noticeable that among all the work of Massinger's long years as collaborator with Fletcher, between 1616 (or earlier) and 1625, there is little or nothing we can call comedy. The nearest to it is *The Elder Brother,* probably written in the year Fletcher died. This is a play on the immortal theme of the bookish recluse being startled into awareness of the real world by a beautiful young woman. There is a well-contrived first act by Massinger, but the disappointing development suggests that the collaborators, whose strongly contrasted talents harmonized so well in tragicomedy and tragedy, could not sustain the singleness of tone needed for comedy. Fletcher was not interested in Massinger's moral positioning (or, if they were writing simultaneously, was not aware of it) and Massinger was left with nothing to bring off in the lame last act.

It was at about the same time as this not very successful attempt at collaborative comedy that Massinger broke away, as it were, with a comedy entirely his own, *A New Way to Pay Old Debts,* which he offered not to the King's Men but to Beeston at the Phoenix. But only one other of the fifteen plays that he wrote on his own did he designate as a comedy. This was *The City Madam* (1632). It seems that Massinger stood by the time-honored definition that comedy concerned itself with abuses in common life, and he was not prepared to call a play a comedy unless it took its theme from contemporary society. Two other plays that we should certainly call comedies, *The Great Duke of Florence* (1627) and *The Guardian* (1633), deal with an Italy of an indeterminate period and contain princes. These plays are designated "comical history."

Even with these two included, comedy still forms only a small area of Massinger's work; his major contribution was in tragicomedy and tragedy. The distinction between comical history and tragicomedy may seem fine to us, but it is real (depending on the gravity of the events and the peril of the situations) and Massinger seems decisive about it. He took a good deal of interest in the printing of his plays, and I am assuming that the title-page designations are his. They mostly echo the head title at the beginning of the text, and so derive from Massinger's manuscript. Perhaps the one tragicomedy which we ought to consider with the comedies and comical histories is *The Picture* (1629), and it is notable that this is a unique case of a title page contradicting the head title. *The Picture* is a 'Tragæcomædie' on the title page but on the head title "A true Hungarian History." (True it is not.) The uncertainty of the designation may be excuse enough to include this interesting feminist play in a discussion of Massinger's comedies.

*   *   *

Massinger's vein of seriousness does not make him a "natural" as a writer of comedy. Perhaps it was his inveterate earnestness which suggested to Fletcher that he was best not employed in comedies and which led Fletcher to appropriate to himself all the comic scenes in the tragicomedies (like *The Custom of the Country* and *The Little French Lawyer,* for example). Massinger's seriousness does not diminish one bit in his comedies (with one vital exception), and he may therefore seem to be forcing himself as he applies himself to the genre, particularly when it comes to social satiric comedy. It would not be extravagant to call *A New Way to Pay Old Debts* and *The City Madam* social studies, so intently do they explore that vexed border-country of the England of Charles I where tradesmen and gentry confronted each other. The plays are about a major social problem: the decline of the status, power, and livelihood of the old landed gentry in the face of the rise of those who have made money in the City and are now reaching out for the lands, titles, and offices of their social superiors. Although *A New Way* and *The City Madam* belong close together in this way, it is of some importance to note that they are not both "city comedies." *A New Way to Pay Old Debts*, set in the Nottinghamshire countryside, is a play about the provinces. The encroachment of city wealth is watched from the estates of the old nobility. In *The City Madam* the gentry have come to town, and we watch the conflict from the counting-houses of the City.

Massinger mapped the social border-country with a loving attention to details of social position, kinship, source of income, the slide downward or the climb upward. Perhaps if he had lived two hundred years later he would have been grateful for the novel as a vehicle for the study of social change. As it was, he had in satirical comedy an advantage the novel could not give, because, besides allowing him to document a swirl of change that alarmed him, it provided, in performance, a kind of ritual for expelling the enemy who was disintegrating society and for affirming the bonds which could cement it. Satiric drama may often claim to be a medicine for the public, but in one of its aspects it carries into civilized days something of the will of primitive satire and invective to disable and cripple enemies, and the tableau of dismissal or banishment at the end of a comedy can be seen as a communal rite of expulsion. In Overreach and Luke, Massinger created images of those whom his social class feared; and, in enjoying their defeat and humiliation, the audience laughed them out of existence (for a time) and flexed its muscles in a new feeling of liberation. These rites of expulsion and consolidation are more easily seen in a comedy writer who, like Massinger, is below the first rank. Very great comedies—such as *The Merchant of Venice, Volpone, The Country Wife, The Man of Mode,* and *The Playboy of the Western World*—tend to subvert the rites they rehearse and undermine the communal values they profess to support. There is not much ambiguity in Massinger's social comedies (though they are sometimes misunderstood), but they are true comedies for all their heavy charge of social concern, and they require—or required—the theater to achieve their full effect.

*   *   *

The explosive opening of *A New Way to Pay Old Debts*, with the gentleman Welborne, in ragged clothing, expelled from a mean alehouse and grossly insulted by the owner (who was formerly his own servant), is a fine image of the Great Inversion, the archetypal nightmare recurrent in both fiction and history, when masters must suddenly cower under the insolence of their former servants. Massinger had already put this revolutionary situation in satiric form in *The Bondman*, when, after their successful revolt, the slaves of Syracuse tyrannized over their former masters and mistresses. There the status quo was restored when the army put down their weapons and shook whips at the slaves, who promptly collapsed in terror. In *A New Way*, the status quo, the restoration of the old gentry, requires more contrivances.

Welborne's father "kept a great house" and relieved the poor in traditional style. His land had been in the family for "twenty descents"—that must take us back to about the Conquest. He was not one of the great nobility, but an important country gentleman who "bare the whole sway of the shire." This patrimony Welborne has carelessly and irresponsibly frittered away on hawks, dogs, horses, drink, and women. Deeply in debt, he was forced to make over the family lands to his uncle Sir Giles Overreach. Now at the nadir of his misfortunes, he is lectured to by a sanctimonious alehouse-keeper who owes his rise in life to a gift of forty pounds that Welborne made him when he was his under-butler. Welborne looks on his past career as "madness" (1.1.182)[1] and the subject of the play is how he mends his fortunes—by imposing on Overreach the elaborate hoax that Lady Alworth is to marry him.

Who is Sir Giles Overreach? He comes from the City (2.1.81), but Massinger gives us little about his early life. There is no indication that he was a merchant. But he is a self-made man. The "industry" that he constantly boasts of consists apparently of shady financial and legal transactions that give him possession of the goods of others. An early step in his progress toward gentility must have been his marriage to Welborne's aunt, the sister of Sir John Welborne (2.1.91). He has acquired a knighthood somewhere along the line, presumably by purchase. In the play's time, he is a widower and a suitor for the hand of Lady Alworth (2.3.90). This is bold, as one of his former successes was ruining her husband (before she married him) and acquiring his estates (1.1.153; 4.1.205–6). This is one of the many tidbits of important information that Massinger, with seeming casualness, drops into the play to give it its remarkably solid circumstantial base. Alworth senior, father of young Tom Alworth by his first wife, was a close friend of Welborne, and Welborne supported him when he was in financial trouble (1.3.99–109). It was Lady Alworth who finally rescued him, by marrying him and making him master of her estate (1.3.110–12). Her gratitude to Welborne for supporting her late husband in his darkest times makes her willing to join in Welborne's deception of Overreach. Her stepson, Tom Alworth, with no inheritance after Overreach's ruin of his father, has taken service with Lord Lovell, living (as Welborne puts it) "At the devotion of a stepmother / And the uncertain favour of a lord" (1.1.174–75).

To return to Overreach: he is continuing, in the play's time, to add to his "many lordships" by intimidation and sharp legal practice. He describes his methods at 2.1.34–48. An essential tool is a magistrate who is in his pocket (Greedy). Overreach is an unfamiliar demon, a whirlwind-like force shattering the gentry by disappropriating them. An important choric passage between two of Lady Alworth's servants runs as follows:

> To have a usurer that starves himself. . .
> To grow rich and then purchase is too common.
> But this Sir Giles feeds high, keeps many servants,
> Who must at his command do any outrage;
> Rich in his habit, vast in his expenses,
> Yet he to admiration still increases
> In wealth and lordships.
>
> He frights men out of their estates,
> And breaks through all law-nets made to curb ill men
> As they were cobwebs. No man dares reprove him.
> Such a spirit to dare, and power to do, were never
> Lodged so unluckily.
>
> (2.2.106, 109–18)

It is the scornful arrogance of Overreach's violent and impetuous career that attracted most of the star-actors of the eighteenth and nineteenth centuries— most notably Edmund Kean—to take on the part of Sir Giles. The swallowing of the estates of Alworth and Welborne takes place before the play's time, but in the play Overreach ruins a poor farmer (2.1.1–8), plans the dispossession of his neighbour Frugal (2.1.34–42), and schemes to get Lady Alworth's lands—first by marrying her and then, when it seems she is to marry Welborne, by getting a legal stranglehold on Welborne.

But what are we to say of his "main work" by which he overreaches himself, the marriage of his daughter Margaret to Lord Lovell? What soft Achilles heel is this in the iron nature of the extortioner? Throughout the play he iterates that all he has ever done has been in order to marry his daughter into the peerage, "to have my daughter 'right honourable.'" To Margaret he says:

> Why foolish girl, was't not to make thee great
> That I have ran and still pursue those ways
> That hale down curses on me?
>
> (3.2.54–56)

To Lord Lovell he says:

> And might I live to dance upon my knee
> A young Lord Lovell, borne by her unto you,
> I write *nil ultra* to my proudest hopes.
>
> (4.1.101–3)

The idea of Cormorant Overreach swooning in delirium over the dream of his humble family entering the peerage is of course nonsense. It is clear that Kean understood the part well, and (according to Hazlitt) in speaking to Lovell he pronounced "right honourable" "with a mixture of fawning servility and sarcastic contempt."[2] The motive force in Overreach's career is hatred. He keeps returning to his pleasure at the abasement of the old nobility.

> And 'tis my glory, though I come from the City,
> To have their issue, whom I have undone,
> To kneel to mine as bond-slaves.
> . . . .
> 'Tis a rich man's pride, there having ever been
> More than a feud, a strange antipathy
> Between us and true gentry.
>
> (2.1.81–83, 87–89)

Massinger's Overreach is powered by a sense of inferiority and fueled by hatred. He has amassed wealth and climbed the social ladder, and he aims at a peerage for his grandson—perhaps an earldom, through purchase (see 4.1.144; the price in 1620 was £10,000).[3] Not only to get even with but to rise above those who are convinced that by birth alone they are superior to him is the Tamburlaine mentality transferred from the steppes of Scythia to the meadows of Nottinghamshire. The demonstration of his ability to enter and occupy the territory of social superiors and to demote those superiors to ignominious positions is almost an end in itself (4.1.135–38).

Marriage was the everyday means to penetrate the barriers of social class, and Overreach is convinced that, given a little sexual enticement by his daughter, the usual quid pro quo of wealth on the one side and title on the other will operate (3.2.103–4). But in marriage-scheming he is no match for the old gentry. His daughter, sent off to marry Lovell, secretly weds the man she loves, Tom Alworth. Sir Giles's ruse to exploit the expected marriage of Welborne and Lady Alworth makes him advance Welborne enough money to pay his debts and rehabilitate himself. But he fails thereby to get Welborne into his clutches, and there is to be no marriage. The final demolition of the raging, baffled tyrant by the discovery that the deeds entitling him to Welborne's lands had been engrossed in a disappearing ink by a treacherous clerk assumes, like the opening scene of the play, considerable symbolic value. It is a wish fulfillment of a very high order: the delighted discovery that the terrible happening was only a nightmare, that the superseding of the old gentry is of no legal force, and that every gentleman (at last awake to his true responsibilities) can have his lands back.

A New Way to Pay Old Debts is an exorcism, an expulsion rite, by which the enemy is turned into a monstrous but recognizable image and triumphantly destroyed. We must remember who is writing. Massinger was a gentleman and the son of a gentleman. He was brought up within the ambit of the highest levels of the English aristocracy, for his father was the Earl of Pembroke's confidential man of business. His father had formerly been a fellow of an Oxford college and had married the daughter of a successful merchant. The death of his father had, however, brought Massinger no inheritance. He left Oxford without a degree and is next heard of in a debtor's prison. Though it is clear from a recently discovered document that he could fiercely defend writing as a profession,[4] he was never proud of the career in the theater to which he was reduced. And here he is in 1635 using comedy's traditional annihilation of the oppressor to restore to the gentry the patrimonial lands that they had lost or were losing by the infiltration of the bourgeoisie. *A New Way to Pay Old Debts* combines a shrewdness in appreciating seventeenth-century social movements with an atavistic belief (shared by those who participated in court masques) in the value of dramatic performances as a means of warding off disaster.

But what of the values that *A New Way* affirms? Lady Alworth, afraid that Lord Lovell is going to marry Overreach's daughter, advises him that the nobility should not seek to repair its worsening economic standing by marrying into City wealth. Her assumptions are that Lord Lovell does not love Margaret and that the money she brings is "ill-acquired." Inherited honor cannot be maintained by tainted money and a loveless marriage. Lovell is not interested in debating the question. However desirable Margaret might be in herself, however great Over-reach's riches (ill-gotten or not), Lord Lovell would never contemplate marrying below his class:

> I would not so adulterate my blood
> By marrying Margaret.
> . . . .
> In my own tomb
> I will inter my name first.
>
> (4.1.223–24, 226–27)

Lord Lovell is a baron, one of the greater nobility. Even Lady Alworth has qualms about social inferiority when the talk of marrying moves to her (5.1.45), though Lord Lovell is kind enough to reassure her about this. There is no question of applying these values lower down the social scale, no question about the fitness of the marriage between Tom Alworth, impoverished member of the old gentry, and Margaret Overreach, rich member of the new gentry. The idea of the unpolluted blood of the old aristocracy, ludicrous though it seems when one thinks of the new creations throughout Tudor and Stuart times, was none-theless an idea of emotional importance to the nobility at a time when honors and titles were freely available for purchase, as Lawrence Stone's *Crisis of the Aristocracy* amply shows. It is associated with a cultivation of what seems to us an empty ideal of traditional honor that also finds its place in the play's conclusion. Having restored his fortunes, Welborne has to restore his reputation, ruined by a life of debauchery. He enlists under Lovell, who is going to fight in the Netherlands:

> I doubt not in my service
> To my king and country but I shall do something
> That may make me right again.
>
> (5.1.397–99)

This echoes Lady Alworth's prosing, that war

> is a school
> Where all the principles tending to honour
> Are taught.
>
> (1.2.100–102)

There is a sad distance between these chivalric notions of military honor and the operations in the Netherlands that were actually going on at the time Massinger was writing his play.[5] These notions are not found in dramatic fiction alone. In 1628, the twenty-five-year-old Sir Kenelm Digby in his own words "resolved to undertake speedily something that might tend to the King's service, and gain himself honour and experience."[6] With a tiny private fleet he set sail for the Mediterranean and involved himself in a series of histrionic misadventures that would have been more suitable and less troublesome in a play. The ways of honor, like the purity of blood, must be seen as ideals that a gentry and nobility, feeling their status, power, and possessions threatened, clung to as a means of self-identification. In *A New Way to Pay Old Debts* honor and purity are rallying cries to a gentry who, in the confines of the Phoenix theater, have seen their enemies routed and who have been restored to their rightful inheritance.

* * *

The City Madam stands much more firmly on the ground than *A New Way* and is perhaps a more subtle play. Sir John Frugal is a very successful merchant—and no wonder, since we see he gets a 500 percent return on his investment in one overseas trading enterprise (1.1.4–5). He has become a gentleman by the purchase of land, and at his wife's instigation he has become a knight (presumably by purchase). Massinger later reveals Sir John as a money-lender on a scale so large that there is "scarce one shire / In Wales or England" where his money is not "lent out at usury" (3.3.40–42). Two of Sir John's apprentices, Tradewell and Goldwire, are the sons of gentlemen, and their fathers are in bond for their sons' good behavior. Sir John's daughters, whose luxury, extravagance, and social ambition are fostered by their silly mother, are being wooed by Sir Maurice Lacy, vain about his social rank as the son of a baron, and by Geoffrey Plenty, a rich self-made farmer, also a gentleman by the acquisition of land, proud of straight-dealing and paying his own way.

It is surprising to find a peer of the realm, Lord Lacy, in this counting-house setting, on intimate terms with Sir John and his family. It is as though he is Lord Lovell from *A New Way* a few years later, knowing now that he cannot keep his estates going without an injection of City money, but thankful that he has a son who can make the necessary alliance and so save his own pride. Goldwire says of Lord Lacy, that he

> needs my master's money
> As his daughter does his honour—

—the sempiternal quid pro quo. Massinger saves until the very end of the play the nugget of information that Lord Lacy has in fact mortgaged his chief estate to Frugal (5.2.64–67).

Sir John has had to make his own way in the world because, though he is the elder brother, his father left "a fair estate" to his favorite son, the younger brother Luke. Luke got through his inheritance in traditional riot and profligacy, living it up as a "gallant" and "companion to the nobility" (1.2.112–15). Eventually he had to be redeemed from a debtors' prison by his brother, in whose house he lives as a drudge, enduring the abuse and petty tyranny of his sister-in-law and his vain nieces with submissiveness and apparent humility. To Lord Lacy, Luke speaks with a special unctuousness, acknowledging his present ignominy as a fit punishment for "such as soar above their pitch," expressing gratitude to his brother for his charity, meekly accepting poverty as a blessing. All this is sweet music to a lord. Luke's tour de force is his appeal to his brother, carefully staged for a concealed Lord Lacy, for clemency for three debtors who have long outrun their time. The student of Massinger will be reminded of the contralto tones of Cleora in *The Bondman,* urging the men of Syracuse to the path of honor and duty as Luke expatiates to his brother on the nobility of compassion. "Shall I be / Talked out of my money?" asks an indignant Sir John. But he agrees to give the debtors more time. Lord Lacy is wholly taken by the Christian deportment of Luke and tries to persuade Sir John to treat him better. Sir John has no faith whatever in Luke, but he and Lord Lacy agree to settle their dispute about him with a *Measure for Measure* deception, by which Luke will be put in sole charge of Frugal's money and his womenfolk, while it is pretended that Sir John has withdrawn to a monastery. This is proposed as a means of chastening the women as well as testing Luke, for the pride of the young ladies has reached the unacceptable danger point of frightening away their suitors.

The one thing that Luke has really learned in the debtors' prison is how to value money, and he expresses his worship in a *Volpone*-style hymn (3.3.1–45). He begins to reveal his true nature to those around him (and to the audience). He arrests the three debtors for whom he has just been pleading, arrests the two gentlemen-apprentices for malpractices that he has himself urged them to perform, and reduces his sister-in-law and nieces to coarse gowns and hard fare. As regards the debtors, he justifies his actions by claiming he has simply assumed his brother's rougher nature. But the cases are quite different. It is not his own money that Luke is demanding back but his brother's, and he has just learned that all these debtors have immediate prospects of large sums which will easily enable them to pay their debts. By his sudden and cruel foreclosure, Luke is able to appropriate all this additional wealth.

The second arrest, of young Goldwire and Treadwell, seems gratuitously cruel unless one realizes Luke's class-hatred. It was because he aped the gentry as a "companion to the nobility" that he was ruined. He taunts the apprentices in an early scene—with an irony that they do not perceive—with not living up to the careless criminality which their birth entitles them to (2.1.51–54). His surprising comment at 5.2.46 that

> the masters never prospered
> Since gentlemen's sons grew prentices

may seem to the unwary to be the dramatist's voice. Not so. It is the class bitterness of a citizen's son who has learned to hate the airs of the gentry and their corrosive pastimes, and who, having amazingly come into a merchant's wealth for a second time, is not willing to let the gentry help him fritter it away *this* time. But it is not sterile vengeance that he visits on the unfortunate apprentices. He has carefully worked matters out and led them into a trap that will involve their fathers, who are sureties for their good behavior. He makes the exorbitant demand of a thousand pounds apiece from the fathers and has them arrested when they are unable to pay (5.3.70–73). His final move against the upper classes, taking him well into the Overreach territory, is to threaten to foreclose the mortgage on Lord Lacy's estate and have him put in prison despite the privilege of his class (5.2.71–74).

It is Luke's action against the women that attracts most attention in the play. Massinger ingeniously gives to the villain of the play the task of demolishing the pride of the bourgeois ladies. Just as Luke's sentiment that the value of mortification, the virtue of poverty, and the nobility of compassion and forgiveness were perfectly correct sentiments for all the insincerity and hypocrisy of the man who uttered them, so Luke's strictures against citizens' wives rising above their stations and emulating the extravagance of the court may contain truth even though uttered by a man dominated by hatred and revenge. Luke's actions do good, but it is not at all the ethics of the play that the wife and daughters of a wealthy merchant should wear "buffin gowns and green aprons" and be without servants, thus achieving their "natural forms and habits" (4.4.133). Holdfast, the steward who remembers the old days, is both delighted and upset by Luke's punishment of the women—it relishes a little, he says, of too much tyranny. Indeed it does. The women who persecuted are now persecuted by their victim. It is a condign punishment, but he who arraigns them is himself on trial, and his victory over them is not a conclusion for himself or for them. Sir John Frugal instituted the trick in order to chasten the women and he is on hand to prevent the chastening getting out of hand. In the superb nonsense of the denouement, the "Indians" demand their human sacrifice, and Luke offers them Lady Frugal and his nieces. A "magic" pageant of all Luke's previous victims fails to move any compassion in him. Sir John and Lord Lacy reveal themselves, and Luke is exposed and disgraced—with a suspended sentence of being sent off to Virginia to repent.

The ending of *The City Madam* is a remarkable coming together and reconcilement. The girls and their mother have been shocked into a sense of responsibility, and they repent of their high-handed treatment of the suitors and of their frivolous behavior generally. Sir Maurice Lacy will marry Anne, and Geoffrey Plenty will marry Mary. Sir John is moved by the cruelty of his brother to promise relief to all the victims—debtors, apprentices, and parents:

> All shall find me,
> As far as lawful pity can give way to't,
> Indulgent to your wishes, though with loss
> Unto myself.
>
> (5.3.126–29)

His last word is to his wife, to instruct "our City dames"

> willingly to confess
> In their habits, manners and their highest port
> A distance 'twixt the City and the Court.
>
> (5.3.153–55)

This is all very proper and becoming, but we reflect that by now this distance is somewhat formal. *A New Way* had a dreamlike elitist ending, with the gentry, back in possession of their manors, marching off to win fantasy-honor. *The City Madam* accepts history, and offers a very practical reconcilement between the classes. Lord Lacy, with his ancestral estates mortgaged in the City, has averted the dread fate of dispossession by marrying his son into the mortgagee's family. City and Court are cheerfully at one here. It was the City that nearly wrecked the alliance—so desirable to the merchant and so indispensable to the aristocrat—by not allowing to the marriage the appearance of a condescension by the nobility. This little difficulty removed with the bride's indicating that she knows her station, there is no talk at all of the pollution of aristocratic blood. The second obstacle was the person of Luke.

What then does Luke represent? What force in *this* play has to be exorcised and expelled to clear the way for a wished-for future? Luke has Overreach's class-hatred and Overreach's callousness, but his dangerousness is more insidious and less obvious than Overreach's. He imposes on the nobility by his obsequiousness and humility. Then, when he has won their trust, snap! He is the confidence man, the smiler with the knife beneath the cloak. In a way, the very center of *The City Madam* is the exchange between Luke and Lord Lacy in 5.2.58–85, in which Luke threatens to foreclose the mortgage unless Lord Lacy pays in the accumulated interest, which has remained unclaimed:

> Pay it in,
> I would be loth your name should sink. Or that
> Your hopeful son, when he returns from travel,
> Should find you, my lord, without land.

Luke invites him to a nearby tavern; "I know you'll drink a health to me." "To thy damnation!" is Lacy's response as Luke exits. "Was there ever such a villain? Heaven forgive me/For speaking so unchristianly—though he deserves it." Overreach and Luke represent two very different threats to the nobility, outright antagonism and clandestine undermining. As I understand the play, the rough but businesslike methods of Sir John Frugal are acceptable to the nobility and promise a means of financial support whose cost in terms of marriage alliances is not too great provided that the distinctions of class are decently observed.[7]

*   *   *

The world of *The Great Duke of Florence*, the first of Massinger's two "comical histories," is very remote from London and Nottinghamshire and very remote from Florence. It is indifferent to time or place; it exists within an idea, the idea of absolute autocracy. How far princes are men and not gods is much discussed (e.g., 1.1.73). The Duke testily rejects in his courtiers "that kind of adoration" shown to emperors who "would be styled gods" (1.2.10). Whether he is adored or not, the Duke has absolute power, and everyone in the play lives in the shadow of his will and thinks constantly about the need for obedience, the consequences of disobedience, the mystery of great place, the inscrutability of the ruler's mind:

> Th' intents
> And secrets of my prince's heart must be
> Served and not searched into.
>
> (2.3.13–15)

Fortunately Duke Cosimo is not a tyrant, but a kindly old widower, anxiously training up his young nephew Giovanni as his successor, giving hospitable protection to Fiorinda, the youthful new Duchess of Urbin, and extending his bounty to his favorite Sanazarro, a dashing fellow who has served his prince well in the wars and is now being advanced to the highest positions "to the envy/Of the old nobility, as the common people" (5.1.104–5).

The plot is fairly simple. Giovanni has fallen in love with Lidia, his tutor's daughter. The Duke sends Sanazarro to find out about this beauty. Whether or not he thinks of making her his duchess is meant to be in doubt. Sanazarro is bowled over by Lidia's beauty and wants her for himself. So it is essential that he conceal from the Duke how beautiful she is. This means recruiting Giovanni into the deception. Both Sanazarro and Giovanni, each trying to preserve Lidia for himself, lie to the Duke about her beauty. Unfortunately, the Duke has good evidence that they are lying, and resolves to see the girl himself. Sanazarro and Giovanni, appalled at the prospect of being found out, arrange for an alcoholic serving-woman to impersonate Lidia. But the substitution is quickly discovered, and the favorite and the prince await the Duke's sentence. Fiorinda, who has always loved Sanazarro—as he knows well enough—pleads his cause and the Duke relents. The Duke disclaims any personal interest in Lidia and gives his blessing to her marriage with Giovanni. Sanazarro accepts Fiorinda and the duchy of Urbin.

Many of Massinger's plays are devised as tests of character, and *The Great Duke of Florence* is clearly one of these. Its basic subject is not the love of Giovanni and Lidia but the temptation, fall, and rescue of Sanazarro. Much is made of how the Duke put his full trust in him and raised him from nothing to being a partner in government (e.g., 1.1.65–95; 5.2.128–40). The fatal sight of Lidia leads him not into great crimes but into the littleness of lying and persuading Giovanni to lie. Their improvisations and intrigues are comic and undignified. Sanazarro is guilty of a double betrayal of trust, the Duke's and Fiorinda's. Fiorinda, a great duchess in love with a man far beneath her in birth who has slighted her, can forgive him, and she makes it a condition of getting his pardon that he should marry her. But how is the Duke to be persuaded to forgive what is not only breach of faith but treason? The extraordinary suggestion is made that Giovanni fell in love with Lidia *to stop the Duke from doing so,* thereby breaking his solemn vow to his dead wife not to remarry. Lidia quickly joins in this absurd excuse:

"He told me so indeed, sir," and Fiorinda as quickly adds her lie, that this was Sanazarro's purpose too (5.2.201–2). The Duke shakes his head; indeed, this is preposterous. "We know/All this is practice, and that both are false" (5.2.206–7). But he pardons them and releases them to their brides.

This ending, which might seem Massinger's facile surrender to the need for a quick happy ending, is both extraordinary and moving. The crisis of the play arose from lies motivated by sexual desire. Here at the end the two women join together in a lie, though it is too absurd to be believed, in order to save the men they are in love with. There can be no possibility that what they say can be received as an extenuation of the conduct of the men. And yet, as a shadow of the previous crime, it becomes a kind of mitigation. The Duke's position seems to be, I cannot believe this excuse *and therefore* I pardon the accused:

> We are pleased
> With our own hand to blind our eyes and not
> Know what we understand. Here Giovanni
> We pardon thee.
> . . . .
> Sanazarro, we forgive thee.
>
> (5.2.209–12, 215)

There *can* be no evading or explaining away of Sanazarro's degrading swerve from rectitude nor of his corruption of Giovanni. Duke Cosimo's act is one of pure forgiveness. The absolute power of the Duke, the inscrutability of his projects, his concern for the future make him a Prospero figure. Though he is concerned throughout the play with the burden of office and the strictness and severity of its demands, yet in the end he is prepared to accept the frailty that affection causes (5.2.165–66), to accept imperfection in clear recognition that it is imperfection. Sanazarro is fortunate all round. Massinger uses the happy ending of comedy to acknowledge a defeat, an acceptance of the second rate, a settling for less, which ought to tinge our pleasure with just a little regret.

*   *   *

Mathias in *The Picture* has a much rougher ride than Sanazarro, in a play of greater psychological interest than *The Great Duke of Florence*. He is a self-satisfied husband, the image of male superiority, and he goes off to the wars to win the riches which he thinks are necessary to maintain his wife Sophia in fitting state, in spite of her protests that she has no interest in status that depends on the display of wealth. He secretly takes with him a magic portrait of his irreproach-able wife that will tell him instantly if she is being unfaithful to him. But it is he who falls, victim of the vanity of Queen Honoria, who enjoys at least the prospect of royal adultery. Exaggerated reports of his infidelity reach Sophia, who quaintly and unconvincingly resolves to reply in kind. Her resolve darkens the magic picture and spurs an offended Mathias on in his liaison with the queen—though adultery is never committed. Mathias sees the magic picture all clear again and gives himself the heady pleasure of a self-righteous denunciation of the queen. He then journeys back to his wife all ready, like the audience, for the happy ending. Sophia, however, refuses to say all's well that ends well; indeed, refuses at first to receive him at all and humiliates him in front of the king. Her anger is not because of his peccadillo with the queen but because of his baseness in suspecting her and taking the magic picture with him to spy on her. She absolutely refuses to forgive him and demands a divorce; only at the behest of the king and queen does she relent. This spirited and unexpected last act is reminiscent of the *coup de théâtre* in *The Maid of Honour,* when Camiola refuses to forgive the inconstant Bertoldo and goes off into a convent. Massinger's discovery of the streak of toughness in the gentle Sophia is excellent, and indeed his handling of the problem of male dominance and female submissiveness throughout the play is sensitive, amusing, and unusual. Once again he has made moral capital out of the required happy ending.

*   *   *

The ending of Massinger's last comedy, *The Guardian,* is undertaken in a different spirit. He wrote it in 1633, when he was fifty. It is one of his last surviving plays, and it seems to have been a theatrical success following a period when he had been failing to carry his audience with him. It is his most light-hearted play, a kind of liberation from himself. It is more farce than comedy. Successive confusions demand the strictest timing of exits and entrances. The treasure chest of tragicomic conventions is ransacked and ridiculed. High-mindedness is treated satirically. Just visible on the horizon is the encroaching cash-nexus that was the main preoccupation of the social comedies. It is to be seen when the musical-comedy bandits, who are presided over by an embittered Robin Hood, the banished nobleman Severino, are instructed in those who are their legitimate prey. The list contains "the grand encloser of the commons" (Overreach was an encloser), the usurer who acquires property by taking advantage of a mortgage "from a prodigal," "builders of iron mills, that grub up forests," and the owners of dark shops. Amongst those to be protected, besides scholars, are

> The rent-racked farmer, needy market folks,
> The sweaty labourer. . . .
>
> (2.4.109–10)

In a dramatist who had so laboriously presented the stern warfare of chastity against the lubricity of men (especially in the uncomfortable *Parliament of Love*), the reduction of every female character to the importunities of the flesh is unexpected; but if Massinger's women have worsened, the men are just the same. The nicest touch about the demands of the flesh concerns the gloomy exile Severino, who every now and again threads his way back to Naples in spite of the risk. "In the change / Of dangers there is some delight" (2.4.47–48). Concerning these visits his prudish wife says to her daughter:

> Yet I have tasted those delights which women
> So greedily long for, know their titillations;
> And when with danger of his head thy father

> Comes to give comfort to my widowed sheets,
> As soon as his desires are satisfied,
> I can with ease forget 'em.
>
>   (1.2.49–54)

It is this severe lady, harsh with her own daughter for talking to men, who is tempted from a lifetime of virtue by the sight of a handsome stranger and makes an assignation with him. (He later turns out to be her own brother in disguise.) This assignation is arranged for just that hour when her daughter plans to elope with her lover. In the virtuoso night scene the daughter is abducted by another suitor whom she has rejected, and the man who turns up in the mother's boudoir is of course the astonished husband Severino. The wife escapes a savage punishment by an ingenious substitution, and claims a miracle when her husband can find no mark on the woman he thought he had just wounded. While he does not believe in the miracle, or in his wife's protestations of injured innocence, he does not understand the trick, and in a pretty exchange of mutual insincerity, makes a sardonic return of her own rhetoric:

> How can I expiate my sin? or hope,
> Though now I write myself thy slave, the service
> Of my whole life can win thee to pronounce
> Despaired-of pardon? shall I kneel? that's poor,
> Thy mercy must urge more in my defence
> Than I can fancy; wilt thou have revenge?
> My heart lies open to thee.
> IOLANTE: This is needless
> To me, who in the duty of a wife,
> Know I must suffer.
> SEVERINO: Thou art made up of goodness,
> And from my confidence that I am alone
> The object of thy pleasures, until death
> Divorce us, we will know no separation.
>
>   (3.6.256–67)

So he prudently takes her back with him to the wild woods. As in Luke's speeches in *The City Madam*, Massinger in this well-controlled scene shows a flexibility of language that he is not often given credit for and uses the more solemn tones of his own earlier heroes and heroines for satiric purposes. Throughout the play, everyone who mounts into high-mindedness is quickly brought down to earth. The guffaws of the old guardian with the roving eye, Durazzo, deflate the raptures of the young hero. A solemn speech of reformation by the rake Adorio is punctured by the discovery that he has eloped with the maid and not the mistress.

The concluding pastoral scenes, in which all confusions are straightened out and the wounds of old feuds healed, are treated with mock seriousness throughout. At the very end, Adorio is still left with the maidservant as a partner, and he indignantly rejects her. "Marry with a servant? / Of no descent or fortune?" But Severino chimes in quickly:

> You are deceived.
> Howe'er she has been trained up as a servant,
> She is the daughter of a noble captain
> Who in his voyage to the Persian Gulf
> Perished by shipwreck. . . .
>
>   (5.4.236–40)

This must be the only birth-discovery in the Fletcher-Massinger canon that is actually played for laughs.

It is quite a triumph that a writer of Massinger's temperament should, once, so successfully achieve unseriousness. With *A New Way to Pay Old Debts*, *The City Madam*, and *The Picture* in mind, it would be silly to call *The Guardian* Massinger's highest achievement in comedy, but it has a special value in making fun of the rhetoric and conventions that he normally lived by. It helps us to distinguish in his own earlier plays the really successful serious work, as in *The Duke of Milan* or *The Maid of Honour*, from its perfunctory shadow, as in *The Parliament of Love* or *The Bashful Lover*. And by writing one comedy which has no observable moral center whatsoever, he emphasizes by contrast the strong determination of the other comedies and comical histories to make the materials of comedy subserve moral and social argument.

NOTES

1. All references to the texts of Massinger's plays are from *The Plays and Poems of Philip Massinger*, ed. Philip Edwards and Colin Gibson, 5 vols. (Oxford: Clarendon Press, 1976). All quotations are given in modern spelling.

2. William Hazlitt, *Works*, ed. P. P. Howe, 21 vols. (London and Toronto: J. M. Dent and Sons, 1930–34), 5:277.

3. See Lawrence Stone, *The Crisis of the Aristocracy, 1558–1641*, abridged ed. (London: Oxford University Press, 1967), p. 55.

4. See P. Beal, "Massinger at Bay: Unpublished Verses in a War of the Theatres," *Yearbook of English Studies* 10 (1980): 199–203.

5. See Edwards and Gibson, eds., *Plays and Poems of Philip Massinger*, 2:274–75.

6. Kenelm Digby, *Private Memoirs*, ed. H. Nicholas (London: Saunders and Otley, 1827), p. 302.

7. A rather different view of the social context of *The City Madam* may be found in Martin Butler's "Massinger's *The City Madam* and the Caroline Audience," *Renaissance Drama*, new series 13 (1982): 157–87.

Three Caroline "Defenses" of the Stage

Jonas Barish

My title contains an equivocation, indicated by the quotation marks around the word *defense*, since of the three plays I propose to discuss—Massinger's *The Roman Actor*, Randolph's *The Muses' Looking-Glass*, and Brome's *The Antipodes*—one is not, I believe, a defense at all, another is one only inferentially, and the third, though intended as such, falls seriously, even grievously, short of its aim.

By the time of Charles I, commentary on the theater within plays themselves had long been a standard feature of English drama, and never more so than during the years when the fundamentalist attack grew so insistent that it finally overwhelmed the theater altogether. The widespread use of inductions and other framing devices, the theatrical chatter in the dialogue, the increasing frequency of plays within plays, all point to a quickened interest on the part of playwrights in the possibilities and limits of their art, its relation to the life it purported to portray, and its vulnerability to attack from those who saw in it nothing but frivolity and illusion. Apologies for it might be more or less explicit, more or less specific. The earlier instances tended to be implicit, even buried, as in Edwardes's *Damon and Pythias* (1565), where the story of the two self-sacrificing friends is acted out on a scaffold before the eyes of the Syracusan tyrant, converting him in the process from a vicious egotist to an aspirant to virtuous friendship himself.[1] In *The Taming of the Shrew* (1594), things are subtler still: a series of pranks and plays and disguises and illusions is mounted, including the central "play," if we may agree to call it such, of Petruchio's wooing, with its whirligig of clatter and antic hubbub designed to provide Katherine with a mirror of her own behavior, as well as to suggest more seemly roles she might choose to play. In cases such as these the stage is being defended in a manner more suited to its truest nature than by simple polemical attacks on those who denounced it as a school of abuse or a shop of Satan.

A slightly later group of plays, mostly Jacobean, mostly Jonsonian, utilizes theatrical commentary for narrower purposes, not so much to defend the theater as to defend one kind of theater against another. In *Every Man Out of His Humour* (1599) we have not an apology for the stage as such, but a theatrically argued rationale for a specific genre, Jonsonian comical satire. The Grex in this play, like the Intermean of Gossips in *The Staple of News* (1623) and the Chorus of *The Magnetic Lady* (1632), serves to expound Jonson's satiric methods, as well as to forestall objections from backward members of the audience, addicted to more comfortable kinds of comedy. In these cases, Jonson is trying not to answer the case against the theater itself, but to build a case for his own theatrical innovations. In the puppet play in *Bartholomew Fair* (1614) he does mount such a defense, a retort to the Puritan adversaries of the stage, but it is a farcical defense. The puppets heap ridicule on their zealous antagonist in mock disputation, reducing him, with little difficulty, to their own level of blockishness, raucousness, and illogicality. In so doing they not only destroy his argument; they very nearly destroy argument itself. The contest becomes a slanging match between rival absurdities. In *The Knight of the Burning Pestle* (1607) we find a theatrically self-conscious play about the performance of a play, focusing on the crude, incoherent, "romantic" stage entertainments favored by the London citizenry, and on the incapacity of that citizenry to grasp the distinction between art and life. The theater's enemies, here, are simply those who willfully, defiantly refuse to learn the distinction.

Caroline playwrights move further into the arena of debate in that they address the question more frontally. They identify specific arguments against the stage. They produce counterarguments, counterdemonstrations. The element of apology becomes more articulate, though not on that account more successful. From the beginning, Massinger's tragedy *The Roman Actor* (1626) was perceived, was indeed hailed, as a stunning refutation of the antitheatrical position, and later generations followed Massinger's own contemporaries in adopting this view of the play. "T. I.," in commendatory verses prefixed to the first published edition, assured the author that "when thy PARIS pleades in the defence/Of Actors, every grace, and excellence/Of Argument for that subject, are by Thee/Contracted in a sweete Epitome" (ll. 13–16),[2]—or, in other words, that in Paris's speech Massinger had brilliantly brought together all the choicest arguments commonly urged in vindication of the actor's craft. Another contributor praises the author for making Paris such a memorable and exemplary figure, exalted by the play as high as Caesar himself: "Each line speakes him an Emperour, ev'ry phrase/Crownes thy deserving temples with the Bayes" (p. 19). Apart from the oddity of hearing Paris praised by being likened to the vicious and degenerate emperor of the play, it is clear that the admiring contributor is thinking only of Paris's speeches to the Senate, for as we shall suggest shortly, Paris in his later appearances does not cut by any means so exalted a figure.

It came about, then, as a natural sequel in the eighteenth and nineteenth centuries, that when *The Roman Actor* was revived, it owed its precarious toehold on the stage almost entirely to the scenes in act 1 in which Paris answers his senatorial accusers. Three celebrated actors—Kemble, Macready, and Kean—converted those scenes into showpieces for the display of their own virtuoso powers of declamation. Kemble led off in 1781 with a playlet entitled "The Defence of the Stage," concocted from the speeches of act 1, scene 3, and later in the same year he produced an abridged version of the Paris-Domitia story as a separate dramatic event. A revival of the latter in 1796 prompted a reviewer to observe that "Mr. Kemble . . . in that noble defence and eulogium of the stage, which Paris makes before the consuls, gave an additional proof of the soundness of his judgement, and the unequalled force of his declamation." Following

Kemble came the elder Macready, with a "petit Piece" of his own, wherein *The Roman Actor* was "corrected, revised, and adapted to the present Time . . . Tending to elucidate the real Purposes for which the Stage was first erected." The "petit Piece" evidently consisted only of scenes 1 and 3 from act 1, and it most likely formed the basis for Kean's version of 1822, played at the inauguration of the Drury Lane Theatre and published in 1854 as *The Drama's Vindication: or The roman Actor. Compressed* [!] *from Massinger's celebrated play.* English provincial troupes, taking their cue from London, followed suit with versions of or excerpts from the same scenes and so, during the same period, did Philadelphia, Boston, and New York.[3]

Such sporadic stage life as the play has enjoyed, then, it has enjoyed mainly in a mutilated, truncated, tendentious version. Paris's eulogium has been lifted from its context as if it contained the core of the play and could be understood without reference to its dramatic surroundings. The editor of a full-scale scholarly reprint in 1929 concludes, from certain resemblances in detail to Heywood's *Apology for Actors* (1612), that Paris's oration before the Senate "was intended as a defence, and not penned simply as a speech appropriate for the actor to recite." Massinger, according to the same editor, may also have been specifically prompted by a just published *Short Treatise against Stage-Plays* (1625), and by subsequent parliamentary debate of its proposal to ban theaters, "to write a play which should be a glowing example of what a drama should be and a defence, with all the arguments he could adduce, not for a specific time, but for all time."[4]

Such a reaction on the part of Massinger's fellow writers, later theatrical impresarios, and scholarly commentators, cannot be dismissed as totally unwarranted. Committed playwrights like Massinger, during the Caroline years, must have felt their professional futures deeply threatened. Massinger, moreover, in a number of his plays, is given to flights of high-minded rhetoric on topics he plainly has at heart—virtue, honor, and true nobility—and Paris's speeches ring with a comparable fervor. In themselves quite without irony or levity, and raised to a certain pitch of passionate eloquence by the injustice of his accusers, they compose an anthology of arguments in behalf of the drama's ethical mission. From Sidney, it would seem, comes the claim that poetry, which shows men in action, instills virtue more effectively than philosophy. From Nashe, Heywood, and others would come the reference to the exceptional vividness of the theater, which can fire spectators to emulation, so that even the viciously inclined "Go home chang'd men" (1.3.106). From Jonson and the satirists would come the disavowal of personal reference, the assertion that plays do not "glance at" specific individuals but deal in types, against whom the onlookers may (but only if they wish) measure their own lives. Paris, moreover, in these early scenes conducts himself in admirably manly fashion, whether rallying his followers to bear with courage whatever may be decided against them, or lecturing the Senate on the moral value of his art. As for his senatorial accusers, they—like the venal senators in Jonson's *Sejanus*, on whom they are modeled—are depicted as toadies and bullies, furious at having been (as they suppose) "touched," "traduced" by the players, and bent on wreaking such vengeance as is available to them.

All this, and especially Paris's resolute manner before his accusers, momentarily confers on him something of the glamor of a fearless champion of a persecuted minority. But the defense and eulogium are only a prelude to the main action, and even at the outset we catch disquieting notes. We learn from the beginning that the company is planning that day to perform "*Agaves* phrensie,/With *Pentheus* bloudie end" (1.1.1–2). Now whether this refers to Euripides' *Bacchae,* or to the version of Statius mentioned in Juvenal, we are not told, nor does it matter.[5] What does matter is the character of the story, an Ovidian tale of madness, of outrage, of wild and orgiastic action, in which the Bacchantes do unspeakable things on behalf of their god. Despite suggestions that Pentheus has blasphemed by refusing to honor Bacchus properly, it is impossible to see this story as a cautionary tale of the sort cited by Paris as evidence of the lofty moral intentions of the theater—tales of the labors of Hercules, of Camillus refusing tribute to Gaul, of Scipio demanding tribute from Carthage, or tales of wicked men turned aside from their evil courses. Even Ovid's moralistic translator, Arthur Golding, expert at unearthing improving meanings in his author, seemed not to know what to do with this particular metamorphosis but passed over it in unaccustomed silence in his otherwise garrulous prefatory epistle.[6]

We may also be slightly unsettled, early on, by the complacency with which Paris stakes his safety, and that of his associates, on the emperor's favor. He gives no hint, either during the early scenes or later, that he comprehends the emperor's baseness, though neither we nor the more clear-eyed among the senators have the slightest doubt about it. No sooner in fact have Paris and his friends been marched off under guard, at the close of scene 1, to answer the charge of treason, than a chorus of right-minded senators, modeled on the Germanican faction in *Sejanus,* remains behind to comment bitterly on their colleagues' servility and on Domitian's criminal megalomania. But Paris, so keenly aware of the former, seems utterly blind to the latter. Immediately following these warnings from his senatorial critics, we have a foretaste of Domitian's own style: his creature, Parthenius, with much calculated insolence, "divorces" the emperor's mistress from her husband. And following Paris's speech to the Senate in act 1, scene 3, we see Domitian making "a bloudie entrance" in person, boasting of his recent triumph before sending the captives off to execution, to "Tast the extreames of miserie" (1.4.18). The fact, finally, that Paris owes his release from jeopardy not to his own pleadings and still less to the validity of his arguments, but purely and simply to an accident of timing that brings his imperial protector back to Rome at the critical moment, hardly makes him a reassuring spokesman for his beleaguered profession.

Act 1, however, as we have said, serves chiefly as a prologue to Paris's later involvement with the imperial pair, which proceeds by way of three plays within the greater play. One would expect, in a drama devoted to defending the drama, introduced with fanfare as a defense of drama, which starts with a rousing eulogium from a celebrated actor, that the illustrative playlets to follow would somehow confirm the eulogium, point the moral and adorn the tale. But Paris's playlets do nothing of the kind. Each, in its own way, undermines the high claims made earlier in the oration to the Senate.

Doubtless it is of small importance that in attempting to cure the avaricious Philargus, Paris is doing what he has just argued actors do *not* do—represent or aim at particular persons.[7] Philargus is known to all as a covetous wretch, and the play is meant to work a change of heart in him. This of course reflects only its contemplated use. The imaginary playwright no more thought of Philargus when he wrote "The Cure of Avarice" than the author of "The Murder of Gonzago" thought of Hamlet's father. Moreover, Paris's motive here is irreproachable—to lift a benighted fellow creature out of his own self-inflicted suffering—even if in doing so he must momentarily violate his own code. What really counts is the spectacular lack of success of the experiment: "The Cure of Avarice" fails dismally in its purpose. Paris hopes that the miser, "looking on a covetous man/Presented on the Stage as in a mirror/May see his owne deformity, and loath it" (2.1.97–99). But this hope is dashed to pieces on the rock of Philargus's obstinacy. Philargus does see his own deformity in the play, but either does not see it *as* deformity, or, worse, sees it as such and is content. The miser in the playlet, persuaded by the eloquence of his Doctor, vows to live henceforth "As neither my heyre should have just cause to thinke/I liv'd too long for being close handed to him,/Or cruell to my selfe" (398–400). But the ruse that converts him has no effect on Philargus at all except to drive him deeper into his fixation. Identifying strongly at first with his stage counterpart, who has taken various grotesque precautions to guard his gold, Philargus rejects him harshly after the conversion. "An old foole to be guld thus!" he jeers, "had he died/As I resolve to doe, not to be alter'd,/It had gone off twanging" (407–9). For his part, Philargus would rather die than lose the least particle of his treasure, or relax an inch of his fanatical vigilance over it. He *chooses* avarice, and chooses it to the death. Caesar's peremptory intervention, ordering him to execution, has the effect only of allowing him to play out his obsession to its grim and bitter end.

The attempt to change him has thus failed, and it is a failure of the theater. Instead of the magical efficacy he thought to display, Paris has revealed only the impotence of his medium. It is not quite enough, with Patricia Thomson, to ascribe this failure to "human intractability."[8] It must also be seen as a rebuff to the pretensions of art, and of theater especially, to effect moral reform. Human intractability, after all, lies all about us. Many men, perhaps most men, are intractable, held rigid in the grip of their ruling passions; few are going to be softened by any amount of theatrical imaging of those passions. Philargus seems to embody a hard-shelled imperviousness to any form of reclamation, whether through art, or exhortation, or the threat of dire punishment. If the stage is helpless to reshape even such an out-and-out gargoyle as he, can it be expected to make much of an impact on the passionate minds of the young? to transform its erring beholders into the likes of Scipio, Camillus, or Hercules? At very least, the episode leaves us doubtful, and it leaves the venerable analogy between art and mirror sadly cracked.

Of the three chief spectators to "The Cure of Avarice," none reacts so as to justify the contentions of the partisans of the stage. Apart from the miser, confirmed in his miserliness rather than shocked out of it, there is a Caesar who takes it on himself to administer the conversion that the play fails to bring about, and there is Domitia, the empress, roused to a reckless passion of lust for the actor whose "tunable tongue and neate delivery" so charm her (2.1.414). Before "The Cure of Avarice" has finished, she is bored, already planning a play of her own for the next day, with Paris in the leading role, on the subject of Iphis and Anaxarete. We hear, shortly, of her ordering the actors about, assigning parts according to her whim, and rewriting the story to suit her own purposes. Now although nothing is said to point expressly to it, the fact is plain that Paris is allowing himself and his talent to be abused, by a patently unworthy empress, for a patently immoral purpose. He acquiesces unprotestingly, so far as we can see, in the story she wishes played, and in her version of it, tailored to enhance his own attractiveness (because she is infatuated with him) and to besmirch her rival, Domitilla. As A. P. Hogan observes, the tale of Iphis and Anaxarete is far from the sort of edifying anecdote instanced by Paris in his speech before the Senate as characteristic of the stage. Rather, it is "a romantic piece of wish fulfillment," an Ovidian tale of passion concerning a despairing suitor who hangs himself, in which "no moral is intended by the actors or taken by the audience."[9] Golding himself could extract from it only a feeble Petrarchan rebuke to the cold-hearted mistress and a warning against aspiring above one's station:

> The tale of Anaxaretee willes dames of hygh degree
> Too use their lovers courteously how meane so ere they bee,
> And Iphis lernes inferior folkes too fondly not too set
> Their love on such as are too hygh for their estate too get.[10]

The excerpt acted by Paris does not even contain this much by way of instruction. It belongs to what Malraux might have termed *"art d'assouvissement"*—the theater of complaisance, as we may call it—and lends no support at all to the view of the stage as an agent of moral education. Paris himself seems, with little resistance, to be sinking into a moral quagmire.

In the scene of his attempted seduction by Domitia, he cuts a depressingly unheroic figure. If we compare his language with that of Rusticus and Sura, who have been tortured to death for their defiance of unjust authority, we find Paris's rhetoric here diffuse, facile, and flattering. It is true that he rejects Domitia's advances at first and enlightens her sensibly concerning the relations between an actor's stage self and his private self. But he lacks persistence; in the face of pressure, he caves in. As an actor, he has been trained to please, and he almost literally does not know how to say no. When Domitia forces the issue, demanding a kiss, he complies, "Since it is your will" (4.2.104)—not by any means, we gather, because he reciprocates her passion. Their love scene rudely interrupted by Domitian, Paris once more adopts a distastefully submissive style: "I know I have deserv'd death. And my suit is / That you would hasten it: yet that your highnes / When I am dead (as sure I will not live) / May pardon me I'll onely urge my frailtie" (177–80). But why has Paris deserved death? And why does he court it so abjectly? Why, if he is to die, should he think a pardon from the depraved Domitian worth begging for? He goes so far as to plead *against* any remission of his sentence: "You must not Sir; / Nor let it to posteritie be recorded / That *Caesar* unreveng'd, sufferd a wrong, / Which yf a private man should sit downe with it/Cowards would baffell him" (193–97). Again, neither an endearing nor a persuasive plea. Why should Paris, coerced by Domitia's advances, declare himself beyond forgiveness? Why should he subscribe, in this huffing vein, to such an exaggerated version of the odious revenge code? Why should he be so much more tender of the supposed honor of this pernicious Caesar than of his own self-respect, let alone of his own survival?

The third playlet, "The False Servant," which now ensues, casts Paris as the title figure. Domitian, by his own request, fills in as the lord who, returning from a journey, surprises his wife embracing the servant left in charge. When it comes his turn, he picks up his cue but gets no farther than the first four words: "O villaine! thankeless villaine!" he rages, following the script, but then breaks off— "I should talke now;/But I have forgot my part. But I can doe,/Thus, thus, and thus. *Kils* PARIS." Paris once safely dead, Caesar explains: it was a tribute, an act of pity, "to distinguish/My *Paris* from all others," so that "as thou didst live/*Romes* bravest Actor, 'twas my plot that thou/Shouldst dye in action, and to crowne it dye/With an applause induring to all times,/By our imperiall hand" (4.2.281–300).

It may be—it is even plausible—that this absurd climax was composed by Massinger with a straight face, to glorify Paris. "Death at the hands of a man of royal rank was considered to be a mark of honour," note Massinger's editors, citing in support another incident from elsewhere in Massinger.[11] Heywood had said the same thing, with specific reference to Roman emperors.[12] And it is true that the scene allows Paris more dignity than the death reported in history. Domitian, it appears, simply butchered him "in the middle of the street."[13] Here he not only kills him in a scene from a play, permitting him to die with his buskin on, but eulogizes him afterward, orders his ashes placed in a golden urn, bids poets write elegies, and the stage mourn its loss forever. But it is difficult to see this as a serious, let alone as a satisfactory, answer to the enemies of the stage. On the contrary, it seems to grant one of their most insistent charges: that acting inflames the passions and pushes them to criminal extremes, both in the actor and in the beholder.

Moreover, the episode testifies once more to the offensively histrionic disposition of Domitian himself, as we have experienced it all along, ruthless in seizing the center of attention and in making himself both chief actor and chief spectator in every scene, the sadistic interrogation of Lamia, Domitia's husband, prearranged so as to humiliate Lamia before killing him, providing a case in point. His one conspicuous failure has been with the dissidents, Rusticus and Sura, for whom he has organized a torture session so that he may enjoy their groans. The pair, however, both Stoics, remain unmoved under torment, until at length the baffled monarch cries out that it is he who is being tortured in their silence. The antitheatricality of the two martyrs thus wins out, in this scene, over the theatricality of their captor, and serves to discredit it.[14] Caesar himself, whose every gesture reflects a craving to place himself on display, provides a repellent example to be shunned. His killing of Paris—less objectionable, to be sure, than most of his other crimes—is nonetheless stamped with the same abhorrent exhibitionism. In his attempt to arouse an applause lasting to all aftertimes, it is not Paris he is thinking of, but himself. The fact that he cannot even momentarily submit to the discipline of reciting his lines but must hurry on to the act of blood—that he must manipulate the script as he manipulates everything else—reflects once more his maniacal need to be in control and to be seen to be in control. Even in a scene orchestrated by himself, with himself as the central personage, he cannot follow the text with proper deliberation but must seize the bit between his teeth and bolt.[15]

We have, then, in act 1, a fine oratorical eulogy of the stage from an actor, Paris, who from the start is tainted by his association with a tyrant. This is followed, in acts 2, 3, and 4, by three plays within the play, each of which in some way undercuts the principles laid down in the eulogy. "The Cure of Avarice" subverts the claim for the stage as an agent of moral therapy; "Iphis and Anaxarete" invalidates the proposition that plays propound useful lessons or, indeed, any lessons at all; while "The False Servant" belies any view of theater as a protected world in which violent actions are merely exemplary because they are make-believe. As for the theater's most illustrious practitioner and revered spokesman, Paris, he shows himself subservient first toward the tyrant, Domitian, and again toward Domitian's self-willed and tyrannical consort. Domitian himself, by his relentless exhibitionism, brings acting into disgrace. The only characters whom we are asked unreservedly to admire are the two Stoics, as devoid of theatrical temperament as the rest are swollen with it. Unlike the professional player, their sense of self does not depend on pleasing. Their passive fortitude, nevertheless, manages to turn the tables, to turn their persecutor into the victim and themselves into curious spectators. No doubt in their indifference to pain they set a standard of *reluctant* theatricality to which it would be vain to expect the generality of men to aspire. Admittedly Paris is weak rather than vicious, and comes closer to reacting as most good men would react in similar circumstances. Nevertheless, his weakness and its consequences, the repeated fiascos of his impromptu theatrical ventures, set the entire theatrical enterprise in an unheroic light and stir our skepticism with regard to its purported power of moral reformation. What one might with more justice infer is that it can be no better than the society around it, that it is more likely to follow society than to lead it, and that it is as prone as any other social institution to take corruption from the shortcomings of human nature.

Looking at the question from a generic point of view, one might conclude that tragedy makes an uncomfortable medium for polemical apologetics. As a social institution, the stage belongs to the world in which the protagonist finds himself and in which he goes down to defeat; it must therefore share somehow in that defeat.[16] The genuine theatrical defenses of the theater tend to be found in comedy, no doubt for the primitive but sufficient reason that comedy, with its happy outcome, tends to celebrate the continuity, the sustaining vitality of institutions, along with the welfare of the individuals who compose them, so that if the theater figures as part of the machinery of the plot, it receives the blessings of the happy ending along with most other elements of the plot.

*   *   *

Thomas Randolph's *The Muses' Looking-Glass* (1630), a less closely wrought, less intellectually challenging piece than *The Roman Actor*, does, however, unlike Massinger's tragedy, attempt to make out a coherent case for the theater,[17] in answer to the perennial Puritan charge against its wickedness. It aims to turn the tables on its critics by showing that the stage surpasses formal religious instruction—catechism, sermon, or lecture—as a mode of moral teaching, and it adopts again the traditional analogy of the mirror, at first rather ingeniously, but then seems disappointingly unable to do much with it. G. E. Bentley has suggested that the play may have originated as an academic piece in Cambridge and later been expanded for performance at the Salisbury Court playhouse in London.[18] This would help account for the curious prologue that concludes act 1, in which the audience is welcomed as though it had just arrived, and for the exceptionally academic, not to say pedantic, nature of the central conceit. We are treated to a parade of no fewer than twenty-four antic characters, emblems of the vicious extremes of the Aristotelian virtues, within a topical frame concerning a brace of visiting Puritans. The Puritans, who have wandered into Blackfriars (the site of the performance) to peddle pins and feathers, first wrangle with their host, Roscius, remaining then, at Roscius's invitation, to see what the theater can have to say for itself. The dispute gives Roscius a chance to ridicule them for their pseudobiblical cant and for the hypocrisy with which they trade in just such vanities as they are given to denouncing from their pulpits—pins, for instance, designed "to joint gew-gawes, and to knit together/Gorgets, strips, neck-cloths, laces, ribbands, ruffs,/And many other such-like toyes as these." As for the feather merchant, his wares serve likewise "But to plume folly,/To give Pride her wings/To deck vain-glory."[19] The stage, avers Roscius, does far better than Puritan moralizing to correct manners. The players live by vices only as physicians do by diseases, in order to cure them. Far from pampering prodigality, they help control it, and a single hearty comedy will often laugh more hearers into virtue than "twenty tedious Lectures drawn from sin." The reason, explains Roscius, lies in the power of the visual image: what we see affects us more keenly than what we merely hear. He invites the visitors to test this proposition for themselves, and they agree to stay, with the excuse that in so doing they will be sending a signal to Satan that they "defie his Engines" (A3v–A4)

One problem with the demonstration that follows is that it lacks forward momentum; it seems tied to one spot. Roscius's act 1 prologue in fact apologizes heavily for the whole enterprise. All that the author can plead, he says,

> Is a desire of Pardon; for he brings you
> No plot at all, but a meer *Olla Podrida,*
> A medly of ill plac'd, and worse pen'd humours.
> His desire was in single Scenes to shew
> How Comedy presents each single vice
> Ridiculous, whose number as their Character
> He borrowes from the man to whom he owes
> All the poore skill he has, great *Aristotle.*

(B1)

"No plot at all" is doubtless too severe, too abject—the self-abasing tone of the passage makes one squirm a little—but it is not altogether inaccurate. Nor, alas, is the further apology, "ill plac'd." Constructive defects do blunt the edge of Randolph's purpose. The pairs of characters succeed each other too haphazardly; no meaningful order is established among them, so that we never know where we are headed next. For the most part, the order is Aristotle's order, but that, arbitrary enough in itself, gives no assistance to the maker of a seventeenth-century comedy. As it is, the pairs fail to build an intelligible architecture of any kind. With each new pair we start all over again, but each time with flagging interest and waning expectation.

Randolph, furthermore, handles the trope of the mirror, of comedy as a truth-telling glass in which the beholder may see his genuine self, both awkwardly and inconsistently. The formula requires that after each set of vices has taken the stage and been put through its paces, the partners learn of the mirror's magical properties and are urged to go in quest of it, to gaze at their own warty selves for the first time. But Colax, the flatterer, who takes over much of the burden of exposition and commentary from Roscius, often lets this thread go slack. Once or twice he recalls the mirror's purpose, assuring the plagiarist, for example, that it will present him with a "Felon's" countenance, and slyly promising the injurious Justice Nimis that it will show him "every close offenders face" (D6, E4ᵛ). But his usual habit is simply to predict that the characters will see in it whatever they wish to see, and he dangles this misleading bait so often that we nearly lose our own sense of what the mirror means. In one or two cases, oddly, the characters already know about the mirror. The miser leaves the scene to seek his scrivener, who has gone "To a strange Glasse wherein all things appear"; Philotimia, the overcurious in her dress, asks the bashful scholar to accompany her "To see an exquisite glasse to dresse me by" (C2, E2). But how have Philotimia and the miser heard of the glass? Why should the latter have learned of it from his scrivener? And if their informants have seen it for themselves, would they not have discovered its true nature and given a different account of it? Would not the miser and the overcurious dresser be anxious to *avoid* looking into it? Why, finally, should Colax himself, aware that he is a flatterer, and already apprised of the properties of the mirror, postpone the moment of his own resort to it until the very end, except as a mechanical contrivance of the plot? There seems something gratuitous in his announcement near the end that "since this age/Is grown too wise to entertain a Parasite,/Ile to the glasse, and there turn vertuous too" (E8). Doubtless this last-minute decision may be traced to the eleventh-hour dishumouring of the envious presenter, Macilente, in *Every Man Out of His Humour*. But Macilente's conversion comes as a strict logical consequence of the plot. Having jolted the other characters out of their humours with his indefatigable intriguing, he has deprived himself of all basis for further envy. Colax can claim no such achievement. The fact that he has sent the various vices off to gaze at their own reflections can hardly warrant his thinking that the age has grown "too wise to entertain a Parasite," or that those he has dismissed have "turned vertuous" offstage, where neither he nor we have been permitted to follow.

Randolph has signally failed indeed to follow through on his own conception. The crucial fact about the mirror, after all, as about the corrective comedy it symbolizes, is the self-recognition it provokes. It requires the offender to confront his own visage, stand appalled at his own ugliness, and set about to mend it.

But once enticed off to view the glass, none of the allegorical characters in the play returns. Once duly flattered and anatomized by Colax and given a moment in which to regale us with their folly, they disappear for good, only to be replaced by yet one more pair of antic extremes related to yet one more golden mean. And this repeated arousing and frustrating of expectation ends by irritating us. Once we grasp the fact that no meaningful confrontation is going to take place, no resolution occur, that we are to be left dangling, we lose our zest for the game. We do not wish to *hear* about the potency of the glass but to *see* it at work, to experience its wondrous cures and conversions with our own eyes. Randolph, very much to the injury of his play, has ignored his own axiom, enunciated by Roscius in the act 1 prologue, that "Men are not wonn by th'eares so well as eies" (A4). What he gives us, in fact, is a series of stage recitations that differ too little from a sequence of verse satires in a printed book.

Occasional local problems betray the same kind of inattention, as when the libertine Acolastus proposes a visit to the theater to cheer up his despondent antithesis, Anaisthetus. Acolastus, after all, represents idle and promiscuous pleasure seeking, whereas Randolph himself is purporting to offer comedy as a wholesome form of moral nourishment. He seems to have let his own creation here undermine his larger purposes. One can almost feel the Puritan spectators stiffen, hear them mutter meaningfully to each other—"Of course, just as we always thought, the one who frequents plays is nothing but a wastrel and an epicure"—though of course Randolph's Puritans say no such thing, being there for the express purpose of being converted *to* the theater.

The vices having at length been exhaustively passed in review, it remains for a final masque and dance of the virtues to conclude matters—not, however, as might have been expected and as would have been dramatically fitting, the vices transformed into virtues after their encounter with the glass, but, simply and lamely, the virtues as independent entities. (We may guess that these were in practical fact danced by the same actors who played the vices, but nothing in the text suggests a connection between them.) The Puritans, by this time enraptured with what they have seen, desire to know of Roscius if there really is such a glass as the one he has been describing. For answer, he spins a charming fable of the sort that could come so readily to the pen of a Renaissance writer. The glass does indeed exist, he tells them. It was created by Apollo, god of medicine, to purge the wicked earth of its folly and heal it of its ignorance:

> He takes out water from the *Muses* spring,
> And sends it to the North, there to be freez'd
> Into a Christall—That being done, he makes,
> A Mirrour with it, and instills this vertue,
> That it should by reflection shew each man,
> All his deformities both of soule and body,
> And cure 'em both—

But the glass proves short-lived, thanks to the ill-temper of Pluto, who is afraid that by ridding men of evil it may empty his realm—"for 'tis sin/That peoples hell." He persuades the Fates, therefore, to shorten its life to a single day. "But

Phoebus to requite the black Gods envy,/Will when the Glasse is broke transfuse her vertue/To live in Comoedie" (F3–F3ᵛ). Whereupon the Puritans, enchanted, hasten in to take their own turn at mirror gazing, and—alone among the characters—to return transformed and dedicated henceforth to a sweeter style of devotion. Roscius, winding up the proceedings, takes his leave of us. In the process, however, he manages to transform the truth-telling mirror into a flattering one: "*A souldier shall himself in* Hector *see,/Grave councellours,* Nestor, *view themselves in thee*" (F4ᵛ), and so forth. Up to this point, the glass has served the purpose of satirical exposure only. The stage abstractions have seen themselves, we presume, as we have seen them, as a parade of grotesques, each one illustrating some vice or folly to be shunned. Suddenly, the mirror turned toward us, we find we are being asked to bask in it, to preen ourselves, to see ourselves not anatomized but idealized. The soldier in our midst will not see himself as a ruffian or a bully but as a Hector, a pattern of heroic courage. The politician among us will see himself not as a pantaloon or a Polonius, but as a Nestor, an elder statesman, a revered vessel of wisdom. So Randolph, in order to ingratiate himself with his audience, waters down the comic astringency of his plot, in another retreat from rigor that his "father" and model, Jonson, would not have countenanced for a moment.

For all his worthy intentions, then, Randolph has at least half bungled his self-imposed assignment. But two further points may be made: first, that the quality of the verse need not have been so strenuously deprecated in the prologue. Whatever the play's shortcomings as a dramatic structure—and they are serious, even disabling—the verse, as verse, has inventiveness and life. One might without absurdity set Acolastus's rapture over nature's sensory delights alongside the enticements of Milton's Comus on the same theme. Viewed solely as a sequence of satiric set pieces, the text possesses merits it lacks as a play. The problem with it lies not so much in Randolph's deficient verbal powers as in his defective grasp of what, given his own premises, the stage requires. The theory of comedy on which he bases his plot, bookish in itself, is embodied in a paralyzingly undramatic structure.

Even so, however, it seems to have found its mark. A contemporary poem makes it clear that Puritans were incensed by it; the same conclusion seems to emerge from a hostile reference in Prynne's *Histriomastix* three years later.[20] Even granting their frequent ineptness as a defense of the theater, then, one can well believe that Randolph's verses, recited from the stage of the Salisbury Court by the talented Children of the Revels, carried a sharper sting than we are able to feel with only the printed page before us.

*   *   *

Brome's *The Antipodes* (1638) succeeds rather better than our other two plays as a defense, perhaps because of its greater reticence. It engages in no polemics against the Puritans or defiances against despotic authority; it advances no formal arguments as to the merits of the stage. But it implies an apology of a sort familiar from earlier plays. Like *The Taming of the Shrew* (1594) and *A Midsummer*

Night's Dream (1595), and doubtless owing something to their example, it concerns the transforming power of the imagination.[21] More specifically than they, it sees that power as exercised through the illusions of the stage, the stage being represented by private theatricals put on under the auspices of an eccentric nobleman named Letoy. Letoy sponsors the theatricals for an express therapeutic purpose: to heal the impotence and barrenness of a young couple whose three-year marriage remains unconsummated. The young man, Peregrine, his head as addled by too much poring over Mandeville's *Travels* as Don Quixote's was by *Amadis de Gaulle,* has neglected his young wife, Martha, whose eagerness to become a mother is exceeded only by her ignorance of where children come from. Martha has searched in parsley beds, in strawberry banks, and in rosemary bushes for the children proverbially said to grow there. She cross-examines other women as to how children are acquired; she "cannot guess/What a man does in child-getting."[22] Considering Renaissance sexual precocity, her ignorance—even allowing for disordered wits in a fantasy world— strains credulity almost as sorely as it would if asserted of a three-year wife of today, and seems prolonged largely in order to permit a certain amount of salacious jesting. The cure of both, in any case, is assigned by Letoy to a Doctor Hughball, to be accomplished at the house of a heraldic painter named Blaze, himself subject to recurrences of the jealousy of which he was supposedly cured years earlier. Unbidden, the doctor undertakes to cure not only Peregrine's melancholia and Martha's long-preserved virginity, but Blaze's jealous relapse, as well as the more serious marital friction between Peregrine's father, old Joyless, and his young wife Diana.

Letoy, who dotes on plays, has fixed ideas about acting and does not hesitate to lecture his cast on their trade. They are not, he tells them, to act in the "scholastic way" they have brought to town; they are not to vent tragical fustian in comic scenes; they are not to interpolate their clownery where the text does not call for it. The most gifted actor of the troupe comes in for special admonition because of his licentious ways with texts, his shameless ad-libbing, his habit of holding "interlocutions" with the audience instead of restricting his attention to his co-actors. When he appeals to the license traditionally accorded clowns, he is reminded frostily by Letoy that that was in the days of Tarleton and Kempe, "Before the stage was purg'd from barbarism" (2.1, p. 279). There is all too little, however, to connect this judicious treatise with Letoy's own whimsical personality. What it suggests is that Brome wishes to say certain things himself, wishes to recommend a certain noneccentric, nonexplosive, nonexaggerated style of playing and has used Letoy as a convenient mouthpiece. Considering how heavily the passage borrows from *Hamlet,* it is surprisingly short on general reflections. It has nothing to say about the theatrical enterprise as a whole; nothing about the purpose of acting; nothing, either, about moral suasion, or (what might have been apt in the present case) about the reclamation of the disordered mind. Such apology as the play does propose will emerge only obliquely, inferentially, in the course of the action.

Byplay, the master extemporizer, assures his lord that Peregrine will have no trouble believing himself truly in the Antipodes, since the actors have often been thought out of their wits, even by normal folk. Peregrine's mind already abuzz with tales of marvels and monsters, he is transported to the Antipodes, first by way of a sleeping drug, and then by the cavortings of the Letoy company, who regale him with vignettes of Antipodean life, in which the customary roles of man and woman, child and parent, ruler and subject, lawyer and client, physician and patient, merchant and customer, beggar and benefactor, are systematically reversed. Waked from his medicated sleep, he retains visions of a "thousand thousand things remarkable . . . Mere shadowy phantasms, or fantastic dreams" (2.2, p. 281). These pave the way for the still vivider phantasms he is about to encounter, as the hallucinations of the drug give way to the hallucinations of the theater. Equally bizarre and skewed from normalcy, the latter conjure up a never-never land that distorts actuality just enough to call it sharply to mind and so provide a thread by which the deranged spirit can grope its way back to sanity.

Quailpipe, the Prologue, garbed antipodally in fur shoes and leather cap, introduces the inner play with a familiar disclaimer: "This play shall no satiric timist be,/To tax or touch at either him or thee,/That art notorious" (2.2, p. 283). The play to follow, that is, will not bow to custom and engage in personal satire, nor will it charge particular persons with offenses for which they may be ill-famed. In fact, of course, it is the disclaimer itself that follows custom. More damagingly, Quailpipe in making it breaches an understanding of the plot according to which it is Peregrine who is the prime spectator of the inner play. Letoy and his guests, seated on the stage opposite Peregrine, may be allowed to be treated like ordinary theatergoers, but why should Peregrine, who genuinely thinks himself in the Antipodes, be addressed as if he were in a London playhouse? Why need *he* be informed that "Our far-fetch'd title over lands and seas/Offers unto your view th'Antipodes"? To say as much is wantonly to destroy the illusion the doctor is laboring to create. What does the reference to a play title have to do with Peregrine? It is really aimed at *us* through him and illustrates Brome's frequent failure to keep the various levels of his plot distinct.[23] Apart from smudging the clarity of the design, it also contributes to a certain desultoriness of effect. Too many hares are started, too few chased down. Here the disavowal of personal reference remains undeveloped. It leads to no fuller protest against the suspiciousness of those in great place, nor does it, like its appearances in Shakespeare or Jonson, form part of a coherent theory of satire. It amounts to little more than a ritual gesture of self-protection on the part of a nervous author, an instinctive raising of the hand to ward off an expected blow from the censor; or, perhaps, even less admissibly, it is an automatic reflex called into play in obedience to the very custom it claims to be repudiating. Paradoxically, however, it sharpens our attention to the details of the scenes to follow, so that we tend to scrutinize them more attentively, not at all to the benefit of Brome's rather casual method.

As the Antipodeans go through their paces, the various spectators react variously. Some, like Martha, identify closely, too closely, with the natives of the Antipodes. Martha, having (conveniently) never before seen a play, throws herself into the scene with an abandon recalling that of the Grocer's Wife in *The Knight of the Burning Pestle,* at one point offering herself in place of the Antipodean wife whose husband has hired a gentleman to impregnate her. Diana, less involved but persecuted by Joyless's jealousy, responds provocatively to the presence of the male actors, inflaming his jealousy further. As for Peregrine, the chief spectator, he finds himself drawn increasingly into the scene, interceding in one moment on behalf of three old men who have been sent like children off to school, and managing to secure a day's happy truancy for them.

In the Antipodes, among other oddities, lawyers go in rags while poets wear finery. The poet we meet has been commissioned by an alderman to write religious madrigals, to be sung "By th' holy vestals in Bridewell, for the/Conversion of our city wives and daughters," as well as a set of hymns for "the choir of Newgate, in the praise/Of city clemency"; as well as to write a distich "graven in his thumb-ring," already incised with the wise sayings of his alder predecessors; inscriptions in hall and parlor, gallery, garden, and outer walls, of his own public acts; an elegy on the death of his wife's coachmare; "a love-epistle for the aldermanikin his son" (3.1, pp. 291–92), and so forth. Plainly poets have their work cut out for them in the Antipodes; they run no risk of unemployment as they do in London. But apart from the philistinism of the London burghers, it is not easy to say who or what is being ridiculed, if indeed anything is.[24] Are the madrigals to be sung by the "vestals" of Bridewell—a "correctional facility," as we might call it, for convicted prostitutes—meant to reflect on the venality of London officials? To what or from what are the city wives and daughters supposed to be converted? And the hymns for Newgate prisoners, in praise of the "city clemency"—are they meant to imply, by ironic contrast, the harshness of London justice, or the squalor of its jails? Are the engraved thumb-ring, the inscriptions in gallery and hall, meant to suggest complacency and self-approval on the part of London magistrates? or merely the greater readiness of their Antipodean counterparts to support poetry? Or are such details simply devices of free-wheeling, fanciful ways of conveying absurdity, flights of pure nonsense? The satire, if it is such, comes scattering forth like buckshot, thickly but a little wildly, directed at no identifiable target. Brome seems insufficiently in control of his own exuberance.

No doubt it is possible to be too solemn about what may be no more than a jeu d'esprit. Nevertheless, the frequent echoes of earlier satire, the references to theatrical practice, tend to force such considerations on us, teasing us into thinking that the details have been chosen and organized with a more rigorous purpose than proves to be the case.

Antipodean perversity provokes Peregrine first to concern, then to anger, at length to crazed intervention. Like a certain doleful knight at a puppet show, he mounts a quixotic assault on the properties of the tiring-house, dons sword and shield, "Rusheth amongst the foresaid properties,/Kills monster after monster; takes the puppets/Prisoners, knocks down the Cyclops, tumbles all/Our jigam-bobs and trinkets to the wall." Spying the emblems of royalty, "He takes the imperial diadem and crowns/Himself king of the Antipodes, and believes/He has justly gain'd the kingdom by his conquests" (3.1 pp. 299–300). The feverish onslaught paradoxically foreshadows Peregrine's release from fever, since the doctor, instead of trying to cure this latest delusion, encourages him in it, seconds his plan "to reduce the manners/Of this country to his own" (p. 300), and even prompts him to wander incognito among his subjects so as to discover what reforms may be most needed. The more Peregrine sees of Antipodean contrariness, however, the less it seems to amuse him and the more urgently he measures it against the standards he has brought from his native place. The climax comes with the revelation of Antipodean justice, which requires criminals to be praised and rewarded while their victims are reviled and punished. Peregrine rises in furious indignation, with a threat to hang all in sight, relenting only when assured that his new subjects will do whatever is needed to bring their laws into conformity with his commands.

At this point, with little warning, his virgin wife, in a masquelike sequence, herself becomes part of the inner play. She enters, royally garbed as a princess of the Antipodes, "*between two boys, in robes, her train borne up by* Barbara [Blaze's wife]," to the playing of soft music. Following a nuptial song, she is introduced as the daughter of the late king, who with his dying breath bequeathed her to the new monarch. Two more spectators have thus been engulfed into the inner play, along with (in some manner) Letoy himself, who is said to enter and mingle with the rest, "*and seems to instruct them all*" (4.1, p. 322). Letoy's anxious mingling and furtive instructing of his troupe has the air of a hasty improvisation designed to account for the suddenness of the episode. For how could the troupe, which has so thoroughly conned and rehearsed its interlude of the Antipodes, have put together this highly studied, highly ceremonial scene on the spur of the moment, especially when the master improviser, Byplay, has remained on stage, extemporizing his own part? How has Martha been recruited into the company? Does she realize, indeed, that she is playing a part? Or does she, like her husband, imagine that she is truly in the Antipodes? We are not told, nor have we any way of guessing. But if we are to hear as much as Brome insists we shall hear, throughout, about theatrical matters—about styles of acting, improvising, reliance on text, about costumes, properties, and seating arrangements—it is merely confusing to be faced, without explanation, by such a collapse of the barrier between players and stage spectators as occurs at this moment. It is hard to resist the suspicion that Brome is once again merely following fashion, inserting a masque into his play because masques in plays are the rage, even if it means destabilizing his own dramatic design.

Peregrine and Martha, at all events, seem to be descending into a gulf of strangeness, immersing themselves in a subterranean or subaqueous fantasy region that will bring them back to health. Assured that his English wife has died, Peregrine kisses his "new" queen and conducts her solemnly to the wedding chamber where, the doctor promises, their mutual cure will finally be accomplished.

Another therapy has meanwhile been in progress with respect to Peregrine's father Joyless, whose young wife Diana, stung by his insistent jealousy, has turned hectically flirtatious. The capers of the Antipodeans stir Joyless to tantrums of suspicion and Diana, in defiant response, to rather desperate bouts of ogling. The climax occurs when Letoy, in a scene based on Volpone's wooing of Celia, attempts to seduce Diana. Diana, in turn, faced suddenly with the consequences of her own loose manners, repels his advances more primly and sactimoniously by far than did Celia, while Joyless, hidden where he can hear, listens shamefaced to her lecture on wifely fidelity. But his chastened mood lasts only a moment—for might not this scene, like so much else he has experienced in Letoy's house, be itself part of a play?—until it is restored, and his mania definitively dispelled, by the revelation that Diana is in fact Letoy's daughter. The startling peripety proves to hinge on a hitherto unmentioned character, True-lock, Diana's supposed father, who now emerges to disclose the true state of affairs: Letoy himself was once an obsessed *jaloux*, who disbelieved his wife's chastity, doubted his own paternity of Diana, gave her for nurture to his friend Truelock, and has since (once persuaded of her legitimacy) watched her benignly from afar—a discovery that extends the circle of delusion as far outward as it can go, unless we carry it farther still to include ourselves.[25] The fact that the originator and ideator of the whole experiment proves to be, or to have been, as much in need of a physician's care as the others may no doubt warn those of us who think we are outsiders, detached witnesses, not to rest too confidently in our own sanity. We too may harbor a lunatical streak. We too may be ready to profit from a dose of homeopathic madness, a moment of liberating folly to keep us in healthy equilibrium, or restore us to it.

A final scene brings the new monarchs back, uncrowned once more, their senses cleared, a loving couple, with "all their melancholy and his travails past,/And but suppos'd their dreams" (5.2, p. 339). Even the wording and the rhythm here suggest the starting up out of nocturnal confusion of the wanderers in the Athenian wood, whose trials appear, in retrospect, "But as the fierce vexation of a dream" (*Midsummer Night's Dream*, 4.1.68). Like Bottom, Peregrine emerges from his fantasy bemused, speaking prose with a wondering hesitancy: "I am . . . so ignorant of mine own condition, whether I sleep, or wake, or talk, or dream; whether I be or be not, or if I am, whether I do or do not anything; for I have had, if I now wake, such dreams, and been so far transported in a long and tedious voyage of sleep, that I may fear my manners can acquire no welcome where men understand themselves" (5.2, p. 340). Half-entranced as yet by the unreality still clinging to him, he approaches reality fearfully, unsure of his footing. The inner play has helped guide him from the labyrinth of his melancholy back to the clear air of reason. And the theater, in the process, has vindicated itself as a place where the imagination can wander freely, even in the fantastic, only to return all the more securely to its moorings in the prosaic.

By way of festive conclusion, the cure is then spelled out emblematically and choreographically in a masque, this one, unlike its act 4 predecessor, introduced with due forewarning. In the antimasque, a quartet of horrid creatures named Folly, Jealousy, Melancholy, and Madness, led by Discord, sing of their effort to overthrow the kingdom. Interrupted by the approach of her rival Harmony—attended by Cupid, Bacchus, Mercury, and Apollo—Discord and her minions grovel, dance briefly, then vanish, routed by the gods of wine and wit and love and health. Disarray having been healed in the microcosm of Peregrine's troubled spirit, it thus is put to flight in the public, ceremonial world of the dance. And as the benign gods retreat in their turn, Letoy promises further mirth to all, Doctor Hughball asks the audience to ratify the cure with its approving hands, and Peregrine, echoing Prospero, begs friendly waftage home, by the same means, from his far-off Antipodean outpost.

Brome gives us, then, not without much incidental blurring and slurring of the effect, an apology for the stage, without, however, identifying it as such or going to buffets with the stage's enemies. Perhaps the lateness of the historical hour would have made any such attempt self-evidently futile. Perhaps, also, Brome, a less combative writer by far than his one-time master, Jonson, and far less rigorous in the working out of his dramatic ideas, was content simply to indulge a certain vein of nonsense, to let his fancy range capriciously over the possibilities for confusion suggested by the Antipodal theme.

In our three plays, then, the element of apology, whether or not consciously intended by the playwrights, comes up against resistances and ineptitudes: against a powerful undertow of skepticism in Massinger, against an imperfect grasp of the theatrical needs of his own material on Randolph's part, and against a somewhat unfocused yearning to abandon himself to the pleasures of pure nonsense in the case of Brome. None of the three attempts seriously to erect a bulwark against the onrushing Puritan tide, nor could plays, frail reeds as they were and are, have prevailed as weapons of controversy in the grim power struggle in which they were destined to be overwhelmed.

NOTES

1. J. E. Kramer, *"Damon and Pythias:* An Apology for Art," *ELH* 35 (1968): 475–90.

2. Philip Massinger, *The Plays and Poems of Philip Massinger,* ed. Philip Edwards and Colin Gibson, 5 vols. (Oxford: Clarendon Press, 1976), 3 : 16. Citations from *The Roman Actor* will be to this text, pp. 21–93 in vol. 3. I have modernized "u" and "v" and "i" and "j"

3. Massinger, *Plays and Poems,* editors' introduction, 3 : 10–12.

4. William Lee Sandidge, Jr., *A Critical Edition of Massinger's The Roman Actor,* Princeton Studies in English 4 (Princeton: Princeton University Press, 1929), pp. 22–23.

It is difficult to believe that the *Short Treatise* (STC 24232) could have had much to do with Massinger's play; its arguments are so remote from those advanced by Paris. One would have expected Massinger, if he had had it in mind, to meet its objections more squarely. Those objections included most of the threadbare complaints, accumulated over centuries of antitheatrical writing, against the iniquity of the stage, the pagan origins of the stage, the sinfulness of plays, their hostility to the word of God, their offenses against Scripture, their unlawful subject matter, their unacceptability as recreation, their infringement of Deuteronomy 20.5, the irreligiousness of those who frequented them, the danger to the souls of those who beheld them, the ungodliness of those who acted in them, the loss of precious time occasioned by them, the long-standing antagonism to them on the part of both "orthodoxall Protestants" (C5) and numerous papists, the censure of them even by "infidell Heathens" (D1), and the disasters that have befallen theaters during performances of them as a consequence of divine wrath. None of these complaints seems especially relevant either to the senatorial attack on Paris and his company or to Paris's own defense.

5. For Massinger's dealings with his varied sources for this play, see C. A. Gibson, "Massinger's Use of His Sources for 'The Roman Actor,'" *AUMLA* 15 (1961): 60–72.

6. A. P. Hogan, "Imagery of Acting in 'The Roman Actor,'" *MLR* 56 (1970): 274n, speaks of a "double tradition" of interpretation with regard to the story, according to which "Pentheus tries to uproot idolatry but is destroyed by the forces of chaos, while he is also [in Sandys's 1632 Englishing of Ovid] 'an implacable tyrant; hating religion, and suppressing it in others.'" But the violence and frenzy of the story alone suffice to cast a shadow over Paris's claims and call them into question, whatever its ultimate meaning might be.

7. See A. K. McIlwraith, ed., *Five Stuart Tragedies,* World's Classics 526 (London: Oxford University Press, 1953), p. xvi, and Patricia Thomson, "World Stage and Stage in Massinger's 'Roman Actor,'" *Neophilologus* 54 (1970): 422–23.

8. Ibid., p. 423.

9. Hogan, "Imagery of Acting," p. 278. My own reading of *The Roman Actor* owes much to, and coincides at a number of points with that advanced in this excellent essay.

10. Arthur Golding, *The xv Bookes of P. Ovidius Naso, entytuled Metamorphosis, translated oute of Latin into English meeter* (London, 1567), a4ᵛ.

11. Massinger, *Plays and Poems*, 5:190.

12. *An Apology for Actors* (1612), facs. ed. Richard H. Perkinson (New York: Scholars' Facsimile Reprints, 1941), E3.

13. *Dio's Roman History*, trans. Earnest Cary, Loeb Classical Library (London: William Heinemann, Ltd., 1925) 8:321–22.

14. See Thomson, "World Stage and Stage," pp. 414–5.

15. A recent discussion, Jonathan Goldberg, *James I and the Politics of Literature: Jonson, Shakespeare, Donne, and Their Contemporaries* (Baltimore and London: Johns Hopkins University Press, 1983), pp. 203–9, analyzing this scene more from Domitian's standpoint than from Paris's, sees it as one of a number of instances in which Domitian's theatricality is intimately, inevitably, bound up with his power: to be an emperor is to be forever on stage, forever acting, forever the prime spectator of others' actions. I would agree. What is equally clear is that the Domitian of the play abuses both his power and his roles as actor and spectator, so that the presentation of him tends to throw a baleful light on the whole phenomenon of theatricality and hence on the calling that embodies it institutionally.

16. The only exception I can think of is one that tests and reconfirms the rule: Rotrou's *Le Véritable Saint-Genest* (1645), another tragedy about a Roman actor. Genest, the leader of an acting troupe, finds himself converted to Christianity while playing the role of a Christian martyr and ends by submitting in earnest to the martyrdom he has often mimed callously in jest. But the finale here is triumphant rather than properly tragic. Genest goes to his death exultantly, with no regrets for the simple human existence he is leaving behind. Even if in purely human terms his action is unhappy for his friends and followers, from the Christian point of view it is comic, and it is by the Christian point of view that we are being asked to judge him. There is no doubt in the end that by embracing marytrdom Genest has conquered the wicked Diocletian, saved his own soul, and been enrolled already in the ranks of the blest.

17. It has been discussed from this point of view by Joe Lee Davis, in "The Case for Comedy in Caroline Theatrical Apologetics," *PMLA* 58 (1952): 353–71, and *The Sons of Ben* (Detroit: Wayne State University Press, 1967), pp. 59–64, 66–70, 76–78.

18. Bentley, *The Jacobean and Caroline Stage*, 7 vols. (Oxford: Clarendon Press, 1941–68), 5:987.

19. Thomas Randolph, *Poems, with the Muses Looking-Glasse, and Amyntas*, 2d ed. (Oxford: F. Bowman, 1640), A3ᵛ-A4. *The Muses' Looking-Glass* is separately signed. Subsequent references will appear parenthetically following text.

20. Bentley, *Jacobean and Caroline Stage*, 2:537–38, and 6:95.

21. *The Antipodes* has been more fully and on the whole more effectively discussed than either *The Roman Actor* or *The Muses' Looking-Glass*, most notably in two essays, that of Ian Donaldson in *The World Upside-Down* (Oxford: Clarendon Press, 1970), chap. 4, pp. 78–98, and that of Jackson I. Cope, in *The Theater and the Dream* (Baltimore: Johns Hopkins University Press, 1973), pp. 143–59. An earlier discussion that concerns itself with theory of comedy is Joe Lee Davis, "Richard Brome's Neglected Contribution to Comic Theory," *SP* 40 (1943): 520–28. Further comment appears in R. J. Kaufmann, *Richard Brome: Caroline Playwright* (New York: Columbia University Press, 1961), pp. 61–66; Davis, *The Sons of Ben*, pp. 64–66 and 70–75; and in the critical introduction to Ann Haaker's Regents Renaissance Drama edition of the play (Lincoln: University of Nebraska Press, 1966), pp. xiv–xxi. Much of the existing criticism is surveyed by Haaker in *The Later Jacobean and Caroline Dramatists*, ed. Terence P. Logan and Denzell S. Smith (Lincoln: University of Nebraska Press, 1978), pp. 179–81.

The commentary being as extensive as it is, and the play so crowded with character, event, and episode, I have made no serious effort to summarize the plot but have merely pointed to elements in it relevant to my own discussion.

22. Act 1, scene 1, p. 264. Citations from *The Antipodes* will be to A. S. Knowland, ed., *Six Caroline Plays*, World's Classics 583 (London: Oxford University Press, 1962), pp. 251–343, with act, scene, and page number supplied parenthetically in text.

23. These have been skillfully disentangled by Donaldson, *World Upside-Down*, pp. 90–95.

24. See Davis, *The Sons of Ben*, p. 72; and Kaufmann, *Richard Brome*, p. 61, with whose blunter judgment I tend to agree: "there is an intellectual awkwardness, a loss of proper proportion that attacks Brome whenever he becomes too abstract or intellectual."

25. See Cope, *Theater and Dream*, pp. 147, 156–57.

Restoration and
Eighteenth-Century Comedy

Understanding Shakespeare in the Seventeenth and Eighteenth Centuries

Rose Zimbardo

> A revaluation of representational idioms comes about only when new elements that invade the environmental field are important enough to demand attention and when there are no traditions to shape visual habits in regard to them.[1]

The seventeenth and eighteenth centuries presented the most crucial "revaluation of representational idioms" that has occurred in Western thought. As C. N. Manlove explains, during this period "phenomena lose their symbolic roles in a teleological scheme and are increasingly seen simply as phenomena . . . . The old network of universal analogy, by which all things could figure one another . . . collapses."[2]

And what, you ask, has this to do with the understanding of Shakespeare in the Restoration and eighteenth century? Quite simply: if we measure the perception/understanding of Shakespeare from Ben Jonson to Samuel Johnson we discover that a major "revaluation," indeed a revolution, in "representational idiom" has occurred. Since the *object* of perception—Shakespeare's plays—remains constant, while the focus of perspective upon them—*what* the viewer *sees*—changes, we find in the response to Shakespeare an invaluable index to what dramatic "imitation of nature" means from the seventeenth to the eighteenth centuries.

During the seventeenth century, as Guillen says, European culture became "interiorized."[3] Rorty goes further and argues that the conception of mind as "inner arena" was invented in the seventeenth century.[4] For the Middle Ages and the sixteenth century the world was "a place of interconnected meanings, not objects,"[5] and consequently the idiom of representation stressed interconnectedness within a whole design and continuity between the microcosm and the metaphysical harmony toward which it pointed or to which it aspired. The seventeenth century brought to human perception, first, separation and locatedness in space and time, and then the invention of an internal arena within the individual, the locus of his special "reality." Inside the human psyche we no

215

longer find Hell Mouth within Hell Mouth, the "center of [man's] sinful earth,"
but rather a new frontier for exploration:

> I turn my gaze inward, I fix it there and keep it busy . . . I look inside myself; I
> continually observe myself . . . I taste myself . . . I roll about in myself,

Montaigne says.[6]

I shall argue here that because the period from Ben Jonson to Samuel Johnson
was so crucially a time when representational idiom was transformed, what each
of these giants actually *saw* in Shakespeare was different. Furthermore, I will
argue that the crux of the revolution in understanding occurred during the
period we loosely call "the Restoration" (1660–1725) and is traceable in three
stages: imitation of nature as the representation of abstract Idea or design;
imitation of nature as representation of the actual; understanding of dramatic
representation as the penetration of an assumed "internal arena" in characters;
and the attempt to "identify with" characters or emulate them.

Gerald Bentley's invaluable decade-by-decade study of allusions to Jonson and
Shakespeare during the course of the seventeenth century indicates a well-
bucket pattern; Jonson allusions fall as Shakespearian ones rise.[7] But, more
significantly, it pinpoints the exact decade when enthusiasm for Shakespeare
begins, and, because Bentley is the careful scholar he is, suggests the reason for
the rise in Shakespeare's popularity. Between 1681 and 1690 there are 151
references to Shakespeare and 175 to Jonson (this represents a significant rise for
Shakespeare); but, as Bentley says, "Upon breaking the figures down into types
[of allusion], one finds certain tendencies becoming apparent—tendencies carrying over into the last decade of the century and clearly indicating the rising tide
of Shakespearian allusions which . . . will far surpass Jonsonian allusions in the
eighteenth century. . . . The significant change is seen in the number of allusions
to the plays and characters [i.e., as opposed to the authors themselves]. . . .
There are 120 references to particular plays of Shakespeare as compared to 137
for Jonson, but *78 character references as compared to Jonson's 26*"[8] [emphasis mine].
Bentley's comment on this change indirectly makes the major point of my
argument:

> The period 1681–90 apparently marks the beginning of a general recognition
> and acknowledgement of Shakespeare's unequalled powers of characteriza-
> tion—a recognition which to the modern taste seems so natural as to be
> inevitable.[9]

The point of this paper is that what seems natural in 1986 was not at all natural in
1660 or 1623; it merely seems so because we stand on the far side of a revolution
that took place during the Restoration period. The "nature" that drama imitates
changed drastically in less than one hundred years, and we, on the far side of the
change, cannot imagine that there ever was another representational idiom,
another way of seeing.[10] Before considering Restoration modes of seeing I
should like to juxtapose the extremes of a continuum of visualization that
stretches from nature as abstract cosmological design to nature as human "inner
arena."

Ben Jonson's conception of dramatic imitation is the medieval/Renaissance conception of proportions among parts within a system of interconnected meanings. That is evident both in his practice and in his theory. As Manlove says, "when considering the structure of a Jonson poem what we find ourselves concerned with are the parts and the way they are married to one another to make a seamless whole . . . the characters [in his plays] *fit in with* rather than act upon one another."[11] And Jonson himself argues that the nature a play imitates is expressed in its architectural design: "For as a house consisting of diverse materials becomes one structure; so an action, composed of diverse parts, may become one fable, epic or dramatic."[12] What Jonson and his early seventeenth-century contemporaries see in Shakespeare is the limitation of nature as microcosmic design. In "To the Memory of my beloved, The Author, Mr. William Shakespeare; And what he hath left us," Jonson writes,

> Nature her selfe was proud of his designes
> And ioy'd to wear the dressing of his lines!
> Which were so richly spun, and wouen so fit

Nature is God's design; art is structured to the lineaments of that design. Jonson goes on,

> Yet must I not give Nature all: Thy Art,
> My gentle *Shakespeare*, must enioy a part
> For though the Poet's matter, Nature be,
> His Art doth give the fashion[13]

The anonymous I.M.S., writing in 1632, makes clearer still that what the early seventeenth century admired in Shakespeare was his ability to feign a world:

> . . . To give a Stage
> (Ample and true with life) voyce, action, age
> As Plato's year and new Scene of the World . . .
> the *Plebian* Impe from lofty throne
> Creates and rules a world. . . .
> And there did sing, or seeme to sing, the choyce
> Birdes of a forraine note and various voyce,
> Here hangs a mossey rock; there playes a faire
> But childing fountaine purled: Not the ayre
> Nor cloudes nor thunder, but were living drawne . . .[14]

In the first half of the seventeenth century Shakespeare, warbling his woodnotes wild, was conceived as the imitator of a world order. It is for this reason, I think, that in the early years of the Restoration period his comedies were as often played as his tragedies (i.e., because comic design consists in multiplicity or variety within a whole) and his tragedies were transformed into heroic drama, a form of comedy; it was not until the turn of the century, when imitation was conceived to be representation of actual persons, that the popularity of his tragedies gained ascendence, and, indeed, that certain of his comedies began to be read as tragedy. In 1709 Nicholas Rowe writes "tho' we have seen [*The*

Merchant of Venice] receiv'd and acted as a Comedy, yet I cannot but think it was design'd tragically by the Author."[15] Neither, alas, can we.

At the other end of the continuum Samuel Johnson sees in Shakespeare not the imitation of cosmic nature but "the mirrour of *life*" [emphasis mine], and he gives evidence that by 1763 our own perceptual method of response to drama— namely, "identifying with," or entering into, its characters—was firmly established. Samuel Johnson was, however, sufficiently close to the earlier perceptual and imitative mode (imitation of Idea) to recognize and condemn it.

> This, therefore, is the praise of Shakespeare, that his drama is the mirrour of life; that he who has mazed his imagination in following the phantoms which others writers raise up before him, may here be cured of his delerious ex- stasies. . . . Other dramatists can only gain attention by hyperbolical or aggra- vated characters, by fabulous and unexampled excellence or depravity [i.e., when character delineates Idea as in Davenant or Dryden] as the writers of barbarous romances . . . and he that should form his expectations of *human affairs* from the play . . . would be equally deceived. Shakespeare has no heroes; *his scenes are occupied only by men, who act and speak as the reader thinks that he himself should have spoken or acted on the same occasion* [emphasis mine].[16]

In the new representational idiom, characterization is conceived to be the imita- tion of actual human behavior. Moreover, once characters are thought to figure human beings the reader presupposes in them an "inner arena." Therefore, Johnson, examining Polonius, not only explores the character's inner space but constructs an imagined psychological history for him.

> Polonius is a man bred in courts, exercised in business, stored with observation, confident of his knowledge, proud of his eloquence, and declining into dotage . . . Such a man is positive and confident because he knows that his mind was once strong, and knows not that it is become weak. Such a man excels in general principles, but fails in particular application. He is knowing in retro- spect, and ignorant in forsight. While he depends upon his memory and can draw from his repositories of knowledge, he utters weighty sentences, and gives useful counsel; but as the mind in its enfeebled state cannot be kept long busy and intent, the old man is subject to sudden dereliction of his faculties, he loses the order of his ideas, and entangles himself in his own thought, till he recovers the leading principle and falls again into his former train.[17]

A character—no longer a figure, a type, or the delineation of an Idea as in the seventeenth century—is believed to have an interior life or reality, which "inner arena" itself has a history. From here to the investigation of Hamlet's Oedipal complex is a very short step.

This comparison of the intelligent critic of 1623 with the intelligent critic of 1763 clearly shows that a transformation in conception occurred. This transfor- mation not only turned the perceiver of Shakespeare in the main from a spectator to a reader, but finally it demanded the invention of the novel and the primacy of that form over the drama as the most serious representational mode.

It is during the course of the Restoration period that we can chart the process of the change by stages. In the first stage, the 1660s and early 1670s, Shake- spearian drama was still perceived as design, but not, as in the early decades of the seventeenth century, the design of a world order. Rather, those "Images of Nature," which, Dryden admiringly asserts "were still present to [Shakespeare]"[18] are Ideas of passions or virtues: as "ambition," "valor," "love," and so on. In his Preface to *The Enchanted Island,* the adaptation he made with Davenant of *The Tempest,* Dryden clearly shows that it is the design of the play he perceives—a design of interacting concepts, upon which, he declares, Davenant has improved:

> It was originally Shakespear's . . . our excellent Fletcher had so great a value for it that he thought fit to make use of the same Design, not much varied. . . . But Sir William Davenant . . . soon found that somewhat might be added to the design . . . and therefore . . . he designed a Counterpart to Shakespear's Plot, namely that of a man who had never seen a woman; that by this means those two *Characters of Innocence and Love* [emphasis mine] might the more illustrate and commend each other.[19]

"Character" here bears its original sense of delineation. What the reader/viewer/ adapter of the 1660s saw in Shakespearian drama were "Images of Nature" as configurations of concepts or Ideas. What he valued was a design that exhibited a variety of such concepts woven skillfully into a whole. "Not an imitation of a fragment of the visible universe, but a model or analogue of the universe itself . . . the shape of reality."[20] Shakespeare's history plays were rejected in the 1660s precisely on the grounds that they imitate "fragment[s] of the visible" world rather than "a shape of reality."

> If you consider the historical plays of Shakespeare, they are rather so many chronicles of kings, or the business of thirty or forty years, cramped into a representation of two hours and a half, which is not to imitate or paint nature but to draw her in miniature, to take her in little; to look upon her through the wrong end of a perspective, and receive her images not only much less, but infinitely more imperfect than the life; this instead of making a play delightful, renders it ridiculous. . . . For the spirit of man cannot be satisfied but with truth.[21]

Early Restoration adapters discerned the meaning of a Shakespeare play as a vision of ideal truth, a shape of reality; their attempt was to reveal that meaning more clearly. Two dramatic designs of reality prevailed in the 1660s: the heroic mounting progression of definition (and heroic includes tragedy, tragicomedy and high comedy), and the three-tiered macrocosmic design, a medieval model secularized by Hobbes. In both modes the "shape of reality" is captured by careful juxtaposition of concept. Consequently, the Davenant-Dryden *Macbeth* (1664) is a heroic structure like *The Indian Queen* or a drama of Corneille; it mounts by careful dialectic juxtaposition to a full definition of heroic ambition. Davenant and Dryden drastically reduce the cast to those figures who in themselves and in their placement with relation to each other represent such ideas as love and valor; love that fosters, as opposed to love that undermines, honor; noble as opposed to ignoble striving, and so on. Five major passages are added: three new scenes of dialogue between the Macduffs to balance against Shakespeare's dialogues between the Macbeths, a new scene between the Macbeths that emphasizes the conflict between love and honor, and a passage between Lady Macbeth and Lady Macduff just before Lady Macbeth receives Macbeth's letter in act 1 that contrasts self-effacing supportive love and self-aggrandizing destructive love. The dialogue between Macduff and his lady, like the male-female debates upon the nature of honor in heroic drama, functions to refine upon a concept:

> LADY MACDUFF. You, by your Pitty which for us you plead
>   Weave but Ambition of a finer thread
> MACDUFF. Ambition do's the height of power affect
>   My aim is not to Govern but Protect.
>
>   (3.2.37–40)

Hecate and the witches, because the adapters understand their function in Shakespeare's play to be the arousal of "wonder" in the minds of the audience the better to prepare them to receive "Ideas of greatness," sound very much as though they might appear with equal facility in *The Enchanted Island:*

> O what a dainty pleasure's this,
> To sail i'th' Air while the Moon shines fair;
> To sing, to Toy, to Dance and Kiss,
> Over Woods, high Rocks and Mountains;
> Over hills, and misty Fountains. . . .
>
>   (3.8.43–47)

As completely ludicrous as this seems to us, it did not seem so to the audience of 1666. Pepys writes of *Macbeth* "a most excellent play in all respects but especially in *divertissement,* though it be a deep tragedy; which is a strange perfection in a tragedy, it being most proper here and suitable" (7 January 1666/67).[22] And he calls *Macbeth* "a most excellent play for variety." What a viewer perceived in the play in the 1660s was a design embracing a variety of concepts. What Davenant saw in *Macbeth,* and sought with Dryden's help to sharpen and improve upon, were the very "Ideas of Greatness and Virtue" freed from "the corruption of manners" and the "familiar" (that is, abstracted from ordinary human behavior) that he himself had attempted in writing *The Siege of Rhodes.*[23] What Dryden saw in this early period, and tried to bring into sharper focus, was a vision of "greatness . . . opposed to greatness" within "a labyrinth of design" that he attempted to improve by a rearrangement of the parts "managed so regularly that the beauty of the whole be kept entire"[24]—the ideal he commended in "Of Dramatic Poesy." We must remember that Davenant's *Macbeth* was performed until 1744 and that then Garrick only partially restored the original. What changed in the course of eighty years was not Shakespeare but the eyes that beheld him.

Pepys admired in *The Tempest,* or *The Enchanted Island,* which he saw three times in as many months in 1667/68, precisely what he admired in *Macbeth,* which he saw twice in two months in 1666/67: its variety. He sees *The Tempest* again and again, he says, because it is so "full of variety." In the early Restoration period dramatic imitation of ideas or concepts of the passions was transgeneric:

Whereas the business of Tragedy is in the highest nature to dispose and elevate the intrigues of the passions and affections; I mean such as depend on Ambition, Revenge, Love, Honour and the like. . . . As it is the duty of Comedy to do the same in those that come nearest our Moralities.[25]

The Tempest was assigned to Davenant's company as early as 1660 but was never acted before it was revised by Davenant and Dryden. Since less than a third of the original was used in the adaptation it is relatively easy for us to determine what the intention of the adapters was, namely, what emendations they considered necessary for the meaning of the play as they understood it to be fitted to the understanding of their audience. All of the changes have as their end sharpening and heightening conceptual design and fitting the original to a three-tiered "shape of reality": a plane of pure idea, indistinguishable from heroic drama, a middle plane of action, wherein pure idea is muddled and direction is lost, and a low plane of mock-heroic parody. In conceptual structure *The Enchanted Island* closely resembles Etherege's *Comicall Revenge, or Love in a Tub* (1664).

On the high plane "Characters of Innocence," heroic ambition, and love dance their stately ideational dance. The two couples (Ferdinand and Miranda, Dorinda and Hippolito) figure faces of love that are played upon and glanced off one another, while points of honor and heroic ambition are debated by Antonio, Alonzo and Gonzalo. The latter are returning not from a wedding but from heroic combat "in defence of Christianity" against the Moors, by which means Alonzo and Antonio have long since "made amends to Heav'n" for their ancient crimes against Prospero. Sebastian is removed from the play altogether so that rebellion, confusion, and appetitive greed can be confined to the lower structural planes.

On the middle plane ideas of ambition and heroic greatness are replayed in another key. In the descent to the world, idea becomes muddled by sense and appetite and all direction is lost. Stephano, Mustacho, and Ventoso figure the woeful inadequacy of clownish man to govern himself or the state in the world of experience:

TRINCULO: I say this island shall be under Trinculo or it shall be a Commonwealth, and so my Bottle is my Buckler and so I draw my Sword.

On the low, mock-heroic plane, of course, monster love and monster ambition parody high plane ideals of love and valor:

From this worshipful Monster and Mistress Monster his Sister, I lay claim to the Island by Alliance.
Monster, I say thy Sister shall be my Spouse.

Caliban is given a sister, Sycorax, so that together these figures of ignorant rebellion and lustful sexuality can be mock-heroic counterparts of Dorinda and Hippolito, the high plane "Characters of Love and Innocence" that Davenant and Dryden added to complete the structural balance of the whole.

But perhaps the best clue to the adapters' intention is the much diminished figure of Prospero. Davenant and Dryden clearly did not understand meaning in *The Tempest* to rest in a single strong character who is torn by inner turmoil, or who is an emblem of the poet-magician, or who, indeed, is any of the interesting people twentieth-century criticism has made him. In *The Enchanted Island* Prospero figures the idea of authority, which is inadequate to bind love or control fate. He is the "character" of an idea, as all the figures in the play are.

The movement toward understanding Shakespeare as imitation of the actual, with the consequent emphasis upon characterization, occurred in two stages. In the first stage—between the late 1670s and the turn of the century—the basic *design* of the drama was thought to be the design of Providence operating within human affairs (clearly a midpoint between design as microcosm and action as the replication of actual behavior). Characterization, too, is midway between the figuration or personification of abstract passions or concepts and the familiar behavior of people like ourselves. Character has become type. Moreover, the effect of drama upon the minds of an audience is no longer believed to be the elevation of our minds to the ideal but, rather, the grounding of the ideal, providential design, to our experience. Thus in 1679 Dryden writes in his "Preface to *Troilus and Cressida*" that "the moral . . . directs the whole action of the play to one centre; and that action or fable is the example built upon the moral, which confirms the truth of it to our experience: when the fable is designed, then, and not before, the persons are to be introduced with their manners, characters, and passions."[26] It is to the better revelation of this providential design that Dryden undertakes to "new-model" *Troilus and Cressida,* for, as he says,

> [Shakespeare's] tragedy is nothing but a confusion of Drums, Excursions and Alarms. The chief persons who give name to the tragedy are left alive: *Cressida* is false and is not punish'd. Yet, after all, because the Play was Shakespear's, and there appear'd in some places of it, the admirable Genius of the Author; I undertook to remove the heap of rubbish under which many excellent thoughts lay wholly bury'd. Accordingly, I new model'd the plot; threw out many unnecessary persons; improv'd those Characters which were begun, and left unfinish'd . . . [and] made with no small trouble an Order and Connection of the Scenes.[27]

Tate, whose "Zeal for all the Remains of Shakespear"[28] makes him approach *King Lear* (1681) with far greater reverence than Dryden shows, finds "the whole" of his original "a Heap of Jewels, unstrung and unpolish't," but what is most curious is that he truly imagines that he *sees* in Shakespeare's play "such Conceptions" as justify the thread on which he strings the "Jewels" he finds:

> 'Twas my good Fortune [he writes] to light on one Expedient to rectifie what was wanting in the Regularity and Probability of the Tale, which was to run through the whole, a Love betwixt Edgar and Cordelia, that never chang'd a word with each other in the Original. This renders Cordelia's indifference and her Father's Passion in the first scene probable. It likewise gives Countenance to Edgar's Disguise, making that a generous Design that was before a poor Shift to save his life. The Distress of the Story is evidently heightened by it; . . .

This Method necessarily threw me on making the Tale conclude in a Success to the innocent distrest Persons.[29]

What is most interesting about Tate's dramaturgic method is that the "persons" or characters *dictate* the necessity of the design rather than, as in the Dryden-Davenant *Macbeth,* the design dictating the figuration and placement of the characters. In the process of descent to experience, character moves to the foreground of perspective. Dryden in "On the Grounds of Criticism" moves sharply from the position he held nineteen years before and envisions character as "that which distinguishes one man from another." In radical departure from "Of Dramatic Poesy," he argues that a "character . . . cannot be supposed to consist of one particular virtue, or vice, or passion only but 'tis a composition of qualities not contrary to one another in the same person. . . . Falstaff is a liar, and a coward, a glutton and a buffoon because these qualities may agree in the same man."[30] We are, however, still a far cry from seeing in Shakespeare's characters persons like ourselves. Verisimilitude is consistency to type. Dryden goes on to explain: "when a poet has given the dignity of a king to one of his persons, in all his actions and speeches that person must discover majesty, magnanimity and jealousy of power, because these are suitable to the general manners of a King."[31]

Paradoxically, in the same decade that Shakespeare's reputation rose above Jonson's for his attention to characterization, it is for error in characterization that he is most often faulted. "I found," Tate writes, "that Newmodelling of this Story, wou'd force me sometimes on the difficult Task of making the chiefest Persons speak something like their Character, on Matter whereof I had no Ground in my Author."[32] And, of course, it is chiefly upon this head that Shakespeare draws the wrath of Rhymer. Just as we read the bitter irony of our own times into Shakespeare, making *King Lear* into *Endgame,* so Rhymer reads into Shakespeare the methods of characterization of the 1690s and chides him for being deliberately perverse:

> Shakespeare knew his Character of Iago was inconsistent. In this very play he pronounces
> > "If thou dost deliver more or less than Truth
> > Thou art no Souldier"
> This he knew; but to entertain the Audience with something new and surprising, against common sense and Nature, he would pass upon us a close, dissembling, false, insinuating rascal instead of an open-hearted, frank, plain-dealing Souldier, a character constantly worn by them for some thousands of years in the World.[33]

It was with the turn of the century that Shakespeare's dramatic imitation of nature came to be understood as the imitation of actual human behavior and, by extension, that our response to characters came to be thought to enter their inner, psychological states. It is not surprising that Rowe could not help thinking *The Merchant of Venice* was "design'd tragically by the Author," for *The Merchant* he saw was Granville's *The Jew of Venice,* which, while it is not designed "tragically" as we understand the term, is at the very least rendered as melodrama. Granville cuts the number of scenes and the cast by half.[34] He drops completely all broadly comic scenes and characters—Launcelot and Old Gobbo, for instance—and pares away anything that can distract us from the central character.

Morocco and Aragon disappear from the play. The richly emblematic casket choices are reduced to one scene because only Bassanio's choice of the casket is important. The positions of Morocco and Aragon are condensed into a short passage that Gratiano speaks as counterpoint to Bassanio's musing over the leaden casket. Like everything else in the play, Gratiano's presence in the choice scene is designed to focus our attention on the admirable qualities of the warm-hearted Bassanio.

Shylock is reduced to the simplest of melodramatic villains who toasts his money when Bassanio and Antonio toast love and friendship, and whose hatred of Christians is without any foundation but his own villainy. Whatever in the original makes the characterization complex is eliminated, and since Granville cuts act 3, scene 1 out and puts the "Hath not a Jew eyes" speech in a context that plays down the opening of the passage and strongly emphasizes its vengeful conclusion, we see nothing of Shylock's suffering. As Spencer has said, "He is fitted into his part in the eternal stage struggle between Villain and Hero."[35] His function in the play is to stand in radical opposition to Bassanio and by his dark shadow to throw into high relief the manifold virtues of the hero. Shylock's unreasonable hatred stands against Bassanio's love for Portia and Antonio. His cruelty is purposeful and reasoned. Granville makes Shylock's motivation in agreeing to the bond a long-range plan to kill two Christians with one stone, since he knows that if Antonio falls forfeit, Bassanio will die of generous grief. Against that dark Machiavellian scheming, Bassanio's warmly emotional self-sacrifice shines bright (he steps in front of Antonio and bares his breast to Shylock's knife in the trial scene).

Bassanio is the central figure in the play. His part is greatly enlarged; he is given the greatest number of sententiae to speak; it is his "inner arena" of feeling that the play directs us to enter. All of Granville's additions to the play deal with love (3.1 and 5.1) or friendship (1.1; 3.1; 5.1) and a whole new scene, act 2, scene 2, is constructed around Antonio's toast to friendship, Bassanio's toast to love, and wicked Shylock's toast to money. However, love and friendship are not rendered as they were by Dryden and Davenant, as Ideas. They are, rather, feelings, qualities *interior* to the characters. In his pioneer study, *Restoration Tragedy*, Eric Rothstein said that the key difference between the "fabulist" play of the 1660s and the "affective" play of the 1690s is that the latter "treats love and honor *as traits of the characters,* to be attained in many possible ways, while the heroic play treats characters against a *fixed grid of love and honor*" [emphasis mine].[36] This is an extremely useful way of discriminating the difference between the Dryden-Davenant *Tempest* and *The Jew of Venice.* "Character" in the former is the delineation of idea and figures are important for their placement within a dialectical design; in the latter characters are people whose feelings we are invited to share. As he embraces Antonio one last time before parting, Bassanio says:

> One more Embrace: To those who know not Friendship
> This may appear unmanly Tenderness;
> But 'tis the frailty of bravest Minds.
>
> (2.2.90–93)

The locus of reality has become the human heart; indeed man has swallowed the cosmos. The great *discordia concors* of the spheres to which Lorenzo directs Jessica's and our attention in act 5 of the original has been domesticated in Granville. The "good" Portia speaks Lorenzo's lines and they have a wholly new direction:

> Play all our Instruments of Musick there
> Let nothing now be heard but sounds of Joy,
> And let those glorious Orbs that we behold,
> Who in their Motions, all like Angels sing,
> Still Quiring to the blew-ey'd Cheribims
> Join in the chorus; that in Heav'n and Earth
> One universal Tune may celebrate
> This Harmony of Hearts.
>
> (5.1.51–58)

Man calls the tune; the angelic spheres are extras.

Providential design, the object of dramatic imitation in the 1680s, is still present, but it has receded in importance to become a mere backdrop against which the characters move:

> Virtue like yours; such Patience in Adversity
> And in Prosperity such Goodness,
> Is still the care of Providence.
>
> (5.1.230–32)

By 1700 the nature that drama imitates is human nature: human motivation and behavior. Pope is the first critic among those with whom I am familiar to use the word *behavior*. He remarks of Cordelia's response to learning how cruelly her sisters have treated Lear that "behavior here is most beautifully painted."[37] Pope's entire assessment of Shakespeare is based upon the assumption that drama draws "images of life," not images of nature. When he praises Shakespeare it is for depicting the actual: "Every single character in *Shakespear* is as much an Individual, as those in Life itself."[38] When he condemns it is upon the assumption that characterization is the meeting ground of the author's "life" and the life of his audience. Pope dislikes Shakespeare's early plays because, aimed at the popular audience, the behavior they imitate is vulgar:

The Audience was generally composed of the meaner sort of people; and therefore the Images of Life were to be drawn from those of their own rank: accordingly we find, that not our Author's only but almost all of the old Comedies have their Scene among Tradesmen and Mechanicks.[39]

In criticism as well as practice the object of Shakespeare's dramatic imitation is clearly understood in the early eighteenth century to be the "inner space" of actual people. The anonymous author of "Some Remarks on the Tragedy of Hamlet" argues that Shakespeare is "so remarkably happy in following of Nature he does it even in Characters which are not in Nature. To clear up this Paradox, my meaning is this, that if we can once suppose such characters to exist, then we must allow they must *think* [emphasis mine] and act exactly as he has described them."[40] The audience, it is thought, enters into the minds and feels the feelings of the characters and vicariously enacts the events of the play. Another anonymous author, writing in 1724, asks "Who can see the filial piety of *Hamlet* without partaking of his sorrows, and with equal Ardor in his Heart, pursuing the good old King's murderer?"[41]

By the end of the period of transition two crucial changes had occurred that have profoundly shaped our own way of understanding Shakespeare—so profoundly, indeed, that it is difficult to imagine that *our* way of seeing is not inevitable and "natural." The first is that Shakespearian tragedy came to seem a better, higher, more seriously artistic mode than his comedy, and those of his comedies that contained powerful figures—like *The Merchant of Venice* or *Measure for Measure*—were thought to be unfinished or mangled tragedies. Clearly this is the consequence of the invention of "inner space" in character. We can more easily experience the illusion of entering into a single central figure than a bustling crowd. The second change, which still affects our investigations of how the drama works upon us, is the conception of emulation that follows inevitably upon the idea of "entering into" characters. Emulation assumes that entering the imagined inner reality of a character changes our own psyches, and we are drawn to emulate the behavior of that character. Working upon this assumption Addison in 1709 proposes productions of Shakespearian tragedy for the moral improvement of society:

> The amendment of these low gratifications [watching the "immoral" comedies of the previous generation] is only to be made by people of condition by encouraging the representation of the noble characters drawn by Shakespeare . . . from whence it is impossible to return without strong impressions of honour and humanity. . . . How forcible an effect this would have upon our minds, one needs no more than to observe how strongly we are touched by mere pictures, who can see Le Brun's picture of the battle of Porus, without entering into the character of that fierce gallant man, and being accordingly spurred to an emulation of his constancy and courage? . . . the apt use of the theatre . . . [is] the most agreeable and easy method of making a polite and moral gentry.[42]

It is from this time and in consequence of this eighteenth-century way of understanding that watching or reading Shakespeare comes to be thought a highbrow or bourgeois activity. It is also from this time that we have lost sight of dramatic imitation *as* artistic imitation, for, as Wallace Stevens said:

> Both in nature and in metaphor, identity is the vanishing point of resemblance.[43]

NOTES

1. Gyorgy Kepes, *Language of Vision* (Chicago: Paul Theobald, 1949), p. 68.

2. C. N. Manlove, *Literature and Reality 1600–1800* (London: Macmillan, 1978), p. 1.

3. Cf. Claudio Guillen, "On the Concept and Metaphor of Perspective," *Literature as System* (Princeton: Princeton University Press, 1971), pp. 306–10.

4. Richard Rorty, *Philosophy and the Mirror of Nature* (Princeton: Princeton University Press, 1972), p. 9.

5. J. Huizinga, *The Waning of the Middle Ages* (New York: Anchor, 1949), p. 201.

6. Montaigne, *Essays*, trans. and ed. Donald Frame (New York: St. Martin's Press, 1963), p. 273.

7. Gerald Eades Bentley, *Shakespeare and Jonson: Their Reputations in the Seventeenth Century Compared* (Chicago: University of Chicago Press, 1945).

8. Ibid., p. 55.

9. Ibid., p. 57.

10. G. Wilson Knight once said that "Victorians tended to make Shakespeare a nineteenth century novelist and that was followed by the twentieth century attempt to see him as a twentieth century dramatist" (*The Christian Renaissance* [New York: Norton and Norton, 1963], p. 4). And, of course, he is right. We read *King Lear* as *Endgame* and call Shakespeare "our contemporary." The point is that every age reads Shakespeare from a contemporary perspective.

11. Manlove, *Literature*, p. 18.

12. Jonson, *Timber or Discoveries*, ed. I. Gollancz (London: J. M. Dent & Sons, 1898), p. 128.

13. Jonson, "To the Memory . . . ," in *Shakespeare Criticism: A Selection 1623–1840*, ed. D. Nichol Smith (1916; reprinted London: Oxford University Press, 1973), p. 4.

14. I.M.S., "On Worthy Master Shakespeare and his Poems," in *Shakespeare Criticism*, pp. 8, 9.

15. Nicholas Rowe, "Some Account of the Life & c. of Mr. William Shakespeare," *Eighteenth Century Essays on Shakespeare*, 2d ed., ed. D. Nichol Smith (London: Oxford University Press, 1962), p. 12.

16. Samuel Johnson, "Preface to Shakespeare (1765)," in *Shakespeare Criticism*, p. 82.

17. Ibid.

18. Dryden, "Of Dramatic Poesy (1668)," in *Shakespeare Criticism*, p. 16.

19. Dryden, "Preface to The Enchanted Island," in *Five Restoration Adaptations of Shakespeare*, ed. Christopher Spencer (Champaign and Urbana: University of Illinois Press, 1965), p. 111.

20. G. D. Josipovici, *The World as Book* (London: Macmillan, 1978), p. 32.

21. Dryden, "Of Dramatic Poesy," in *Of Dramatic Poesy and Other Critical Essays*, ed. George Watson, 2 vols. (London: Dent, 1962), 1:47.

22. Samuel Pepys, *Diary*, 9 vols., ed. Dennis Wheatley (London: G. Bell, 1893–99), vol. 7, 3 February 1667/68.

23. See Davenant's 1663 dedication to the Earl of Clarendon in Sir William Davenant, *Love and Honour and The Seige of Rhodes*, ed. James W. Tupper (Boston and London: D. C. Heath & Co., 1910), pp. 187–88.

24. Dryden, "Of Dramatic Poesy," *Of Dramatic Poesy and Other Critical Essays*, 2 vols., ed. George Watson (London: Dent, 1962), 1:61.

25. Edward Howard, Preface to *The Womens Conquest* (London: Herringman, 1671).

26. Dryden, "The Grounds of Criticism in Tragedy, prefixed to *Troilus and Cressida*," in *Of Dramatic Poesy*, 1:248.

27. Ibid.

28. Tate, *The History of King Lear*, in *Five Restoration Adaptations*, p. 203.

29. Ibid.

30. Dryden, "On the Grounds of Criticism," in *Of Dramatic Poesy*, 1:247.

31. Ibid., p. 249.

32. Tate, *The History of King Lear*, in *Five Restoration Adaptations*, p. 203.

33. Thomas Rhymer, "A Short View of Tragedy (1693)," in *Critical Essays of the Seventeenth Century*, 3 vols., ed. J. E. Spingarn (Bloomington: Indiana University Press, 1957), 2:224.

34. He eliminates 2.1–4; 2.7–9; 3.1; and 3.4–5.

35. Spencer, *Five Restoration Adaptations*, p. 30.

36. Eric Rothstein, *Restoration Tragedy* (Madison: University of Wisconsin Press, 1966), p. 34.

37. Pope, "Preface" to *The Works of Shakespear*, 6 vols. (London: J. Tonson, 1723–25), 1:iii.

38. Ibid., 1:iv.

39. Ibid.

40. Anonymous (attributed to Thomas Hanmer), "Some Remarks on the Tragedy of Hamlet"

(1736), reprinted in Augustan Reprint Society, 3rd series, iii, ed. Clarence Thorpe (Ann Arbor, 1947), p. 2.

41. "The Universal Journal," 4 July 1724, reprinted in John Loftis, ed., *Essays on the Theatre from Eighteenth-Century Periodicals*, Augustan Reprint Society 85–86 (Los Angeles: Clark Library, 1960), p. 11.

42. *The Tatler,* ed. George A. Aitkens, 4 vols. (London: Duckworth, 1898), 2:330.

43. Wallace Stevens, *The Necessary Angel* (New York: Knopf, 1951), p. 72.

The Shadow of the Burlador: Don Juan on the Continent and in England

Anthony Kaufman

I want a hero: an uncommon want,
When every year and month sends forth a new one,
Till, after cloying the gazettes with cant,
The age discovers he is not the true one;
Of such as these I should not care to vaunt,
I'll therefore take our ancient friend Don Juan—
We all have seen him, in the pantomime,
Sent to the devil somewhat ere his time.

Lord Byron, *Don Juan*

When the narrator of Byron's *Don Juan* decided that the heroes of his age were ephemeral, merely, as we should say, celebrities, he settled for a somewhat shopworn but durable hero. Don Juan was at least lasting: he had to be, to have survived the violence of the eighteenth-century pantomimes, and perhaps he was a puppet empty enough to be reformed to the poet's conceit. We all know that Don Juan is malleable—he changes with the form and pressure of his time. He begins in the seventeenth century as a mocking, blasphemous swashbuckler, a character in search of a Barrymore or Fairbanks or Flynn. Then comes the philosopher-seducer of Molière: he talks and talks of free thought and conquests and such, but fails to become a hero to his valet. When it comes to actual seduction, he is a philosopher. Don Juan gains a little gaiety and insolence in the opera by Da Ponte and Mozart, but loses it back to E. T. A. Hoffmann. He dances in the puppet shows of London but is discussed seriously by Kierkegaard. He regains every bit of his Spanish arrogance in the first part of Zorrilla, but in the second, he is born again. He runs scared in Shaw, the prey of something rather creepy called the Life Force. But he achieves in the twentieth century what splendor the age can give: first he becomes in the hands of Otto Rank the subject of Freudian analysis (and thus the equal of the Wolf Man)—then he becomes the very symbol of the times: the Absurd Man. From the narrow streets of Seville and hellish flames to the analyst's couch—at least he is a survivor.[1]

His plasticity owes much to the curiosity that no one work of art defines the

229

real Don Juan. And there is another reason for his chameleon-like quality: his appeal has always been highly ambiguous. Today, in our culture, it may be difficult to present any version of Don Juan other than the self-mocking Juan—the man who doubts his sexuality, who wants to *relate* to women, the schlemiel.

But not so in the traditional theater of Don Juan, the Don Juan of the seventeenth century. Here, in the major plays, Don Juan has not lost his macho qualities: the only *relationship* Don Juan has with women is that of predator to prey. Although he begins to lose his virility early in his career, becoming a figure of fun, a parody of his former self, the classic Don Juan is a figure of strength. But it is important to see clearly one central fact about him: his extraordinary sexual antagonism, his anger toward those whom he wants to make his victims. As he is first seen in *El burlador de Sevilla,* by Tirso de Molina (published 1630), his sexual hostility is clear and unambiguous; indeed, it is at the center of the play. Although Molière did not use *El burlador* directly, he retained the essence of Tirso's Don Juan: the sexual hostility. I want to point out that when Don Juan crossed the channel into England, into the fog and damp of a climate generally lacking in sympathy toward him, he did change somewhat. There appears to be only one true Don Juan play in seventeenth-century English drama: Thomas Shadwell's *The Libertine* (produced in June 1675). Here we find the two components of the classic Don Juan story: the serial seduction (although obviously seduction is not always the right word), and the punishment by means of the avenging statue. Don Juan merges at times with another figure in the seventeenth-century English theater: that of the libertine, the rake, the hostile seducer who appears in a number of plays. I do not say a number of comedies, because very often the exact generic form of the plays in which this figure appears is ambiguous. But the essence of the Don Juan figure is retained—his sexual hostility—and it is this hostility that occupies the center of the play and is an important source of its interest to the modern reader. And inherent in this figure are two elements: he is, whatever the generic ambiguities of the play may be, essentially a comic figure, and he is essentially a self-defeating figure.

El Burlador de Sevilla y Convidado de Piedra

The myth of Don Juan is transcultural and takes many forms, but it is generally acknowledged that the first full literary crystalization of the story is found in Tirso de Molina's *El burlador de Sevilla y convidado de piedra,* published first in 1630, although written about 1612–16.[2] Scholars differ on the immediate source of *El burlador;* the play may derive from the *auto sacramental,* one-act religious plays that flourished from the sixteenth to the eighteenth centuries, or perhaps Tirso developed his drama from medieval folklore, ballads, or romances. It has been suggested that an actual historical figure stands behind Tirso's Don Juan Tenorio.[3]

As presented in Tirso, Don Juan is a young Spanish nobleman, the son of a high official at the Spanish court, a grandee of "pure blood." He has undertaken a series of sexual escapades: his delight is in the *burla,* the cruel sexual, sadistic joke at the expense of an unwitting woman, who is then abandoned.[4] We enter the play at the culmination of one such *burla*, the tricking of the noblewoman Isabel, and we witness the seduction of two lower-class women and the attempted (or perhaps successful) rape of another woman of high birth, Ana. In the attempt to rape Ana, Don Juan kills her father, thus introducing the second motif of the play: the revenge of the "stone guest." Don Juan is accompanied by his servant, Catalinón, a comic figure who not only provides amusement but comments on his master's escapades and is a constant reminder of the wicked-ness and cruelty of the don and of his inevitable punishment. The play ends with the final encounter with the statue of Gonzalo and Don Juan's descent into hell.

Readers and viewers of Don Juan have long noted that the play, both in Tirso's version and in Molière's, contains two elements: first, the sexual career of Don Juan, his trickery, his capture of the woman, and his quick getaway. This is the Don Juan, then, of popular currency: "He's a real Don Juan." The second element is his punishment via the agency of the man he has murdered: Don Gonzalo in the play by Tirso. In *El burlador*, the drama is structured on the reciprocal interplay between the two motifs: Don Juan's continued amused insistence that the day on which he must pay his debts is far away, that there will always be time to repent and to gain salvation—and the recurrent warnings throughout the play that his due date grows near indeed and that no person can be sure of time enough to prepare for death. Tirso's Don Juan is no atheist; he believes in the existence of God, but he thinks that he need not repent for a long time yet. Repeatedly warned of his damnation throughout the play by many people and by divine warning, Don Juan gaily waves off such ominous threats:

> CATALINÓN: The way you tempt the thunderbolt!
> Those who cheat women with base sham
> In the long run their crime will damn
> After they're dead. You'll find out when!
> DON JUAN: Well on the credit side I am
> If you extend my debt till then
> You'll wait till death to punish me.
>
> (1, pp. 257–58)[5]

¡Que largo me lo fiáis! "How much time you're giving me"—Don Juan's refrain could provide a subtitle for the play and reveals his amused contempt for orthodoxy and restraint.[6] Yet throughout the play another phrase becomes increasingly ominous and provides the dramatic answer to Don Juan's audacity: *Quien tal hace, que tal pague.* "What you've done, you pay for." (Or perhaps in current American: "You pay for your thrills.") *Quien tal hace, que tal pague* gains resonance when one learns that "this phrase, which occurs quite often in Golden Age literature, was that chanted by the town crier who preceded criminals on their way to execution."[7] Although readers of *El burlador* or of Molière's *Dom Juan* know the unavoidable outcome of the play, the tension between the don's audacious defiance and the increasingly ominous and forceful reminders of his real powerlessness continues the suspense and keeps our interest.

One may approach the play by Tirso in many ways, but what becomes obvious to the modern reader is the hostile aggression of Don Juan toward his victims, a hostility that achieves catharsis through the *burla*. To sense this is not just to reflect the legitimate concerns of our own age concerning misogyny and aggression, for the *burla,* the sadistic joke, is at the heart of Tirso's own imagination in the creation of Don Juan—El Burlador de Sevilla.

Don Juan glories in the name, El Burlador, the sexual trickster, and he proclaims: "In Seville/I'm called the Trickster; and my greatest pleasure/Is to trick women, leaving them dishonoured" (2, p. 269). Don Juan's hostility toward women amounts, as one critic suggests, to a "virtual declaration of war,"[8] and central to his enjoyment of the *burlas* he plays is the release of hostility, the triumph in sadism rather than the act of sexuality itself. He needs the display of technique, the daring risk, and, indeed, the notoriety that he hopes (and here he succeeds) will extend into posterity. Tirso's Don Juan is portrayed as Machiavellian: his means are the deliberate lying promise; his end, the sadistic infliction of pain on a deceived woman. Don Juan's servant, Catalinón, cries out:

Towns should be warned: "Here comes the plague
Of women in a single man
Who is their cheater and betrayer,
The greatest trickster in all Spain."
DON JUAN: You've given me a charming name.

(2, p. 273)

Throughout the play he is associated with the devil: "Poor unhappy man/To fall into the hands of Lucifer!" says Catalinón (2, p. 282) of one of Don Juan's victims. Gerald Brenan notes the similarity of Don Juan to Milton's Satan:

Don Juan, though presented to us as a real man, has also an aura of mystery and daemonic possession that makes him, in a certain sense, the Spanish equivalent of Milton's Satan. He is the corruptor, the destroyer, and the key to his actions is pride.[9]

Don Juan is silent as to his motivation; he does not explain or justify his sadistic trickery. To deceive and dishonor is his nature, he claims: "As a seducer/You've always known me. Why, then, ask me/And with my own true nature task me?" he asks Catalinón (1, p. 257). Indeed, he glories in his skill and reputation, and he is concerned with posterity—how he will appear to the future as well as the present. Although terrified after the first encounter with the statue of Don Gonzalo, he accepts the challenge to dine with him, "that all of Seville/May make a living legend of my valour" (3, p. 302). That Don Juan should persist in his striking out against women, despite the obvious and ominous warnings throughout the play that the divine is not mocked, leads to his horrific end—one that has obvious and profound psychological implications.

Who then is Don Juan and what is the *burla?* Why does he persist in his self-destructive and extraordinary actions, and why does the *burla* become the means to his destruction? What needs are being satisfied?

The psychology of Tirso's own day, the "humours" notion of human make-up, is of limited use. Like Hamlet, Don Juan has been a crux for the psychoanalyst and for the literary critic employing the psychoanalytic method of analysis.

Perhaps the classic definition, in status rather like Ernest Jones's portrait of Hamlet, is that provided by Otto Rank. Rank, who based his ideas about Don Juan largely on the Mozart/Da Ponte opera, saw well the element of guilt and punishment in the myth of Don Juan, which, following Freud, he attributes to the Oedipus complex. He notes that the serial form of seduction, together with the hostility toward the husband or fiancé—Freud's "injured third party"— confirms a psychoanalytic interpretation. "The many women whom Don Juan has to replace again and again represent to him the irreplaceable mother, while his adversaries, deceived, fought and eventually even killed, represent the un-conquerable mortal enemy, the father." Rank says, fairly, that "this is a basic psychological fact uncovered in individual analysis. Applied to the extra-ana-lytical situation, however, it can be used only as a hypothesis to further our desire to understand; it is not a hypothesis whose correctness we are trying to prove." He adds: "The change from a man who in his subconscious remained faithful to his untouchable mother to a cynical deserter of women, presupposes repres-sions, displacements, and revaluations."[10] What Rank offers, then, is a possible insight into the genesis of "Don Juanism," a psychological malfunction, seen both in clinical studies and in fictional character.

Another student of Freud, another Otto—perhaps a valuable credential—Otto Fenichel, derives his ideas about the Don Juan figure from Freud and Rank. He writes of the Don Juan character as seen not in literature but in clinical observa-tion. He agrees with the notion of the primacy of the Oedipal complex and notes the presence in the Don Juan character of narcissistic needs. Most important for the study of the Don Juan character as seen in Tirso and his inheritors, Fenichel points out the distinct possibility of sadistic impulses directed at the woman:

> Don Juan's behavior is no doubt due to his Oedipus complex. He seeks his mother in all women and cannot find her. But the analysis of Don Juan types shows that their Oedipus complex is of a particular kind. It is dominated by the pregenital aim of incorporation, pervaded by narcissistic needs *and tinged with sadistic impulses.* In other words, the striving for sexual satisfaction is still condensed with the striving for getting narcissistic supplies in order to main-tain self-esteem. *There is a readiness to develop sadistic reactions if this need is not immediately satisfied* [emphasis mine].[11]

Fenichel argues, then, that Don Juan's actions are not primarily for the enjoy-ment of sex, but generated by narcissistic problems, and he adds a convincing explanation of what is evident to readers of Tirso: the sadistic element of Don Juan's actions.

A third and widely read interpretation, that of the Spanish analyst Gregorio Marañón, may be mentioned. Marañón derives his theory of the Don Juan type from both clinical studies and literature, notably the Don Juan of Tirso. For Marañón, Don Juan is less than fully masculine. He is indiscriminate in his choice of women, whereas "the love of a perfect male is strictly monogamous or reduces its preference to a small repertory of women, generally resembling one an-other." In his lack of discrimination, he is essentially adolescent and animalistic. He feels no jealousy of his mistresses for he has no "instinct of possession." He brags of his conquests, enjoying "the evil satisfaction of displaying his triumphs."

Every villainy seems a joke to him; he is Machiavellian in his continual pursuit of new victims. In short, "Don Juan possesses an immature, adolescent instinct, arrested in the generic stage, when face to face with the attraction of women. . . . He loves women, but is incapable of loving *the woman*. The man most truly man, is the one who, like Dante, has been able to devote his entire male life to a single Beatrice; even when she is Dulcinea, that is to say when she is only a dream."[12] Marañón dismisses the notion of the eminent Don Juan scholar Gendarme de Bévotte who speaks of the "puissance superbe de sa virilité," insisting that Don Juan, while not effeminate or homosexual, is less than a full man.

Freudian theory is currently the center of much dispute (along with much else in the study of human psychology), and its usefulness in the analysis of fictional characters and situations is also in dispute (along with much else in the study of literature). But in Rank, Fenichel, and Marañón, we see an attempt to explain, with as much accuracy as an inexact and complex craft is capable of, a genuine psychological disorder, observed in both literature and in clinical observation. Rank and Marañón are especially aware of the firm junction between psychological disorder as observed in life and its reproduction in literature. Although there are points of disagreement among the three analysts, all believe that Don Juan's motivations are hidden, aberrant, and destructive. They suggest that Don Juan's actions toward women are not characteristic of healthy sexual relations, that they show an underlying hostility toward women, and that we can understand something of his motivations, despite the fact that they are not spelled out for us in the manner of the overtly "psychological" novel or drama.

Tirso's *El burlador*, then, begins the presentation of what psychologists call "the Don Juan character." Typically this character seeks out a series of brief sexual affairs with women and, after seduction, moves on to further "conquests." The idea of "triumph" is present; such characters are responding to inner feelings of masculine inadequacy—feelings that require perpetual denial. And central to the Don Juan's psychology is his need to act toward women with "small regard to her wishes and perhaps with positive pleasure in her degradation."[13] Indeed, the Don Juan of Tirso dwells on the degradation of the various prostitutes of his acquaintance in his shocking conversation with the Marquis of La Mota in act 2. Here the emphasis is on the physical decay of these women and the tone of the passage is amused contempt and disgust. Later he roars with laughter at the seduction and humiliation of the ruined Aminta:

DON JUAN: For two whole weeks Aminta has not known
How she's been tricked.
CATALINÓN: So thoroughly she's hoaxed
She goes about calling herself the countess!
DON JUAN: God, what a funny hoax!
CATALINÓN: Funny enough;
And one for which that girl must weep forever.

(3, p. 295)

¡Graciosa burla será! Once again we understand the *burla* as a means of sexual humiliation.

Other commentators on the Don Juan character suggest that the Don Juan figure reacts against feelings of latent homosexuality.[14] But more directly significant to the present study is the suggestion that the Don Juan character does not find the sexual conquest gratifying.[15] In *El burlador* this is evidenced by the don's continual flight from the seduced woman to find a replacement and his obvious enjoyment of the woman's degradation. The Don Juan character is a man obsessed, attempting to resolve through sexuality a need essentially nongenital, and this accounts for the sense that many readers may gain from the text of his joylessness in sex. Surely this is suggested by his insistence that "*my greatest pleasure*/Is to trick women, leaving them dishonored." His successful but unsatisfying seductions are gestures of hatred toward women, a desire to revenge himself for the initial erotic attachment to the mother that is inevitably betrayed.[16]

Thus Don Juan's career in *El burlador* is best seen as a series of hostile gestures directed toward women. The pattern of seduction and abandonment provides Don Juan with the release, the feelings of exultation, necessary to him. He glories in what he believes to be his nature: El Burlador.

Dom Juan ou le Festin de Pierre

Apparently Molière did not know Tirso's play directly. His *Dom Juan ou le festin de pierre* (1665) is Tirso as filtered through intermediate sources.[17] But Molière reproduces the essence of the Spanish figure: the aggressive hostility toward women. For neither the Spanish nor the French Don Juan is there the possibility of love; instead, there is only the satisfaction of a seduction that is in fact a sadistic gesture. Some years ago, John Palmer noted that Molière's Dom Juan exhibits a moral sadism and deliberately inflicts suffering and humiliation;[18] and in a somewhat different context, Lionel Gossman suggests that

Dom Juan can find no peace or happiness in a real relation with another human being. As with the sexual maniacs of our times (and not all of them are in psychiatric clinics), there is no end, because no substance to his desire. His desire is not for any person or persons.[19]

Dom Juan's aggression toward women is set out very clearly early in the play. In act 1, scene 2 he explains his motives to the wondering Sganarelle (the counterpart of Catalinón): he speaks of his delight in the corruption of the innocent, the painstaking seduction of "innocent modesty . . . in forcing, step by step, the little obstacles with which she resists, in conquering the scruples in which she takes honor" (1.2, p. 322).[20] Throughout the play Dom Juan justifies his actions as part of his allegiance to *libertinage*. Although his quasi-philosophical justification of life is continual, we see that his *libertinage* is a mere facade to conceal his desire to use seduction as a weapon. Indeed, this Dom Juan anticipates his eighteenth-century successor, Valmont of *Les liaisons dangereuses*, especially when he confides that

In short, there's nothing so sweet as to triumph over the resistance of a beauty; and in this matter I have the ambition of the conquerors who perpetually fly from victory to victory and cannot bring themselves to limit their aspirations. (1.2, p. 322)[21]

The idea of conquest and triumph is clearly present: "like Alexander, I could wish there were other worlds, so that I might extend my amorous conquests there" (1.2, p. 322). Earlier he had suggested obliquely his dread of being himself captured; his language presented images of binding, burying, death:

Do you want us to bind ourselves for good to the first object that captivates us, give up the world for her. . . . to bury ourselves forever in one passion, and to be dead from our youth on. . . . I may be bound; but the love I have for one beautiful woman does not bind my soul to do injustice to the others. (1.2, p. 322)

His fear of being captured or bound, subject to the whim of the other party, is reflected ironically in his characteristic use of oaths to bind the woman to him. Repeatedly in the play he swears, or offers to swear, oaths that of course he intends to break. He has indeed married repeatedly; Sganarelle informs Elvire's servant, Gusman:

You tell me he married your mistress; believe me, he would have done more than that for his passion, and besides her he would have married you, his dog, and his cat as well. A marriage costs him nothing to contract; he uses no other snares to catch beauties, and he's a marrier for all comers. . . . if I told you the names of all the women he has married in various places, it would be a chapter to last us until evening. (1.1, pp. 319–20)

J. D. Hubert has noted that "It is . . . mainly through words, those Trojan horses of temptation, that Don Juan gains access to the minds of his victims."[22] We must see that such vows are indeed weapons: aggressive instruments of his hostility, with their promise of permanence and emotional intensity.

As in Tirso, this Don Juan is associated with the diabolic, although here Dom Juan is not as effective as his Spanish original. Nevertheless, the play's emphasis is on his Satanic nature. Sganarelle, played by Molière himself, describes Dom Juan in the opening exposition: "Enough to say that the wrath of Heaven must crush him someday; that I'd be much better off belonging to the Devil than to him" (1.1, p. 320). Dom Juan's description of his intention to separate and destroy the happiness of "a couple of sweethearts" is suggestive of his destructive quality. In a curious and striking way, the passage parallels Milton's Satan's confused and angry emotions upon observing Adam and Eve in the Garden:[23]

Never have I seen two people so happy with each other and displaying more love. The visible tenderness of their mutual passion stirred me; I was struck to the heart by it, and my love began in jealousy. Yes, from the first, I couldn't bear seeing them so happy together; vexation alerted my desires, and I imagined an extreme pleasure in being able to disturb their understanding. (1.2, pp. 324–25)

That Dom Juan's "love" begins in jealousy is suggestive of his anger, of the inextricable knot that ties his sexuality to destructiveness.

Dom Juan's principal victim is Elvire; he has caused her to break her vows and has taken her from her convent. She is the very type of woman he most delights in; here he has indeed conquered "the scruples in which she takes honor." When she overtakes him in his flight from her and demands an explanation, he contemptuously forces the frightened and incoherent Sganarelle to answer her. He mocks her, playing the hypocrite as he will again in the last act of the play: "I admit, Madam, that I do not have the talent to dissimulate, and that I have a sincere heart" (1.3, p. 327). He taunts her by reminding her of *her* broken vows; he is not the only one to have betrayed certain oaths:

> Scruples came to me, Madame, and I opened the eyes of my soul upon what I was doing. I reflected that in order to marry you I stole you from the enclosure of a convent, that you broke vows that bound you elsewhere, and that Heaven is very jealous of this kind of thing . . . in short I should strive to forget you and give you a way to go back to your first bonds. (1.3, pp. 327, 328)

Elvire reappears in act 4, scene 6. Here it is Dom Juan's contemptuous silence that wounds. She pleads for his reformation, but his only response is a partial reawakening of his lust.

Elvire is Dom Juan's principal female antagonist in this play. His only other encounter is with the two country girls, Charlotte and Mathurine, whom he coolly and with great amusement baffles and humiliates. Elvire's pathos recalls that of the deceived Thisbe of Tirso; it is a disturbing element of *Dom Juan*. Molière wishes to suggest the damage done by Dom Juan's destructive neurosis. We may admire his clever encounters with M. Dimanche, perhaps even with Charlotte and Mathurine. But the humiliation and degradation of Elvire goes beyond the conventional contrivances of the trickster. They are suggestive of the abnormality of the dom, of how dangerous his neurosis can be. For it is in his freedom, his privilege, to act out his compulsions that we find the real meaning of Sganarelle's "a great lord who is a wicked man is a terrible thing."

When reviewing the Don Juans of Tirso and Molière we see that they are derived, in part at least, from the ancient figure of the trickster. Several recent works have illuminated this complex mythic figure and suggested how deeply he (and at times she) is rooted in our cultural imagination.[24] He is pancultural, appearing in the legends of North American Indians and, in his European version, stemming from the ambiguous figure of Hermes, or perhaps earlier, Mercurius. His story seems always to suggest doubleness: he fools others and is fooled; he triumphs and is defeated; he exults and suffers. He dominates; he is rejected as a scapegoat. This figure is seen clearly in both *El burlador* and *Dom Juan;* and when Don Juan is identified as a variation of this mythic figure, we understand better his perennial appeal and the ambivalent feelings he inspires. This ambivalence is crystalized in centuries of criticism of the Don Juan versions: we read of Don Juan as superman and weakling, triumphant and damned. He is male and less than fully masculine. He seeks the ideal; he seeks momentary gratification.

In both plays our expectations concerning the comic hero are belied. We expect to identify with the trickster's clever overturning of authority. We expect him to combat the older authority figures successfully and to emerge triumphant at the conclusion. We expect him to embody a life force, to scorn arbitrary conventions, the abstract, the metaphysical, and to insist in word and deed on the real, the physical, the enjoyable, the here and now. But although the predominant tone of both plays is comic, neither playwright allows the traditional and familiar comic pattern to develop fully. It is clear in both plays that Don Juan is excessive in his actions, indeed perverse. El Burlador's defiance of authority, his contempt for and mockery of the divine go too far: *tan largo me lo fiáis*. To this I would add that to seventeenth-century as well as twentieth-century readers and viewers, Don Juan's acting out of his *burlas* would have seemed excessive and perverse. Tirso emphasizes the pathos of Thisbe and Aminta.[25] Images of destruction by fire and allusions to the destruction of Troy run throughout the play, suggesting the danger Don Juan represents. Far from embodying a life force, he is a force of death. Tirso's play, then, works to make us aware of the religious implications of Don Juan's defiance—this has always been clear—and also, I suggest, of the self-defeating quality of his aggressive and hostile sexuality.

In *Dom Juan,* Molière's dramatic intentions are much less clear and have been the subject of extensive debate. Molière's attitude toward Dom Juan is not obvious: Is there a covert admiration for the defiant freethinker and rebel, whose hypocrisy is in itself a mockery of hypocrisy? Or must we see him as excessive in acting out the libertine, comic in his repetition of excessive actions? What is clear, I believe, is that Dom Juan's urge to "triumph over the resistance of a beauty," to "force step by step the little obstacles with which she resists, in conquering the scruples in which she takes honor," is presented as a dangerous form of perverse sexuality, a monomania. The trickster dominates the action but is at the end self-defeating, the victim of his own unacknowledged disorder.

The conclusions of the plays are emblematic of Don Juan's self-destruction. His defiance, his contempt for the ominous warnings he receives, his mockery of the divine agent, the statue—all are suggestive of his compulsion. To see this is not to ignore the clear and obvious religious theme defined earlier by Tirso in *El burlador:* God is not mocked and man knows not the time of his death. *Tan largo me lo fiáis* is deadly ironic. Nor do I ignore the possibility that Molière in *Dom Juan* wished to demonstrate the blindness of the fashionable libertine. But both plays emphasize the rapidity of Don Juan's career toward death; his rush from locale to locale; and, finally, his defiant rendezvous with the divine—here is the perfect emblem of sexual compulsion, the illusion of control belied by the inability to halt. The fire and brimstone of the conclusion are a perfect emblem of the man consumed by his own anger and hostility.

As seen in Tirso and Molière, Don Juan and Dom Juan are provocative figures: vital, yet diabolical in their need to strike out at women, they use sex as a means of venting their anger. Both playwrights have portrayed a recurrent psychological type. They dramatize for us a familiar, if disturbing, disorder: the Don Juan character. The psychological truth central to the myth is not, I must urge, extrinsic to the literary works: it is central. There is no question of importing a psychological model; the plays dramatize the disorder that lies at the center of the very conception of Don Juan. Nor does the analysis of this psychological situation reduce Don Juan to a case study; the psychological truth of the plays is the very source of their dramatic vitality, and in neither Tirso nor Molière does Don Juan lack fictional power. I suggest, moreover, that the psychological truth central to the Continental Don Juan helps explain the re-emergence of Don Juan in various guises in England.

The Country Wife

Sexual hostility is central to the English comedy of the 1670s and 1680s. F. W. Bateson suggested quite rightly that the sex jokes lie near the heart of Restoration comedy,[26] and it seems obvious that the often described "battle of the sexes," analyzed variously as an expression of *libertinage*, an offshoot of *préciosité*, or as an effort to rationalize sex relations, is in fact a symptom of far deeper malaise. Horner, the central character of *The Country Wife* (1675), stands alone in his society, with no close friends or confidants, alienated and isolated, incapable of any meaningful action except repeated and unsatisfactory seduction. He pretends to be impotent in order to deceive myopic and inadequate husbands and gain admission to their wives—and his pretended impotence is obviously symbolic, pointing to the very real sterility of his emotions.[27] What isolates Horner, what is central to his motivation, and what links him to the Don Juans of Tirso and Molière, is his abnormal hostility toward women. Horner's depth of feeling goes far beyond that of the conventional Restoration "rakehell." Everywhere in the play Horner insists that all women are whores, and his central concern is to prove them so: his repeated "ay, a pox on them all," distills the savagery of his hatred. Much of the repartee of the play is composed of obviously hostile jokes: verbal gestures of hatred. And like his prototypes, Horner works through trickery; the affinity of the Don Juan character and the Machiavellian is seen again in Horner's remark: "I am a Machiavel in love."[28]

It is difficult to view Horner as the "hero" of *The Country Wife*, as the moral norm of the play, a "truewit" who demonstrates a right way of conduct or a definition of true masculinity. Although he is a wonderful comic character, his world view is diseased: Alithea and Harcourt are intended to demonstrate a reasonable life style and the healthy emotions of normal people. They stand in deliberate contrast to the obsessive Horner, although it is obviously true that Horner is the dramatic center of the play. It is quite true also that like the conventional libertine, Horner wittily exposes the affectation and hypocrisy around him, that he is genuinely admired by the wits who surround him, that he is capable of honorable action, that the conclusion of the play finds him spared overt comic punishment. But Horner's neurotic view of the world is announced in the opening lines: "A quack is as fit for a pimp as a midwife for a bawd; they are still but in their way both helpers of nature" (1.1.1–2).[29] Nature, or "human nature," is for Horner irrevocably corrupt, and his sense of human degradation is close to that of Volpone and Mosca.

Although Horner ostensibly devotes himself to a free sexuality, his real relation to women is summed up, unwittingly perhaps, by the jealous Pinchwife, who forbids his country wife to see her unknown gallant, Horner, "for he would but ruin you, as he has done hundreds. He has no other love for women but that; such as he look upon women, like basilisks, but to destroy 'em" (2.1.109–12). Pinchwife has unknowingly touched the essence of Horner's motivation. Horner states his own attitude succinctly in the same scene, when the complacent fool, Sir Jaspar, urges Horner to frequent "that sweet, soft, gentle, tame, noble creature, woman, made for man's companion." Horner replies characteristically, saying woman is like

> that soft, gentle, tame, and more noble creature a spaniel, and has all their tricks—can fawn, lie down, suffer beating, and fawn the more; barks at your friends when they come to see you; makes your bed hard; give you fleas and the mange sometimes. And all the difference is, the spaniel's the more faithful animal, and fawns but upon one master. (2.1.451–57)

It is significant that Horner, who compulsively exploits women, insists that they are animalistic and incapable of love.

Such sentiments might be dismissed as part of Horner's "act," intended to delude the likes of Sir Jaspar, but they are repeated incessantly throughout the play and with such intensity as to reveal Horner's motivation. In act 3, scene 2, Dorilant asks Horner, "Did I ever think to see you keep company with women in vain?" Horner answers, "In vain! No—'tis, since I can't love 'em, to be revenged on 'em." And a few lines later: "Because I do hate 'em, and would hate 'em yet more, I'll frequent 'em; you may see by marriage, nothing makes a man hate a woman more than her constant conversation. In short, I converse with 'em, as you do with rich fools, to laugh at 'em and use 'em ill" (6–9; 16–20).

In act 4, scene 3, Horner again displays contempt for women, ostensibly to deceive Sir Jaspar, but revealing in fact the truth of his psychological situation. "Oh, women," he says, "more impertinent, more cunning, and more mischievous than their monkeys, and to me almost as ugly!" (119–20). One could easily cite similar expressions throughout the play; they form a motif always associated with Horner. Perhaps one last example will be conclusive: in act 4, scene 3, he again, as he has done throughout the play, equates women with the devil: "I love a woman only in effigy and good painting. . . . I could adore the devil well painted" (217–19). Horner's language is a constant barrage of hostile wit, discharging hostility that cannot, at the moment, be directly expressed. His characteristic action, verbally, is to "unmask" women in the sense in which Freud uses the term in *Jokes and their Relation to the Unconscious*:

> Under the heading of "unmasking" we may also include a procedure for making things comic with which we are already acquainted—the method of degrading the dignity of individuals by directing attention to the frailties which they share with all humanity, but in particular the dependence of their mental functions on bodily needs.[30]

Horner satisfies certain psychological needs that are essentially nongenital through a joyless and perverse sexuality. His successful but unsatisfying seductions are a gesture of hatred toward women, a desire to revenge himself on them, for the initial erotic attachment to the mother, inevitably betrayed, may lead to the hostile charge that all women are fickle, are whores—and this is precisely the charge that Horner makes and attempts to document through his actions. It is interesting and significant that in act 2, scene 1, after the speech in which Horner equates women with spaniels, Sir Jaspar unwittingly makes a telling point as he remonstrates with Horner: "For shame, Master Horner, your mother was a woman." It is dramatically remarkable that Horner, who has dominated the action to this point, is silent for the next twenty-five lines.

Horner's revenge against the betraying female is twofold: the continual barrage of hostile wit, expressing a hatred that cannot be directly expressed, and the act of seduction. Sexuality, for Horner, the "Town-bull," is not, quite obviously, a mature love; instead it is an act of hostility and revenge.

Was Wycherley aware of such a neurosis? The question may be irrelevant, but there is evidence in the play that he was. Horner is flanked by three characters who, I think, are drawn deliberately to reflect Horner's malaise. All three seem to be drawn in sharp contrast to Horner: they are all sexually inadequate and ineffective, while Horner appears as the brilliantly successful "Town-bull." But I suggest that there is an underlying affinity among them. They share a sharply defined hostility toward women. First, the neurotically jealous Pinchwife, who is obsessed with his wife's sexuality in a manner quite removed from his prototype in Molière's *L'Ecole des femmes* and *L'Ecole des maris*. Norman Holland has noted the neurotic quality of Pinchwife's attitude toward his wife: after pointing out that Pinchwife continually speaks of women in hostile images of conflict ("damned love—well—I must strangle that little monster whilst I can deal with him") and that Pinchwife threatens his wife with his sword twice, and with a penknife elsewhere, Holland concludes:

> Pinchwife—his name is significant—fears and distrusts women; these fears create a hostility that tends to make him an inadequate lover: unconsciously, he satisfies his aggressive instincts by frustrating and disappointing women he makes love to.[31]

In this character, also, we observe the sense of inadequacy, the feeling that women inevitably betray: "If we do not cheat women, they'll cheat us; and fraud may be justly used with secret enemies, of which a wife is the most dangerous," says Pinchwife after locking his wife into her bedroom (4.2.192–95). When asked why at age forty-nine he married—was it not better to keep a whore?—Pinchwife replies: "A pox on't! The jades would jilt me; I could never keep a whore to myself" (1.1.431–32). Pinchwife's hostility toward women ("tormenting fiend!" he calls his wife at one point, echoing a motif in Horner's speech) is discharged through his furious attempts to keep his wife prisoner and by brandishing his sword; Horner's hostility through sexual aggression. Perhaps Pinchwife's sense of his own inadequacy and his fear of women are best observed when he asks himself: "Why should women have more invention in love than men? It can only be because they have more desires, more soliciting passions, more lust, and more of the devil" (4.2.56–58). Women are more sexually appetitive than men and this is terrifying to the inadequate Pinchwife.[32]

Diametrically opposed to Pinchwife, seemingly at least, is Sparkish, whose hostility toward women is seen in his dehumanization of his fiancée Alithea, whom he treats carelessly as a possession: "Sir, you dispose of me a little before your time," she protests (2.1.194). Affecting the fashionable negligence of the wits in matters of jealousy, Sparkish actually reveals an egotistical contempt for Alithea—a contempt that she finally must acknowledge. Withdrawal is obviously a symptom of hostility; like Pinchwife, Sparkish satisfies his hostility by frustrating and disappointing Alithea's legitimate expectations that Sparkish act his role as fiancé. Instead he prefers to act another role: that of the fashionable negligent "wit." Until the conclusion of the play Sparkish refuses to deal directly with Alithea, preferring instead, interestingly enough, that his "friend" Harcourt make addresses to her. Sparkish's sense of hostility, revealed in his withdrawal from a relationship with his fiancée, is finally revealed when he berates her on the streets for her supposed infidelity, and in this scene we see again the sense of inadequacy that lies behind the accusation that all women are betrayers: "for shall I tell you another truth? I never had any passion for you till now, for now I hate you. . . . I'll come to your wedding, and resign you with as much joy . . . as I would after the first night, if I had been married to you" (5.3.66–73).

Horner's malaise is also reflected in a third inadequate male, Sir Jaspar Fidget, a "cit," or London businessman. In the self-important and complacent Sir Jaspar we see once again a deliberate neglect of women as he foists off his wife onto the supposedly "safe" Horner in order to absorb himself entirely in his business affairs. Lady Fidget's contempt for her middle-aged and indifferent husband is expressed in her marital infidelity. Sir Jaspar lumbers off to the City, urging his wife and Horner to "get you gone to your business together; go, go to your business, I say, pleasure, whilst I go to my pleasure, business." Lady Fidget notes that: "Who for his business from his wife will run,/Takes the best care to have her business done" (2.1.568–70; 575–76). Again, we see masculine withdrawal as a symptom of hostility and contempt; both Sir Jaspar and Sparkish dehumanize women, and both, we must assume, are inadequate as males. In Sir Jaspar, however, we see a skillful variation: Sir Jaspar's sense of inadequacy is reflected in his preoccupation with Horner's supposed impotence. Throughout the play, Sir Jaspar plays a ham-fisted hostile wit around this subject: "ha, ha, ha! I'll plague him yet," giggles Sir Jaspar as he refers again to the subject of impotence.[33]

Horner is a comic character, despite his obvious neurotic condition, and this suggests that very often the comic springs from neurosis: comedy is often about people who hoard money, fall in love with girls too young, eat too much, pretend to despise society, become too involved in their work, and so on. That Horner too is one of these neurotics should not puzzle or disturb the critic; Horner's neurosis is not an idea imported into a literary work to "explain" it; it energizes a play that many have found comic over a long period of time. To point out his neurosis is not to "psychoanalyze" a literary character (whatever that may mean) but to point out the very source of his comedy.

The Man of Mode

The Man of Mode (1676) is linked by critics with *The Country Wife*. Although there are significant differences between Horner and Dorimant, it is clear that both characters are essentially similar: they share Don Juan's sexual antagonism. Critics have made efforts to ignore or to justify the evident hostility of Dorimant in various ways, suggesting that modern readers who find Dorimant's brutality disturbing are being quite simply "ahistorical"—a word thrown about perhaps too casually. I think it doubtful that Etherege was not aware of his character's antagonism: it lies at the center of the play, and perhaps it is precisely because this antagonism is so disturbing to modern readers and viewers that there has been so much effort to justify Dorimant's actions. But the tone of the play is determined primarily by the pervasive sexual antagonism, and it must be said at once that a principal difference between *The Man of Mode* and *The Country Wife* is that we experience not only the sexual hostility of Dorimant toward his victims but also the intense hostility of the various women toward Dorimant. If, as John Wain suggested some years ago, Dorimant embodies the mentality of a "fighter pilot,"[34] his hostility is reciprocated by his antagonists, Loveit, Bellinda, and Harriet.

Like Horner, Dorimant is a variant of the traditional Don Juan figure: his aggressive hostility toward women parallels that of his Spanish and French predecessors.[35] To note this is not of course to deny his very real charm, poise, and elegance. Indeed, such qualities are very much in line with the traditional Don Juan figure; Don Juan is nothing if not poised, urbane, capable of generosity and of expressing his peculiar version of honor. Etherege, like his Restoration colleagues, was a student of Molière; his Sir Fopling derives, it has been noted, from the Mascarille of *Les précieuses ridicules*. And like Don Juan, Dorimant subscribes to the pervasive *libertinage* of his milieu.[36] He justifies his breaking of his promises to Loveit by reference to the "frailty" of love. Such sentiments are not denied directly in the play; indeed, Emilia, who represents a norm of good sense within the play, also believes that "Our love is frail as is our life, and full as little in our power; and are you sure you shall outlive this day?"[37] Yet in the figure of Dorimant, such beliefs coexist with what is more central to his personality: his struggle for power, the desire to manipulate others, to exert control, to humiliate and wound.

Just as the opening of *The Country Wife* establishes Horner's emotional situation, act 1, scene 1 of *The Man of Mode* suggests that Dorimant's fashionable *libertinage* is merely the facade for more intense psychological urges. His impudent note to Loveit is in itself, as he well understands, a hostile gesture: "What a dull, insipid thing is a billet-doux written in cold blood, after the heat of the business is over! It is a tax upon good nature" (1.3–5). He immediately afterwards entertains a bawd in the guise of a fruit seller, whom he employs for information concerning the eligible women of the town. Foggy Nan's basket of fruit suggests Dorimant's attitude toward women; the parallel between the fruit and the women Nan offers leads to a pattern of double entendre:

> DORIMANT: How now double tripe, what news do you bring?
> ORANGE-WOMAN: News! Here's the best fruit has come to town t'year. Gad, I was up before four o' clock this morning and bought all the choice i' the market.
> DORIMANT: The nasty refuse of your shop.
> ORANGE-WOMAN: You need not make mouths at it. I assure you, 'tis all culled ware.
> . . . .
> Good or bad, 'tis all one; I never knew you comend anything. Lord, would the ladies had heard you talk of 'em as I have done.
>
> (1.28–39)

Dorimant's verbal hostility toward women, like Horner's, reveals deeper feelings of anger than has been recognized; Dorimant can indeed be treated, as Underwood does so well, as the Machiavel-Libertine, or as a version of the contemporary gentleman à la mode; neither treatment need interfere with our sense of Dorimant as a man driven by subconscious feelings of anger and the desire to humiliate, control, revenge. These feelings are announced early in the play when Dorimant reveals to his acquaintance, Medley, that he would enjoy conflict with his gull, Loveit:

> Next to the coming to a good understanding with a new mistress, I love a quarrel with an old one. But the devil's in't, there has been such a calm in my affairs of late, I have not had the pleasure of making a woman so much as break her fan, to be sullen, or forswear herself, these three days.
>
> (1.189–94)

As was true in the case of Horner, we may read these lines as being in some sense a pose, an effort to disguise true motivation. But that Dorimant's aggression is recognized by others is clear: when Lady Townley notes Loveit's distress at being mistreated by Dorimant, Medley, who is valued for his knowledge of the town, says "She could not have picked out a devil upon earth so proper to torment her" (2.1.117–18), a statement that is suggestive not only of Dorimant's ulterior aggression but also of Loveit's willingness to be tormented. This suggestion of masochism is emphasized some lines later when Loveit tells her maid, "I know he is a devil, but he has something of the angel yet undefaced in him" (2.2.15–16). Critics note the repeated associations of Dorimant with the devil; as in Tirso, Molière, and Wycherley, the Don Juan figure is portrayed as diabolical. Here such association defines clearly Don Juan's characteristic destructive aggression. Loveit speaks the truth later in the play when she rebukes Dorimant, telling him that: "You . . . have more pleasure in the ruin of a woman's reputation than in the endearments of her love" (5.1.183–84). Bellinda too rebukes him a few lines later: "Other men are wicked, but then they have some sense of shame. He is never well but when he triumphs—nay glories—to a woman's face in his villainies" (5.1.261–63). A dramatic center of the play is found in act 2, scene 2, when, in a lengthy passage, Dorimant torments Loveit with cool insolence, forcing her to reveal her helpless dependence on him. That this scene is central is emphasized at the end of act 2 when Bellinda, also attracted to Dorimant, remains alone on the stage: "H'as given me the proof which I desired of his love; but 'tis a proof of his ill nature too. I wish I had not seen him use her so./I sigh to think that Dorimant may be/One day as faithless and unkind to me" (2.2.270–73).

Bellinda herself remains a shadowy figure in the play; it is by no means certain what exactly her role is. She sees Dorimant very well and realizes his compulsion to deceive, control, humiliate. Yet she gives herself to him (and at five o' clock in the morning!) in this full realization. The scene, act 4, scene 2, begins with the servant alone, "tying up linen," an apt pre-Hogarthian comment on the scene that has just taken place. Bellinda's impulse is to leave—at once and secretly. She repeats her need for secrecy, although she has little faith in Dorimant's ability to keep the secret. Her unrationalized attraction to Dorimant is suggestive of his power to fascinate. She leaves by the backstairs, having received his con-temptuous gesture: "*(Kissing her hand.)* Everlasting love go along with thee" (4.2.64–65).

Critics have suggested that in Harriet Dorimant meets his match. Surely she is as witty, malicious, verbally aggressive, as Dorimant himself, and their duel of wits seems to end in a stalemate. It is far from certain what their relationship will be after the play concludes. But in their several encounters, one sees again the intense aggression of Dorimant as he attempts to control Harriet as he has his other female victims. Harriet's realization of what Dorimant is, rather than leading her to capitulate like the masochistic Loveit, leads her to resist, to be equally aggressive. What is emphasized in their passage at arms is their fear that the inner turmoil they feel will lead to weakness, that it will be revealed, that it will mean surrender and being controlled. There are a number of passages in which both Dorimant and Harriet struggle to maintain the mask, to conceal their intense feelings. The fear of such exposure is the key to the play: Dorimant wishes to expose and, in doing so, to control and humiliate. This is expressed in his desire to "pluck off this mask and show the passion that lies panting under" (3.3.309–10). The sense, shared by both Dorimant and Harriet, that love means a failure of control, weakness, capitulation, humiliation, exposure, is seen even in the song ordered up by Harriet when the talk turns to Mr. Dorimant, act 3, scene 1. Here the emphasis is on love as "fatal," a "dang'rous passion you must shun,/Or else like me be quite undone" (64–65). It becomes clear that the word *love* (used rather indiscriminately in discussions of the play) does not here suggest an ordering impulse but, as used by Dorimant and Harriet, an impulse that erodes control and leads to failure and helplessness. Thus the repeated suggestions that all signs of love must be concealed, lest the enemy triumph. When he first sees Harriet, Dorimant, fond of quotation, muses: "In love the victors from the vanquished fly;/They fly that wound, and they pursue that die" (3.3.36–37). The conventional sentiments of Waller suggest Dorimant's sense of encounter as warfare. Harriet responds at once to the presence of Dorimant; again we observe the dangerous attraction of Dorimant, the Don Juan figure. He remarks: "Overcast with seriousness o' the sudden! A thousand smiles were shining in that face but now. I never saw so quick a change of weather." To which Harriet replies: *"(aside)*. I feel as great a change within, but he shall never know it" (3.3.58–61). This psychological action is repeated and becomes the central motif of the play. At another encounter Dorimant says aside: "I love her and dare not let her know it. I fear sh'as an ascendant o'er me and may revenge the wrongs I have done her sex" (4.1.139–41), perhaps the most crucial statement of the play's dynamics. It is important here to see that "love" is not of the greeting card variety: the word suggests infection, loss of control, weakness—as is made clear in a passage only a few lines later:

> HARRIET: Take heed; sickness after long health is commonly more violent and
>   dangerous.
> DORIMANT: *(aside)*. I have took the infection from her and feel the disease now
>   spreading in me.
>
> (4.1.147–50)

Harriet (5.2.92–93) echoes this sense of danger: "My love springs with my blood into my face. I dare not look upon him yet." We are far from the "gay" or "witty couple" of traditional criticism where the sexual antagonism is less intense, more playful and gamelike. One need only compare the earlier figures of Beatrice and Benedick of *Much Ado about Nothing*, Oriana and Mirabel of *The Wild Goose Chase*, or the later figures of Angelica and Valentine of *Love for Love*, to see that the impulse underlying the dramatic conflict of *The Man of Mode* is that of sexual antagonism: aggression and defense. One foresees a satisfactory marriage for the gay couple, but it is difficult to agree with those critics who foresee a happy union or any marriage at all for Dorimant and Harriet. The steadfast trust and openness of the second couple, Emilia and Young Bellair, is deliberately intended to contrast with the high-intensity antagonism of Dorimant and Harriet.

The psychological dynamics that mark Dorimant's character are essentially those of the Don Juan figure as I have traced it thus far. As his aside clearly reveals (4.1.139–41), Dorimant fears that a woman may revenge the wrongs done her sex. His distrust of women, his fear of them, is apparent when he says: "There is an inbred falsehood in women which inclines 'em still to them whom they may most easily deceive" (5.1.137–38). To Dorimant, as to Horner, women are aggressive, false, quick to revenge. Such interior feelings are central to Dorimant and one reason that we respond (and respond so variously) to *The Man of Mode* is because of Etherege's ability to delineate these psychological pressures.

The Libertine

Thomas Shadwell received his notions of Don Juan not through Molière directly, but primarily through the French version of Rosimond, whose Dom Juan is far more violent, more criminal, than in Molière.[38] Produced in June 1675, the play was intended to meet the taste for sex comedy then attractive to London theatergoers, and Shadwell was aware of the need to "make it new": in his dedication he asks the reader to "excuse the Irregularities of the Play, when they consider, that the Extravagance of the Subject forced me to it: And I had rather try new ways to please, than to write on in the same road, as too many do."[39] *The Libertine* is apparently the only true Don Juan play in seventeenth-century English drama; that is, it offers both the element of Don Juan's sexual adventures and the element of divine retribution in the guise of the statue of the murdered father.[40] But what Shadwell seems to refer to by "the Extravagance of the Subject" is his extraordinary presentation of Don John, the libertine, a figure who goes well beyond any earlier Don Juan or Don Juan analogue I have discussed in his criminal violence and sadistic joy in the blending of sex and violence. In his prologue the playwright calls his play, "The most irregular Play upon the Stage,/As wild, and as extravagant as th' Age" (p. 23), again suggesting that he intended to go beyond, indeed to belie, conventional expectations concerning characterization and decorum.

Critics have suggested that in Don John and his companions Shadwell intends to satirize the fashionable devotion to Hobbes and libertinism seen among the witty courtiers who surrounded Charles II; such men included Rochester and Buckingham.[41] Certainly for the modern reader Rochester's most famous poem, "A Satyr against Reason and Mankind," provides a subtext to Shadwell's play. There Rochester praises "right reason"—the wisdom of the appetites—and damns the false reason of orthodoxy. Shadwell's libertines parrot such sentiments:

> DON JOHN: . . . there is no right or wrong, but what conduces to, or hinders pleasure. . . .
> DON ANTONIO: We live in the life of Sense, which no fantastick thing call'd Reason, shall controul.
> DON LOPEZ: My reason tells me, I must please my Sense.
> DON JOHN: My appetites are all I'm sure I have from Heav'n, since they are Natural, and them I always will obey.
>
> (1.1, p. 28)

And so on. The automatic reiteration of these commonplaces, juxtaposed to acts of sex and violence, serves to mock both the idea of and the living out of *libertinage*.[42]

Thus Shadwell's Don John follows only the dictates of his "natural appetites," which lead him to disregard the orthodox pieties of social behavior in favor of murder, incest, rape, and blasphemy. Shadwell dramatizes a fictional world closer perhaps in atmosphere and action to that of the modern theater of the absurd than to that of "Restoration comedy." The actions of Don John and his followers are violent, brutal, bizarre. The only modern editor of the play notes that "Shadwell's world goes berserk with evil."[43] The actions of Don John and his two interchangeable followers, Antonio and Lopez, are outrageous; yet Shadwell carefully controls our response through laughter. John and his devotees are not literary characters at all, if literary characterization suggests a degree of probability, but caricatures intentionally exaggerated, made grotesque and wildly comic. Shadwell's bent was for satire, not the subtleties of characterization. Don

Lopez has cut his elder brother's throat for an estate; Don Antonio has got both his sisters with child. But they are as nothing compared with their peerless leader, Don John, whose praises they never tire of singing. Indeed, his career seems unparalleled, even in the equally bizarre world of the Restoration heroic play. He murders his own father, the Commander of Seville, his lovers, his rivals—the stage presents an extraordinary amount of violence. Yet the very extravagance of his career insures that the play is finally comic. The very rapidity and the mechanical repetition of violent crime distances us from the action and the result is laughter.[44] A typical moment comes when he casually has his servant haul into his room the first woman he encounters by chance on the street. He is miffed when the victim turns out to be a beldame of some years, but honor is honor and he proceeds. Or perhaps he is best seen when he kills Maria's lover, Octavio, in order to get at her, but insists on dragging the dying man aside so "that his groans may not disturb our pleasure."

The play, then, presents a grotesque fantasy. Coleridge pointed out that "the play is throughout *imaginative*. Nothing of it belongs to the real world, but the names of the places and persons. The comic parts, equally with the tragic; the living, equally with the defunct characters, are creatures of the brain; as little amenable to the rules of ordinary probability, as the *Satan* of *Paradise Lost* or the *Caliban* of *The Tempest*."[45]

I have noted the element of aggressive misogyny central to the plays of Tirso and Molière. Shadwell modifies the Continental Don Juan. He emphasizes the character's implicit violence, his rebellion against society, indeed, his latent misanthropy. Don John's career is without limits, and the result produces not only the shocked laughter of disbelief but also a certain dreamlike quality to this play. It is difficult to speak only of his aggression toward *women*, for his aggression is the entire play; it is extended beyond any sense of probability, and thus the play takes on the quality of a fantasy at once comic and disturbing.

So magnified is the Don John of this play that the possibility of parody emerges. I do not mean to suggest that we find the Don Juans of Tirso and Molière realistic in any simple sense, but Shadwell's Don John seems to burlesque the very conception of "Don Juanism." Perhaps it is possible to find in Shadwell an anticipation of later Don Juan versions in which the Don Juan character is in one way or another diminished, forced to burlesque or discredit in various ways the power that seemed his essence. His grotesque joy in violence, his incredible treachery, his automatic reiteration of a conventional libertinism that seems to mock itself—these seem to undermine the sense of hostility toward women that energized and made serious the two earlier Continental versions and the two analogous English versions. Shadwell's tendency here, as elsewhere in his drama, is toward satire and burlesque, and he makes impossible the psychological portrayal so evident in Tirso, Molière, Wycherley, and Etherege.

Yet Shadwell is far from ignoring the consequences of Don John's living out of his absurd libertinism. His destructive career leaves a trail of human debris, and all of Don John's female victims are portrayed as emotionally desolate. Two, Leonora and Maria, are given long speeches in which they express their dismal situation. These speeches, I believe, are to be taken straight, and yet such pathos jars uneasily with the determined mockery of what Don John is: the libertine as automaton.

If such pathos presents a problem of tone, the ending of the play is even more surprising. The conclusions of *The Country Wife* and *The Man of Mode* follow from the psychological action we have read or witnessed: the highly ambiguous triumph of the Don Juan figure. I have suggested that the comedy of Horner and Dorimant is that of the self-defeating man, whose wit is striking and socially successful, but whose ulterior motivation is ultimately dangerous both to himself and to those whom he dominates and in varying degrees harms. At the conclusion of *The Country Wife*, Horner stands in an emblematic scene, surrounded by his gulls and willing, unindicted co-conspirators, to witness the mocking "dance of cuckolds." The tone of Horner's final quatrain is one of detached, contemptuous amusement. It is difficult to regard this conclusion as "joyous"; Horner stands alone, to engage over and over, we assume, in the sterile if comic antics we have witnessed. Neither does the dance that concludes *The Man of Mode* suggest the future happiness of Dorimant the married man. There is little evidence in the text that Dorimant will undertake the ordeal of following Harriet to the dreaded country, there to conclude a marriage. Instead we see him speaking the same dissembling rhetoric to Harriet that he has spoken throughout—there is no change in tone—and at act 5, scene 2, line 252 and following, we see him attempting to satisfy both Loveit and Bellinda of his continuing interest. The concluding couplet refers to the forthcoming marriage of Young Bellair and Emilia, and we understand that given Dorimant's psychological situation, he too might well speak Horner's lines from *The Country Wife:* [a husband?], "I, alas, can't be one" (5.4.386). The endings of both plays are acute and realistic enough, unsentimental enough, to dramatize the ambiguous triumph of the Don Juan character.

But in *The Libertine*, the ending seems to jar with the rest of the play. Don John, portrayed throughout as puppetlike, a burlesque figure, suddenly becomes heroic! Faced with the traditional confrontation with the forces of divine retribution, Shadwell makes Don John entirely courageous. He faces his destruction with bravery, without compromising his horrible principles. The emphasis on heroism goes beyond the more ambiguous endings of Tirso and Molière, where we may or may not find Don Juan a heroic figure.

Were we to identify a unifying principle in this shifting, dreamlike play—one that informs the fantasy we witness—it would be, I think, the curious joining of absurdity to heroic self-assertion. Everywhere we witness the danger of Don John: his destruction of happiness, of innocence, his betrayals, his violence. He is an absurd and obsessive character; his mechanical justification according to the tenets of *libertinage* is merely the mask for open and uncontrollable hostility. Yet at the end of the play Shadwell is not able to dismiss his monster as simply absurd. Perhaps it is the nature of the myth, with its subtle invitation to identify with power, aggression, and sexuality, that led Shadwell to belie his satiric conception of Don John in favor of an almost romantic figure. The comparison between Satan and the Don Juan figure is constant throughout criticism, and in Shadwell Don John is at first absurd, then glorious. Perhaps Shadwell (without being a true poet) was of the devil's party without knowing it.

Conclusion

The attraction of Don Juan is enduring and profound. Although today our sensibility may demand a debased Don Juan, his shadow has not diminished. As seen in the seventeenth-century plays I have discussed, Don Juan speaks to our deepest emotional selves. He defines a psychological type not only of his own time and place but of ours. The plays offer a central fantasy: that of sexual hostility and aggression, and this fantasy offers the chance for identification and wish fulfillment.[46] That such identification may be displeasing to some readers may account for a certain critical resistance to this central element of the story. His intense sexual antagonism is disturbing. But ultimately the appeal of the Don Juan myth is to the subconscious self—to the dream of power and perfect freedom to act out aggression:

> The rest of us men live tormented by the consciousness of our limitations or those which social laws impose on us, and by the anticipation of the consequences of our acts. Natural law, social law and reason oppress us: Moira, Dike and Logos. Don Juan hurdles the three. He has shaken off the three yokes.[47]

The Don Juan figure, then, tends to become universal, an Everyman. In Tirso, the first realization of the figure, this universality becomes strikingly apparent in the first scene. Don Juan has by trickery gained Isabel, who, realizing her error, cries out: "What man are you?" Juan replies cryptically, "I am a man without a name." And when the King of Naples suddenly (and rather unexpectedly, given the context) appears and inquires "Who's there?" Juan answers again only "Why, can't you see—/A man here with a woman?" (1, p. 235.).

But if the central fantasy offered within the outline of the old story and the dramatic conventions of the time is one of sexual aggression and hostility, there is a second and powerful component: that of anxiety and guilt. Don Juan is punished; although in Tirso, Molière, and Shadwell, he easily overcomes the authority figures that oppose him, throughout these plays there are warnings of his inevitable punishment. Rank suggested that Don Juan and his servant are split-off parts of the same personality: the master represented the sexual aggression, the servant the voice of conscience; aggression versus the ego ideal.[48] As I have suggested, the conclusions of the versions of Tirso, Molière, and Shadwell are symbolic of his inevitable defeat.

This sense of defeat is present, more covertly, in the two other plays I have discussed. The sexual hostility is obvious; perhaps the sense of anxiety, guilt, and punishment less so. But even in *The Country Wife* and *The Man of Mode*, vestiges of the authority figures are present in the older men, whose power, of course, is debased and mocked. The endings of the two plays are ambiguous and suggest in Horner and Dorimant a psychological sterility even in the midst of socially defined success.

If this freedom represented by the Don Juan figure is central to the myth, in one important sense he is never free: he is a prisoner of sex, of his own neurosis. He is the free man; yet he is doomed to repeat over and over the one act that can give him no satisfaction. He is doomed always to the rigidity of action that Bergson saw as the essence of comedy. His freedom and success are illusory, and we are to see this as clearly in Don Juan as in Milton's Satan.

I do not wish to ignore or deny the other sources of the appeal of Don Juan, either in the seventeeth century or later. He is a protean figure and takes many shapes. It is obvious that there are strong religious implications in Tirso's *El burlador*, strong philosophical ones in Molière's *Dom Juan*, and social implications in both. I have emphasized here what seems to me to lie at the core of these versions of Don Juan: a fantasy of aggression that is powerful and peculiarly striking in our own times. For I think that much of the literature we read now redramatizes this image of male aggression and hostility, linked to anxiety and guilt. Granted there are today few stone statues lumbering forth bearing dinner invitations, but the psychological truth of Don Juan in whatever modern dress he chooses to wear remains a constant and powerful source of his perennial appeal.

NOTES

1. The standard sources on the development of the Don Juan story are Georges Gendarme de Bévotte, *La Légende de Don Juan*, 2 vols. (Paris: Hachette, 1911); Leo Weinstein, *The Metamorphoses of Don Juan* (Stanford: Stanford University Press, 1959); Oscar Mandel, *The Theatre of Don Juan: A Collection of Plays and Views, 1630-1963* (Lincoln: University of Nebraska Press, 1963). There is a bibliography by Armand E. Singer, *A Bibliography of the Don Juan Theme*, West Virginia University Bulletins, ser. 54, no. 10–11 (Morgantown, W.Va.: 1954), with supplements.

2. See the Introduction to Gerald E. Wade's edition of *El burlador de Sevilla y convidado de piedra* (New York: Scribner's, 1969) for questions of authorship and date of composition.

3. Gregorio Marañón, "Grandeur and Misery of the Count of Villamediana," *Partisan Review* 24 (1957):391–96. See also Wade, *El burlador*, pp. 29, 35.

4. Wade discusses the meaning of the word *burla* in *El burlador*, pp. 41–51.

5. *El burlador de Sevilla y convidada de piedra*, trans. Roy Campbell as *The Trickster of Seville and His Guest of Stone*, in *The Classic Theater*, vol. 3, *Six Spanish Plays*, ed. Eric Bentley (Garden City, N.Y.: Doubleday, 1959). Further citations will be found in the text.

6. Indeed there is another and puzzling version of the El Burlador story, obviously related to *El burlador*, but unclear as to its exact relationship. Its title, *Tan largo me lo fiáis*, suggests its proximity to *El burlador*, and, as Oscar Mandel points out, "half of the lines of the two plays are identical, or nearly identical." See Mandel, *Theatre of Don Juan*, pp. 39–41, and Wade, *El burlador*, pp. 3–11.

7. Margaret Wilson, *Tirso de Molina* (Boston: Twayne, 1977), pp. 110, 151.

8. Weinstein, *Metamorphoses*, p. 13.

9. Gerald Brenan, *The Literature of the Spanish People* (1953; reprint, Cambridge: Cambridge University Press, 1962), p. 217.

10. Otto Rank, *Die Don Juan-Gestalt* (Leipzig, Vienna, Zürich: Internationaler Psychoanalytischer Verlag, 1924), pp. 11–12. The relevant passage I quote may be found in Mandel, *Theatre of Don Juan*, pp. 625–34, translated by Walter Bodlander. Rank has written extensively on the Don Juan figure. See *The Don Juan Legend* (Princeton: Princeton University Press, 1975), and *The Double* (Chapel Hill: University of North Carolina Press, 1971).

11. Otto Fenichel, *The Psychoanalytic Theory of Neurosis* (1945; reprint, London: Routledge and Kegan Paul, 1963), p. 243.

12. Gregorio Marañón, *Don Juan ensayos sobre el origen de su leyenda*, 11th ed. (Madrid: Espasa-Calpe,

1967), pp. 74–83. The translation of this passage by Lloyd D. Teale can be found in Mandel, *Theatre of Don Juan*, pp. 637–41.

13. Dallas Pratt, "The Don Juan Myth," *American Imago* 17 (1960):331.

14. Fenichel supports this conjecture concerning the possible homosexuality of the Don Juan figure: "His sexual activities are primarily designed to contradict an inner feeling of inferiority by proof of erotic 'successes' . . . An unconsciously homosexual man, for example, may be aroused by sexual contact with women but not satisfied; he then vainly seeks satisfaction in more and more sexual activity" (*Psychoanalytic Theory of Neurosis*, pp. 243–44). There are indeed at least two suggestions of Don Juan's homosexuality in *El burlador*.

15. Dr. Ira Miller points out that after consummation there is a feeling of disappointment. "The relationship has not provided him with a release from inner tensions. This feeling of dissatisfaction causes increased frustration in him, and as often as not he blames the woman. *This may cause him to behave somewhat sadistically toward her* and will impel him to seek another woman who might provide him with his longed-for gratification and relief. This, too, results in failure, and the process is cyclically perpetuated" [emphasis mine]. See "The Don Juan Character," in *Medical Aspects of Human Sexuality* 3, no. 4 (April 1969):43–44. Miller adds: "Typically, the Don Juan character is incapable of a love affair in the true sense of the word. . . . Indeed, because of his essential loneliness, it would be accurate to describe the Don Juan's sexual exploits as a form of compulsive, vaginal masturbation" (p. 44). Miller points out that "Another possible dynamic instigator to the Don Juan complex is its use as a defense against unconscious, homosexual strivings" (p. 44).

16. For a discussion of the significance of the mother in the formation of the sadomasochistic personality, see Wilhelm Stekel, *Sadism and Masochism: The Psychology of Hatred and Cruelty*, trans. Louise Brink (1929; reprint, New York: Washington Square Press, 1968). Dallas Pratt maintains of the Don Juan character that "Unconsciously . . . he sees his mother, and any woman who has given herself to another, (husband, favored sibling) as a deceiver. She is beyond the pale of his defense. The Don Juan with whom he identifies is he who sexually enjoys the woman-possessed-by-another, with small regard for her wishes and *perhaps with positive pleasure* in her degradation" [emphasis mine] ("Don Juan Myth," p. 331). Gerald E. Wade presents an insightful and provocative analysis in "The Character of Tirso's Don Juan of *El burlador de Sevilla:* A Psychoanalytical Study," *Bulletin of Comediantes* 31 (1979):33–42. Wade points out the element of sadism and the need to degrade the female partner in Don Juan's sexuality, and he notes the possibility of Don Juan's homosexuality. Wade grounds his analysis to a great extent on Dr. Robert J. Stoller's *Perversion: The Erotic Form of Hatred* (New York: Pantheon, 1975).

17. See Georges Gendarme de Bévotte, ed., *Le festin de pierre avant Molière* (Paris: Connelly et Cie., 1907), and his *Le légende de Don Juan*. Oscar Mandel discusses the sources in *Theatre of Don Juan*, pp. 100–10.

18. John Palmer, *Molière* (1930; reprint, New York: Blom, 1970), p. 365.

19. Lionel Gossman, *Men and Masks: A Study of Molière* (1963; reprint, Baltimore: Johns Hopkins University Press, 1969), pp. 47–48. J. D. Hubert notes Dom Juan's "diabolical side," and suggests that Juan provides a "catalyst of evil," testing characters with whom he comes into contact. See *Molière and the Comedy of Intellect* (Berkeley and Los Angeles: University of California Press, 1962), pp. 113–29. W. G. Moore maintains that "Don Juan is alone in his world, despising the company of both God and man." *Molière A New Criticism* (1949; reprint, Oxford: Clarendon Press, 1968), p. 97.

20. *Tartuffe and Other Plays by Molière*, trans. Donald M. Frame (New York: New American Library, 1967). Further citations appear in the text.

21. W. D. Howarth notes that twice in the play "there are even touches of the refined, sadistic pleasure one associates with the Lovelaces and the Valmonts of the following century, for whom seduction was to be such a cerebral exercise." *Molière: A Playwright and His Audience* (Cambridge: Cambridge University Press, 1982), p. 207.

22. Hubert, *Comedy of Intellect*, p. 120.

23. I am thinking of *Paradise Lost*, 4, 356 ff.

24. Paul Radin. *The Trickster* (1956; reprint, New York: Schocken, 1973); Edith Kern, *The Absolute Comic* (New York: Columbia University Press, 1980), especially chapter 4: "The Absolute Comic and the Trickster Figure." Kern discusses Don Juan as a trickster, pp. 191–97, in relation to Rank's idea of the "The Double," and on pp. 199–205 she discusses the character of Don Juan and the tricks he plays.

25. Critics have suggested that the scenes including Batricio, Aminta, and Don Juan were presented as comic. It is difficult, however, to view the scenes as comic today. The emotions evoked and the damage done seem far too severe.

26. "Second Thoughts: II. L. C. Knights and Restoration Comedy," *Essays in Criticism* 7 (1957):59,

reprinted in *Restoration Drama: Modern Essays in Criticism,* ed. John Loftis (New York: Oxford University Press, 1966), p. 25.

27. Northrop Frye suggests that Horner's pretended impotence "would be recognized in real life as a form of infantile regression" (*The Anatomy of Criticism: Four Essays* [1957; reprint, New York: Atheneum, 1966], p. 181). Bonamy Dobrée maintains that, like Tartuffe, Horner is a "grim, nightmare" figure (*Restoration Comedy: 1660–1720* [Oxford: Oxford University Press, 1924], p. 94), and Anne Righter says of Horner: "His purely behaviourist point of view is limited and distorting; like Jonson's Volpone, he is a monomaniac who pays too great a price for his undeniable success" ("William Wycherley," in *Restoration Theatre,* ed. John Russell Brown and Bernard Harris [1965; reprint, New York: Capricorn Books, 1967], p. 79).

28. *The Country Wife,* ed. Thomas H. Fujimura (Lincoln: University of Nebraska Press, 1965), 4.3.65–66. Further citations appear in the text.

29. The figure of the "Quack" aligns Horner with the Don Juan tradition, since the Quack seems to be a vestige of Juan's servant, called Catalinón in Tirso and Sganerelle in Molière. We note Horner's readiness to explain his methods to the Quack, whose wonderment at and somewhat rueful admiration of Horner's success recalls the earlier servants. The Quack's function, of course, is to assist Horner's ruse, for which he is paid money.

30. Sigmund Freud, *Jokes and Their Relation to the Unconscious,* in *The Standard Edition of the Complete Psychological Works of Sigmund Freud,* trans. James Strachey, 24 vols. (London: Hogarth Press, 1960), 8:202.

31. *The First Modern Comedies* (Cambridge, Mass.: Harvard University Press, 1959,) p. 74. See also Katharine M. Rogers, *William Wycherley* (New York: Twayne, 1972), pp. 66–67, concerning Pinchwife's hostility toward women.

32. David M. Vieth speaks to this point in "Wycherley's *The Country Wife:* An Anatomy of Masculinity," *Papers on Language and Literature* 2 (1966):339.

33. David M. Vieth notes (ibid., p. 340) that Sir Jaspar is indifferent to his wife as a woman and that "although he evades a truly masculine role, perhaps because of inferiority feelings, he is neurotically absorbed in the subject of sex." Vieth also notes Sir Jaspar's preoccupation with Horner's supposed impotence (p. 340) and suggests (p. 339) that Sir Jaspar is a well-known type, "the man who tries to sublimate his masculinity in his occupation instead of fulfilling it with a woman."

34. "Dorimant, in his relationships with women, has the fighter-pilot's mentality; he wants to get them before they get him. He is at war with the sex, and they immediately feel it and feel a very real wish to injure him (which doesn't prevent their feeling attracted to him)." John Wain, *Preliminary Essays* (London: Macmillan, 1957), p. 16.

35. Horner derives of course not merely from the Don Juan tradition; his sources are various and plainly defined in the earlier English comedy. But it is equally clear that the Don Juan story fed into the English tradition, and, as Dale Underwood points out, "In seventeenth-century drama the Don Juan legend . . . had itself become a focus of libertinism . . . and had assimilated most of the libertine doctrines and practices reflected in the Restoration comedy of manners." See *Etherege and the Seventeenth-Century Comedy of Manners* (New Haven: Yale University Press, 1957), p. 11. Later Underwood notes other similarities between Dorimant and the Don Juan figure (p. 74, n.5):

> The libertinism, the seeming rationality, the wit and general polish of manner, the physical attractiveness, the "Machiavellianism," the Satanic egoism, pride, and malice are among the specific characteristics which they share. The similarity is especially apparent in the Don Juans of Molière, Rosimond, and Shadwell—the versions with which Etherege and the Restoration were most familiar. (Shadwell's *The Libertine* was produced in June 1675, nine months before Etherege's play.) At the same time it seems apparent that the 17th-century concerns reflected in Dorimant and Don Juan are to be related to those which produced the "Machiavellian villain" of pre-Restoration English drama.

John Traugott, "The Rake's Progress from Court to Comedy: A Study in Comic Form," *Studies in English Literature* 6 (1966), distinguishes between the Don Juan figure and that of the rake, but I am not inclined to believe that in Shadwell's *The Libertine,* "Don John is wholly unlike his fellow actor; he remains a morality play figure, a mindlessly malicious rapist, an absurd puppet calling down God's vengeance" (p. 385). I would argue instead that the two figures merge in such characters as Horner and Dorimant.

36. Underwood accounts for the Restoration's fascination with libertinism; see *Etherege,* especially chap. 2. The question of the character of the rake and his relation to the intellectual milieu of the later seventeenth century is discussed in some detail by Robert Jordan, "The Extravagant Rake in Restoration Comedy," in *Restoration Literature: Critical Approaches,* ed. Harold Love (London: Meth-

ANTHONY KAUFMAN

uen, 1972), pp. 69–90; Robert D. Hume, "The Myth of the Rake in 'Restoration' Comedy," *Studies in the Literary Imagination* 10, no. 1 (Spring 1977): 25–55, and Maximillian E. Novak, "Margery Pinchwife's 'London Disease': Restoration Comedy and the Libertine Offensive of the 1670's," in the same collection, pp. 1–23.

37. *The Man of Mode*, ed. W. B. Carnochan (Lincoln: University of Nebraska Press, 1966), 2.1.27–28. All citations from the play are from this edition.

38. See *Le nouveau festin de pierre ou L'athée foudroyé*, in *Les contemporains de Molière*, ed. Victor Fournel, vol. 3 (Paris: Firmin-Dedot, 1875).

39. Preface to *The Libertine*, in *The Complete Works of Thomas Shadwell*, ed. Montague Summers, vol. 3 (1927; reprint, New York: Blom, 1968), p. 21. All citations from the play are from this edition.

40. Some scholars see a trace of the legend in Sir Aston Cockain's *The Tragedy of Ovid*, 1662, where one finds a version of the double-invitation motif.

41. Michael W. Alssid, *Thomas Shadwell* (New York: Twayne, 1967), suggests that "Don Juan's career etches the darkest extreme of libertinism," while Don R. Kunz, *The Drama of Thomas Shadwell* (Salzburg: Institut für Englische Sprache und Literatur, 1972), maintains that "the fact that scenes, characters, and action were passed off as Spanish scarcely concealed Shadwell's criticism of English manners and art. Don John, Don Antonio, and Don Lopez were only Charles II, Sir Charles Sedley, the Earl of Rochester . . . substantially exaggerated. . . . This bombast and the libertine philosophy blended together, comprise a most irregular play filled with comic absurdities and tragic implications. The libertines were viewed as spreading an infection throughout the land" (p. 177).

42. Although it seems clear that Shadwell is satirizing libertinism, one must be cautious. Shadwell remained on cordial terms with Rochester after May 1675. See David Vieth, *The Complete Poems of John Wilmot, Earl of Rochester* (New Haven: Yale University Press, 1968), p. xxx. *The Libertine* was produced in June of that year. The exact feelings of Shadwell about Rochester, that magnet for strong feelings, and about libertinism are far from clear. If libertinism was au courant, so was antilibertinism. See Novak, "Margery Pinchwife's 'London Disease,'" p. 15. I disagree of course with Novak's assertion that "in *The Libertine* (1675), he had made Don John into a protagonist in the Caligula tradition rather than in the Don Juan tradition."

43. Mandel, *Theatre of Don Juan*, p. 167.

44. John Loftis notes that "the multiplicity and gravity of Don John's sins convey an impression that borders on the burlesque." See *The Spanish Plays of Neoclassical England* (New Haven: Yale University Press, 1973). p. 174.

45. *Biographia Literaria*, ed. J. Shawcross, vol. 2 (1907; reprint, London: Oxford University Press, 1958), p. 185.

46. I am aware of an important, indeed crucial, critical question here: that the Don Juan story offers the male the opportunity for wish fulfillment and identification is obvious; but do women respond in the same way as men to the Don Juan figure? It hardly seems likely; yet this question has not received extended treatment, and such treatment is beyond the scope of this paper.

47. Ramiro de Maeztu, *Don Juan or Power*, trans. Lloyd D. Teale, in Mandel, *Theatre of Don Juan*, pp. 635–36.

48. Rank, in Mandel, *Theatre of Don Juan*, pp. 629–34.

Romance and Finance: The Comedies of William Congreve

Albert Wertheim

It is often the case that in the works of second- and third-rate writers we come closest to seeing the preoccupations of an age. For in their works, unalloyed by authorial talent or invention, we find baldly stated the attitudes and ideas artfully and inventively presented in the works of their more gifted contemporaries. Such is the case of *A Wife to be Lett* (1724) by Mrs. Eliza Haywood, whom Pope took to task in *The Dunciad* and whom Swift described as "A stupid, infamous, scribbling woman." The conflict in Mrs. Haywood's play centers around the idea of the union of the sexes as a strictly monetary arrangement rather than as a consummation of romantic love. In the closing couplet of the second act, Toywell, a mercenary fop, asserts:

> When her Fortune's gone, the loveliest of Woman
> In this wise Age is fit Wife for no man.
>
> (E1)[1]

The contrasting view is given at the close of the fourth act by a reformed rake:

> Ye false-nam'd Pleasures of my Youth farewel,
> They charm'd my Sense, but you subdue my Soul.
> Tho fix'd to you alone, I've pow'r to change,
> While o'er each Beauty of your Form I range.
> Nor to those only need I be confin'd,
> But changing still, enjoy thy beauteous Mind.
>
> (H4ᵛ)

With little subtlety, Mrs. Haywood pits extremes of thoroughly crass behavior against extremes of thoroughly romance attitudes. In the plot that gives the play its title, a thoroughly exploitative husband is prepared to rent out his wife for a fee of £2000. In another plot, Celemena has no second thoughts at all about losing her £10,000 portion in order to follow the dictates of her heart:

Well, let me consider—Here's a Coach and Six with my Father's Commands and 10,000*l.* to back it—On the other hand, 16 *s.* a Day, and the Title of a Captain's Lady, with a reasonable Suspicion of being turn'd out of doors with never a Groat—But then, on this side, I've a Fool—on that, a Man not disagreeable, and of allow'd sense—One marries me upon Compact, the other

255

generously runs the risque of a Fortune—Well, *Gaylove,* I think you carry the day. (I2)

Mrs. Haywood paints her portraits without life, color, or shading.

The conflict of marriage based on romantic feeling versus marriage based on a cash nexus, so flatly and unsubtly presented in *A Wife to be Lett,* is also the one that informs most of the best getting-married plays from the 1690s to Sheridan's *The Rivals* (1775). It is the conflict central to plays like Farquhar's *The Constant Couple* (1700), *The Recruiting Officer* (1706), and *The Beaux' Stratagem* (1707); Steele's *The Tender Husband* (1705) and *The Conscious Lovers* (1722); Gay's *The Beggar's Opera* (1728) and *Polly* (1729); Fielding's *A Modern Husband* (1732); and Colman and Garrick's *Clandestine Marriage* (1766). Viewing Congreve as a transition figure between the love-game comedies of Etherege and Wycherley, which appeared a quarter of a century before *The Way of the World,* and the marriage comedies of the eighteenth century, which so often dwell on questions of portions and jointures, one can see how economic matters make their presence felt in comic drama after 1688, the date usually cited as the onset of England's Commercial Revolution.

The "Glorious Revolution"—the ascension of William and Mary to the throne of England in 1688—is a major landmark in English political, constitutional, and social history. As historians are becoming increasingly aware, however, 1688 is an even more important landmark in English economic history, largely because of the consequences of British commercial interests in the New World and the growing wealth derived from trade as opposed to land.[2] By 1688, as W. W. Rostow and others have shown, England was ready for economic "take-off" and ready to become the first industrial nation.[3] Although in drama before 1688 the opposing claims of romance versus finance had already made their mark in Elizabethan plays[4]—for example, Shakespeare's *The Taming of the Shrew* (1594) and *The Merchant of Venice* (1596), Middleton's *A Trick to Catch the Old One* (1605), Fletcher's *Wit without Money* (1614), and Shirley's *The Brothers* (1641)—in the period following 1688, the new economic circumstances in England and the new wealth created through entrepôt trade make the economic questions in courtship and marriage comedies particularly acute ones.[5] As the major comic playwright writing in the decade following 1688, Congreve provides us in his four comedies with a useful measure for gauging the growing importance of financial concerns in marriage comedies.

As it is found in the four comedies of Congreve, the question of the conflation of love and money is recognizable but muted. Though financial marriage arrangements are central to the plots of *The Double Dealer* (1693), *Love for Love* (1695), and *The Way of the World* (1700), and though Sir Joseph Wittol's desire to marry Araminta's £12,000 fortune forms one plot interest in *The Old Bachelor* (1693), Congreve's main characters are at once wise enough to know that marriage for money alone is foolish and urbane enough to recognize that London courtship and romance courtship are incongruent. It is only the most excessive of all Congreve's characters, Lady Wishfort, who seems to read romances with any seriousness. Her comparison of her maid to "*Maritornes* the *Asturian* in *Don*

Quixote" (3.1.37–38),[6] probably in Durfey's version, is only less excessive than her idea that she and Mrs. Marwood head for the nearest pastoral landscape:

> Well Friend, you are enough to reconcile me to the bad World, or else I wou'd retire to Desarts and Solitudes; and feed harmless Sheep by *Groves* and *Purling Streams.* Dear *Marwood,* let us leave the World, and retire by our selves and be *Shepherdesses.* (5.1.131–35)

The very thought of Lady Wishfort, the foppish, "superannuated" would-be coquette and Mrs. Marwood, the most jaded of all Congreve's town ladies, as shepherdesses is as ludicrous as it is inconceivable. It is, at the same time, only Congreve's two out and out villains, Fainall in *The Way of the World* and Maskwell in *The Double Dealer,* who consider marriage strictly in its nonromantic context, as a means to pecuniary ends.

Though Congreve sees the possibilities of romantic and mercenary excess, he nonetheless maintains an urbane distance from the fundamentally antithetical demands of marriage as the fruition of courtship on the one hand and marriage as the culmination of economic negotiation on the other. This is evident in his first comedy, *The Old Bachelor,* which separates the courtship plots involving Bellmour and Vainlove from the money plot concerning the bilking of the foolish Wittol by the confidence man Sharper. In *The Old Bachelor,* two young men about town, Vainlove and Bellmour, are united by their complementary amoristic tastes. Vainlove relishes only pursuit and courtship; his friend, Bellmour, enjoys the consummation of an affair. They work happily in tandem: the one tracks down agreeable young women and woos them; the other beds them down. It is striking, however, that although Vainlove and Bellmour's activities are not shaped by a profit motive, their association is like a business partnership, as their friend Sharper aptly underlines when he describes their union of Neoplatonic friendship and physical consummation with a monetary image: "He does the drudgery in the Mine, and you stamp your image on the Gold" (1.1.220–21). Throughout *The Old Bachelor,* moreover, the love games of Vainlove and Bellmour are juxtaposed to the confidence game of Sharper, who hopes to fleece Sir Joseph Wittol. Picking up Sharper's monetary imagery, Bellmour says of the Sharper-Wittol relationship, "a little of thy Chymistry *Tom,* may extract Gold from that Dirt" (1.1.345–46). Here as elsewhere, the plots of *The Old Bachelor* are related metaphorically, but metaphorically only. The love plots exist separately from the money plot.

In the main plot or plots, the fortunes of the two women are hardly spoken of. Vainlove pursues the airy Araminta who is described as "a kind of floating Island; sometimes seems in reach, then vanishes and keeps him busied in the search." Bellmour pursues the witty and disdainful Belinda. Although it is known that Araminta is a "great fortune," Vainlove seems unconcerned about Araminta's financial assets. The less idealistic Bellmour is aware of his Belinda's wealth but surely does not treat it with great seriousness:

> SHARPER: Faith e'en give her over for good-and-all; you can have no hopes of getting her for a Mistress, and she is too Proud, too Inconstant, too Affected

and too Witty, and too handsome for a Wife.

BELLMOUR: But she can't have too much Mony—There's twelve thousand
Pound *Tom*—'Tis true she is excessively foppish and affected, but in my
Conscience I believe the Baggage loves me, for she never speaks well of me her
self, nor suffers any Body else to rail at me. Then as I told you there's twelve
thousand Pound—Hum—Why faith upon second Thoughts, she does not
appear to be so very affected neither—Give her her due, I think the Woman's a
Woman, and that's all. As such I'm sure I shall like her; for the Devil take me if
I don't love all the Sex.

(l.l.161–75)

These speeches sensitize the audience to Belinda's considerable fortune and
make them aware, too, that Bellmour is not entirely ignorant of her £12,000.
Still, the pursuit of Belinda is almost entirely an amorous one, and John Harrington Smith rightly asserts that Congreve's audience must have delighted in "a
love game as had not been seen since the time of Etherege."[7]

The minor plot of *The Old Bachelor* is quite another matter. In it, the foppish
Sir Joseph Wittol and his *miles gloriosus* companion, Captain Bluffe, lose their
gold in hopes of gaining the rich Araminta. Setter, Bellmour's pimp, ruminating
aloud so that Wittol and Bluffe can be sure to hear him, inspires their fortune
hunting:

Were I a Rogue now, what a noble Prize could I dispose of! A goodly Pinnace,
richly laden, and to launch forth under my Auspicious Convoy. Twelve Thousand Pounds, and all her Rigging; besides what lies conceal'd under Hatches.
(5.1.221–25)

Both Wittol and Bluffe take the gilded bait, each bribing Setter to match him
with Araminta. And in their pursuit of Araminta's £12,000, both Wittol and
Bluffe are deprived of courtship and even of the sight of their betrothed. Their
comic punishment is that they are married off respectively to Bellmour and
Vainlove's shared former mistress, Silvia, and her maid Lucy. Although the love
games of Bellmour and Vainlove may be linked metaphorically to the monetary
duping of Wittol and Bluffe, Congreve keeps the two plots largely separate, and
there seems a distinct reluctance on Congreve's part to recognize the con game
and the love game not merely as analogous but as conflated social realities.

In the later comedies, some of that reluctance is overcome, but Congreve's
world is, for the most part, homogeneously aristocratic; and neither Mellefont in
The Double Dealer, nor Valentine in *Love for Love,* nor Mirabell in *The Way of the
World* is *forced* to consider a wealthy match either outside or within his class. True,
Mellefont and Valentine face the possibility of disinheritance and financial ruin,
but Congreve does not have either think of recouping his losses through marriage. Quite the contrary: Mellefont is prepared to marry Cynthia without
money, and Valentine hopes to outwit his father so that his own fortune may be
commensurate with Angelica's. Mellefont's and Valentine's views are not, however, those of the playwright, and it is the women who must teach them what
appears to be Congreve's concept of happiness in marriage.

The Double Dealer is unique among Congreve's comedies, for Mellefont, its hero, is neither rake nor wit. Those traits belong instead to the mercenary villain, Maskwell. Mellefont's innate virtue, his ingenuous and blind trust in the unscrupulous Maskwell, and his near loss of Cynthia bring him dangerously close to sentimentality and to the heroes of sentimental comedy. He is, however, like Valentine in *Love for Love,* both rescued and educated by his more discerning female counterpart. The central difficulty in *The Double Dealer* turns on a financial issue: through the scheming of various characters and of Maskwell in particular, Mellefont stands to lose his own inheritance as well as the hand and fortune of Cynthia. But Mellefont's boyish romantic attitude is such that he is prepared to surrender his monetary interests if he can marry Cynthia. And he is prepared to have her with or without her money. Mellefont's idealistic enthusiasm is, however, significantly adjusted and redirected by a wiser, more pragmatic Cynthia:

MELLEFONT: I don't know why we should not steal out of the House this moment and Marry one another, without Consideration or the fear of Repentance. Pox o'Fortune, Portion, Settlements and Joyntures.
CYNTHIA: Ay, ay, what have we to do with 'em; you know we Marry for Love.
MELLEFONT: Love, Love, down right very Villanous Love.
CYNTHIA: And he that can't live upon Love, deserves to die in a Ditch—Here, then, I give you my promise, in spight of Duty, any temptation of Wealth, your inconstancy, or my own inclination to change—
MELLEFONT: To run most wilfully and unreasonably away with me this moment and be Married.
CYNTHIA: Hold—Never to Marry any Body else.
MELLEFONT: That's but a kind of Negative Consent.—Why, you wont baulk the Frollick?
CYNTHIA: If you had not been so assured of your own Conduct I would not—But 'tis but reasonable that since I consent to like a Man without the vile Consideration of Money, He should give me a very evident demonstration of his Wit: Therefore let me see you undermine my Lady *Touchwood,* as you boasted, and force her to give her Consent, and then—
MELLEFONT: I'll do't.
CYNTHIA: And I'll do't.

(4.1.27–51)

Mellefont's stress upon marriage based on love is applauded, but his easy surrender of both money and wit are not. Of course, Mellefont's proper demonstration of wit, the successful undermining of Lady Touchwood, will, in effect, secure the "Fortune, Portion, Settlements and Joyntures" against which he has just so vocally protested.

Mellefont's education about wit, money, and love is done in the context of Lord and Lady Froth on the one hand and of Machiavellian Maskwell on the other. The Froths are poetasters and false wits, who celebrate their affection by writing "Songs, Elegies, Satires, Encomiums, Panegyricks, Lampoons, Plays, or Heroick Poems" (2.1.1–26), but whose supposed wit has as its end only self-adulation, self-admiration, and self-congratulation. The use of wit—or in this case false wit—merely for egocentric and nonutilitarian purposes is presented and rejected by

Congreve as well as by Cynthia (3.1.626–34). Maskwell is a character not as easily rejected, for he has both true wit and utilitarian purpose. For these reasons he is not rendered foolish like the Froths and almost defeats Mellefont. He is a forerunner of Fainall, who is very nearly a match for Mirabell in *The Way of the World*, and like Fainall, he is rendered a Machiavel by the primacy of his utilitarian ends, his acquisitiveness.[8] He tells Mellefont that he has tricked Lady Touchwood and "if I accomplish her designs (as I told you before) she has ingaged to put *Cynthia* with all her Fortune into my Power" (2.1.427–29); and when Mellefont exits, Maskwell, in a long Machiavellian soliloquy, exclaims:

> Success will attend me; for when I meet you [Mellefont], I meet the only Obstacle to my Fortune. *Cynthia*, let thy Beauty gild my Crimes; and whatsoever I commit of Treachery or Deceit, shall be imputed to me as a Merit. (2.1.439–43)

Later, when he seems nearly successful in obtaining Cynthia and the inheritance Lord Touchwood had planned to settle on Mellefont, Maskwell soliloquizes, "This is prosperous indeed—Why let him find me out a Villain, settled in possession of a fair Estate, and full fruition of my Love, I'll bear the railings of a losing Gamester" (5.1.85–88). What makes Maskwell reprehensible and villainous from Congreve's point of view is not that his wit is used to betray others, for certainly this could be said of Bellmour, Valentine, and Mirabell. It is, rather, his concentration upon the acquisition of money. Whether Maskwell has any affection for Cynthia beyond his affection for her fortune is never clear. Even Cynthia's beauty is transmuted into precious metal by Maskwell, for it will "gild" his crimes. He sees, moreover, that Cynthia's money is something to be held and controlled, for he speaks of having Cynthia's fortune put "into my Power" and of being "settled in possession of a fair Estate." Maskwell's possessiveness is such that he wishes to use his wit primarily to bring him a bundle of money and only secondarily the young lady who accompanies it.

To a ruthless business mentality like Maskwell's, a friend like Mellefont is expendable when he becomes a competitor in the economic marketplace. If he can possess Cynthia's estate, says Maskwell, "I'll bear the railings of a losing Gamester." The object of Maskwell's game playing is the possession of money, and here Congreve has Mellefont differ radically and importantly from him. Early in the play, Cynthia and Mellefont describe marriage through the imagery of games. Cynthia quips, "Still it is a Game, and Consequently one of us must be a Loser," to which Mellefont replies, "Not at all; only a Friendly Tryal of Skill, and the Winnings to be Shared between us" (2.1.168–71). For Maskwell, marriage is a game of winners and losers with the former in control of the marriage settlement. For Mellefont, by contrast, marriage and getting married are a game, but the "Tryal of Skill," the play, is more important than any monetary prize; and, furthermore, "the Winnings" are to be *shared* or, as some editions read, "laid out in an Entertainment." What Mellefont and the audience are taught through Cynthia and through Congreve is that the reasons for getting married should be based upon love and should transcend fortune, which is not to say that a loving couple should marry without money if it is in the power of their wit to secure it.

In *The Double Dealer* wit must be used to secure the love of a young lady and then to secure the settlement she should bring with her, but step one must greatly outweigh and precede step two.

By making Maskwell such an outright villain and Mellefont so amiable and trusting a fellow, Congreve allows the question of romance versus finance in marriage to be one that need not engage much of the audience's attention.[9] Mellefont's values are after all largely in the right place. He prefers love to settlements and jointures; and he sees any money brought into the marriage by either partner as funds that the married couple may jointly enjoy. Cynthia's task is simply to encourage Mellefont not to lose what, by virtue of the marriage arrangements already drawn up, is nearly his. The questions of money and love are furthermore pushed into the background by Congreve's satiric portraits of three other couples, the Froths, the Plyants, and the Touchwoods. These comic characters and the plots in which they move serve to draw the audience's attention away from the issues besetting the Mellefont-Cynthia-Maskwell triangle. It is in *Love for Love* that Congreve places the questions concerning the relationship between money and love in the foreground and at the center of his comedy. This play abounds in talk of fortunes, inheritances, settlements, deeds of conveyance, and estates. A loan broker and an estate lawyer receive extended comic treatment.[10] And a sometimes nasty, frequently comic, world driven nearly mad by the precedence of material values is the potent image that Congreve has pass before the eyes of his audience.

Love for Love has no fewer than eleven characters of major importance, all of whom are, with the exception of Mrs. Foresight and Scandal, directly affected by the financial state of affairs in the play. Mrs. Foresight, who is financially secure in her marriage to Foresight and who has no children to marry off, has nothing to lose or gain by the monetary transactions of the play. Since, however, she has in the past made a presumably financially advantageous marriage to Foresight, she can use her experience to counsel and abet her sister in Mrs. Frail's attempts to attain financial security through marriage. Likewise, Scandal, whom the play pairs with Mrs. Foresight and who is her worldly-wise male counterpart, has no personal loss or gain at stake in the money that will pass hands in the play; but he serves, nonetheless, to advise and abet his friend Valentine in affairs of the pocketbook as well as of the heart. At the center of Congreve's witty but acquisitive world stand Valentine and Angelica, whose positions toward courtship, marriage, and money create the central interest of the comedy. Those positions not only are treated directly but also are examined indirectly through each of the several other actions of the comedy. In part, the point of *Love for Love* can be located in its title, for although there is much courtship for purely sexual ends and much courtship for purely acquisitive ends, there is no true love for love except that displayed betweeen Angelica and Valentine during the final moments of the play.

The two most patent fortune hunters in *Love for Love* are Mrs. Frail and Mr. Tattle, who, through Congreve's poetic justice, emerge married to each other. Yet Congreve is no harsh judge, for he knows that Mrs. Frail is no mean-spirited, avaricious Maskwell but rather is a victim of the way of the world who must do what she can to mend or make her fortune. Sight unseen, therefore, she is prepared to set her cap for the rough tar, Ben, whose promise of inheritance obliterates his unpromising personality. To her successful sister, she dispassionately explains:

> You have a Rich Husband, and are provided for, I am at a loss, and have no great Stock either of Fortune or Reputation; and therefore must look sharply about me. Sir *Sampson* has a Son that is expected to Night; and by the Account I have heard of his Education can be no Conjurer: The Estate You know is to be made over to him:—Now if I cou'd wheedle him, Sister, ha! You understand me? (2.2.489–96)

And when the estate is taken from Ben and seems to revert to Valentine, she can just as dispassionately have no qualms about marrying Valentine despite his seemingly demented state. That Ben is crude or that Valentine is mad makes little difference, for it is the estate that matters. As Mrs. Foresight shrewdly comments, "after Consummation, Girl, there's no revoking. And if he should recover his Senses, he'll be glad at least to make you a good Settlement" (4.1.473–75).

As in most love comedies, there are winners and losers in *Love for Love,* but—in a way that sets them apart from Etherege's and Wycherley's characters—the wins and losses are realistically reckoned in pounds sterling rather than in mistresses. This sense of gain and loss informs Tattle's as well as Mrs. Frail's *Weltanschauung.* Valentine's servant Jeremy convinces Tattle that, in return for some tangible rewards, Angelica can be tricked into marrying Tattle. Jeremy's lure is Angelica's fortune, to which Tattle has already shown himself not indifferent. "'Tis an Act of Charity, Sir," observes Jeremy, "to save a fine Woman with Thirty Thousand Pound, from throwing her self away" (5.1.209–11). Tattle's assurance of success is expressed with images, like Mrs. Frail's, stressing marriage as a game of chance played for monetary stakes:

> I have some taking Features, not obvious to Vulgar Eyes; that are Indications of a sudden turn of good Fortune, in the Lottery of Wives; and promise a great Beauty and great Fortune reserved alone for me, by a private Intriegue of Destiny. (5.2.267–71)

When Mrs. Frail marries Tattle believing him to be Valentine, and when Tattle married Mrs. Frail believing her to be Angelica, Congreve momentarily allows Tattle and Frail to be comic proxies for Valentine and Angelica in order to project what it would be like for the main couple to marry for fortune and estate only. Despite their dislike for one another, however, the two fortune hunters, Mrs. Frail and Tattle, do not make a bad match;[11] and they will likely survive even more swimmingly than Silvia and Sir Joseph, their forerunners in *The Old Bachelor.*

The economics of getting married are delineated in another key through the marriage preparations for Ben and Miss Prue. Here Congreve presents a radically mismatched couple, he "a Sea-Beast" and she "a Land-Monster," who are brought together by Sir Sampson and Foresight, their parents, to unite jointure and settlement. Sir Sampson is perhaps the character most corrupted by the material values that color the way of *Love for Love's* world, but even the other-worldly astrologer Foresight, comically lost in the stars, seems not completely oblivious to the prime mover, prosperity, that guides the realities of the beau monde:

> SCANDAL: But I fear this Marriage and making over this Estate, this transfer-ring of a rightful Inheritance, will bring Judgments upon us. I prophesie it, and I wou'd not have the Fate of *Cassandra*, not to be believ'd.
> . . . .
> FORESIGHT: But as to this marriage I have consulted the Stars; and all Ap-pearances are prosperous—
> SCANDAL: Come, come, Mr. *Foresight*, let not the Prospect of Worldy Lucre carry you beyond your Judgment, nor against your Conscience—You are not satisfy'd that you act justly.
>
> (3.1.543–57)

Congreve does not take pains to let us see exactly how much worldly wisdom resides beneath Foresight's otherworldly humour, but he is pellucid in his por-trayal of Sir Sampson Legend.

If there is a villain in *Love for Love*, Sir Sampson is it; and he is, appropriately, the one character publicly exposed, disgraced, and punished at the close of the comedy. Sir Sampson not only plans to dispose of Ben as he would a piece of property, but in his treatment of Valentine he replaces the obligations of parental love with loveless legal and monetary obligations. When Valentine sues for his father's blessing, Sir Sampson tellingly replies, "You've had it already, Sir, I think I sent it you to day in a Bill of Four Thousand Pound" (2.1.274–75). Valentine continues to urge the obligations of paternal love; Sir Sampson counters with an argument for paternal despotism and the divine right of the father, un-ashamedly setting forth the purely capitalistic paradigm of the family as an arrangement of economic exploitation and dependence:[12]

> why Sirrah, mayn't I do what I please? Are not you my Slave? Did not I beget you? And might not I have chosen whether I would have begot you or no? Ouns who are you? Whence came you? What brought you into the World? How came you here, Sir? . . . Did you come a Voluntier into the World? Or did I beat up for you with the lawful Authority of a Parent, and press you to the service? (2.1.323–32)

Valentine rightly terms his father's behavior "Barbarity and Unnatural Usage," an unnaturalness and barbarity bred by a monstrous materialism that allows children to become inanimate goods or property to be disposed of according to the whims of their fathers, the despotic property holders. The monstrosity of Sir Sampson's attitude is brought out to its fullest by Angelica, who wins his favor by feigning to share his materialism, "If I marry, Sir *Sampson*, I'm for a good Estate with any Man, and for any Man with a good Estate" (3.1.253–54). She aph-

oristically echoes his depersonalization of human relationship in favor of economic egotism. Her trick works so well that Sir Sampson proposes marriage and
reveals himself prepared unfeelingly to disinherit both his sons:

> SIR SAMPSON: Odd, Madam, I'll love you as long as I live; and leave you a good
> Jointure when I die.
> ANGELICA: Aye; But that is not in your Power, Sir *Sampson;* for when *Valentine*
> confesses himself in his Senses; he must make over his Inheritance to his
> younger Brother.
> SIR SAMPSON: Odd, you're cunning, a wary Baggage! Faith and Troth I like
> you the better—But, I warrant you, I have a Proviso in the Obligation in favour
> of my self—Body o'me, I have a Trick to turn the Settlement upon the Issue
> Male of our Two Bodies begotten. Odsbud, let us find Children, and I'll find
> an Estate.
>
>   (5.1.119–29)

The voice of intelligence, judgment, and wit in *Love for Love* belongs to
Angelica, and it is she, therefore, who teases both Valentine and his father to
show their best and worst selves respectively. She tests both father and son, and
rewards them accordingly:

> I was resolv'd to try him [Valentine] to the utmost; I have try'd you [Sir
> Sampson] too, and know you both. You have not more Faults than he has
> Virtues; and 'tis hardly more Pleasure to me, that I can make him and my self
> happy, than that I can punish you. (5.1.574–78)

For his generous love, Valentine receives a public declaration of Angelica's love
for him. For his unnatural and materialistic barbarity, Sir Sampson is publicly
exposed; and for his plan to disinherit his sons and marry Angelica, he is
rendered a fool open to both the ridicule and scorn of all.

The events involving the Foresights, Mrs. Frail, Ben and Prue, and Sir
Sampson and Angelica merely form a dramatic context for the education of the
comedy's central character, Valentine. That education is, furthermore, the
product of Valentine's two principal teachers, Scandal and Angelica. When at the
close of *Love for Love,* Angelica gives heart and hand to Valentine, she says she
"was resolv'd to try him to the utmost"; but in the course of that trial, Valentine
learns what no character other than Angelica knows: the importance of love for
love.

In the first act of the play, Congreve introduces a Valentine impoverished by
courtship. At heart a romantic, Valentine takes pleasure in the prospect of
becoming a misogynist poet or philosopher, roles his reduced finances will
support. He hopes as well to gain Angelica's love, the love he had not gained
through prodigality, through the charm of his current romantic poverty. At the
same time that he maintains a romantic pose, Valentine also possesses a sharp
wit, has fathered a bastard, and has not been untouched by the way of the world.
His worldly education has taught him what it has taught the other characters: in
this world money triumphs over love. That knowledge, combined with his innate

romanticism, has led Valentine first upon a mad course of proving his affection for Angelica by spending vast sums in her behalf and then to a belief that his current resultant poverty is the ultimate demonstration of his love:

> Well; and now I am poor, I have an opportunity to be reveng'd on 'em all; I'll pursue *Angelica* with more Love than ever, and appear more notoriously her Admirer in this Restraint, than when I openly rival'd the rich Fops, that made Court to her; so shall my Poverty be a Mortification to her Pride, and perhaps, make her compassionate that Love, which has principally reduc'd me to this Lowness of Fortune. (1.1.49–56)

This romantic view would justify Valentine's further impoverishing himself by signing away his inheritance to his brother Ben.

Signing a deed of conveyance would be, as Scandal chides, "A very desperate demonstration of your love to Angelica," and he argues astutely, "you have little reason to believe that a Woman of this Age, who has had an indifference for you in your Prosperity, will fall in love with your ill Fortune; besides, *Angelica* has a great Fortune of her own; and great Fortunes either expect another great Fortune, or a Fool" (1.1.343–44, 350–54). The correctness of Scandal's comment on the monetary basis of love relationships specifically and on social behavior generally is brought home to Valentine by various characters who are heard from in act 1. They include the pragmatic, philosophizing Jeremy, who speaks of the need to leave a master bereft of credit; the past mistress who now writes for child support; the loan broker Trapland, whose friendliness in flush times has been replaced by an uncharitable readiness to clap insolvent debtors into irons; Mrs. Frail, who carries the news of the proposed, economically motivated arranged match between Ben and Prue; and Sir Sampson's steward, sent to act on his master's barbarous demand for Valentine's deed of conveyance.

By the end of the first act, Valentine, in the context of the other characters, does indeed seem to have acted naively, and Scandal's observation and couplet, which close the act, are well taken:

> I'll give an account of you, and your Proceedings. If Indiscretion be a sign of Love, you are the most a Lover of any Body that I know: you fancy that parting with your Estate, will help you to your Mistress.—In my mind he is a thoughtless Adventurer,
>
> > Who hopes to purchase Wealth, by selling Land;
> > Or win a Mistress, with a losing hand.
>
> > (1.1.675–81)

Apparently, it is Scandal's worldly teaching upon which Valentine then proceeds to act. His feigned madness is principled by a pragmatic, materialistic outlook that will enable him to keep his estate, and provide him with the land and the winning hand that Scandal asserts are necessary for marriage to Angelica. Valentine's feigned madness is, furthermore, simply his satiric exaggeration of the mad, unprincipled proceedings of the rest of society. "All mad, I think–Flesh,

I believe all the *Calentures* of the Sea are come ashore for my part" (4.1.356–57), is, after all, what the plain-dealing Ben so aptly says of the entire cast of *Love for Love*.

As the play shows it, Scandal's teaching may have the ring of truth, but it is, nonetheless, flawed; and as Valentine's teacher, his *magister ludi*, Congreve replaces Scandal with Angelica. In act 4, Valentine recites to Angelica the lessons he has mastered under Scandal and receives reproof instead of expected reward. He admits that he "has worn this Mask of Madness, only as the Slave of Love, and Menial Creature of your Beauty" (4.1.702–4), and that, furthermore, his efforts to retain his estate and inheritance, to match fortune for fortune (which Scandal has said is necessary for winning "Women of this Age"), are proof of his affection. Instead of falling into his arms and ending the comedy, as Valentine anticipates, Angelica gives him a telling and heuristic rebuff:

> VALENTINE: The Comedy draws toward an end, and let us think of leaving acting, and be our selves . . . my seeming Madness has deceiv'd my Father, and procur'd me time to think of means to reconcile me to him; and preserve the right of my Inheritance to his Estate . . .
> ANGELICA: How! I thought your love of me had caus'd this Transport in your Soul; which, it seems, you only counterfeited, for mercenary Ends and sordid Interest.
> VALENTINE: Nay, now you do me Wrong; for if any Interest was considered, it was yours; since I thought I wanted more than Love, to make me worthy of you.
> ANGELICA: Then you thought me mercenary—But how am I deluded by this Interval of Sense, to reason with a Madman.
>
> (4.1.707–8, 715–30)

Angelica here affirms that Valentine has acted as madly and as badly as the rest of the world. Placing mercenary interests above love, Valentine has adulterated and transmogrified the love between the sexes in precisely the same way that Sir Sampson has adulterated and transmogrified the love between parent and child. In this short exchange, Angelica successfully reveals that neither prodigality nor avarice need mix with love and that to posit mercenary ends as a necessary prelude to marital love, as most of the characters in *Love for Love* do, is for her nothing short of madness.

Congreve's title, of course, is the core of Angelica's educational philosophy; and Valentine must come to understand the concept of generosity that avoids and transcends both prodigality and avarice which is implicit in the title.[13] It is only when, through Angelica's guidance, he masters the idea of generosity that Valentine can have both his woman and his money:

> VALENTINE: I never valu'd Fortune, but as it was subservient to my Pleasure; and my only Pleasure was to please this Lady: I have made many vain Attempts, and find at last, that nothing but my Ruine can effect it: Which, for that Reason, I will sign to—Give me the Paper.
> ANGELICA: Generous *Valentine!*. . .Had I the World to give you it cou'd not make me worthy of so generous and faithful a Passion: Here's my Hand, my

Heart was always yours, and struggl'd very hard to make the utmost Tryal of your Virtue.

(5.1.544–64)

Of all his comedies, Congreve's *Love for Love* is the one that turns most centrally on the conflation of money and the affairs of the heart. *The Old Bachelor* separates the two concerns by dividing them into two plots, and *The Double Dealer* overwhelms the concern for Mellefont's and Cynthia's fortunes with a strong Machiavel and a constellation of manners comedy stock figures. In *Love for Love*, however, no character is unaffected by the impact of money, yet Congreve seems to shy away from the implications of his own satire. Perhaps this is Congreve's own form of generosity. Clearly Angelica and Valentine rise above the other characters as they affirm a relationship based upon love for love instead of love for money or money for money; but at the same time, the other characters are not, except Sir Sampson, really condemned or punished. Scandal and Mrs. Foresight consummate their affair, Mr. Foresight remains unchanged, Ben happily returns to the sea, and Miss Prue will, as she herself predicts, probably fulfill her destiny and run off with one of the servants. Tattle and Mrs. Frail are married but even they realize that they will likely manage quite well; and though Tattle's fortune is not what Valentine's is or what Ben's would have been, it will nevertheless serve the purpose of rescuing Mrs. Frail from her economic dilemma. Even Sir Sampson, who is condemned and punished, is not in a class with Congreve's out and out villains, Maskwell and Fainall, and his punishment is merely the exposure of his failures as a parent and suitor; there is no concomitant economic punishment as there is for Maskwell and Fainall. Even with Angelica, the central intelligence of the play, Congreve seems to skirt some of the realities of economics by placing Angelica's fortune entirely in her own hands. This rare situation, in short, frees Angelica from any economic control including that of her guardian Foresight. As a totally free agent, absolute mistress of her vast £30,000 fortune, she can enjoy the luxury of teaching Valentine to be generous.

In *The Way of the World*, which is less centrally about money than *Love for Love*, Congreve nonetheless comes closest to treating the question of money convincingly. In *The Double Dealer*, Cynthia's settlement is not in question, it is only a matter of whether it will go to Maskwell or Mellefont; in *Love for Love*, Angelica's considerable fortune is entirely at her own disposal; but in *The Way of the World*, Millamant's £12,000 is only partially in her own hands, for Lady Wishfort controls £6,000, exactly half of it. Millamant, therefore, can only in part be her own mistress and affirm the primacy of love, for she is also in part liable to the loss of half her monies if she marries without her aunt's consent. How Mirabell and Millamant deport themselves, consequently, seems a more true test and more convincing example of Congreve's attitudes toward marriage than those found in his earlier comedies.

Dividing the control of Millamant's £12,000 fortune equally between the heroine and her aunt, Congreve places Millamant at the theoretical center of *The*

Way of the World. She could conceivably marry for love thereby forfeiting £6,000; or she could marry the unsuitable Sir Wilfull Witwoud, her aunt's choice, thereby losing Mirabell but keeping her fortune intact. Neither choice is a happy one, but, the conventions of comedy being what they are, an audience has every right to expect that Millamant either alone or together with Mirabell will use her wit to trick Lady Wishfort and the other blocking characters in such a way that Millamant can have Mirabell as well as her full £12,000 intact. The desired result is achieved, but how it is achieved has not been given enough consideration. It is remarkable indeed that in a society where jockeying for financial position seems so much the way of the world, and in a plot where the disposal of Millamant's fortune is so central an issue, Millamant herself never once discusses her money nor does Mirabell ever once discuss with Millamant his elaborate plotting to secure the £6,000 pounds under Lady Wishfort's control. Millamant is, nonetheless, certainly aware of what is happening around her, as she reveals the one time Mirabell unsuccessfully attempts to broach the subject:

MIRABELL: Can you not find in the variety of your Disposition one Moment—
MILLAMANT: To hear you tell me that *Foible's* married, and your Plot like to speed—No.
MIRABELL: But how came you to know it—
MILLAMANT: Unless by the help of the Devil you can't imagine; unless she shou'd tell me her self. Which of the two it may have been, I will leave you to consider; and when you have done thinking of that; think of me.   *Exit.*
(2.2.480–89)

Millamant parries before Mirabell can thrust, at once acknowledging her awareness of Mirabell's doings and forbidding him to speak to her of them. Before the astonished Mirabell can react, she turns with physical and linguistic flourish to exit, but leaves him with the injunction, "think of me." Like so much that happens in *The Way of the World* between Mirabell and Millamant, much of the communication is effected precisely by what is *not* said. Unlike Angelica, Millamant need not stop to reprove the hero's acquisitiveness or remind him to concentrate more on love than on fortune. She merely deflects the topic of conversation, yet wittily and pointedly reminds Mirabell not to lose sight of his real object: "think of me."

The singular and superior relationship between Mirabell and Millamant is made by Congreve to look all the more singular and superior by the characters around them. As everyone who has ever seen or read *The Way of the World* immediately senses, consciously or unconsciously, the foppish Petulant and Witwoud, the plain-spoken but boorish Sir Wilfull, and the passionate Lady Wishfort set off by their various flaws the patently superior wit and style of the lead couple. More discrimination is necessary to measure Mirabell and Millamant against Marwood, Fainall, and Mrs. Fainall, for these three are no fools and fall only slightly short of Mirabell and Millamant's level of intelligence and poise. Yet Mirabell and Millamant do emerge superior and not merely because they are less passionate and less malicious, though that has something to do with placing them above Marwood and the Fainalls. What distinguishes Mirabell and Millamant is, finally, what also distinguishes Valentine and Angelica from the rest of the characters in *Love for Love*, namely their generosity and their attitude toward the relative importance of money as a basis for marriage or love relationships.[14]

If Mirabell and Millamant fail to talk of money, the two characters who are most closely compared to them, Fainall and Marwood, can think of little else. Their relationship to the other characters and even to each other is repeatedly marked, often dominated, by their prodigality and acquisitiveness. Reminiscent of the union of Jonson's Subtle and Face, the relationship between Fainall and Marwood is an explosive one and one that is a business partnership held together by money:

> MRS. MARWOOD: It shall be all discover'd. You too shall be discover'd; be sure you shall. I can but be expos'd—If I do it my self I shall prevent your Baseness.
> FAINALL: Why, what will you do?
> MRS. MARWOOD: Disclose it to your Wife; own what has past between us.
> FAINALL: Frenzy!
> MRS. MARWOOD: By all my Wrongs I'll do't—I'll publish to the World the Injuries you have done me, both in my Fame and Fortune: With both I trusted you, you Bankrupt in Honour, as indigent in Wealth.
> FAINALL: Your Fame I have preserv'd. Your Fortune has been bestow'd as the prodigality of your Love would have it, in Pleasures which we both have shar'd. Yet had not you been false, I had e'er repaid it—'Tis true—Had you permitted *Mirabell* with *Millamant* to have stoll'n their Marriage, my Lady had been incens'd beyond all means of reconcilement: *Millamant* had forfeited the Moiety of her Fortune; which then wou'd have descended to my Wife;—And wherefore did I marry, but to make lawful Prize of a rich Widow's Wealth, and squander it on Love and you?
> MRS. MARWOOD: Deceit and frivolous Pretence.
>
> (2.1.187–208)

Marwood's passion is conflated with prodigality. Fainall's circuitous plotting to obtain everyone's money is as complex and extravagant as Mirabell's scheme to gain Lady Wishfort's blessing and loosen her grip on Millamant's £6,000 by extricating the aunt from a marriage with a valet. What distinguishes the two schemes, however, is that for Fainall all things and all women are sacrificed to his egotistical desire for money. Any feeling for Marwood is at best an afterthought, as is clear in the priorities revealed in Fainall's declaration that he desires money to "squander it on Love and you." He loves for money, he marries for money, and he plots for money. Mirabell, by contrast, acts with greatest honor toward Mrs. Fainall, his former mistress, and toward the money she has placed in his trust, and he omits all question of money in his discourses with Millamant. His plotting is meant to place at her disposal the money that is rightly Millamant's and not to secure it for himself. Mirabell's elaborate plot is, after all, well under way long before Millamant has given any consent, verbal or written, to marry him.

At the heart of Mirabell and Millamant's relationship is the famous "Contract" or "proviso" scene of act 4. For every critic this scene takes on signal importance as the representation of what the relationship between the hero and heroine actually is and what it will be after marriage. Norman Holland[15] and Virginia Birdsall[16] stress the harmony of temperament and the maturation of Millamant;

Kathleen Lynch places the proviso scene in the context of the dramatic sources and analogues Congreve likely knew,[17] and Maximillian Novak goes on to show that against the literary background Lynch documents, Mirabell and Millamant play wittily with the proviso convention because their understanding is already such that provisos are superfluous.[18] Ian Donaldson notes in passing that the proviso scene does not touch "upon the cold mercantile facts" raised in Wycherley's *The Gentleman Dancing-Master,* an analogue Lynch overlooked.[19] Donaldson here indicates precisely what is remarkable about the verbal contract Mirabell and Millamant agree to. In the mock formality of its legal language, its *imprimis* and *item,* it calls to mind the usual marriage contracts in which the clauses concerned settlements and jointures, the financial arrangements that were to provide the legal setting for a union officially recognized in a church ceremony. Mirabell and Millamant "convenant" a great many things, most of them trifles that are nonetheless indicative of the social and love relationship they already have and wish to foster in the future.[20] As is often the case, however, in the discourses between Mirabell and Millamant, what is unspoken is as important as what is stated. That the issue of money is never once part of their legalistic convenant, though in the world outside the theater it was always the heart of the legal marriage convenant, shows at once Mirabell and Millamant's awareness of the monetary ways of the world as well as their determination not to define their love verbally by the economic strictures of the traditional marriage contract. The content of the proviso scene italicizes the primacy of love and personal relationships that Mirabell and Millamant affirm as the proper basis for marriage. Money, in not being mentioned, is given a distinctly peripheral place. The actual monetary agreements that would have to have been reached in the written contract, seemingly drawn up off stage somewhere between the fourth and fifth acts, are never either specified or discussed by the principals. Congreve's emphasis upon the importance of love over concerns about money is further italicized by providing Mirabell and Millamant with a real financial issue, namely, Lady Wishfort's control over half of her niece's fortune. For Angelica, whose fortune is entirely in her own hands, her attitudes, however laudable, can be judged a luxury. Millamant's is an attitude that must necessarily be more hard won and, therefore, more credible.

In the concluding scene of *The Way of the World* the avarice of Fainall and the generosity of Mirabell collide. In a proviso scene of his own, Fainall proposes a contract that would enable him to control Lady Wishfort and, consequently, her estate; he demands that Mrs. Fainall "settle on me the remainder of her Fortune, not made over already" (5.1.268–69), and insists upon immediate possession of the half of Millamant's fortune held by Lady Wishfort. Since all things seem to be going Fainall's way, he gives vent to what is for him obviously the optimum social relationship, malevolent economic despotism. Lady Wishfort may enjoy her "own proper Estate during Life; on the condition you oblige your self never to Marry, under such penalty as I think convenient" (5.1.252–54). Mrs. Fainall not only is to make over her fortune to her husband but must, says Fainall, "for her Maintenance depend entirely on my Discretion" (5.1.269–70). As Fainall senses his strength, he revises his demands to insist upon his sole control of Lady

Wishfort's estate as well as his wife's (5.1.433–36). His machinations are, however, foiled by Mirabell and the contents of the black box:

MIRABELL: Mr. *Fainall*, it is now time that you shou'd know, that your Lady while she was at her own disposal, and before you had by your Insinuations wheedl'd her out of a pretended Settlement of the greatest part of her fortune—
FAINALL: Sir! pretended!
MIRABELL: Yes Sir. I say that this Lady while a Widdow, having it seems receiv'd some Cautions respecting your Inconstancy and Tyranny of temper . . . she did I say by the wholesome advice of Friends and of Sages learned in the Laws of this Land, deliver this same as her Act and Deed to me in trust, and to the uses within mention'd. You may read if you please—tho perhaps what is inscrib'd on the back may serve your occasions.
FAINALL: Very likely, Sir, What's here? Damnation! *A deed of Conveyance of the whole Estate real of* Arabella Languish *Widdow in trust to* Edward Mirabell. Confusion!
MIRABELL: Even so Sir, 'tis *the way of the World*, Sir: of the Widdows of the World.

(5.1.535–54)

Why, one is led to ask, should Congreve allow his comic plot to hinge on a providential black box and its hitherto obscure contents? Why, too, is Mirabell's elaborate hoax necessary when he might so easily compel Lady Wishfort to permit his marriage to Millamant by flourishing Mrs. Fainall's deed of conveyance? The obvious answer is that Congreve forces his audience to dwell upon Mirabell's generosity, especially in contrast to the exposition of Fainall's character. There is, however, a still more important answer, namely, that the audience in asking the second question comes to realize that Mirabell could not have won Millamant through blackmail that threatened the financial ruin of her cousin or aunt. In the 162 lines (432–594) comprising Fainall's seeming triumph and his consequent defeat, Millamant remains silent, but consistent with her presentation throughout *The Way of the World*, she is not only present on the stage but eloquent in her silence. Her presence amid the revelations whereby Mirabell saves Mrs. Fainall and Lady Wishfort makes the audience realize that had Mirabell used the black box to obtain Lady Wishfort's consent he would have shown that he sought Millamant's money more than the lady herself, and, more important, would have revealed a culpable, mercenary character, not unlike Fainall's, by the very nature of blackmail based upon economic mastery. In the last speech of the play, Mirabell relinquishes the deed of conveyance to its owner and projects a new, enlightened view of money in marriage:

For my part I will Contribute all that in me lies to a Reunion, (*To Mrs.* Fainall) in the mean time, *Madam,* let me before these Witnesses, restore to you this deed of trust. It may be a means well manag'd to make you live Easily together. (5.1.615–19)

Mirabell conveys the sense that in those marriages like the Fainalls' where love does not overshadow economics there is a second best choice, namely, to use economics so that the couple may "live Easily together."

Although in the courtships that take place in his comedies Congreve acknowledges the importance of money in a way that Wycherley and Etherege do not, he finally avoids having his characters make their choices in the context of real monetary pressures. In *The Old Bachelor* marriage for love and marriage for money are separate issues relegated to separate plots; and characters like Mellefont, Valentine, and Mirabell, who acknowledge the need for both love and money, never have to make a serious choice *between* them. Congreve's world is a game board that includes a desired young lady and a bundle of money. To win the game, the male player must bring these two objects to the same square on the board, and the game is not over until there is a winner. Like the witty couples found in the comedies of Elizabethan dramatists such as John Fletcher or in the comedies of Congreve's more immediate forebears, Etherege and Wycherley, Congreve's main couples are primarily expert players of the mating game. Their game has, however, been made more complex and difficult by adding financial obstacles to the sexual ones. And it is precisely those financial obstacles that will increasingly come to occupy the descendents of Valentine and Angelica and of Mirabell and Millamant as they are found in the comedies of Steele, Gay, Fielding, Garrick, and Sheridan.

NOTES

1. All quotations from *A Wife to be Lett* are from the first edition of the play, London, 1724. Parentheses following quotations indicate page signatures.

2. Christopher Hill, *The Century of Revolution, 1603–1714* (Edinburgh: Thomas Nelson and Sons, 1961), pp. 262–74; and Ralph Davis, "English Foreign Trade, 1660–1700," *Economic History Review* 7 (1954): 150–66.

3. W. W. Rostow, *The Stages of Economic Growth* (Cambridge: Cambridge University Press, 1964), pp. 31–33. See also Phyllis Deane and H. J. Habakkuk, "The Take-Off in Britain," in *The Economics of Take-Off into Sustained Growth*, ed. W. W. Rostow (New York: St. Martin's Press, 1963), pp. 53–82; Phyllis Deane, *The First Industrial Revolution* (Cambridge: Cambridge University Press, 1965), pp. 51–68; Bert F. Hoselitz, "Entrepreneurship and Capital Formation in France and Britain since 1700," reprinted in *Readings in the History of Economic Growth*, ed. Malcolm E. Falkus (Nairobi: Oxford University Press, 1968), pp. 95–133; and Paul Mantoux, *The Industrial Revolution in the Eighteenth Century*, rev. ed. (London: Jonathan Cape, 1961), pp. 134–35.

4. See Raymond Williams, *The Country and the City* (New York: Oxford University Press, 1973), p. 51.

5. See John Loftis, *Comedy and Society from Congreve to Fielding* (Stanford: Stanford University Press, 1959), chap. 1.

6. *The Complete Plays of William Congreve*, ed. Herbert Davis (Chicago: University of Chicago Press, 1967). All quotations from the plays of Congreve are from this edition. Parentheses following quotations indicate act, scene, and line numbers.

7. John Harrington Smith, *The Gay Couple in Restoration Comedy* (Cambridge, Mass.: Harvard University Press, 1948), p. 149.

8. Thomas H. Fujimura, *The Restoration Comedy of Wit* (Princeton: Princeton University Press, 1952), pp. 172–74.

9. The ways in which the virtues and foibles of all the characters in *The Double Dealer* give way to the dominant villainy of Maskwell is well described in Laura Brown, *English Dramatic Form, 1660–1760* (New Haven: Yale University Press, 1981), pp. 127–28.

10. See Maximillian E. Novak, *William Congreve* (New York: Twayne, 1971), pp. 108–11.

11. See Aubrey L. Williams, *An Approach to Congreve* (New Haven: Yale University Press, 1979), p. 165.

12. An excellent discussion of the philosophical underpinnings inherent in the conflict between Sir Sampson and Valentine is given in William Myers, "Plot and Meaning in Congreve's Comedies," in *William Congreve*, ed. Brian Morris (London: Ernest Benn, 1972), pp. 79–82.

13. See Ben R. Schneider, Jr., *The Ethos of Restoration Comedy* (Urbana: University of Illinois Press, 1971), p. 21.

14. See ibid., p. 143.

15. Norman Holland, *The First Modern Comedies* (Cambridge, Mass.: Harvard University Press, 1959), pp. 183–86.

16. Virginia Ogden Birdsall, *Wild Civility* (Bloomington: Indiana University Press, 1970), pp. 243–45.

17. "D'Urfe's *Astree* and the 'Proviso' Scene in Dryden's Comedy," *PQ* 4 (1925): 302–8 and *The Social Mode of Restoration Comedy* (New York: MacMillan, 1926), pp. 201–3.

18. Novak, *William Congreve*, pp. 150–51.

19. Ian Donaldson, *The World Upside-Down* (Oxford: Clarendon Press, 1970), pp. 140–41.

20. The underlying idea behind the items agreed upon is "mutual forbearance" for Williams, *An Approach to Congreve*, p. 209.

Plot, Character, and Comic Language in Sheridan

Robert Hogan

Oliver Goldsmith and Richard Brinsley Sheridan—these two Irishmen are inevitably considered the preeminent comic talents of the English-speaking theater in the eighteenth century. Indeed, many literary historians have said that from the retirement of Congreve and the death of Farquhar early in the eighteenth century, until the appearance of Oscar Wilde, Bernard Shaw, and W. B. Yeats late in the nineteenth century, there were no dramatists who even approached the quality of Goldsmith and Sheridan.

Like all generalizations, this one is a bit too general. This long period hardly saw the profusion of masterpieces that appeared during the reign of Elizabeth I or of Charles II, and an overwhelming number of the plays produced between 1700 and 1890 now strike us as too full of high fustian and low theatrics, and too evocative of easy tears and brainless belly laughs. Still, John Gay's *The Beggar's Opera* has outlasted Sheridan's *The Duenna,* and Henry Fielding's *Tom Thumb* stands up nicely to Sheridan's *The Critic,* while some of the straight comic work of Macklin, Murphy, Garrick, Colman the Elder, and Sheridan's own mother Frances did not in the eighteenth century fall that far short of the best of Goldsmith and Sheridan themselves. And even from the more arid nineteenth century, Dion Boucicault's *Old Heads and Young Hearts* and T. W. Robertson's *Caste* might be revived with pleasure, while the airy operettas of Gilbert and Sullivan have never been out of favor.

Still, when all of the qualifications have been made, Goldsmith and Sheridan remain unlikely to be challenged in their historical preeminence, just as their best works remain unlikely to lose their popularity on the stage.

When Sheridan's first play, *The Rivals,* was initially produced at Covent Garden in 1775, it failed. It was too long, insufficiently rehearsed, and in one instance badly cast. Sheridan quickly cut the play and replaced the offending actor with a better, and in less than two weeks, *The Rivals* had become a solid success. The play has never lost its popularity. It is one of those plays that takes a perverse genius to do badly. It is almost actor-proof and director-proof, and mediocre or even distinctly bad productions can still arouse delight. It has, nonetheless, been generally considered a lesser work than *The School for Scandal.* Yet, if there is to be any revision in the critical opinion about Sheridan, it can only be in the upgrading of *The Rivals,* and a convincing case can be made that *The Rivals* in many ways equals and in some surpasses the worth of *The School for Scandal.*

Neither play is what one would call well made, and, indeed, construction was never Sheridan's strong point.[1] However, a tidy plot construction is probably an overrated quality in comedy, and even in tragedy the English-speaking theater has preferred Elizabethan sprawl to neoclassical trimness. Sheridan's faults in plotting *The Rivals* have been no better isolated than by the perceptive Tom Moore, who noted that

> For our insight into [the] characters, we are indebted rather to their confessions than their actions. Lydia Languish, in proclaiming the extravagance of her own romantic notions, prepares us for events much more ludicrous and eccentric, than those in which the plot allows her to be concerned; and the young lady herself is scarcely more disappointed than we are, at the tameness with which her amour concludes . . . and the wayward, captious jealousy of Faulkland, though so highly coloured in his own representation of it, is productive of no incident answerable to such an announcement.[2]

This point can be applied to the relations of other characters in the play. Bob Acres and Lydia are never brought together for a confrontation; little is made of the "love affair" of Mrs. Malaprop and Sir Lucius. Despite his usefulness to the "real" plot, Acres might just as well be cut out of the play. It would have been dramaturgically tidier for the Jack-Lydia-Mrs. Malaprop-Sir Lucius imbroglio if Jack confronted Sir Lucius without the distraction of Acres. Acres's cowardice is, however, so delicious that one would no more sacrifice it than one would the windmill episode in *Don Quixote.* Such academic strictures are sometimes just theatrically beside the point. Despite, then, the omission of several "obligatory scenes," an audience does not miss or even note what Sheridan might or should have done, because what he has done is totally absorbing and increasingly delightful: he has written a series of irresistible scenes, based either on ludicrous situations or characterizations. As each droll scene is succeeded by another of equal or greater interest, the audience remains so caught by the pleasure of the moment that the static or erratic quality of the plot is simply not noticed. Nevertheless, the plot must at least seem to move, and in *The Rivals* Sheridan's plot does lurch on toward the aborted duel. A difficulty of *The School for Scandal* is that for the first two acts the plot *seems* static.

Tom Moore sets up a persuasive but wrong-headed comparison between the language and characterization of the two plays:

> With much less wit, it [*The Rivals*] exhibits perhaps more humour than *The School for Scandal,* and the dialogue, though by no means so pointed or sparkling, is, in this respect more natural, as coming nearer the current coin of ordinary conversation; whereas, the circulating medium of *The School for Scandal* is diamonds. The characters of *The Rivals,* on the contrary, are *not* such as occur very commonly in the world; and, instead of producing striking effects with natural and obvious materials, which is the great art and difficulty of a painter of human life, he has here overcharged most of his persons with whims and absurdities.[3]

This view—that the dialogue is natural but the characters are exaggerated—strikes me as only half true. Sheridan was dealing with "humours," types, exaggerations, but the characters were not extravagant exaggerations, and so, for instance, the stage-Irishness of Sir Lucius was played down when Sheridan revised the play. The excellence of Sheridan's comic characterizations is that his types are handled with such a verve, freshness, and panache that they reinvigorate their stockness. Sir Anthony is basically the tyrannical father; Mrs. Malaprop, the superannuated dame; Sir Lucius, the Stage Irishman; and Bob Acres is a combination of rustic booby, false beau, and braggart soldier. Among the comic characters (as opposed to the straight characters of Jack and Julia), Lydia and Faulkland are the most touched with originality. Both possess the dull youth and handsomeness of innumerable young heroes and ingenues, but in Sheridan's treatment they become comic rather than straight characters because their admirable qualities are exaggerated until they become faults. In Lydia, romance becomes exaggerated to absurdity; in Faulkland, love becomes exaggerated to neurosis. Even the stock servant—a figure that has a centuries-old provenance and is little different in Wodehouse, Wilde, Vanbrugh, Machiavelli, or Terence—is made original in Sheridan. What he adds to the character of the pert servant is a charming falsity of language that the audience finds both refreshing and novel, and this addition revivifies most of Sheridan's otherwise stock characterization.

The individuality of Lydia, Faulkland, and all the less original characters, then, is established largely by their language. Rather than the natural dialogue that Tom Moore saw, the play contains a dazzling degree of unnatural and absurd dialogue. Sheridan took great pains with the writing of *The Rivals*, and it has throughout a graceful fluency that gives the impression of naturalness. It is, however, the unimportant parts of the play that are the most easy, natural, and realistic. The strongest parts, with the biggest laughs, are those in which a character uses language in a finely foolish fashion.

To take the most obvious example: the great comic lines of Mrs. Malaprop spring from an inspired misuse of words that is far too outlandish to be thought realistic or natural. Set in a surrounding dialogue of fluent naturalness, her marvelous mistakes of diction appear in bold relief. Mrs. Malaprop is funny because she is doubly pretentious: she is an aging woman who regards herself as still young and beautiful enough to be the object of a romantic love affair, and she is a stupid and vain woman who regards herself as a bluestocking. Her first pretension is deflated by the plot and by how the other characters regard her; her second pretension is deflated by her own language and by how the audience regards it. A character using the wrong word has long been a source of theatrical and fictional comedy.[4] The laughter has traditionally come from the character using a wrong word that sounds like the right one. Mrs. Malaprop's best mistakes improve on this device, for the word that she chooses not only sounds like the word she meant, but it also contains a meaning that either reduces her thought to inspired nonsense or makes her say the opposite of what she intended. In her great speech about the education of young women (act 1, scene 2), she desires Lydia to know "something of the contagious countries," and her choice of "contagious" for "contiguous" contains a brilliant bit of nonsense that, of course, indicates her own ignorance and delights the audience.

If Mrs. Malaprop's language deflates her claims to learning, Sir Anthony's deflates his own false reasoning. In his attempts to persuade Jack to be married, Sir Anthony is thwarted, and, instead of becoming more cogent and reasonable, he becomes more incoherent and emotional. So far Sheridan follows tradition: a stock father who would be the repository of wisdom, reason, and tolerance is shown to be dense, irrational, and splenetic. Sheridan again goes beyond tradition, however, for Sir Anthony's language does not merely become incoherent with anger; at its climactic and funniest it actually becomes a parody of reasoning. His brilliant exit speech of act 2, scene 1, uses the trappings of reason but winds up in the depths of infantilism.

The success of these scenes requires two characters: the faulty speaker and the clear-eyed critic. The critic is a straight character who helps the audience see what is wrong with the comic character's language and, therefore, with his character. Thus, after Sir Anthony's great outburst, Jack acts the role of critic with his ironic remark:

> Mild, gentle, considerate father—I kiss your hands—What a tender method of giving his opinion in these matters Sir Anthony has![5]

Or, in Mrs. Malaprop's great scene in act 1, it is Sir Anthony, elsewhere himself a faulty speaker, who acts the role of critic and says:

> I must confess, that you are a truly moderate and politic arguer, for almost every third word you say is on my side of the question.[6]

In the Faulkland-Julia scenes, Julia acts as the critic, and so her language needs to contrast sharply with Faulkland's. In contrast to his circuitous, emotional floridness, she must be direct, simple, and reasonable. To emphasize what is wrong with his language and character, her language and character must set the rhetorical and the moral norm. Early in their first meeting (act 3, scene 2), Sheridan controls her language well, and she makes direct and terse remarks: "I had not hoped to see you again so soon," for example, or, "Nay then, I see you have taken something ill. You must not conceal from me what it is." Such sentences contrast effectively with Faulkland's purple effusions:

> For such is my temper, Julia, that I should regard every mirthful moment in your absence as a treason to constancy:—The mutual tear that steals down the cheek of parting lovers. . . . [7]

Although the young Sheridan was already a master of comic language and here effectively mocks the language of sentiment, he was far from a master of serious language used to convey emotional intensity.[8] Consequently, Julia's later, more intense speeches become as stiff, florid, and false as Faulkland's, and we find her saying in act 5, scene 1:

Then on the bosom of your wedded Julia, you may lull your keen regret to slumbering; while virtuous love, with a Cherub's hand, shall smooth the brow of upbraiding thought and pluck the thorn from compunction.[9]

Aside from the failure of serious language, the play is the performance of a virtuoso of dialogue fit to be ranked with Wilde and Shaw. The play may have a rather untidy plot, but the plot does provide a multitude of effective comic situations. The play may use stock types, but it also works original variations on these types. Finally, the play does provide a variety of false language hardly seen in English drama since the comedies of Congreve and Ben Jonson. The language of *The Rivals* has secured the play its high position in the English theater. It is a language that civilizes by involving its audience. It is a language that makes its audience become active critics of false language and, therefore, of false behavior.

*   *   *

The two main kinds of comic language are the language of humor and the language of wit. The language of humor predominates in *The Rivals,* and the language of wit in *The School for Scandal.* The language of humor misuses grammar and sentence structure and rhetorical devices to produce speech that amusingly and ignorantly diverges from a norm of commonly accepted good speech and writing. The language of wit uses grammar and sentence structure and rhetorical devices with such uncommon fluency that its speech diverges from a norm of good speech and writing by its more considerable excellence. In other words, the language of humor is purposely bad writing, and the nature of its badness is a symptom of what is wrong with the speaker. The language of wit, on the other hand, is purposely superb writing, and the nature of its excellence is a symptom of what is right with the speaker. Using the language of humor, the speaker may fail to attain a civilized norm by innate stupidity such as Dogberry's, or by lack of education such as Sam Weller's, or by provincial ignorance such as the quaint dialect flaws of the stage Irishman and Scotsman or Frenchman. Using the language of wit, as Shakespeare's Benedick and Beatrice do poorly, or as Congreve's Millamant and Mirabell do well, or as Shaw's Don Juan and Devil do consummately, the speaker exceeds the civilized norm and makes us admire his urbanity, insight, and wisdom. In the language of humor, the audience perceives a misuse of words that stems from a character fault, and the resultant laughter is critical. In the language of wit, the audience perceives a consummate use of words that stems from excellences of character, and the resultant laughter is admiring. More simply, the language of humor occasions critical laughter at stupidity, and the language of wit occasions admiring smiles at brilliance.

As the appreciation of wit is of higher worth than the perception of stupidity, so the language of wit is thought of greater worth than the language of humor. Thus a play like *The School for Scandal* is more highly regarded than a play like *The Rivals.* Yet this attitude may be suspect, for both comic languages actively engage the judgment of their auditors, and both comic languages use quite complex techniques. If there is an innate difference of value between the two comic languages, it must lie in the content. The language of wit has occasionally been used, notably in some plays by Shaw, to discuss more complex themes than the drama usually handles.

The School for Scandal, largely because of its witty language, has been Sheridan's most admired play. The play was first produced at Drury Lane on 8 May 1777 and has held the boards ever since. The scandal scenes in particular have been considered a triumph of witty language, and they will only work, indeed, because they are witty. The danger of these scenes, particularly in a poor production, is that they are static. Nothing happens in them. The plot does not advance, and one of the viewers at the play's brilliant premiere was even heard to grumble that he wondered when the author was going to get on with the story.

But, of course, the stories themselves are not well structured. To take only one example, the heroine, Maria, has quite a small part. She is off the stage through most of the crucial acts and, amazingly, is not even confronted with the hero until the very denouement in act 5. As with *The Rivals,* one could pile up a dozen instances of what Sheridan had to do with his plot and did not do. But, also as with *The Rivals,* one must admit that what he did do instead is so delightful and absorbing that his audience is thoroughly satisfied.

Sheridan makes some use of more individualized characterization in this play. There are well-defined stock types such as Mrs. Candour and Sir Benjamin Backbite, but Sir Peter and Lady Teazle are rather fuller than types, and in Charles and particularly in Joseph, Sheridan cuts beneath the surface and finds contradictions and something approaching complexity. Joseph, the apparently good but actually hypocritical brother, was regarded by Sheridan's sisters as a sketch of their own older brother, Charles. In any event, Joseph is a meaty acting role, even if not quite a fully fleshed-out one. He is, however, closer to reality than the great comic monsters of a Volpone or a Tartuffe. In Charles, it may not be stretching a point to see some of Richard Sheridan's own carelessness and casual mismanagement. But, like everyone, Sheridan had a good deal of tolerance for his own foibles, and so does his audience have a good deal of tolerance for the erring but basically good-hearted Charles. From this crucial attitude, much of the sunniness of the play can be traced.

The rhetorical showpieces of the play are the great scandal-mongering scenes of acts 1 and 2, in which the chorus of gossips, with bubbling spirits and brilliant technique, rends and shreds reputations. It is curious that the strength of these scenes arises from exquisitely phrased malice. Lady Sneerwell says in explanation that "there's no possibility of being witty without a little ill nature: the malice of a good thing is the barb that makes it stick."

Certainly it is true that Maria and Sir Peter, the unmalicious characters in the scandal scenes, are able to counter the witty malice with no more than direct statement, which is ineffective, and with honest dignity, which appears stuffy. Yet, while neither Maria nor Sir Peter is a match for witty malice, that does not mean that a match could not be found. A well-equipped Shavian wit, such as Sidney Trefusis or Don Juan, could have more than upheld the side of sense and worth with equal rhetorical cleverness and by substituting gaiety for malice.

It seems generally taken for granted that Sheridan's scandalmongers are deplorable, but it has not been much noticed that their critiques are correct. An audience would not laugh at their jokes unless their victims deserved laughter. Mrs. Evergreen, discussed in act 2, is mutton trying to pass as lamb; Miss Simper and Miss Prim are foolishly vain; Mrs. Pursy, although too fat, attempts to appear slim; Lady Stucco, although too old, attempts to appear beautiful. All of these victims deserve the lash of satire, and the audience laughs at popular pretensions deservedly deflated. The scandalmongers, then, are joke makers and, like all joke makers, are necessarily moralists. Why, then, are they themselves funny?

The reason, of course, is that they live in glass houses. The delight they take in other people's failings is wedded to their perfect ignorance of their own. Once again Sheridan worked a new twist upon old material and conveyed his truths by the vehicles of folly.

In the language of humor, which Sheridan basically used in *The Rivals,* the audience laughs at language faultily used and so becomes, en masse, a literary critic. In the language of wit, which Sheridan frequently used in *The School for Scandal,* the audience laughs at language cleverly used and becomes a literary appreciator. The point might be proved by taking any of *The School for Scandal*'s well-turned jokes and rephrasing them. Almost invariably the rephrasing lessens—if not, indeed, destroys—the strength of the joke. For instance, in act 1, the poetaster Sir Benjamin Backbite unknowingly makes a joke against his own vapid verses when he describes the appearance of his forthcoming slim volume: "a beautiful quarto page, where a neat rivulet of text shall meander through a meadow of margin." The delight of the joke comes from two sources, one obvious and one rather subliminal. The obvious point is the originality of the metaphor; the subtler point is the reinforcement of sound, first in the *t*'s of "neat Rivulet of text," and next in the *m*'s of "meander through a meadow of margin." To rephrase the remark in unmetaphorical and unalliterative statement is to arrive at something like: "a beautiful quarto page, where a few lines are set off by a wide margin."

We catch Sheridan's neatly conceived and deftly turned statement on the wing, and our appreciative laughter is instantaneous. It is, therefore, unnecessary as well as uncivilized to spend more space in reducing clearly successful jokes to baldly tedious statements. However, it might be noted that Sheridan pushes his audience to appreciate wit in another way, and he does so by smoothly inserting some literary criteria. Several times he actually ensures that his audience will laugh by telling them what and even how to appreciate.

For instance, in the play's opening dialogue, Snake and Lady Sneerwell almost immediately launch into a rhetorical consideration of Lady Clackitt's gossip:

LADY SNEERWELL: She certainly has Talents, but her manner is gross.
SNAKE: 'Tis very true—she generally designs well—has a free tongue and a bold invention—but her colouring is too dark and her outline often extravagant. She wants that delicacy of Hint—and mellowness of sneer which distinguish your ladyship's Scandal.[10]

In a similar manner, Sheridan sets up the rhetorical techniques of Crabtree and Mrs. Candour.

But perhaps to say more about the high quality and the manifold techniques of Sheridan's comic language would be tedious. A good joke does not need to be explained. It startlingly explodes into perfect and unexpected obviousness, and our instantaneous laughter results from our perfect but unexpected perception. Let it merely be asserted, then, that Sheridan's command of the widest variety of rhetorical techniques is consummate. When one thinks of the flabby badinage that passes for wit between Shakespeare's Beatrice and Benedick, one can only turn with relief and delight to a Congreve, a Wilde, a Shaw—or a Sheridan.

But perhaps the greatest quality of Sheridan's comic writing is one that he shares with Goldsmith—a sunny good nature deriving from a benevolent tolerance. Neither Sheridan nor Goldsmith says much in his plays, but in their one shared, pervasive quality they imply an attitude that imparts to their work something often lacking in the work of even their greatest colleagues. That attitude is charm. Charm is usually an underrated quality, assigned to minor writers such as Charles Lamb or Kenneth Grahame. Perhaps it is easier to allow them a trivial excellence than to analyze their excellence seriously. But is charm so trivial? In Sheridan, are we not charmed because we are reminded of the vital fact that it is awfully nice to be alive? This humanity, as Virginia Woolf noted, "was part of his charm" and "still warms his writing."[11]

*   *   *

It is too arbitrary to limit comic language to two kinds only, the language of humor and the language of wit. There is at least one other, albeit minor, kind. What of the language of imitation, the language of parody that satirizes presumptive excellence by exaggerating its faults? This is a rarer use of comic language, limited mainly to the criticism of literary forms, but it certainly does appear in plays.

The three great examples of parody or burlesque in English drama are Buckingham's *The Rehearsal* (1671), Fielding's *Tom Thumb* (1731), and Sheridan's *The Critic* (1779).[12] *The Critic* pushed *The Rehearsal* off the stage, and Fielding's delightful play presents such problems of staging that it has always been more popular in the study than on the boards. Only *The Critic* is still occasionally performed today, even though the stage style it lampooned is two centuries out of date.

Sheridan's second and third acts in *The Critic* have some brilliantly bad writing, although not nearly the profusion found in Fielding. Sheridan compensates, however, by satirizing the complete theatrical experience. Thus, he has many more visual and aural gags than does Fielding. Indeed, if we are to consider the play solely as literature, it tails off disappointingly because Sheridan does not rely on words at the conclusion but, rather, on a parody of excessive stage spectacle. In the original staging at Drury Lane, the spectacular visual conclusion satisfyingly topped everything that had gone before. On paper, little of this effect can be apparent; on the modern stage, all of this effect can be a problem.

The purely literary content, however, is so fine that the play has always been admired as the third of Sheridan's masterpieces. Indeed, he himself regarded the first act as the most finished piece of dramatic writing he had done. The act is a brilliant piece of work, and a chief excellence is that it gets its laughs while actually establishing the rules for laughing. Some of the generalizations established in act 1 are also aids for judging the ineptitudes of the play-within-the-play of acts 2 and 3.

Act 1 falls into three major scenes: the dialogue between Mr. Dangle and Sneer, the baiting of Sir Fretful Plagiary, and the rhetorical exhibition of Mr. Puff. In the Dangle-Sneer dialogue, some criticisms are made about the incompatibility of comedy and overt moralizing, which had been joined in popular sentimental comedies of Richard Steele and others. There is briefly even some criticism of the bad writing of sentimental comedy. It has too much nicety: "No double entendre, no smart innuendo admitted; even Vanburgh [sic] and Congreve obliged to undergo a bungling reformation!"[13] The Sir Fretful scene is a humorous criticism of a poor but egotistical playwright, à la Buckingham's Bayes, and the character is something of a cartoon of Richard Cumberland.[14] But even in this scene a number of axioms about false and inflated language are insinuated. For example:

> In your more serious efforts . . . your bombast would be less intolerable, if the thoughts were ever suited to the expression; but the homeliness of the sentiment stares thro' the fantastic encumbrance of its fine language, like a clown in one of the new uniforms![15]

Later, in the play-within-the-play, this fault is illustrated abundantly and with delightful inanity. Then, after the broad interlude of non-English and broken English in the little scene of the Italian singers and the French interpreter, comes the great scene in which Mr. Puff analyzes the varieties of false language that composed contemporary advertising. The passage is too long to quote in full, but in it Sheridan bombards his audience with false fluency and, in effect, forces each member to see that it is false and to become a literary critic. For instance, part of Mr. Puff's illustration of the Puff Direct reads:

> Characters strongly drawn—highly coloured—hand of a master—fund of genuine humour—mine of invention—neat dialogue—attic salt! Then for the performance—Mr. DODD was astonishingly great in the character of SIR HARRY! That universal and judicious actor Mr. PALMER, perhaps never appeared to more advantage than in the COLONEL;—but it is not in the power of language to do justice to Mr. KING!—Indeed he more than merited those repeated bursts of applause which he drew from a most brilliant and judicious audience! As to the scenery—The miraculous power of Mr. DE LOUTHERBOURG's pencil are universally acknowledged!—In short, we are at a loss which to admire most,—the unrivalled genius of the author, the great attention and liberality of the managers—the wonderful abilities of the painter, or the incredible exertions of all the performers![16]

Sheridan has set up Mr. Puff's lecture on Puffing so that the audience is primed to look closely at language that Puff asserts will be effective and seem sincere in any instance. Hence, all of the descriptive phrases and all of the admiring epithets stand out in bold relief as indications of insincerity and gush. This is a considerable achievement and a healthy one.

To test Sheridan's feat, I took down from my shelves the first four volumes of contemporary dramatic criticism I put my hands on; books by Kenneth Tynan, Robert Brustein, Stanley Kauffmann, and Martin Gottfried. Still seeing with a Brinsleyan clarity, I opened each volume at random and was astonished to see that certain phrases now leapt off the page. From Mr. Tynan: "admirable, transfigured, one of the noblest performances I have ever seen, marvelously characterized, I shall never forget the skill with which. . . ."[17] From Mr. Brustein: "a spirited performance, the season's triumph, and a triumph for the American theatre. Though superlatives have a habit of sticking in my throat, I must not temporize here: this was the finest production of a Shakespeare comedy I have ever seen." [18] From Mr. Kauffmann: "production is outstandingly happy, setting is almost miraculous, vitality of the born actor and the fine control of the skillful one, we will be allowed to watch an extraordinary career develop."[19] From Mr. Gottfried: "wonderfully fluid use of stage possibilities, genuinely poetic, apt and funny, hilarious, brilliant. He is part of our theater's great tomorrow." [20]

We have seemingly wandered far afield here, but the difference between the muddy fustian of the critics and the piercing clarity of the dramatist may indicate not only how pertinent Sheridan's strictures still are but also how valid his excellence still is. It may also suggest that the clearest, shortest way to truth is not through criticism but through the work of art itself.

The language of the remaining two acts of *The Critic* illustrates, by broad parody, various kinds of bad dramatic writing. Particularly droll is the flat and intentional inadequacy of the blank verse in the "butler-maid" scene of exposition between Raleigh and Hatton. Here, of course, Sneer's axiom about homely sentiment and fine language is illustrated. Such a prosaic lameness of thought couched in words of pseudo-Shakespearian grandeur is not far-fetched. Many worthless tragedies with scarcely less awful language have succeeded for the moment on the stage: see much, if not quite all, of the work of Sheridan's young kinsman, James Sheridan Knowles.

An equally fine parody is Tilburnia's lyric purple passage that begins with the superbly stale

> Now has the whispering breath of gentle morn,
> Bad Nature's voice, and Nature's beauty rise;
> While orient Phoebus, with unborrow'd hues,
> Cloaths the wak'd loveliness which all night slept
> In heav'nly drapery! Darkness is fled.[21]

The speech ends with a lengthy catalogue of birds and flowers. Ophelia has a lot to answer for.

A chief symptom of Sheridan's parodic success is that quoting it is so irresistible. Here, then, is one final, fine, brief parody, this time of the language of rant and fustian:

WHISKERANDOS: Thou liest—base Beefeater!
BEEFEATER: Ha! Hell! the lie!
          By heav'n thou'st rous'd the lion in my heart!
          Off, yeoman's habit!—base disguise!—off! off![22]

By precept and example, Sheridan has established what bad theatrical language is. One does not need to be a scholar to appreciate his fun, but he has joked and punned so well that he has momentarily created an audience of laughing pundits. *The Critic* is not about life or human nature. It is about good and bad literary form; it is about taste. That fact must make it a work of lesser import than *The Rivals* or *The School for Scandal*, but it is not a work of lesser pleasure.

*   *   *

Three conclusions and a concluding generalization sum up Sheridan's accomplishments in his three great plays.

The plotting, although academically slovenly, is so continuously absorbing in its successive incidents that it is theatrically irresistible.

The characterization contains no original elements and scarcely ever diverges from the stereotypes worked over by Congreve, Molière, Shakespeare and Jonson, Goldoni and Plautus; upon these stock figures, however, Sheridan has mixed such new combinations and insinuated such fresh fancies of detail that they have not lost the illusion of bloom for the last two hundred years.

The comic writing, similarly, contains no original elements; and indeed, I suspect that no writer in the last two thousand years—with the dubious exception of Beckett—has discovered a new way of making a joke. What Sheridan's comic writing does is to utilize each of the comic modes—humor, wit, and parody—and to invest these traditional manners with such fresh inventiveness of detail as to make the three great plays a perennial source of linguistic delight and even of civilized apprehension.

Sheridan wrote in one of the most constricting, simplistic, and naive forms of art, the drama. Unlike Ibsen or Strindberg or Chekhov or Granville-Barker, he did not attempt to expand the form either in technique or in content. He was a traditionalist, albeit a consummate one. A greater comic artist who did attempt to expand the form but who also thoroughly understood its traditionalism, was Bernard Shaw who remarked—not with entire truth—that dramaturgically he himself merely appropriated the characterization of Dickens and the plotting of Molière. But what Shaw further said of himself is an appropriate final generalization about Brinsley Sheridan: "He touches nothing that he does not dust and polish and put back in its place much more carefully than the last man who handled it."[23]

NOTES

1. In comedy, tidy construction has given us the mechanical plots of a Feydeau or a Labiche farce, as intricate and insanely logical as clockwork and just about as inhuman. And in our own day, tidy construction in comedy has given us the rigid formula of television's half-hour "sit-com." If we recollect the glories of comic writing in the English theater, however, we might well conclude that the greatest comedy is that which diverges from or even destroys the form. Shakespeare's comedies are more often than not hopelessly slapdash in construction. In *A Midsummer Night's Dream,* the plot is concluded by the end of act 4, and nothing remains to do in act 5 except get on with the funniest part of the play, the amateur dramatic company of Bully Bottom, which really has nothing whatsoever to

do with the plot. Aside from *Volpone,* the great comedies of Ben Jonson are little more than illustrative incidents effectively jumbled together; yet the warmth, vigor, and vitality of *Bartholomew Fair, The Alchemist,* and *Epicoene* are inordinately more comfortable than the cold logic of *Volpone.* The plot of Congreve's *The Way of the World* is so convoluted that no one pays much attention to it; the joy is in the glittering wit. Even the consummate comic artist Molière hastily winds up *Tartuffe* by the limpest deus ex machina. And in our own time the masterpieces of Chaplin are composed of little more than a succession of unrelated comic situations. It might almost be thought that the best made comic plots have little room for the other major elements of character and language, while the best comedies have little room for plot.

2. Thomas Moore, *Memoirs of the Life of the Right Honourable Richard Brinsley Sheridan* (London: Longman, Hurst, Rees, Orme, Brown, and Green, 1825), p. 104.

3. Ibid., pp. 103–4.

4. In her character as in some of her funniest lines, Mrs. Malaprop owes much to Mrs. Tryfort in Sheridan's mother's play, *A Journey to Bath.* See *The Plays of Frances Sheridan* (Newark: University of Delaware Press, 1984). As Sheridan's sister, when she was also borrowing some of Mrs. Tryfort's language and character in her novel *Strathallan,* remarked, however, "I am of the opinion of Charles, in *The School for Scandal.* that it is very hard if one may not make free with one's relations."

5. Cecil Price, ed., *The Dramatic Works of Richard Brinsley Sheridan* (Oxford: Clarendon Press, 1973), p. 99.

6. Ibid., p. 86.

7. Ibid., p. 106.

8. This is not an unusual fault in masters of comic language. Thus, we find Dickens's handling of Sam Weller brilliant and of Little Nell mawkish. Or we find the language of Captain Boyle and Joxer Daly consummately comic in *Juno and the Paycock;* and yet in the same play we find a serious but maudlin line like, "Ah God, Mary, have you fallen as low as that?"

9. Price, ed., *Dramatic Works,* p. 132.

10. Ibid., p. 360.

11. Virginia Woolf, *Books and Portraits* (New York: Harcourt Brace Jovanovich, 1977), p. 49.

12. One modern play might possibly be added—the first (not the revised) version of Elmer Rice's forgotten but delightful *Not for Children.*

13. Price, ed., *Dramatic Works,* p. 501. In part, Sheridan is here poking fun at his own bad practice, for in 1777 he himself had made a bungling reformation of Vanbrugh's *The Relapse,* which he staged as *A Trip to Scarborough.*

14. In his edition of Sheridan's *Works* (1874; reprint, London: Chatto & Windus, 1913), p. 630, F. Stainforth relates the following story:

> Cumberland's children induced their father to take them to see *The School for Scandal.* Every time the delighted youngsters laughed at what was going on on the stage, he pinched them, and said, "What are you laughing at, my dear little folks? you should not laugh, my angels; there is nothing to laugh at"; and then, in an undertone, "Keep still, you little dunces."—Sheridan, having been told this, said, "It was very ungrateful in Cumberland to have been displeased with his poor children for laughing at *my comedy,* for I went the other night to see *his tragedy,* and laughed at it from beginning to end."

15. Price, ed., *Dramatic Works,* p. 507.

16. Ibid., pp. 514–15.

17. Kenneth Tynan, *Curtains* (New York: Atheneum, 1961), pp. 272–73.

18. Robert Brustein, *Seasons of Discontent* (New York: Simon and Schuster, 1965), p. 276.

19. Stanley Kauffmann, *Persons of the Drama* (New York: Harper and Row, 1976), p. 175.

20. Martin Gottfried, *Opening Nights* (New York: G. P. Putnam's Sons, 1969), pp. 203–4.

21. Price, ed., *Dramatic Works,* p. 529.

22. Ibid., pp. 545–46.

23. Bernard Shaw, *Sixteen Self Sketches* (New York: Dodd, Mead, 1949), p. 183.

Bibliography of Eugene Mersereau Waith

BOOKS

The Pattern of Tragicomedy in Beaumont and Fletcher (New Haven: Yale University Press, 1952).

Edition of *Macbeth* in The Yale Shakespeare (New Haven: Yale University Press, 1954).

The Herculean Hero (New York: Columbia University Press, 1962).

Edition of *Bartholomew Fair* in The Yale Ben Jonson (New Haven: Yale University Press, 1963).

Shakespeare: The Histories, ed. Eugene M. Waith, Twentieth Century Views (Englewood Cliffs, N.J.: Prentice-Hall, 1965).

The Dramatic Moment (New York: Prentice-Hall, 1967).

Restoration Drama, ed. Eugene M. Waith (New York: Bantam Press, 1968).

Ideas of Greatness: Heroic Drama in England (London: Routledge and Kegan Paul, 1971).

Edition of *Titus Andronicus* in The Oxford Shakespeare (Oxford: Clarendon Press, 1984).

ARTICLES

"The Ascription of Speeches in *The Revenger's Tragedy*," *Modern Language Notes* 57 (1942): 119–21.

"Samuel Rowlands and *Humor's Antique Faces*," *Review of English Studies* 18 (1942): 213–19.

"Characterization in John Fletcher's Tragicomedies," *Review of English Studies* 19 (1943): 141–64.

"A Tragicomedy of Humors: Fletcher's *The Loyal Subject*," *Modern Language Quarterly* 6 (1945): 299–311.

"The Sources of *The Double Marriage* by Fletcher and Massinger," *Modern Language Notes* 64 (1949): 505–10.

"Manhood and Valor in Two Shakespearean Tragedies," *Modern Language Notes* 17 (1950): 262–73.

"John Fletcher and the Art of Declamation," *PMLA* 66 (1951): 226–34.

"*Pericles* and Seneca the Elder," *Journal of English and Germanic Philology* 50 (1951): 180–82.

"The Poet's Morals in Jonson's *Poetaster*," *Modern Language Quarterly* 12 (1951): 13–19.

"*Controversia* in the English Drama: Medwall and Massinger," *PMLA* 68 (1953): 286–303.

"*Macbeth:* Interpretation versus Adaptation," in *Shakespeare: Of an Age and for All Time*, ed. Charles Tyler Prouty, pp. 101–22 (Hamden, Conn.: The Shoe String Press, 1954).

"The Calling of Stephen Dedalus," *College English* 18 (1957): 256–61.

"The Metamorphosis of Violence in *Titus Andronicus*," *Shakespeare Survey* 10 (1957): 39–49.

286

"Landino and Maximus of Tyre," *Renaissance News* 13 (1960): 289–94.

"Eugene O'Neill: An Exercise in Unmasking," *Educational Theatre Journal* 13 (1961): 182–91.

"The Staging of *Bartholomew Fair*," *Studies in English Literature* 2 (1962): 181–95.

"The Voice of Mr. Bayes," *Studies in English Literature* 3 (1963): 335–43.

"*Edward II:* The Shadow of Action," *Tulane Drama Review* 8 (1964): 59–76.

"*Macbeth:* History and Poetry in the Theater," in *Reports and Speeches*, Tenth Conference of the Masters in Art of Teaching Program (Spring 1964).

"Marlowe and the Jades of Asia," *Studies in English Literature* 5 (1965): 229–45.

"Dryden and the Tradition of Serious Drama," in *John Dryden*, ed. Earl Miner, pp. 58–89 (London: Bell, 1972).

"Tears of Magnanimity in Otway and Racine," in *French and English Drama of the Seventeenth Century* (Los Angeles: William Andrews Clark Library, 1972).

"Spectacles of State," *Studies in English Literature* 13 (1973): 317–30.

"Things as They Are and the World of Absolutes in Jonson's Plays and Masques," in *The Elizabethan Theatre IV*, ed. George Hibbard, pp. 106–26 (Hamden, Conn.: The Shoe String Press, 1974).

"Heywood's Women Worthies," in *Concepts of the Hero in the Middle Ages and the Renaissance*, ed. N. T. Burns and C. J. Reagan, pp. 222–38 (Albany: State University of New York Press, 1975).

"Struggle for Calm: The Dramatic Structure of *The Broken Heart*," in *English Renaissance Drama: Essays in Honor of Madeleine Doran and Mark Eccles*, ed. Standish Henning, Robert Kimbrough, and Richard Knowles, pp. 155–66 (Carbondale: Southern Illinois University Press, 1976).

"Aristophanes, Plautus, Terence, and the Refinement of English Comedy," *Studies in the Literary Imagination* 10 (1977): 91–108.

"'Give Me Your Hands': Reflections on the Author's Agents in Comedy," in *The Author in his Works: Essays in Honor of Maynard Mack*, ed. Louis L. Martz and Aubrey Williams, pp. 197–211 (New Haven: Yale University Press, 1978).

"*King John* and the Drama of History," *Shakespeare Quarterly* 29 (1978): 192–211.

"Richard Cumberland, Comic Force, and Misanthropy," *Comparative Drama* 12 (1978–79): 283–99.

"Admiration in the Comedies of Thomas Southerne," *Evidence in Literary Scholarship: Essays in Memory of James Marshall Osborn*, ed. René Wellek and Alvaro Ribeiro, pp. 89–103 (Oxford: Clarendon Press, 1979).

"The Appeal of the Comic Deceiver," *Yearbook of English Studies* 12 (1982): 12–23.

"The English Masque and the Functions of Comedy," in *Elizabethan Theatre VIII*, ed. George Hibbard, pp. 154–63 (Port Credit, Ont.: Meaney, 1982).

"Shakespeare and the Ceremonies of Romance," in *Shakespeare's Craft*, ed. Philip Highfill, Jr., pp. 113–37 (Carbondale: Southern Illinois University Press, 1982).

"The Ceremonies of *Titus Andronicus*," in *Mirror up to Shakespeare: Essays in Honour of G. R. Hibbard*, ed. J. C. Gray, pp. 159–70 (Toronto: University of Toronto Press, 1984).

"Mad Lovers, Vainglorious Soldiers," *Research Opportunities in Renaissance Drama* 27 (1984): 13–19.

"*Titus Andronicus* and the Wounds of Civil War," in *Literary Theory and Criticism*, ed. Joseph P. Strelka, pp. 1351–62 (New York: Peter Lang, 1984).

Contributors

Jonas Barish, *University of California, Berkeley*

Lee Bliss, *University of California, Santa Barbara*

Philip Edwards, *University of Liverpool*

R. A. Foakes, *University of California, Los Angeles*

Marjorie Garber, *Harvard University*

Robert Hogan, *University of Delaware*

Jean E. Howard, *Syracuse University*

G. K. Hunter, *Yale University*

Anthony Kaufman, *University of Illinois*

Alvin B. Kernan, *Princeton University*

John Lemly, *Mount Holyoke College*

Maynard Mack, *Yale University*

Kenneth Muir, *University of Liverpool*

Gail Kern Paster, *George Washington University*

Albert Wertheim, *Indiana University*

Rose Zimbardo, *State University of New York, Stonybrook*

A. R. Braunmuller, *University of California, Los Angeles*

J. C. Bulman, *Allegheny College*

Index of Plays Discussed

This index cites only the more extensive discussions of the respective plays rather than cataloguing each allusion or mere reference; plays mentioned in the notes are not entered here. Authors' names and the titles of plays appear in their customary modern forms; plays in languages other than English are listed in the form chosen by the various authors of this volume. Plays in the "Beaumont and Fletcher canon" appear under Beaumont's name; other plays of corporate authorship are entered under the name of the author commonly listed first, and later versions of Shakespeare's plays appear under their adapters' names. Anonymous plays are entered by title in the main alphabetical series.